ハヤテのごとく!
Hayate the combat butler

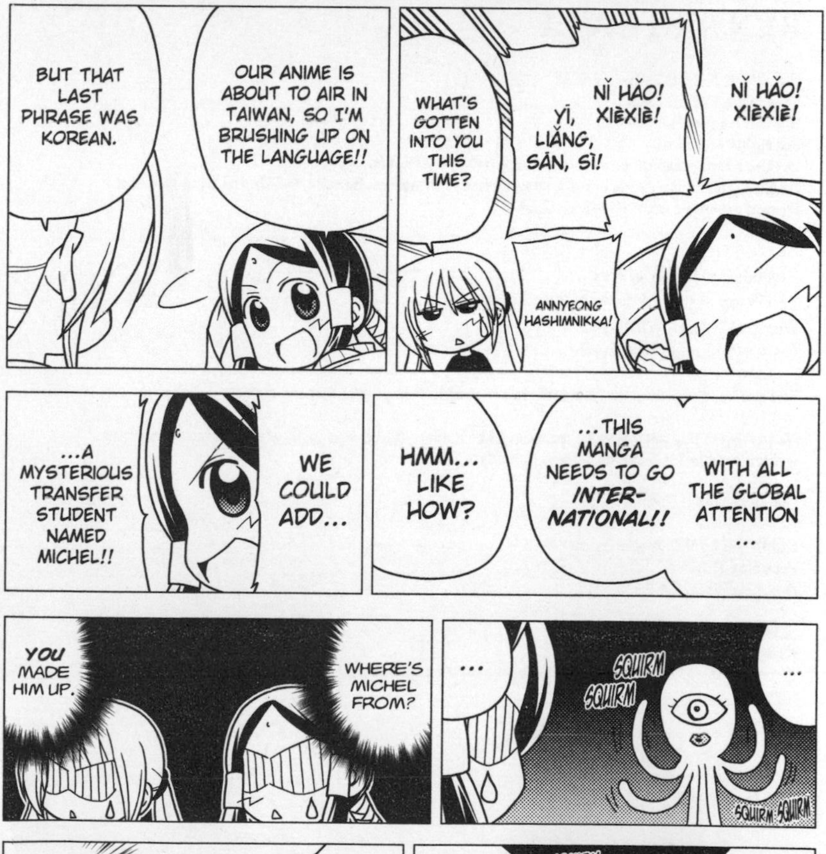
NǏ HǍO! XIÈXIÈ!
NǏ HǍO! XIÈXIÈ!
YĪ, LIǍNG, SĀN, SÌ!
WHAT'S GOTTEN INTO YOU THIS TIME?
ANNYEONG HASHIMNIKKA!
OUR ANIME IS ABOUT TO AIR IN TAIWAN, SO I'M BRUSHING UP ON THE LANGUAGE!!
BUT THAT LAST PHRASE WAS KOREAN.
WITH ALL THE GLOBAL ATTENTION ...
...THIS MANGA NEEDS TO GO INTERNATIONAL!!
HMM... LIKE HOW?
WE COULD ADD...
...A MYSTERIOUS TRANSFER STUDENT NAMED MICHEL!!
...
SQUIRM SQUIRM
...
SQUIRM SQUIRM
WHERE'S MICHEL FROM?
YOU MADE HIM UP.
HI! ♥ I'M MICHEL.
SQUIRM SQUIRM
I'M A MYSTERIOUS TRANSFER STUDENT FROM FAR AWAY.
SQUIRM
AND WE'RE INVADING THIS PLANET!
KSHAK
A SQUID INVASION !!

HAYATE THE COMBAT BUTLER
VOL. 26
Shonen Sunday Edition

STORY AND ART BY
KENJIRO HATA

HAYATE NO GOTOKU! Vol. 26
by Kenjiro HATA
© 2005 Kenjiro HATA
All rights reserved.
Original Japanese edition published by SHOGAKUKAN.
English translation rights in the United States of America, Canada, the United Kingdom and
Ireland arranged with SHOGAKUKAN.

Translation/John Werry
Touch-up Art & Lettering/John Hunt
Design/Yukiko Whitley
Editor/Shaenon K. Garrity

The stories, characters and incidents mentioned in this publication are entirely fictional.

Printed in the U.S.A.

Published by VIZ Media, LLC
P.O. Box 77010
San Francisco, CA 94107

10 9 8 7 6 5 4 3 2 1
First printing, September 2015

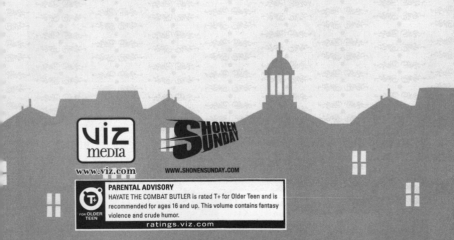

Hayate the Combat Butler

26

KENJIRO HATA

*The window reads "Table of Contents."

Episode 1:
"B-DMP! ♥ Operation Maiden's Heart ★ Pitter-Patter ♥ Or Whatever"

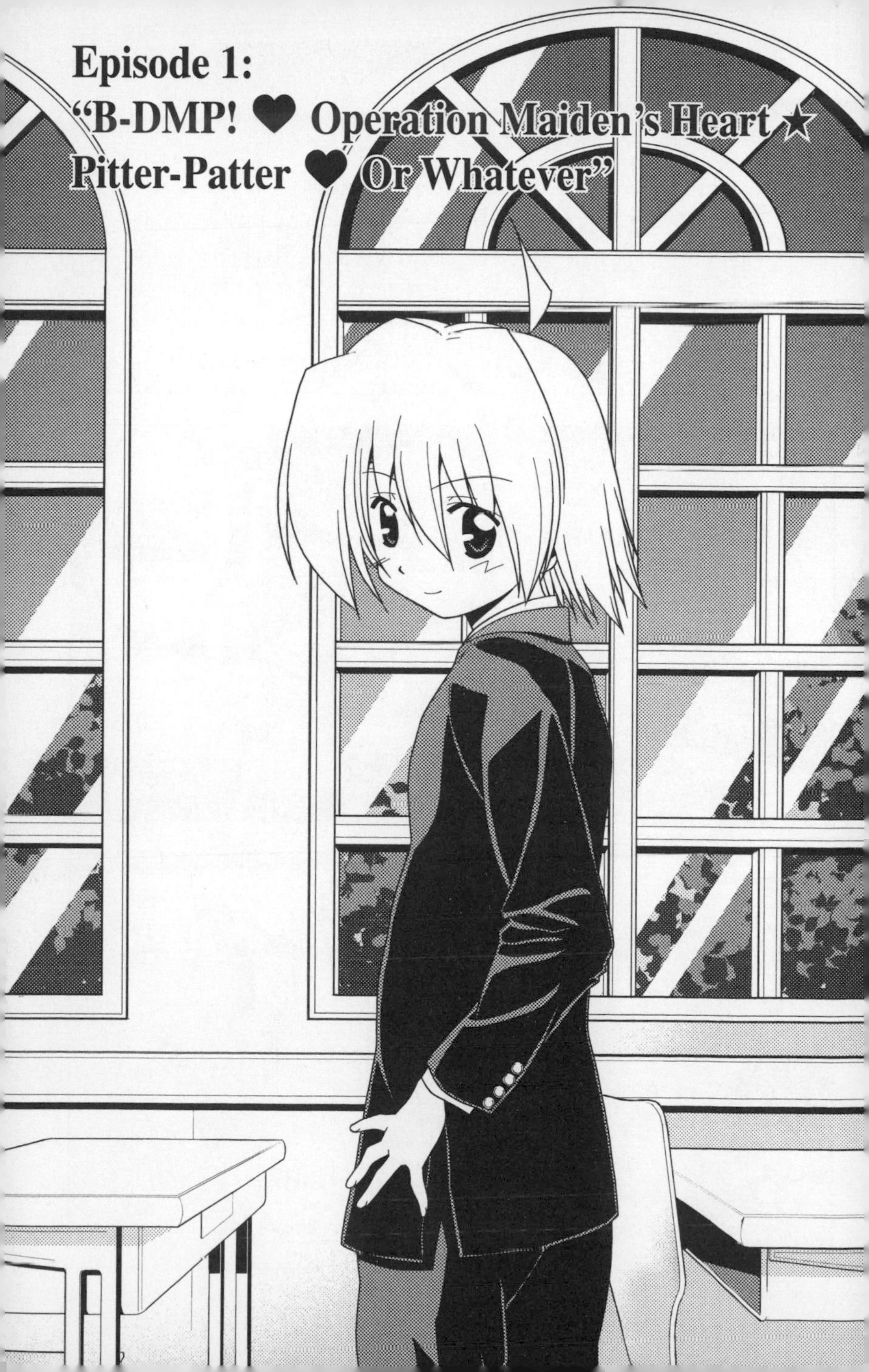

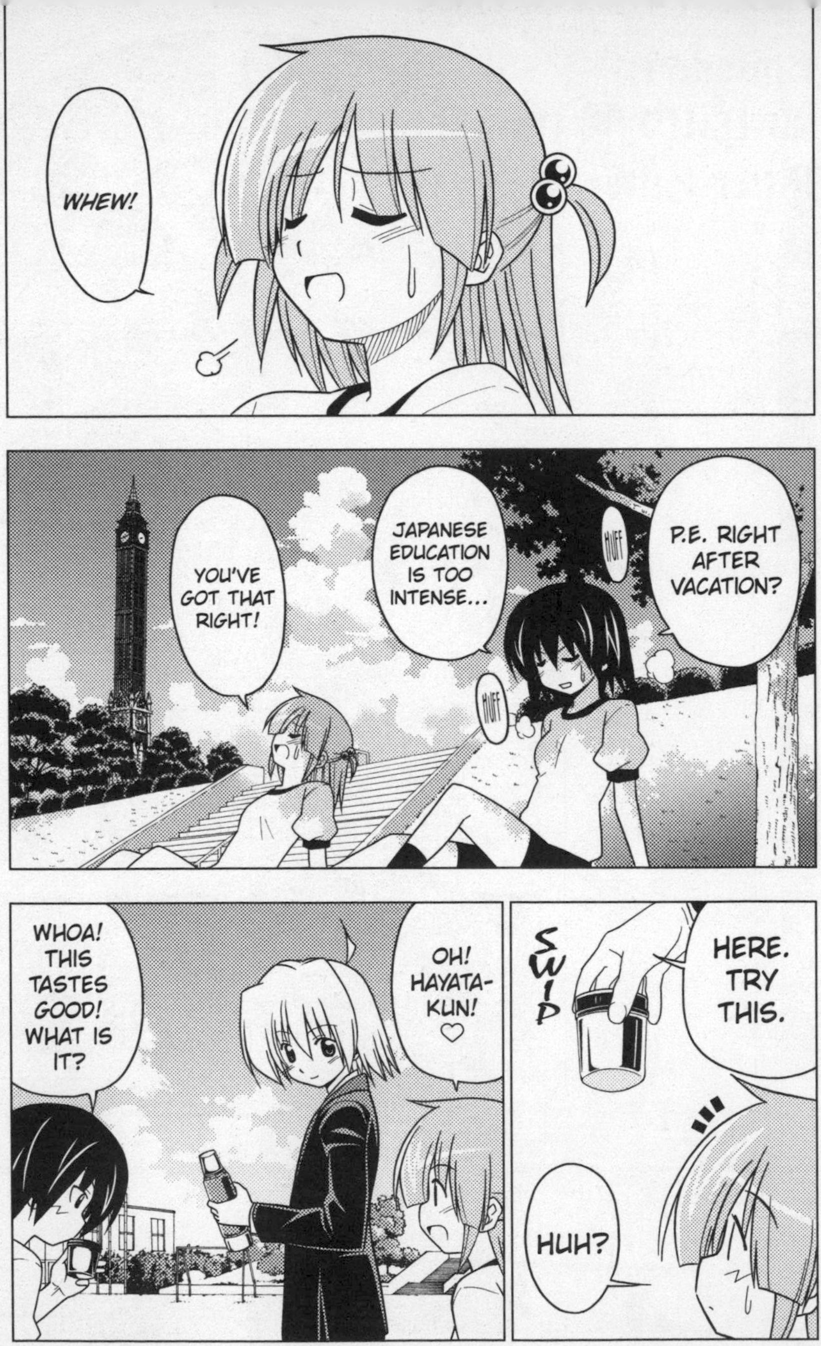
WHEW!
P.E. RIGHT AFTER VACATION?
HUFF
JAPANESE EDUCATION IS TOO INTENSE...
YOU'VE GOT THAT RIGHT!
HUFF
HERE. TRY THIS.
SWIP
HUH?
OH! HAYATA-KUN! ♡
WHOA! THIS TASTES GOOD! WHAT IS IT?

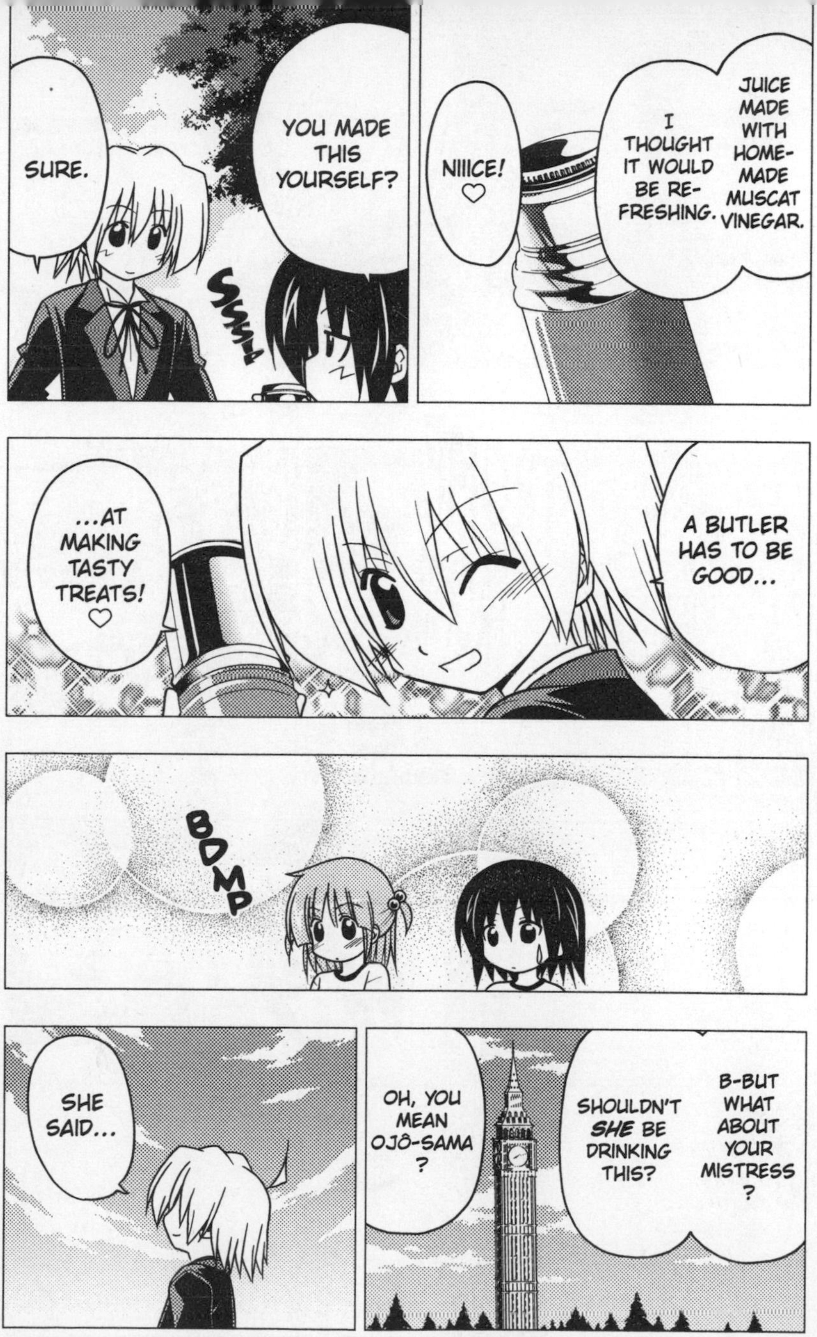
JUICE MADE WITH HOME-MADE MUSCAT VINEGAR.
I THOUGHT IT WOULD BE RE-FRESHING.
NIIICE! ♡
YOU MADE THIS YOURSELF?
SURE.
A BUTLER HAS TO BE GOOD...
...AT MAKING TASTY TREATS! ♡
BDMP
B-BUT WHAT ABOUT YOUR MISTRESS?
SHOULDN'T *SHE* BE DRINKING THIS?
OH, YOU MEAN OJÔ-SAMA?
SHE SAID...

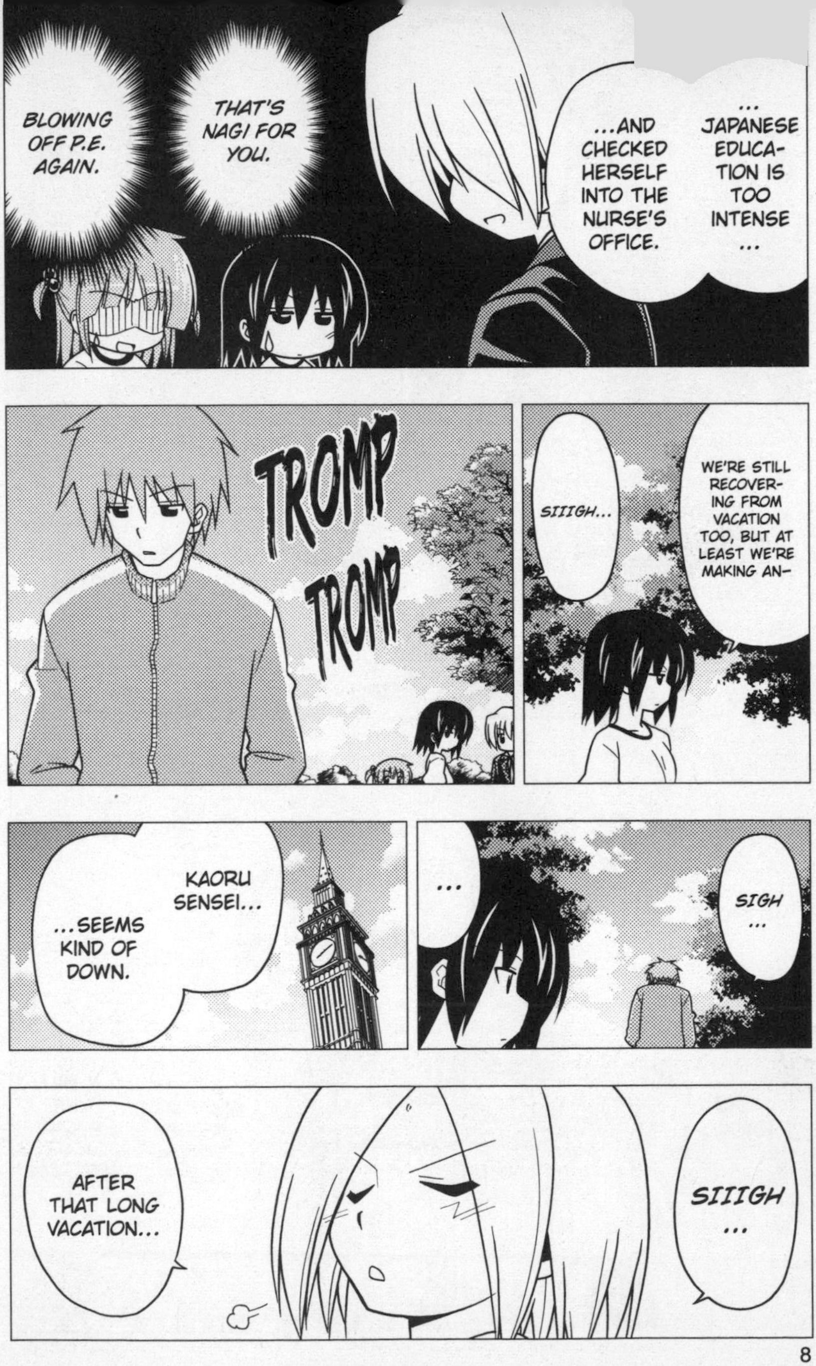
...JAPANESE EDUCATION IS TOO INTENSE...
...AND CHECKED HERSELF INTO THE NURSE'S OFFICE.
THAT'S NAGI FOR YOU.
BLOWING OFF P.E. AGAIN.
WE'RE STILL RECOVERING FROM VACATION TOO, BUT AT LEAST WE'RE MAKING AN-
SIIIGH...
TROMP
TROMP
SIGH...
...
KAORU SENSEI...
...SEEMS KIND OF DOWN.
SIIIGH...
AFTER THAT LONG VACATION...

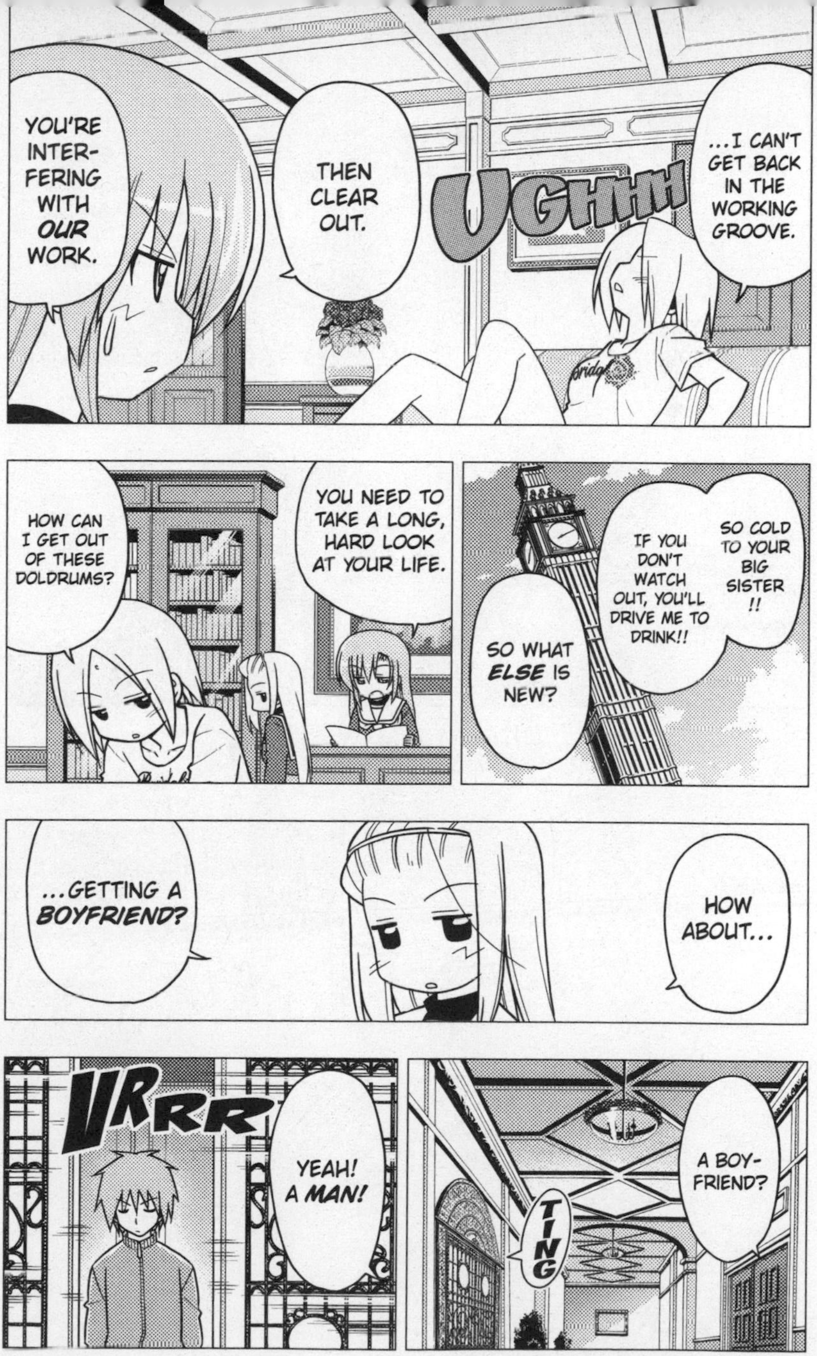
...I CAN'T GET BACK IN THE WORKING GROOVE.
UGHHH
THEN CLEAR OUT.
YOU'RE INTER-FERING WITH OUR WORK.
SO COLD TO YOUR BIG SISTER !!
IF YOU DON'T WATCH OUT, YOU'LL DRIVE ME TO DRINK!!
SO WHAT ELSE IS NEW?
YOU NEED TO TAKE A LONG, HARD LOOK AT YOUR LIFE.
HOW CAN I GET OUT OF THESE DOLDRUMS?
HOW ABOUT...
...GETTING A BOYFRIEND?
A BOY-FRIEND?
TING
YEAH! A MAN!
VRRR

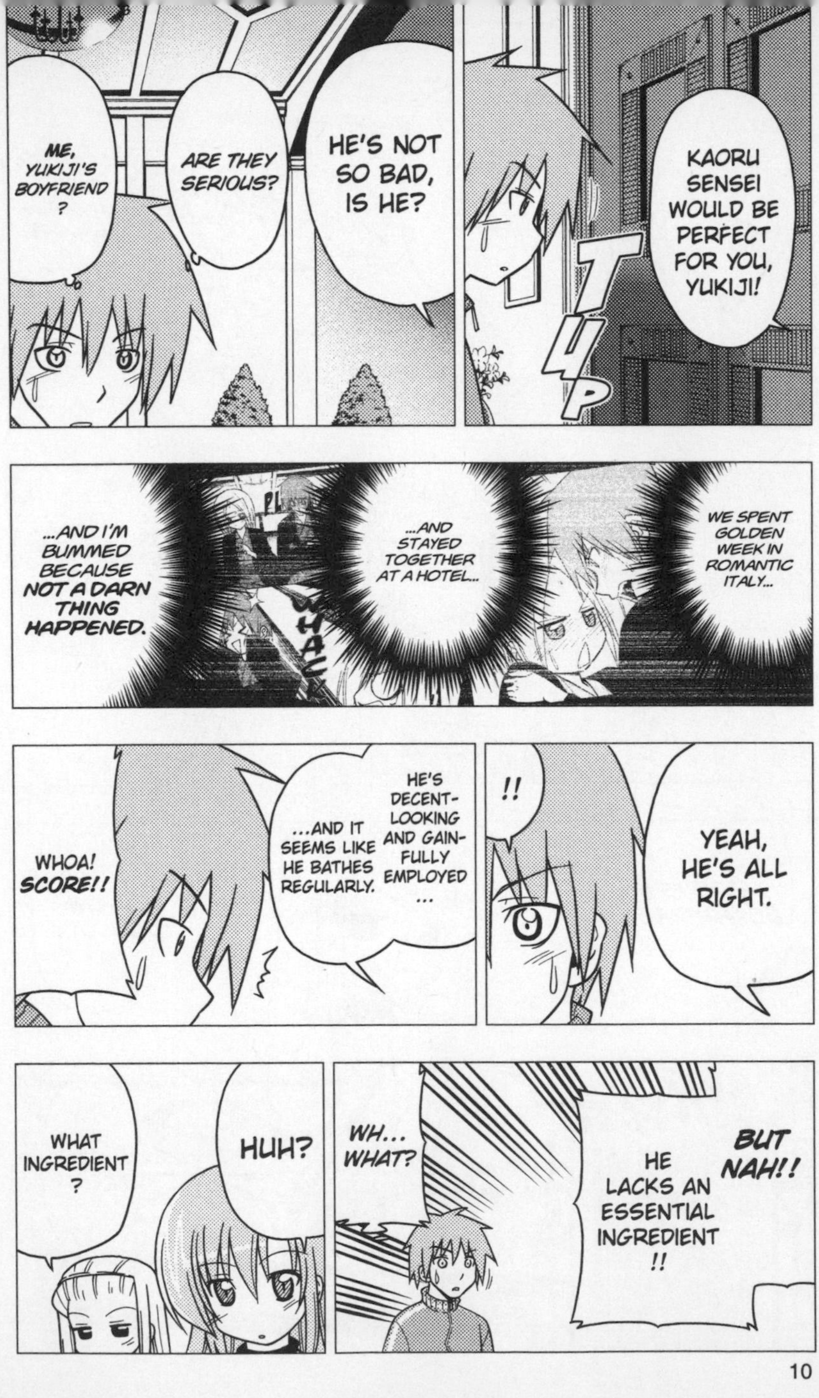
KAORU SENSEI WOULD BE PERFECT FOR YOU, YUKIJI!
TUP
HE'S NOT SO BAD, IS HE?
ARE THEY SERIOUS?
ME, YUKIJI'S BOYFRIEND ?
WE SPENT GOLDEN WEEK IN ROMANTIC ITALY...
...AND STAYED TOGETHER AT A HOTEL...
...AND I'M BUMMED BECAUSE **NOT A DARN THING HAPPENED.**
YEAH, HE'S ALL RIGHT.
!!
HE'S DECENT-LOOKING AND GAIN-FULLY EMPLOYED ...
...AND IT SEEMS LIKE HE BATHES REGULARLY.
WHOA! **SCORE!!**
BUT NAH!!
HE LACKS AN ESSENTIAL INGREDIENT !!
WH... WHAT?
HUH?
WHAT INGREDIENT ?

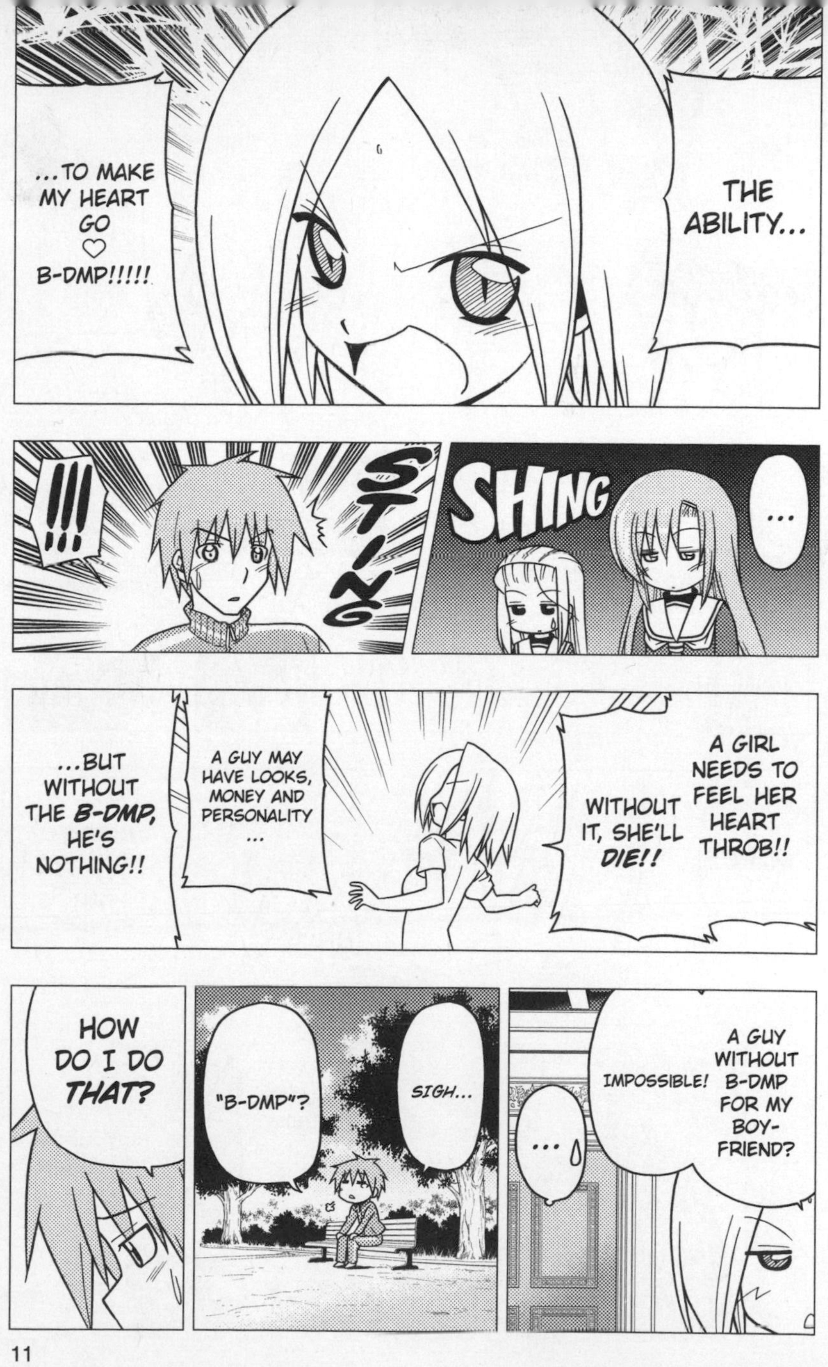
THE ABILITY...
...TO MAKE MY HEART GO ♡ B-DMP!!!!!
...
SHING
STING
!!!
A GIRL NEEDS TO FEEL HER HEART THROB!!
WITHOUT IT, SHE'LL *DIE!!*
A GUY MAY HAVE LOOKS, MONEY AND PERSONALITY ...
...BUT WITHOUT THE *B-DMP,* HE'S NOTHING!!
A GUY WITHOUT B-DMP FOR MY BOY-FRIEND?
IMPOSSIBLE!
...
SIGH...
"B-DMP"?
HOW DO I DO *THAT?*

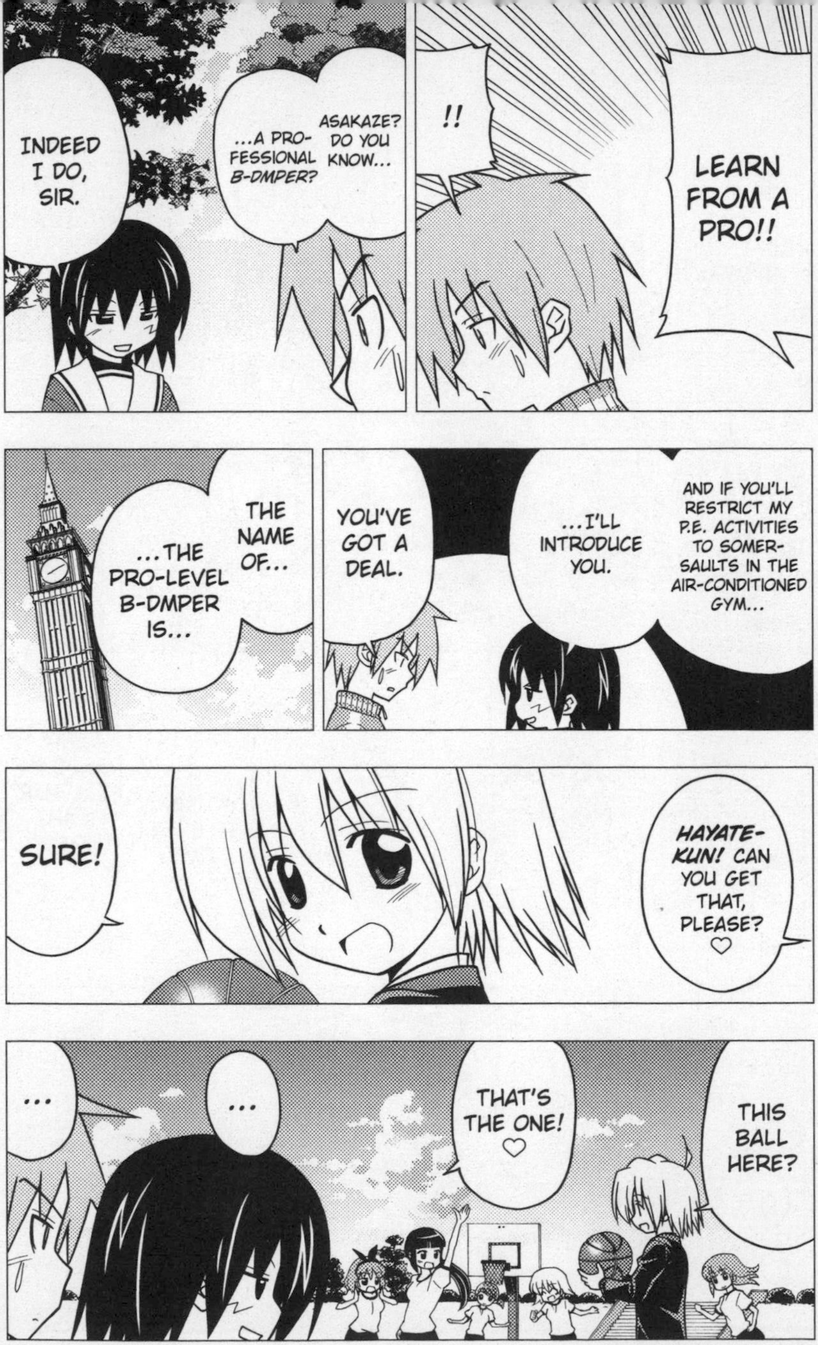

LEARN FROM A PRO!!
!!
ASAKAZE? DO YOU KNOW...
...A PRO-FESSIONAL B-DMPER?
INDEED I DO, SIR.
AND IF YOU'LL RESTRICT MY P.E. ACTIVITIES TO SOMER-SAULTS IN THE AIR-CONDITIONED GYM...
...I'LL INTRODUCE YOU.
YOU'VE GOT A DEAL.
THE NAME OF...
...THE PRO-LEVEL B-DMPER IS...
HAYATE-KUN! CAN YOU GET THAT, PLEASE? ♡
SURE!
THIS BALL HERE?
THAT'S THE ONE! ♡
...
...

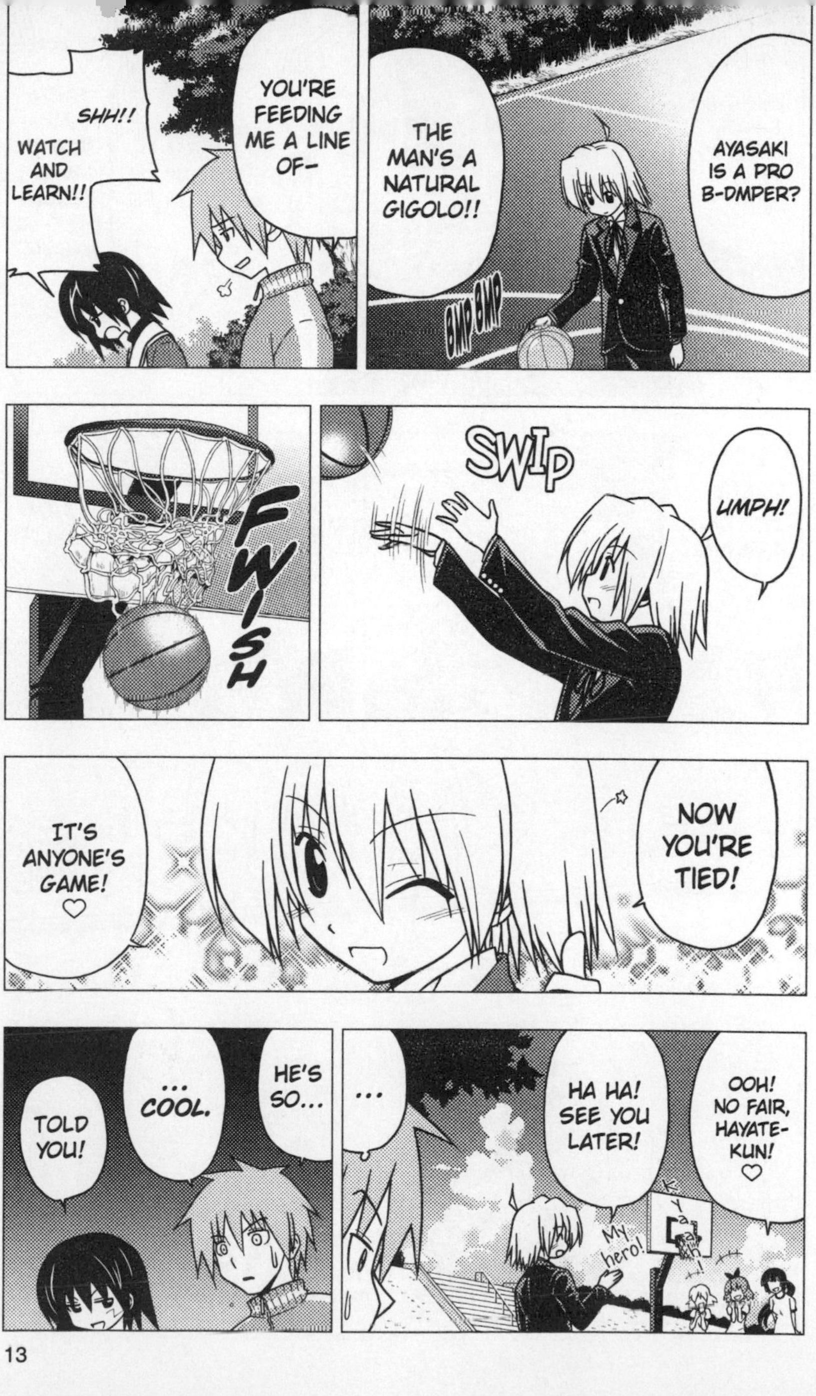
AYASAKI IS A PRO B-DMPER?
THE MAN'S A NATURAL GIGOLO!!
BMP BMP
YOU'RE FEEDING ME A LINE OF–
SHH!!
WATCH AND LEARN!!
UMPH!
SWIP
FWISH
NOW YOU'RE TIED!
IT'S ANYONE'S GAME! ♡
OOH! NO FAIR, HAYATE-KUN! ♡
HA HA! SEE YOU LATER!
My hero!
...
HE'S SO...
... COOL.
TOLD YOU!

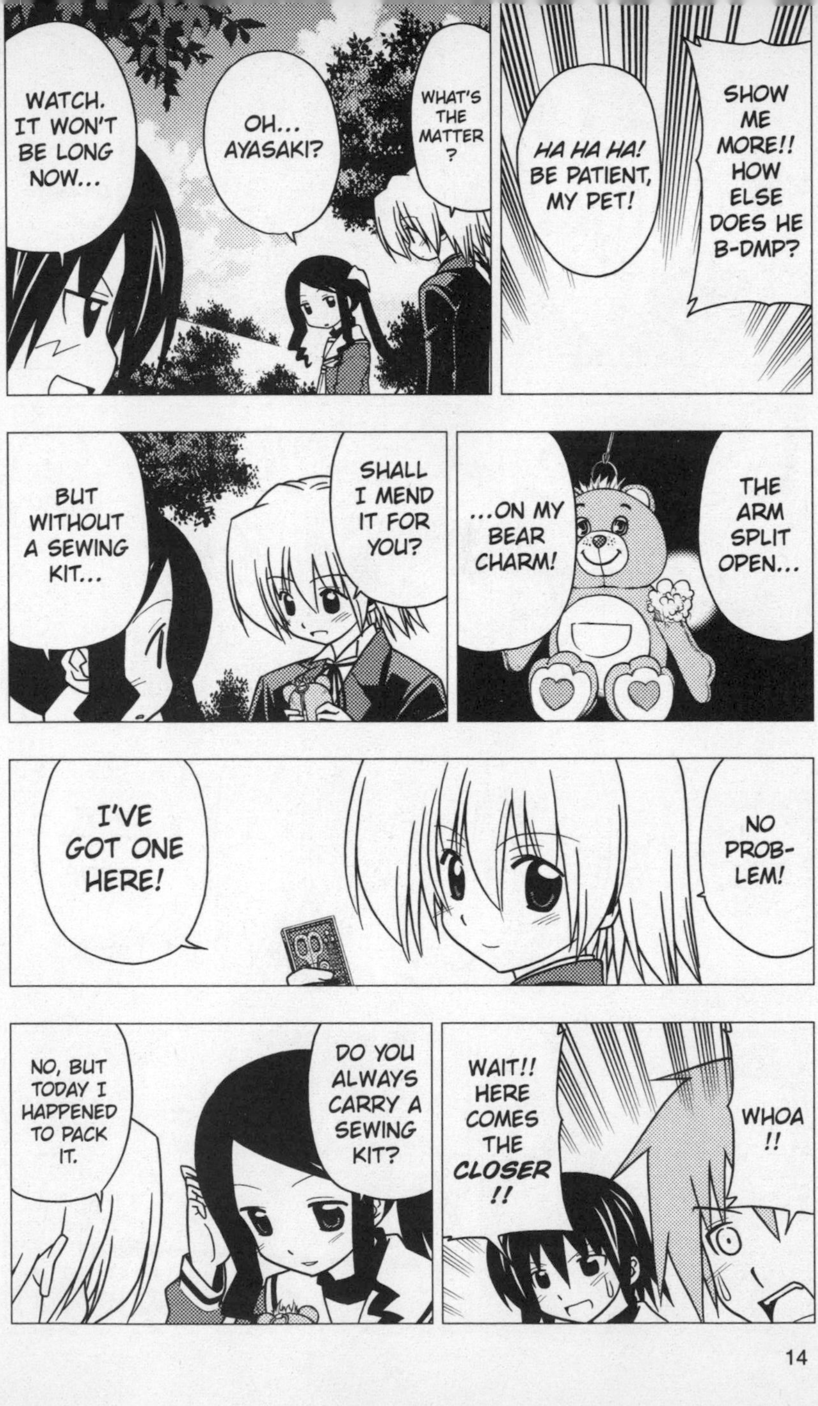
SHOW ME MORE!! HOW ELSE DOES HE B-DMP?
HA HA HA! BE PATIENT, MY PET!
WHAT'S THE MATTER?
OH... AYASAKI?
WATCH. IT WON'T BE LONG NOW...
THE ARM SPLIT OPEN...
...ON MY BEAR CHARM!
SHALL I MEND IT FOR YOU?
BUT WITHOUT A SEWING KIT...
NO PROBLEM!
I'VE GOT ONE HERE!
WHOA!!
WAIT!! HERE COMES THE CLOSER!!
DO YOU ALWAYS CARRY A SEWING KIT?
NO, BUT TODAY I HAPPENED TO PACK IT.

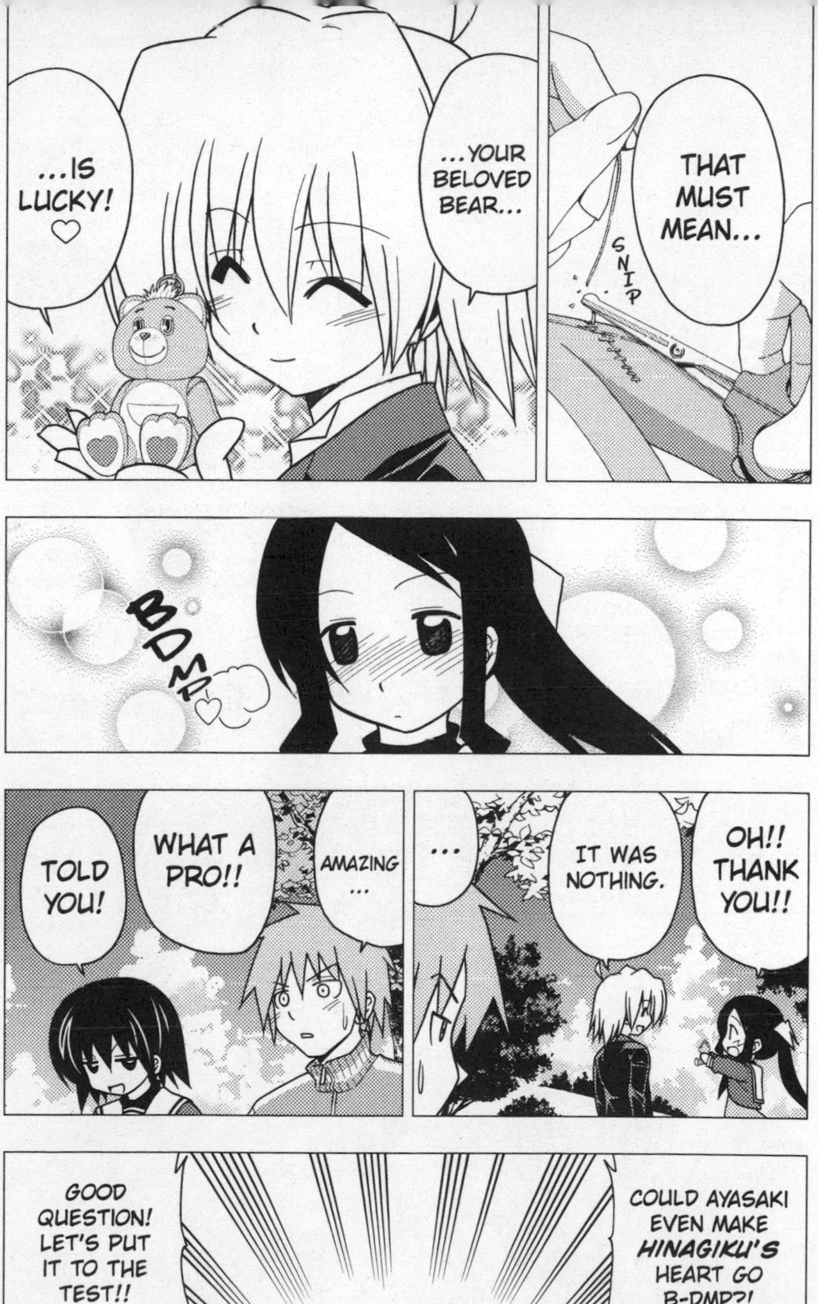
THAT MUST MEAN...
SNIP
...YOUR BELOVED BEAR...
...IS LUCKY! ♡
BDMP ♡
OH!! THANK YOU!!
IT WAS NOTHING.
...
AMAZING ...
WHAT A PRO!!
TOLD YOU!
COULD AYASAKI EVEN MAKE *HINAGIKU'S* HEART GO B-DMP?!
GOOD QUESTION! LET'S PUT IT TO THE TEST!!

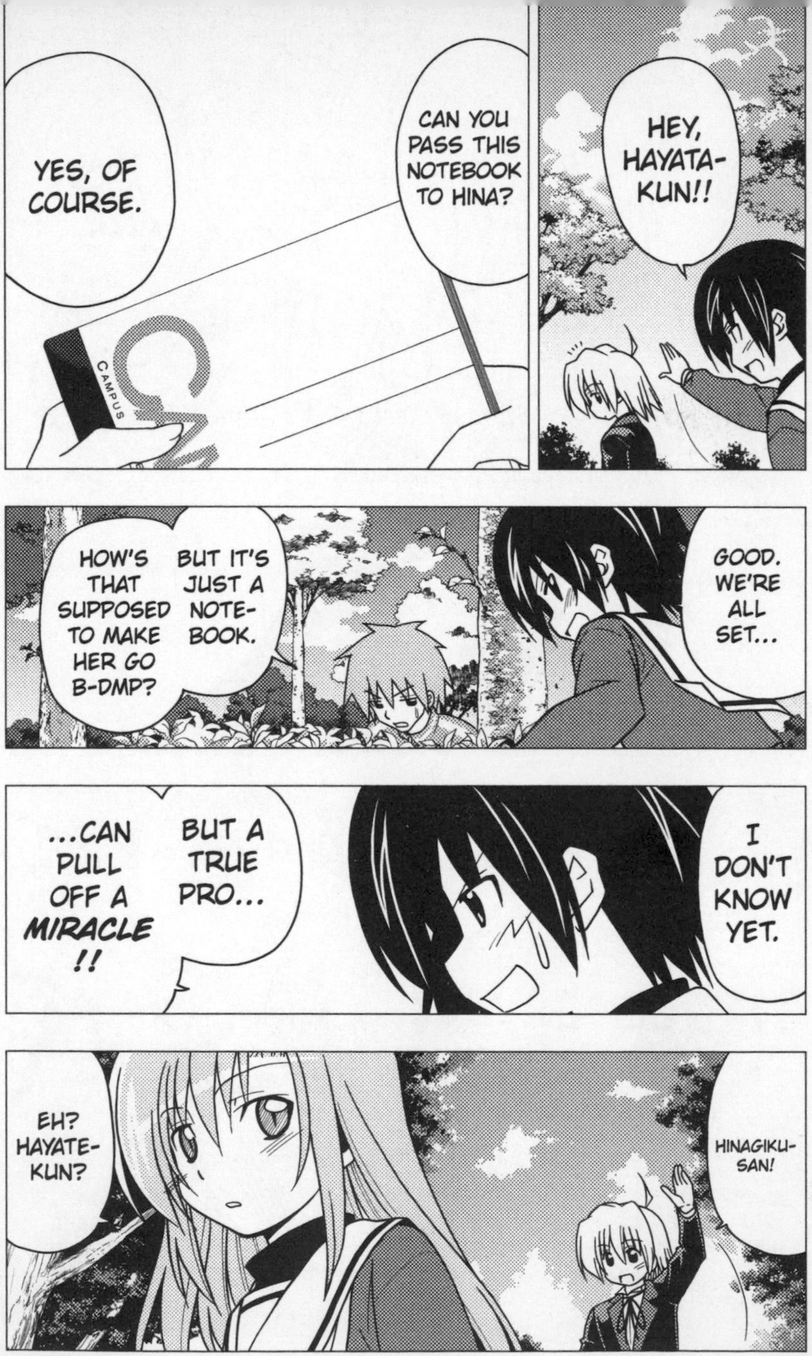
HEY, HAYATA-KUN!!
CAN YOU PASS THIS NOTEBOOK TO HINA?
CAMPUS
YES, OF COURSE.
GOOD. WE'RE ALL SET...
BUT IT'S JUST A NOTEBOOK.
HOW'S THAT SUPPOSED TO MAKE HER GO B-DMP?
I DON'T KNOW YET.
BUT A TRUE PRO...
...CAN PULL OFF A *MIRACLE*!!
HINAGIKU-SAN!
EH? HAYATE-KUN?

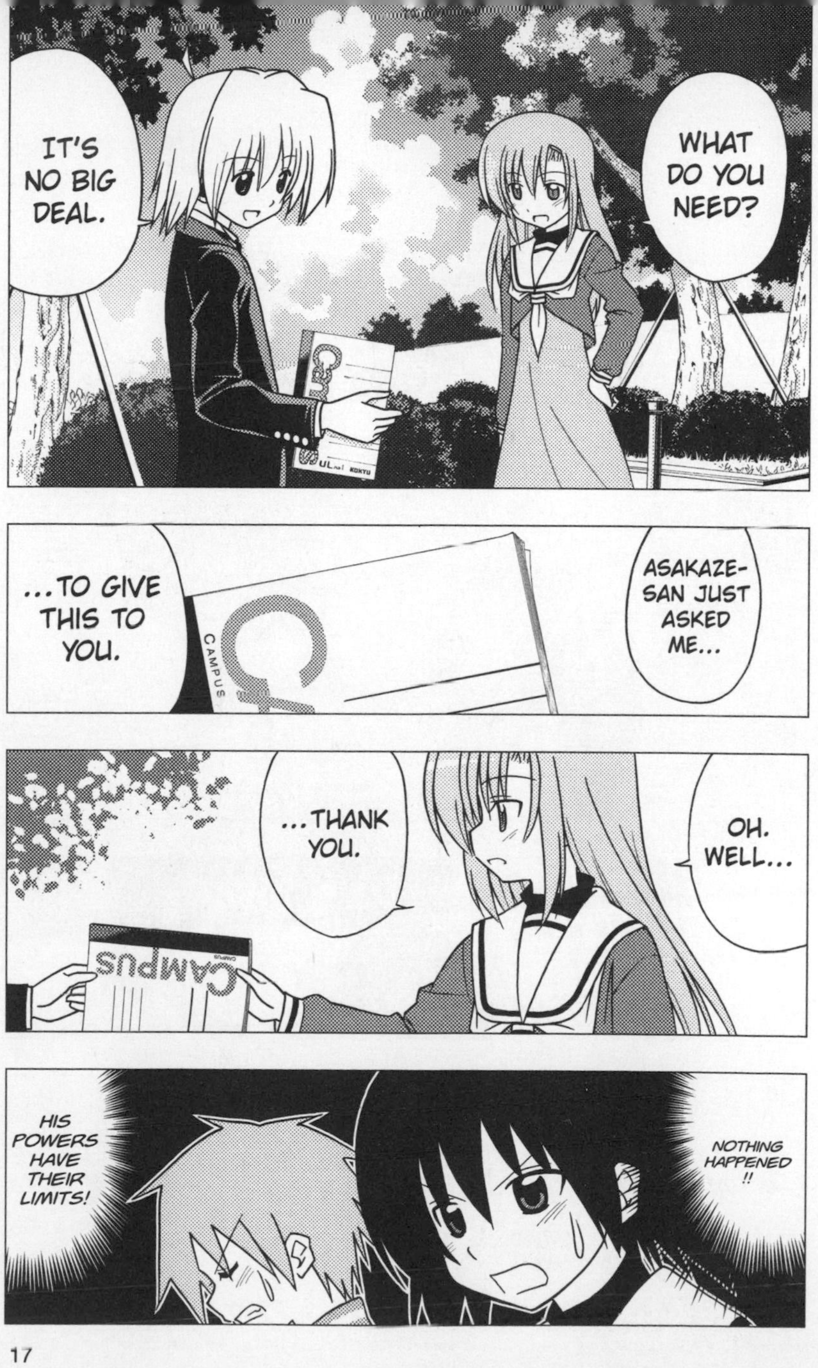
WHAT DO YOU NEED?
IT'S NO BIG DEAL.
ASAKAZE-SAN JUST ASKED ME...
CAMPUS
...TO GIVE THIS TO YOU.
OH. WELL...
...THANK YOU.
NOTHING HAPPENED!!
HIS POWERS HAVE THEIR LIMITS!

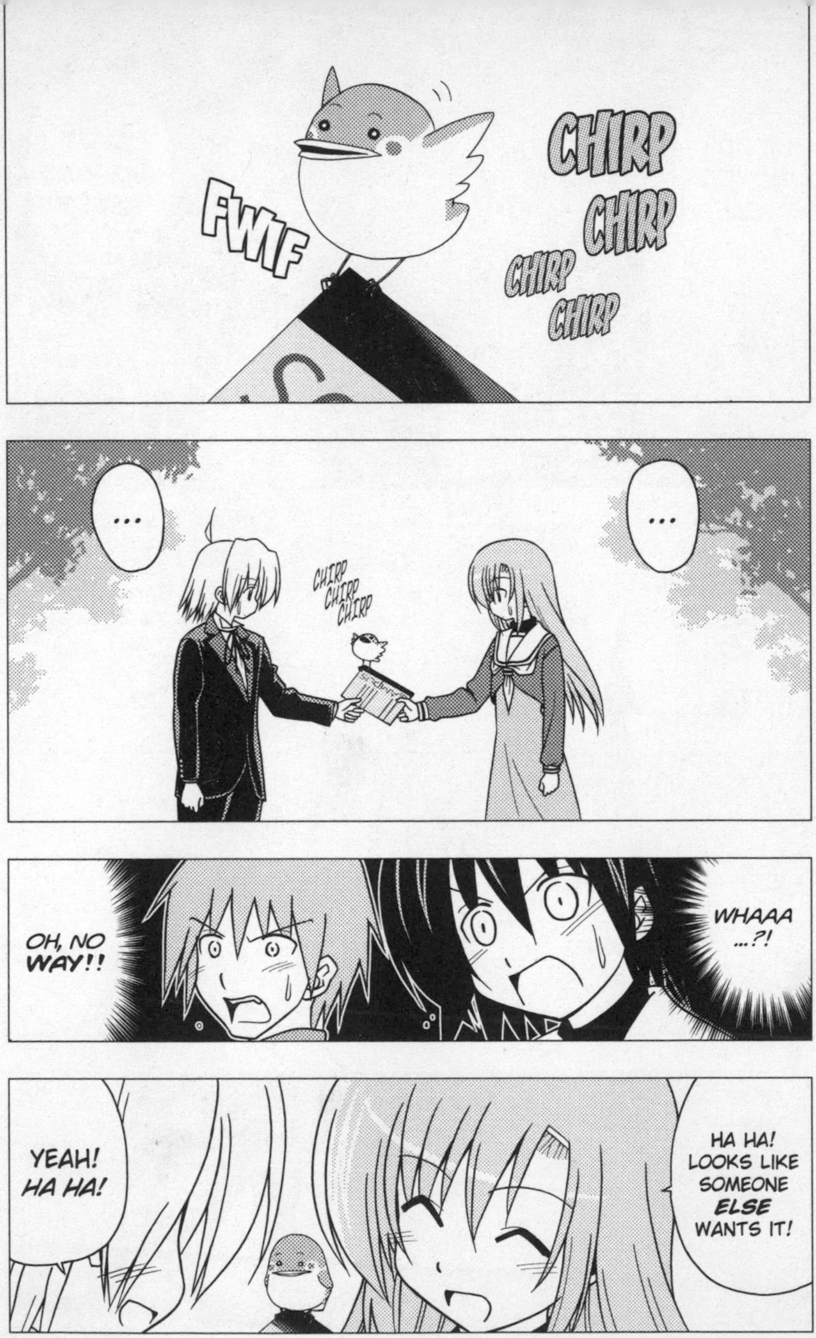
CHIRP
CHIRP
CHIRP
CHIRP
FWIF
...
...
CHIRP CHIRP CHIRP
WHAAA ...?!
OH, NO WAY!!
HA HA! LOOKS LIKE SOMEONE ELSE WANTS IT!
YEAH! HA HA!

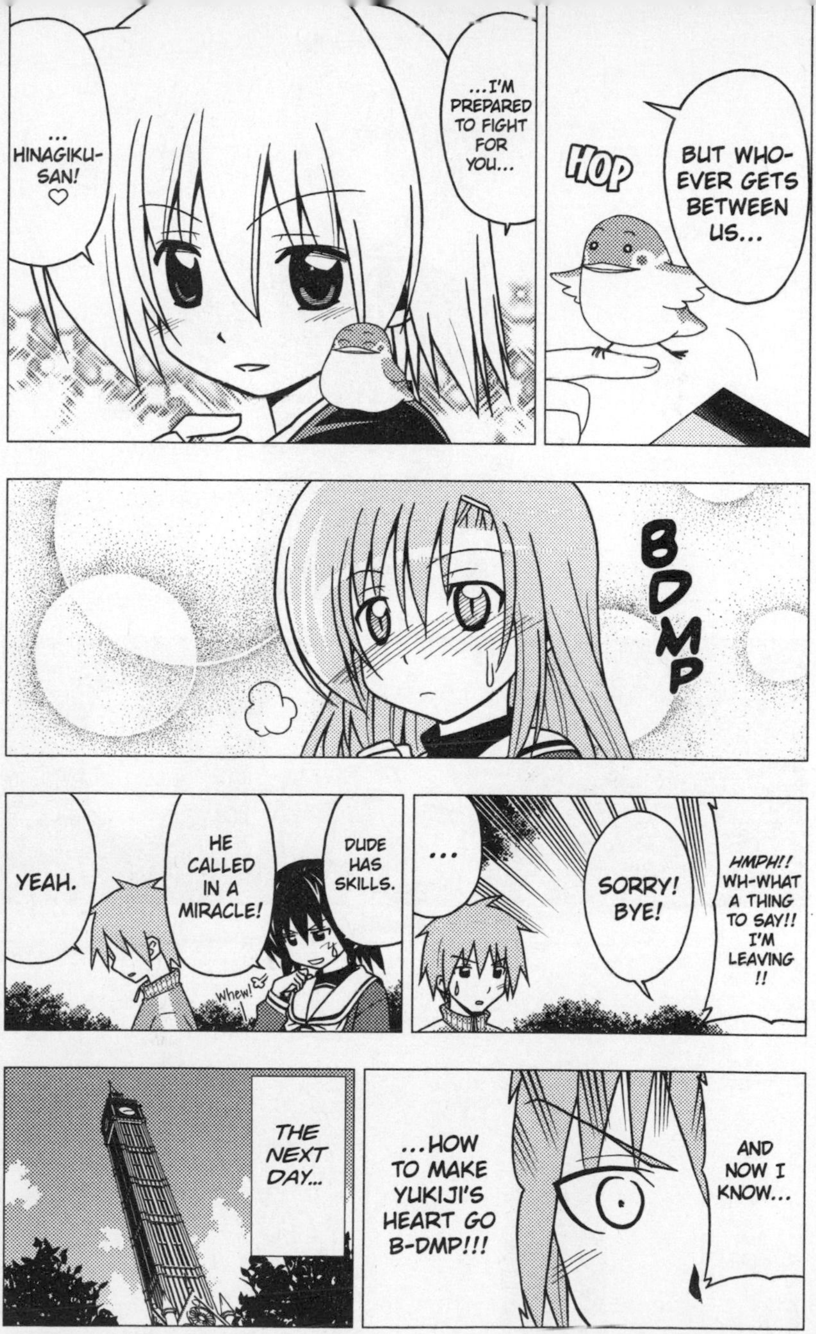
BUT WHO-EVER GETS BETWEEN US...
HOP
...I'M PREPARED TO FIGHT FOR YOU...
...HINAGIKU-SAN! ♡
BDMP
HMPH!! WH-WHAT A THING TO SAY!! I'M LEAVING!!
SORRY! BYE!
...
DUDE HAS SKILLS.
HE CALLED IN A MIRACLE!
Whew!
YEAH.
AND NOW I KNOW...
...HOW TO MAKE YUKIJI'S HEART GO B-DMP!!!
THE NEXT DAY...

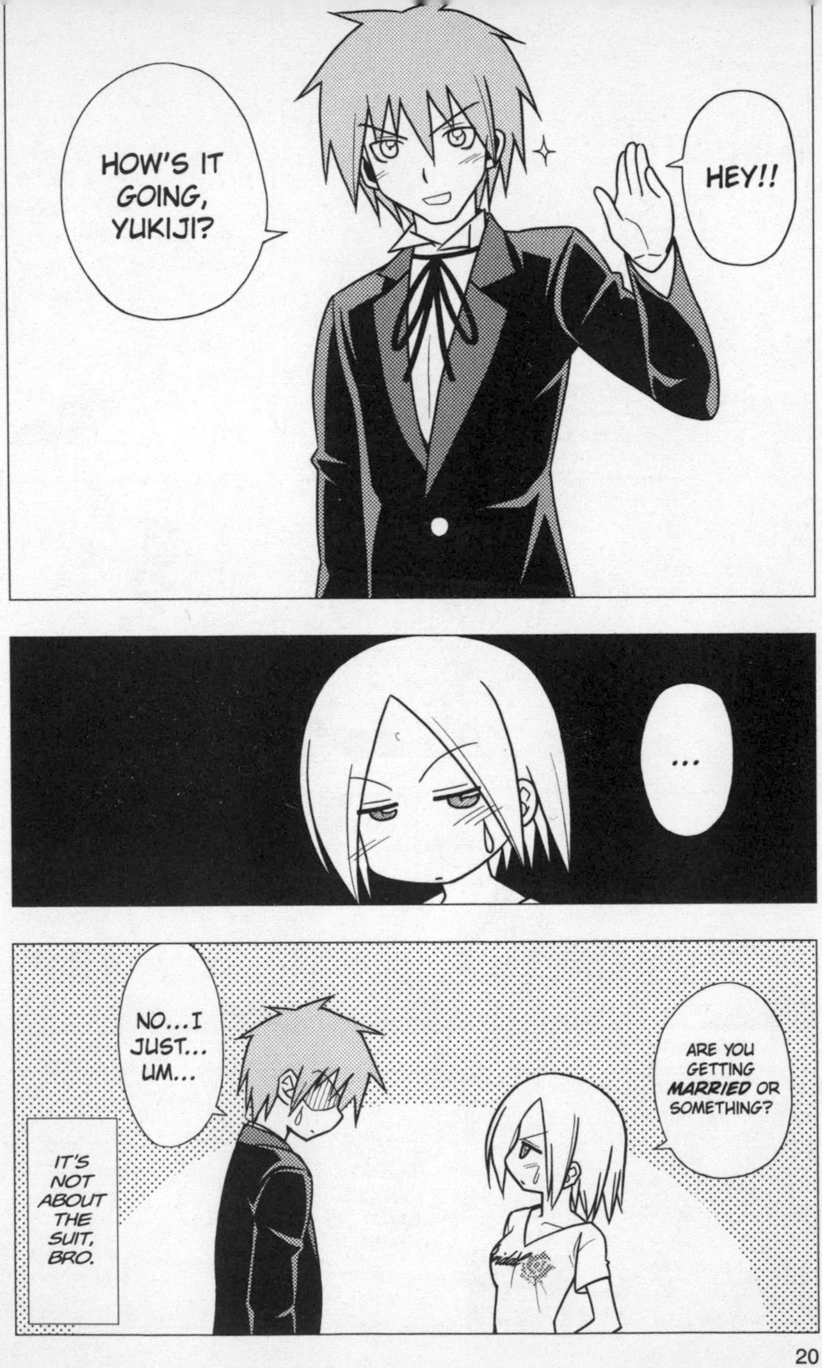
HEY!!
HOW'S IT GOING, YUKIJI?
...
ARE YOU GETTING *MARRIED* OR SOMETHING?
NO...I JUST... UM...
IT'S NOT ABOUT THE SUIT, BRO.

Episode 2: "M-m-m-m-meow!"

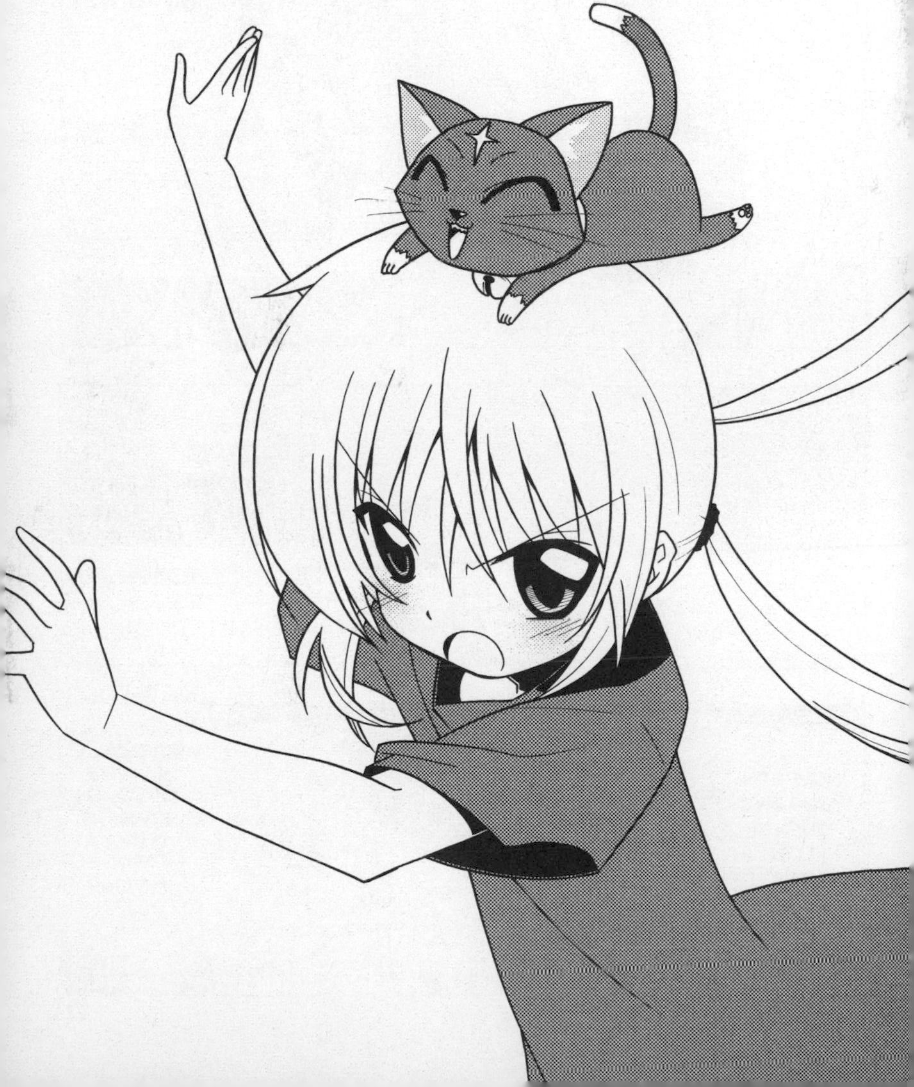

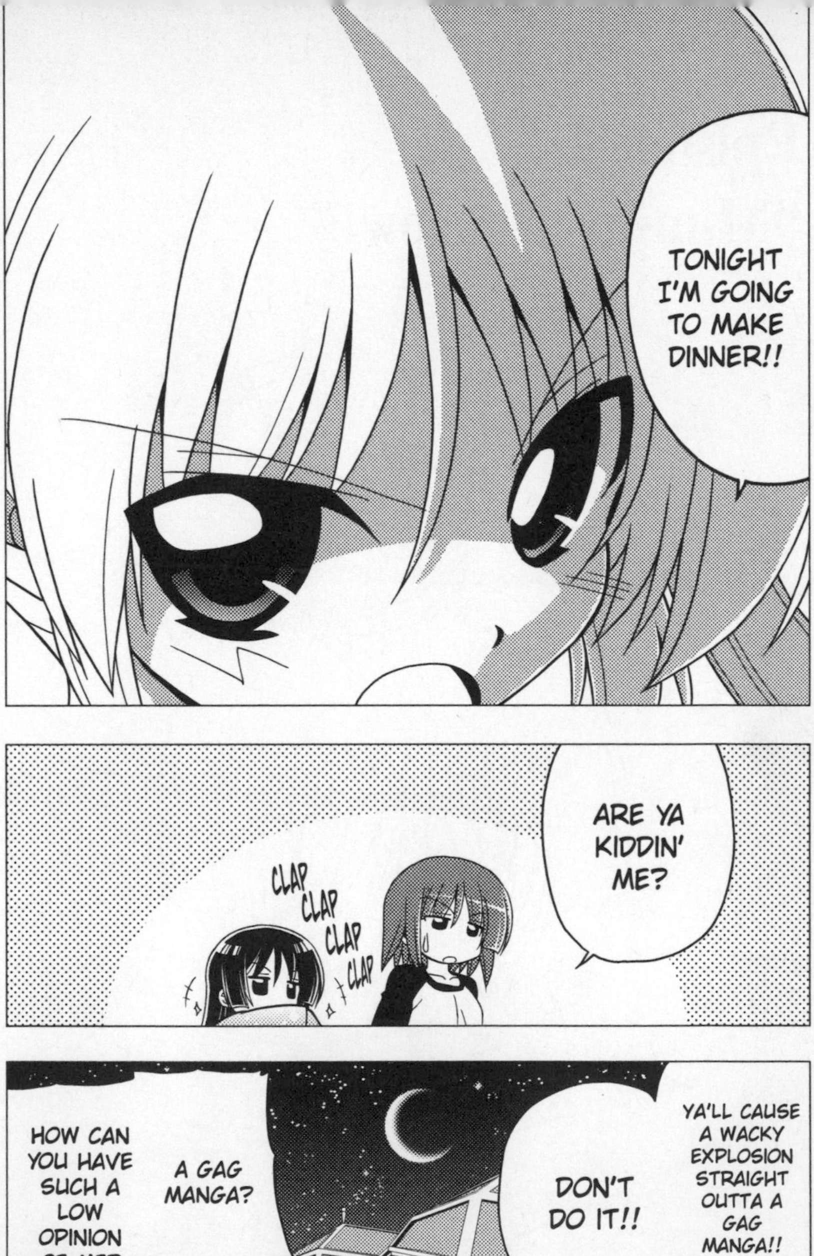
TONIGHT I'M GOING TO MAKE DINNER!!
ARE YA KIDDIN' ME?
CLAP CLAP CLAP CLAP
YA'LL CAUSE A WACKY EXPLOSION STRAIGHT OUTTA A GAG MANGA!!
DON'T DO IT!!
A GAG MANGA?
HOW CAN YOU HAVE SUCH A LOW OPINION OF ME?

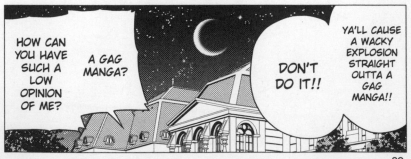

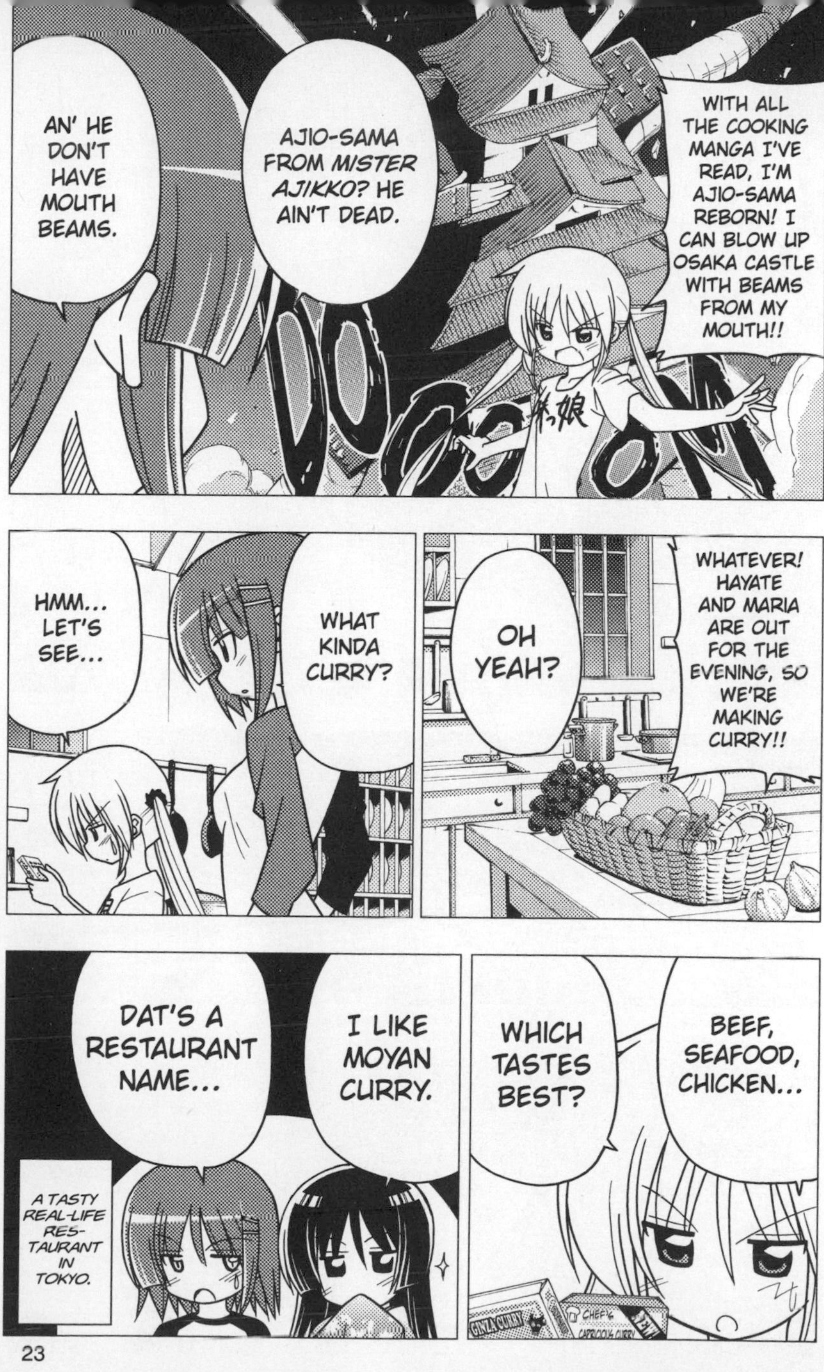
WITH ALL THE COOKING MANGA I'VE READ, I'M AJIO-SAMA REBORN! I CAN BLOW UP OSAKA CASTLE WITH BEAMS FROM MY MOUTH!!
AJIO-SAMA FROM *MISTER AJIKKO*? HE AIN'T DEAD.
AN' HE DON'T HAVE MOUTH BEAMS.
WHATEVER! HAYATE AND MARIA ARE OUT FOR THE EVENING, SO WE'RE MAKING CURRY!!
OH YEAH?
WHAT KINDA CURRY?
HMM... LET'S SEE...
BEEF, SEAFOOD, CHICKEN...
WHICH TASTES BEST?
GINZA CURRY
CHEF'S CAPRICIOUS CURRY
I LIKE MOYAN CURRY.
DAT'S A RESTAURANT NAME...
A TASTY REAL-LIFE RES-TAURANT IN TOKYO.

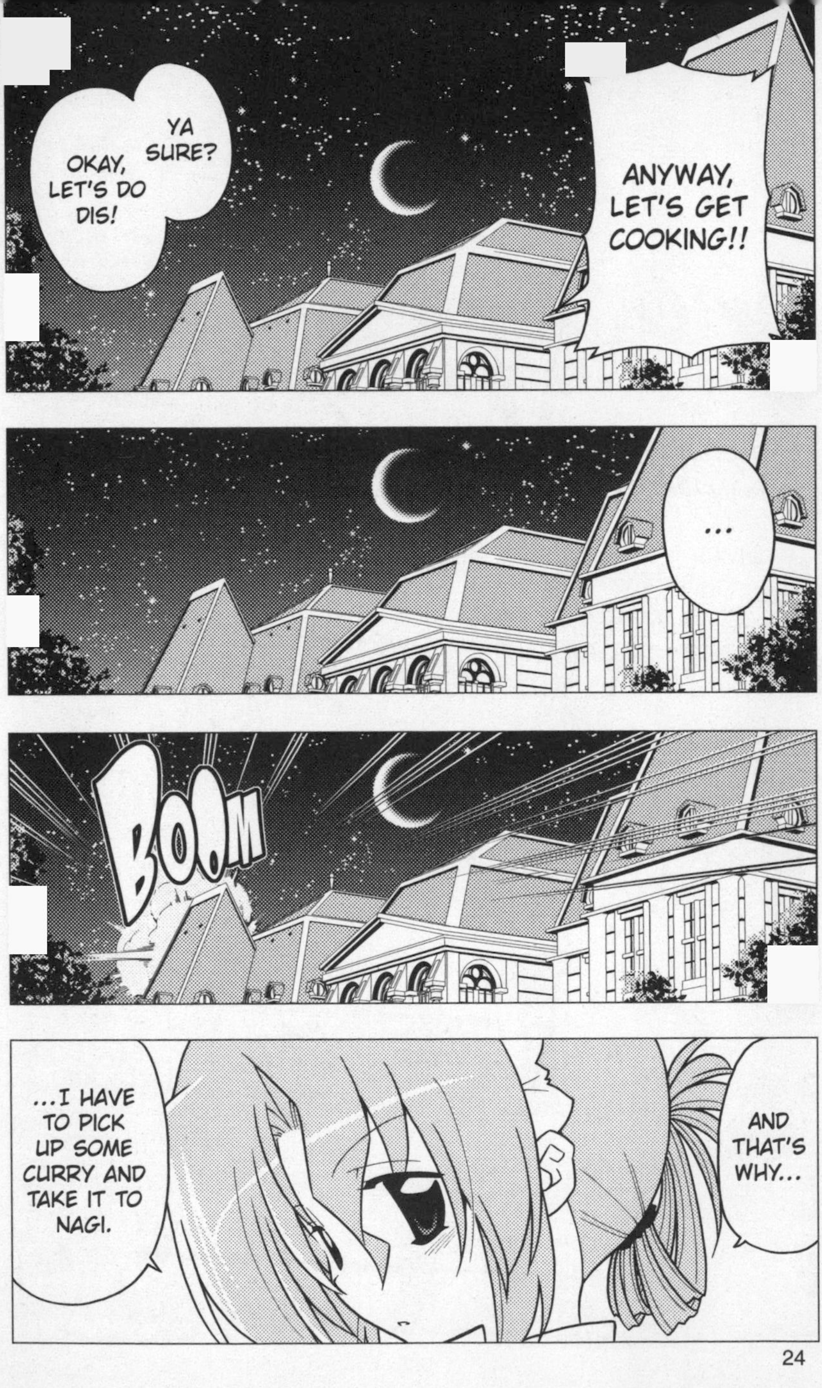
ANYWAY, LET'S GET COOKING!!
YA SURE?
OKAY, LET'S DO DIS!
...
BOOM
AND THAT'S WHY...
...I HAVE TO PICK UP SOME CURRY AND TAKE IT TO NAGI.

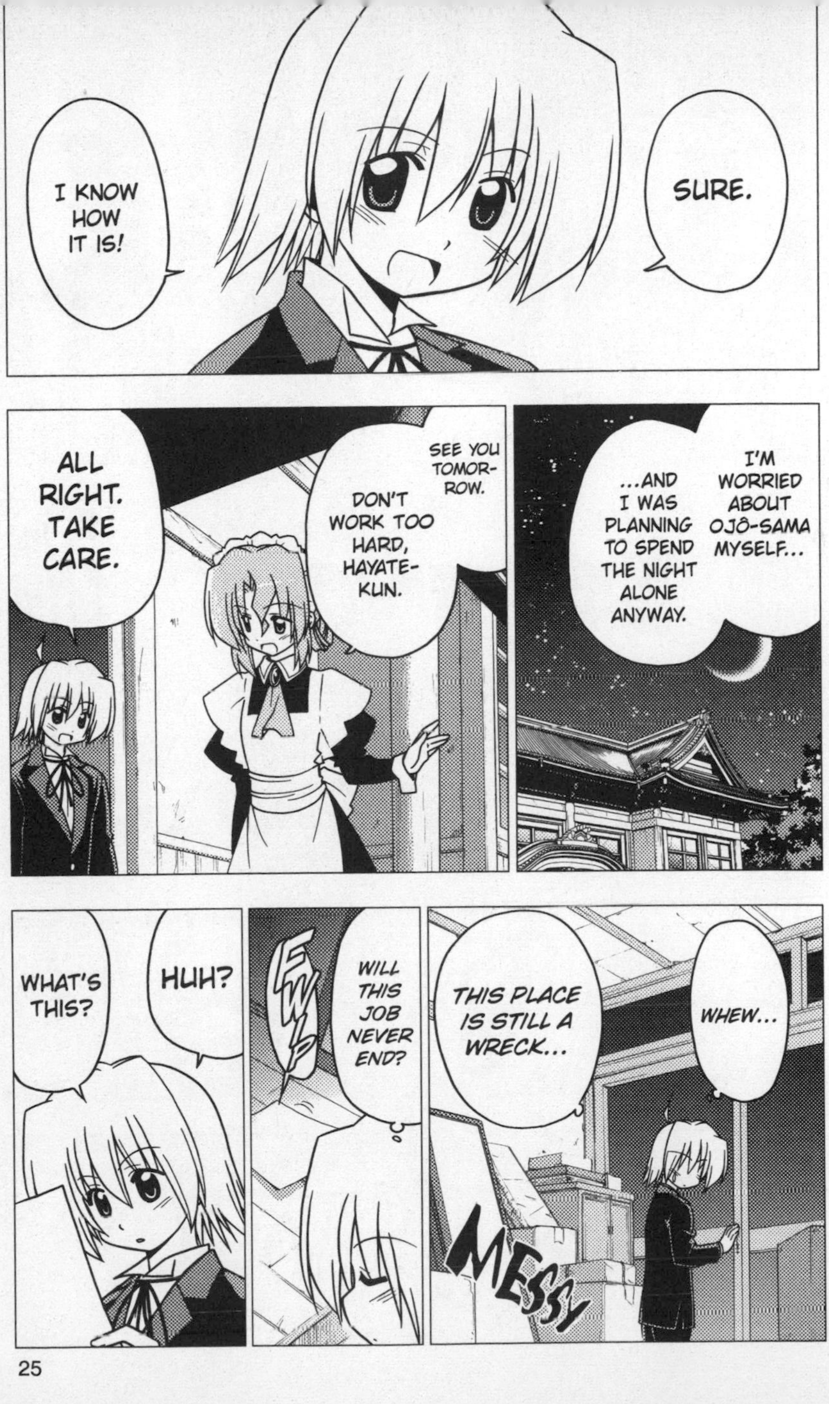
SURE.
I KNOW HOW IT IS!
I'M WORRIED ABOUT OJÔ-SAMA MYSELF...
...AND I WAS PLANNING TO SPEND THE NIGHT ALONE ANYWAY.
SEE YOU TOMOR-ROW.
DON'T WORK TOO HARD, HAYATE-KUN.
ALL RIGHT. TAKE CARE.
WHEW...
THIS PLACE IS STILL A WRECK...
MESSY
WILL THIS JOB NEVER END?
FWIP
HUH?
WHAT'S THIS?

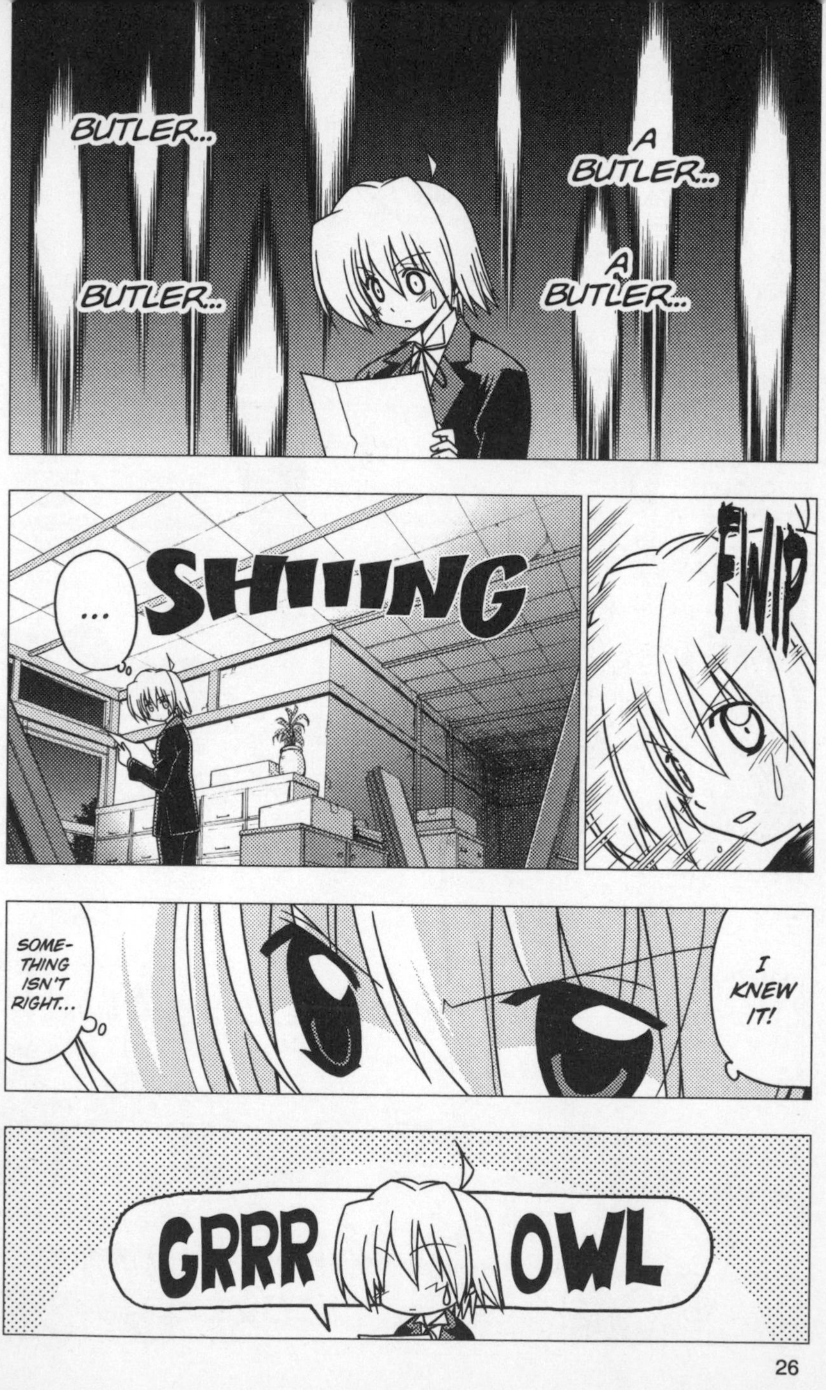
A BUTLER...
A BUTLER...
BUTLER...
BUTLER...
FWIP
...
SHIIIING
I KNEW IT!
SOME-THING ISN'T RIGHT...
GRRR OWL

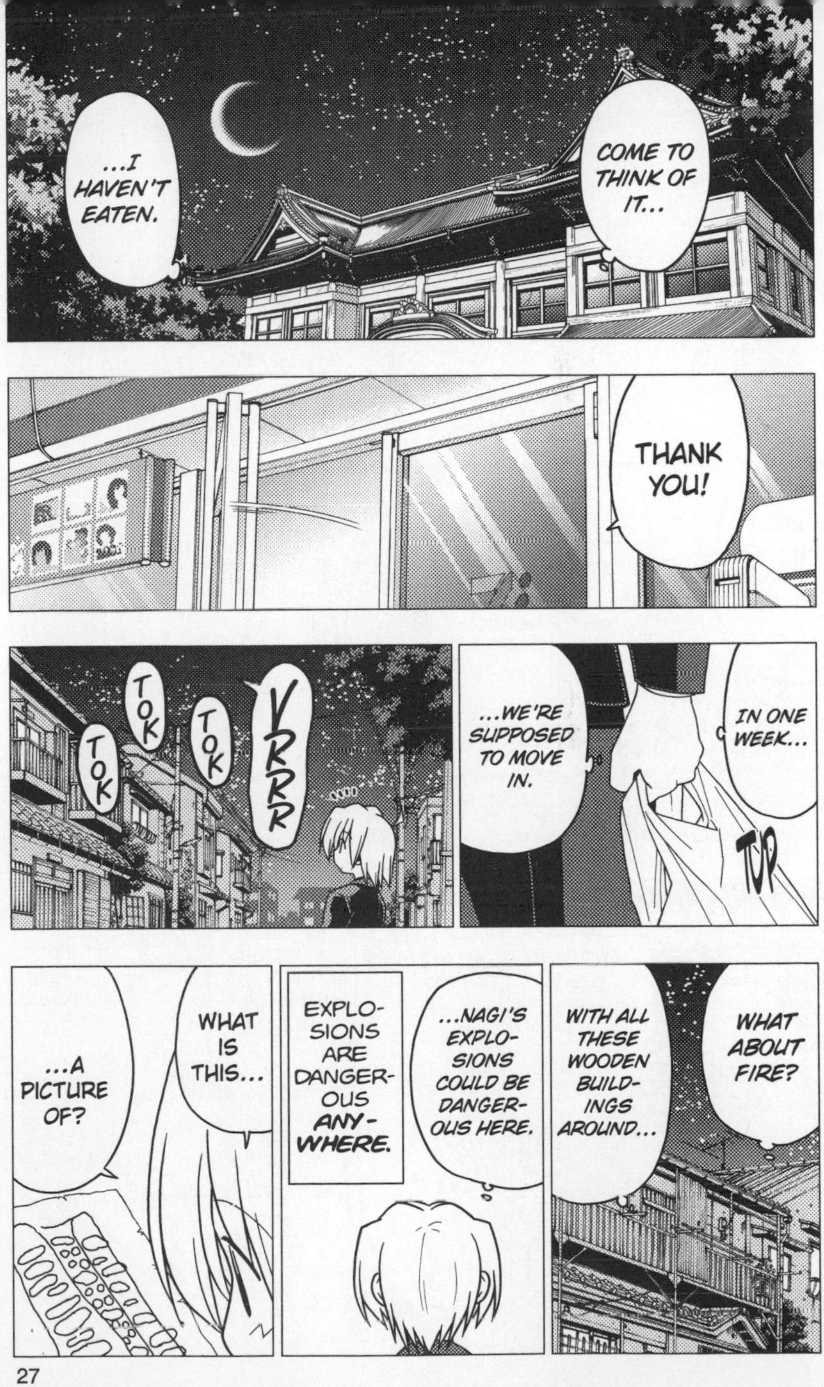
COME TO THINK OF IT...
...I HAVEN'T EATEN.
THANK YOU!
IN ONE WEEK...
...WE'RE SUPPOSED TO MOVE IN.
TUP
VRRRR
TOK
TOK
TOK
WHAT ABOUT FIRE?
WITH ALL THESE WOODEN BUILDINGS AROUND...
...NAGI'S EXPLOSIONS COULD BE DANGEROUS HERE.
EXPLOSIONS ARE DANGEROUS ANYWHERE.
WHAT IS THIS...
...A PICTURE OF?

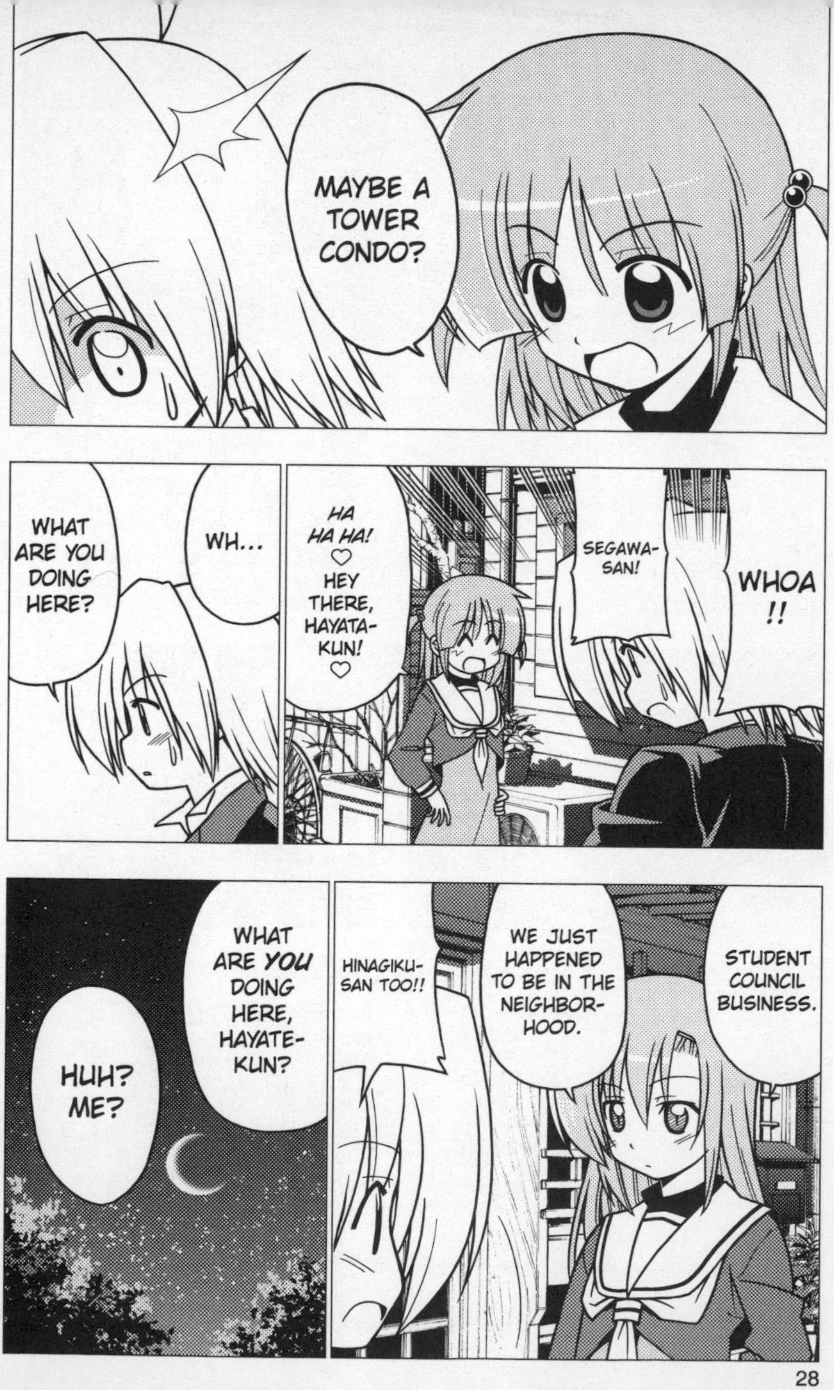
MAYBE A TOWER CONDO?
WHOA!!
SEGAWA-SAN!
HA HA HA! ♡ HEY THERE, HAYATA-KUN! ♡
WH...
WHAT ARE YOU DOING HERE?
STUDENT COUNCIL BUSINESS.
WE JUST HAPPENED TO BE IN THE NEIGHBOR-HOOD.
HINAGIKU-SAN TOO!!
WHAT ARE *YOU* DOING HERE, HAYATE-KUN?
HUH? ME?

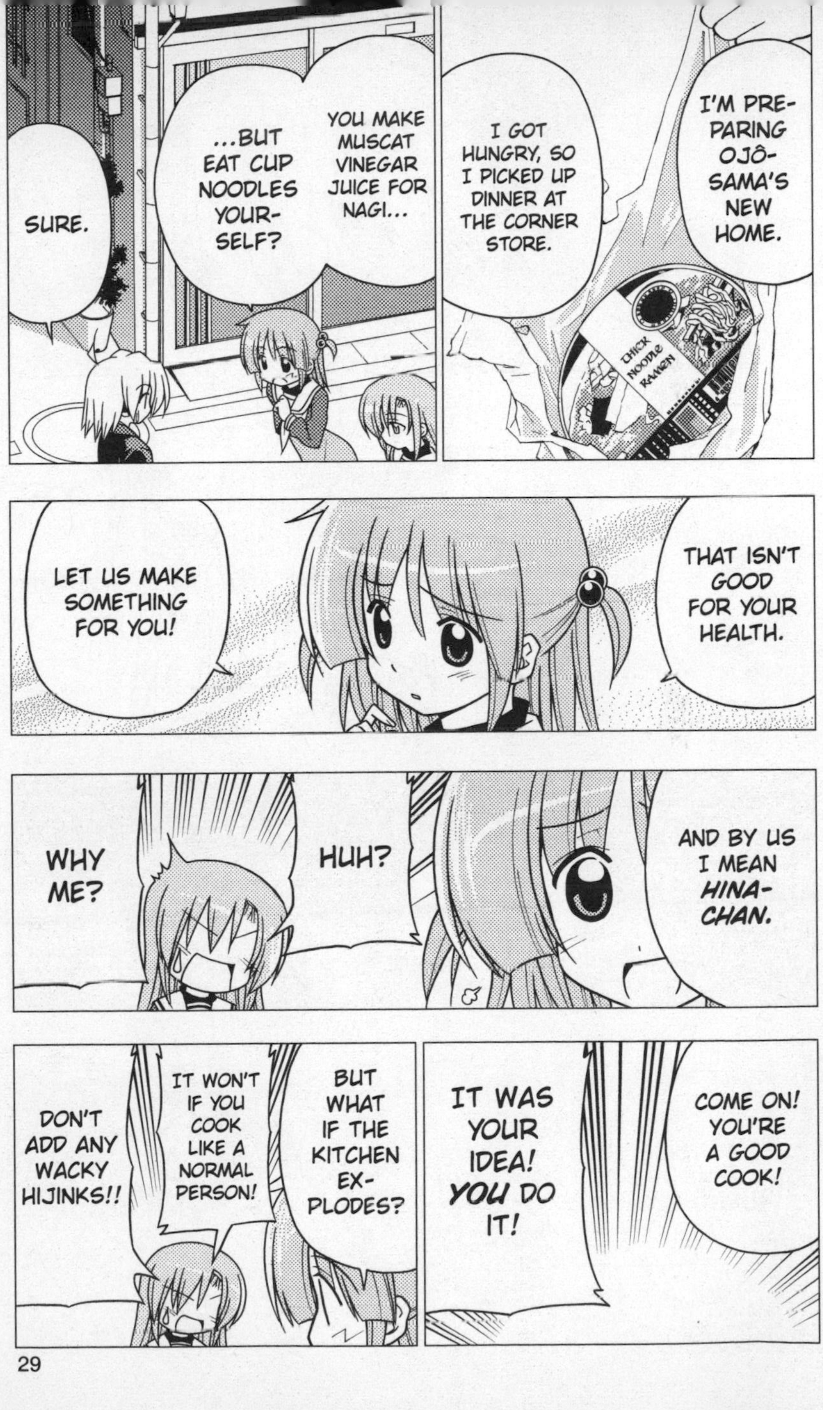
I'M PREPARING OJÔ-SAMA'S NEW HOME.
I GOT HUNGRY, SO I PICKED UP DINNER AT THE CORNER STORE.
THICK NOODLE RAMEN
YOU MAKE MUSCAT VINEGAR JUICE FOR NAGI...
...BUT EAT CUP NOODLES YOURSELF?
SURE.
THAT ISN'T GOOD FOR YOUR HEALTH.
LET US MAKE SOMETHING FOR YOU!
AND BY US I MEAN *HINA-CHAN.*
HUH?
WHY ME?
COME ON! YOU'RE A GOOD COOK!
IT WAS YOUR IDEA! ***YOU*** DO IT!
BUT WHAT IF THE KITCHEN EXPLODES?
IT WON'T IF YOU COOK LIKE A NORMAL PERSON!
DON'T ADD ANY WACKY HIJINKS!!

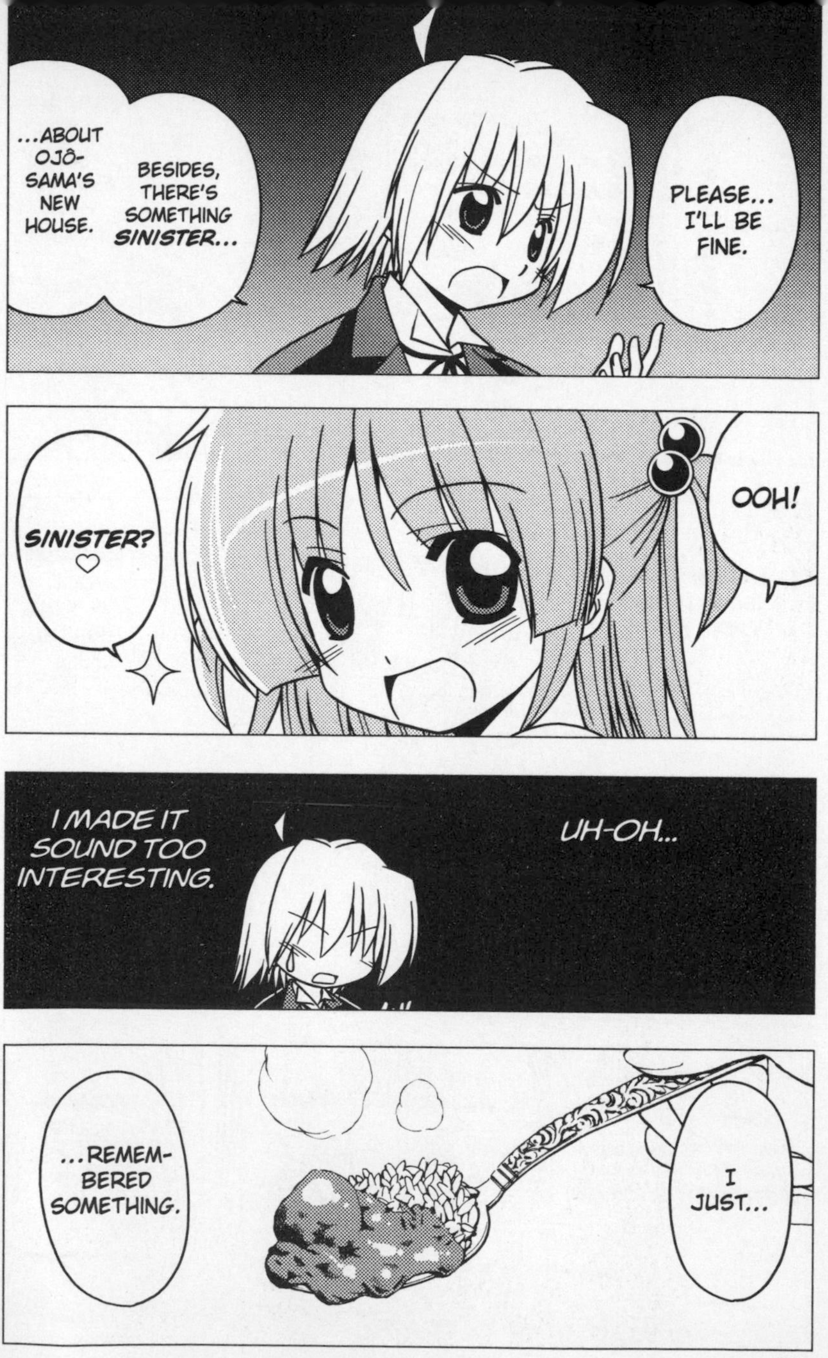
PLEASE... I'LL BE FINE.
BESIDES, THERE'S SOMETHING SINISTER...
...ABOUT OJÔ-SAMA'S NEW HOUSE.
OOH!
SINISTER? ♡
UH-OH...
I MADE IT SOUND TOO INTERESTING.
I JUST...
...REMEMBERED SOMETHING.

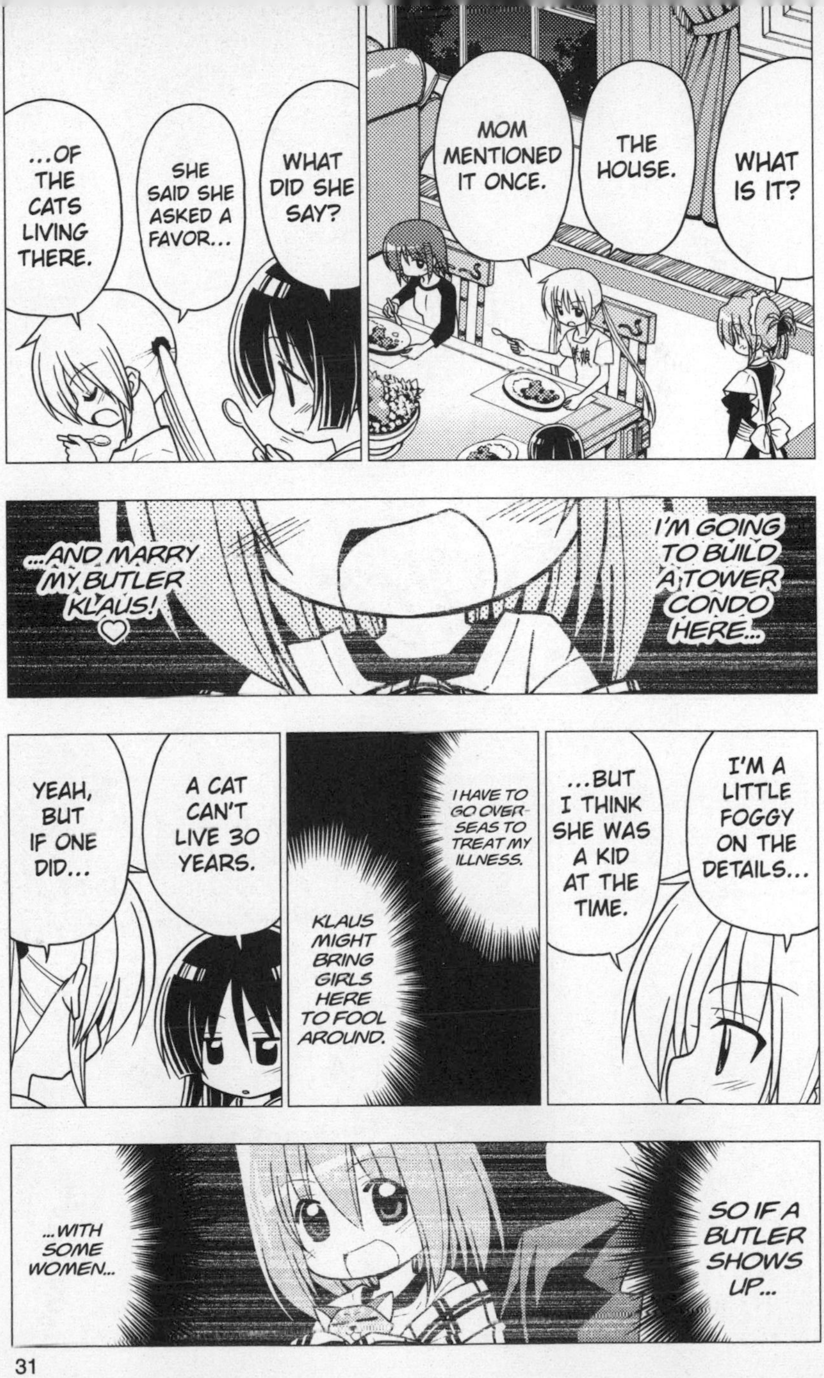
WHAT IS IT?
THE HOUSE.
MOM MENTIONED IT ONCE.
WHAT DID SHE SAY?
SHE SAID SHE ASKED A FAVOR...
...OF THE CATS LIVING THERE.
I'M GOING TO BUILD A TOWER CONDO HERE...
...AND MARRY MY BUTLER KLAUS! ♡
I'M A LITTLE FOGGY ON THE DETAILS...
...BUT I THINK SHE WAS A KID AT THE TIME.
I HAVE TO GO OVER-SEAS TO TREAT MY ILLNESS.
KLAUS MIGHT BRING GIRLS HERE TO FOOL AROUND.
A CAT CAN'T LIVE 30 YEARS.
YEAH, BUT IF ONE DID...
SO IF A BUTLER SHOWS UP...
...WITH SOME WOMEN...

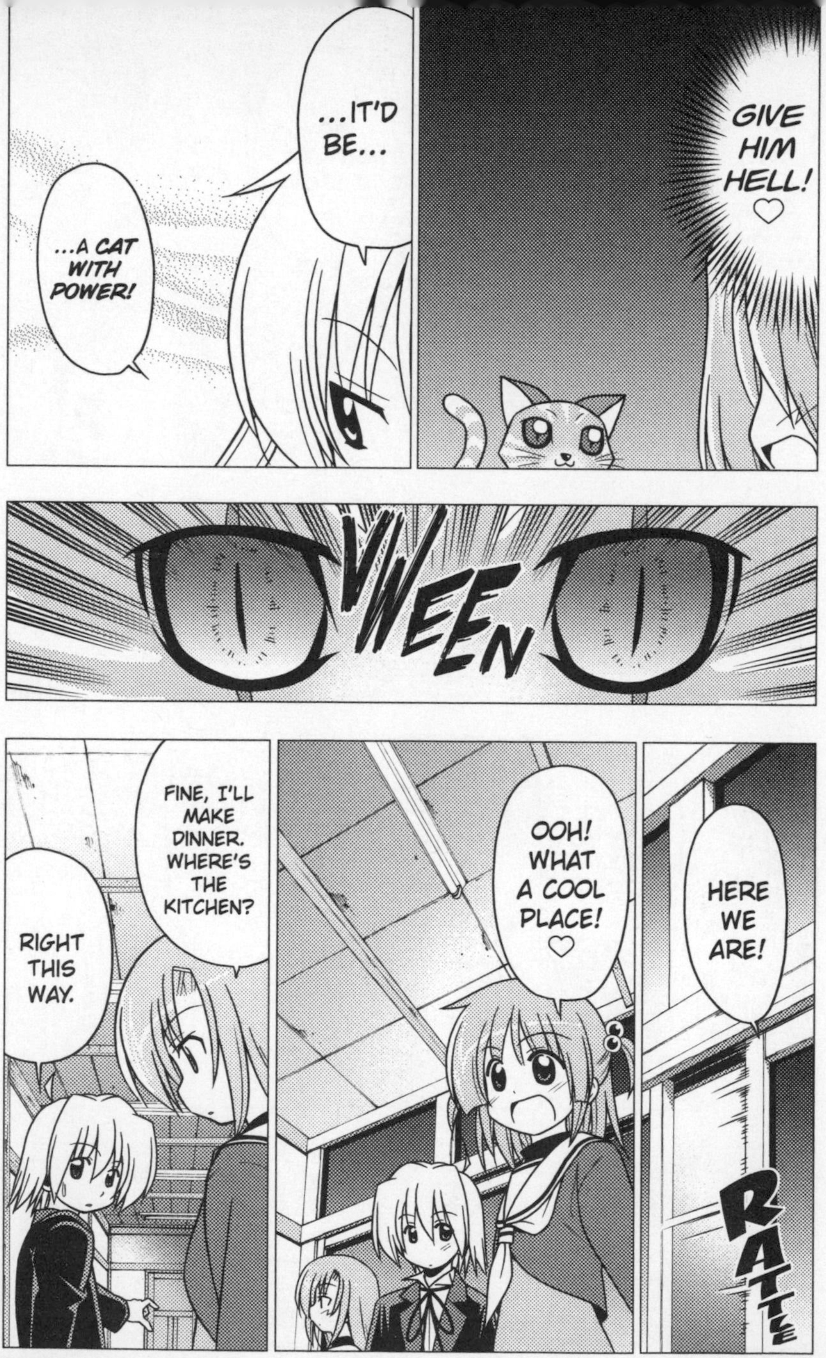
GIVE HIM HELL! ♡
...IT'D BE...
...A CAT WITH POWER!
VWEEN
HERE WE ARE!
RATTLE
OOH! WHAT A COOL PLACE! ♡
FINE, I'LL MAKE DINNER. WHERE'S THE KITCHEN?
RIGHT THIS WAY.

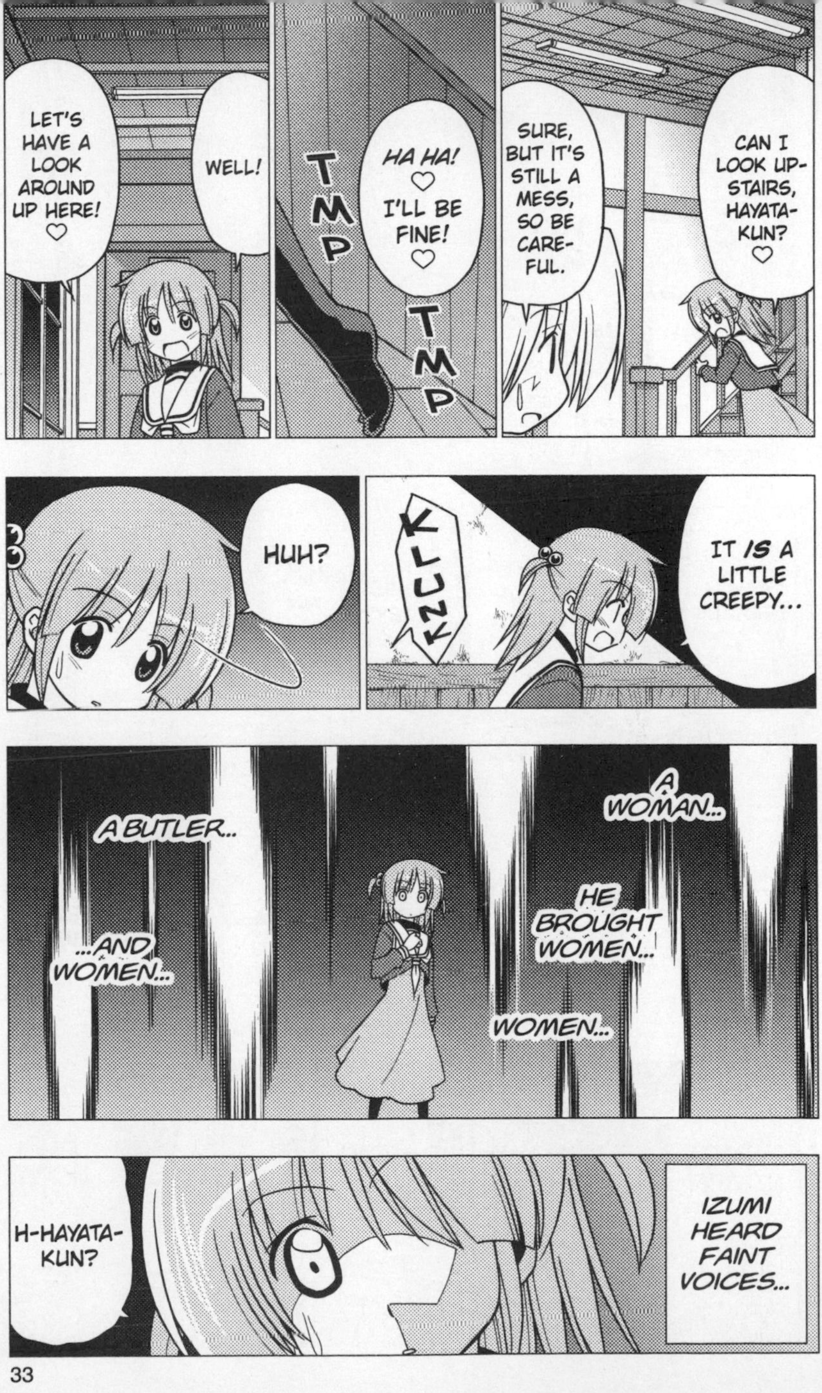
CAN I LOOK UP-STAIRS, HAYATA-KUN? ♡
SURE, BUT IT'S STILL A MESS, SO BE CARE-FUL.
HA HA! ♡ I'LL BE FINE! ♡
TMP
TMP
WELL!
LET'S HAVE A LOOK AROUND UP HERE! ♡
IT *IS* A LITTLE CREEPY...
KLUNK
HUH?
A WOMAN...
HE BROUGHT WOMEN...
A BUTLER...
WOMEN...
...AND WOMEN...
IZUMI HEARD FAINT VOICES...
H-HAYATA-KUN?

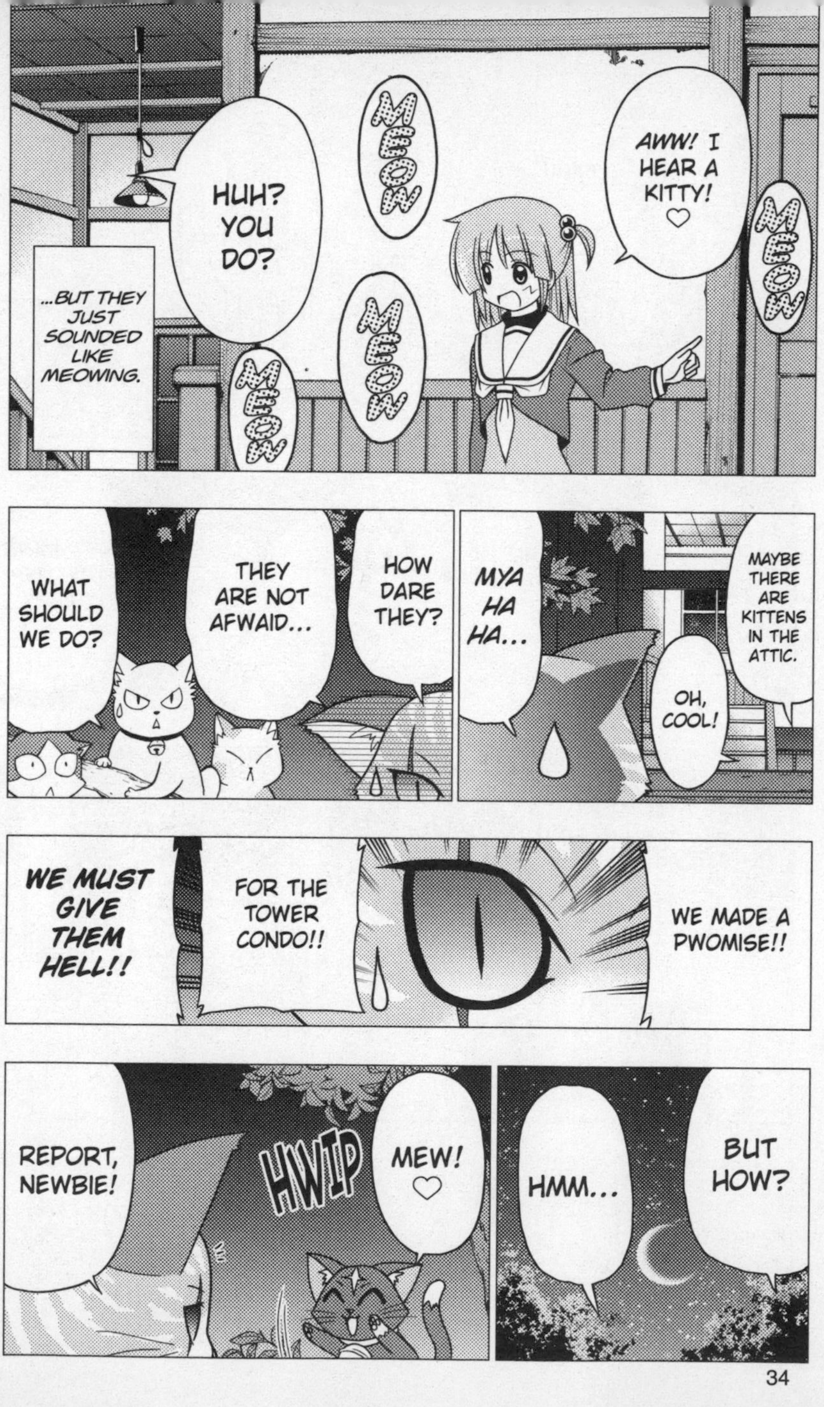
MEOW
AWW! I HEAR A KITTY! ♡
MEOW
HUH? YOU DO?
MEOW
MEOW
...BUT THEY JUST SOUNDED LIKE MEOWING.
MAYBE THERE ARE KITTENS IN THE ATTIC.
OH, COOL!
MYA HA HA...
HOW DARE THEY?
THEY ARE NOT AFWAID...
WHAT SHOULD WE DO?
WE MADE A PWOMISE!!
FOR THE TOWER CONDO!!
WE MUST GIVE THEM HELL!!
BUT HOW?
HMM...
MEW! ♡
HWIP
REPORT, NEWBIE!

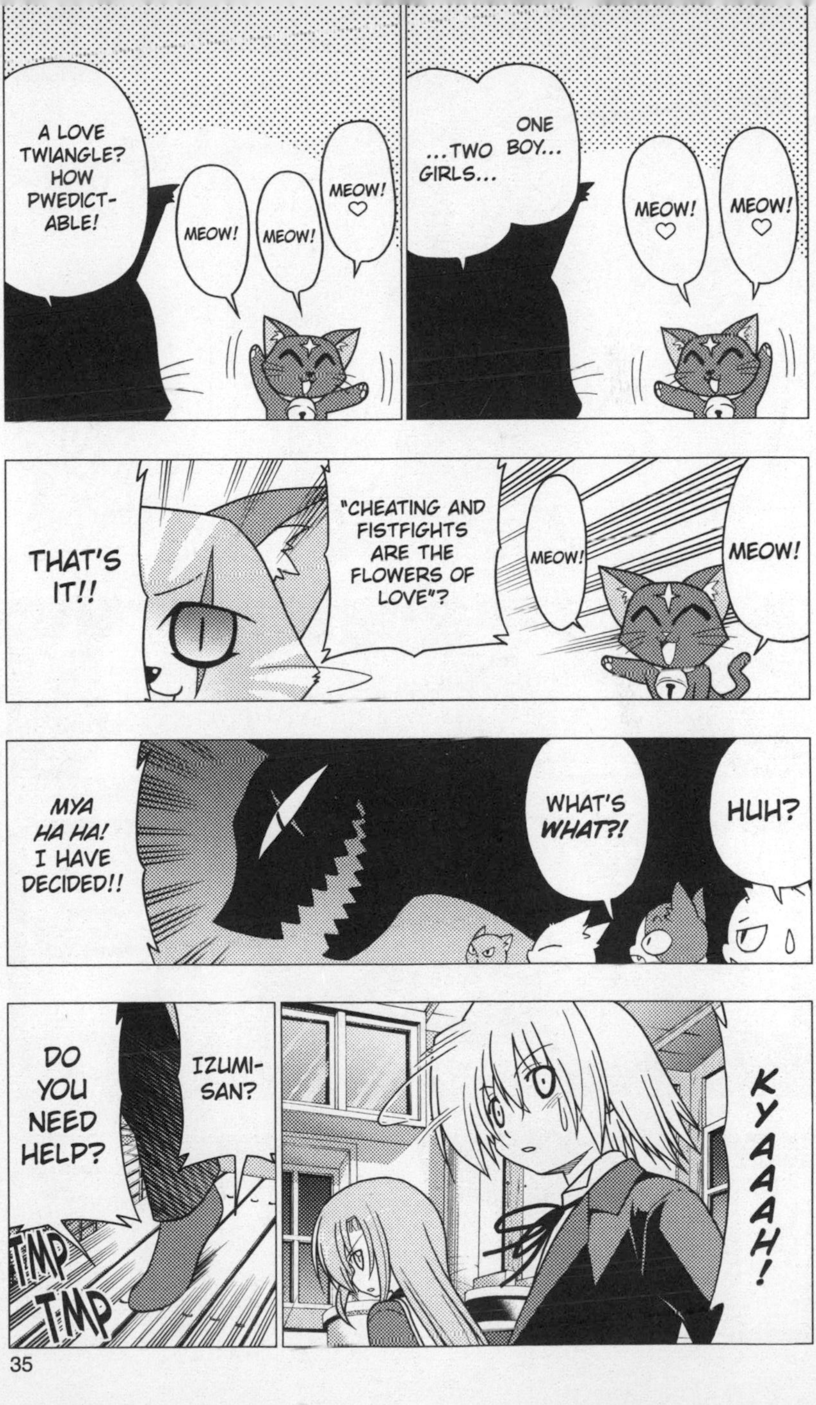
ONE BOY... ...TWO GIRLS...
MEOW! ♡
MEOW! ♡
MEOW! ♡
MEOW!
MEOW!
A LOVE TWIANGLE? HOW PWEDICT-ABLE!
MEOW!
MEOW!
"CHEATING AND FISTFIGHTS ARE THE FLOWERS OF LOVE"?
THAT'S IT!!
HUH?
WHAT'S *WHAT?!*
MYA HA HA! I HAVE DECIDED!!
KYAAAAH!
IZUMI-SAN?
DO YOU NEED HELP?
TMP
TMP

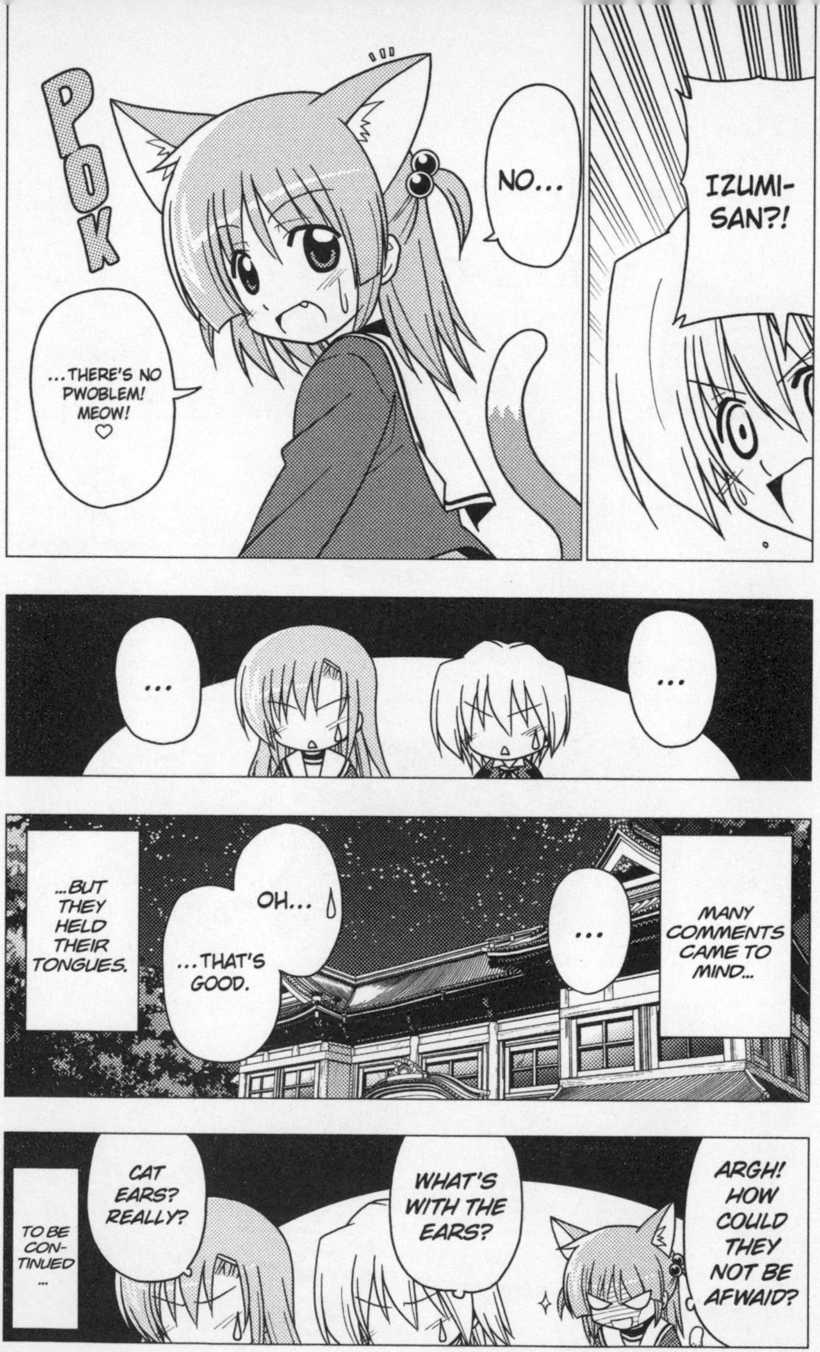
IZUMI-SAN?!
NO...
POK
...THERE'S NO PWOBLEM! MEOW! ♡
...
...
MANY COMMENTS CAME TO MIND...
...
OH... ...THAT'S GOOD.
...BUT THEY HELD THEIR TONGUES.
ARGH! HOW COULD THEY NOT BE AFWAID?
WHAT'S WITH THE EARS?
CAT EARS? REALLY?
TO BE CON-TINUED ...

Episode 3: "Meow Meow M-m-m-m-m-m-meow ♥ "

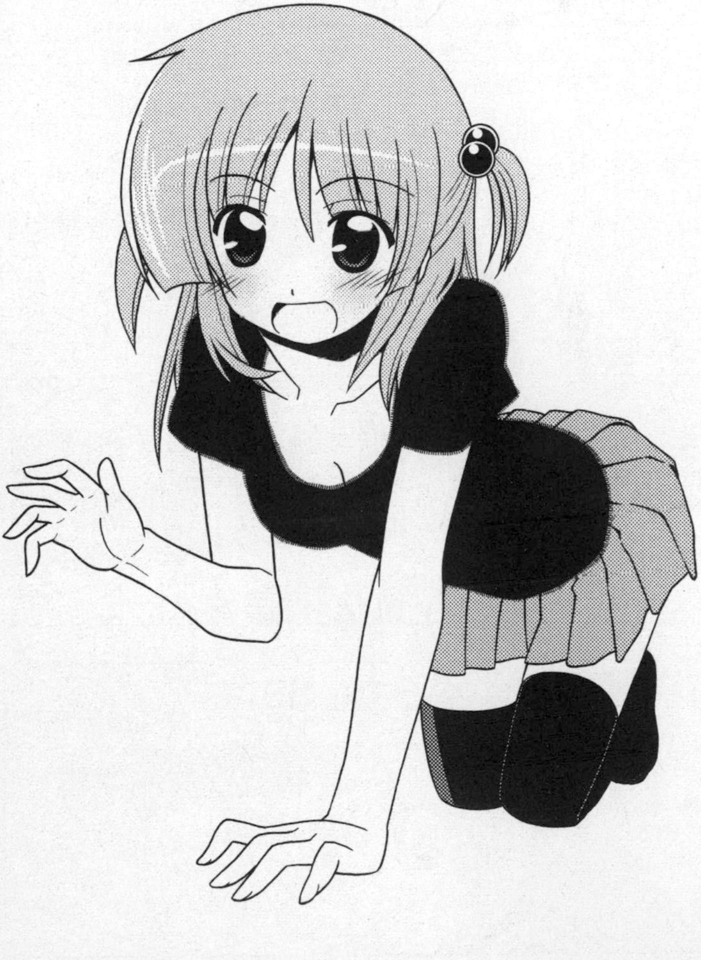

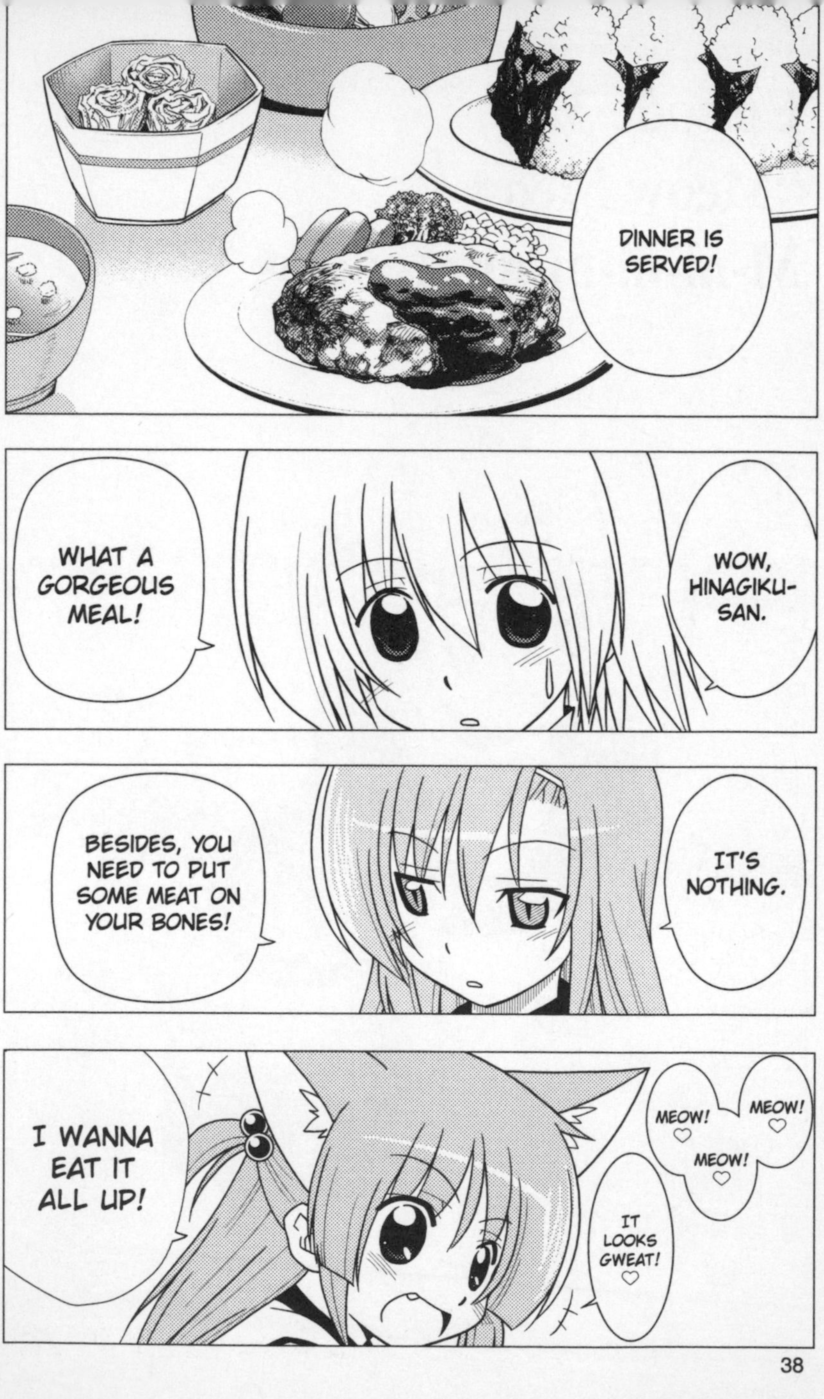
DINNER IS SERVED!
WOW, HINAGIKU-SAN.
WHAT A GORGEOUS MEAL!
IT'S NOTHING.
BESIDES, YOU NEED TO PUT SOME MEAT ON YOUR BONES!
MEOW! ♡
MEOW! ♡
MEOW! ♡
IT LOOKS GWEAT! ♡
I WANNA EAT IT ALL UP!

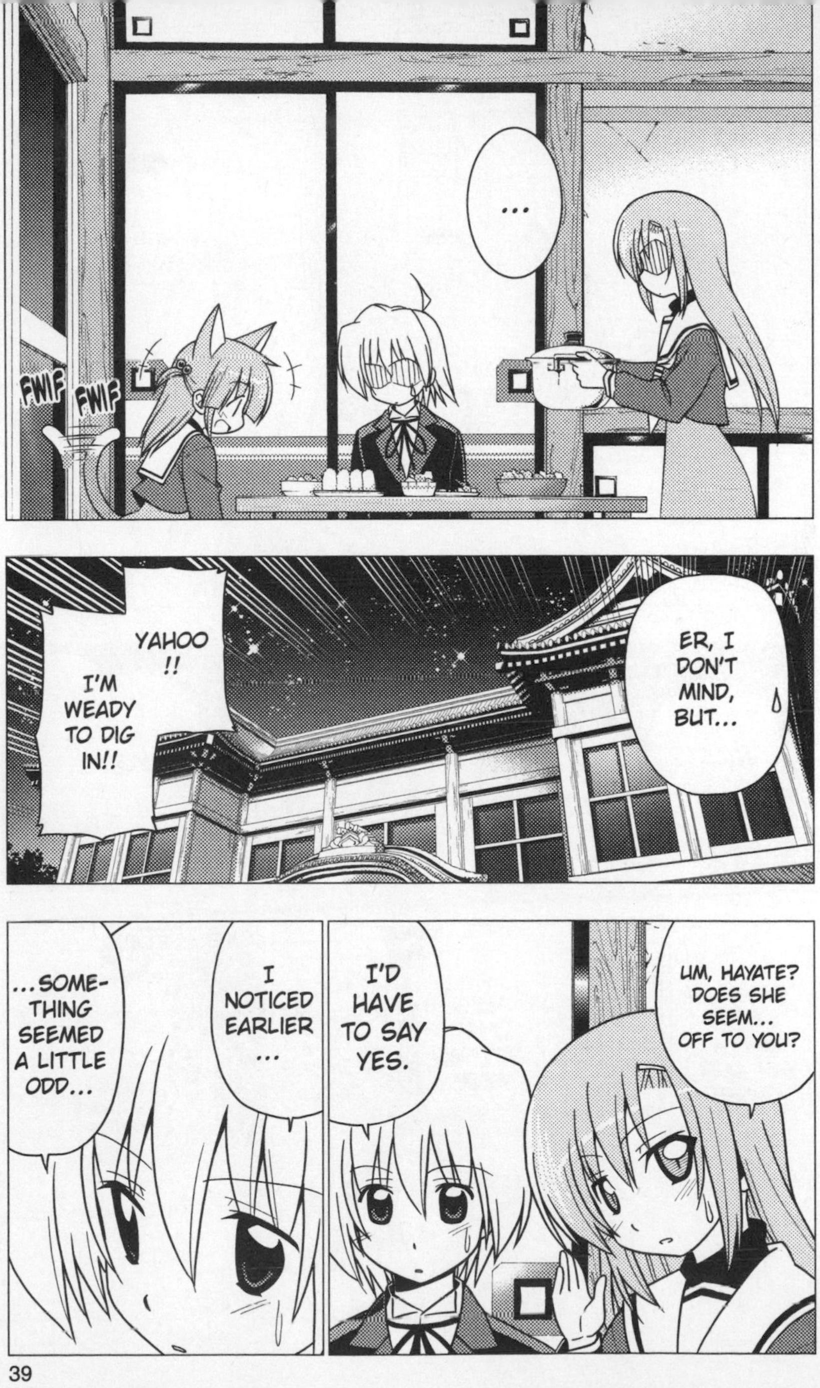
...
FWIF FWIF
ER, I DON'T MIND, BUT...
YAHOO!!
I'M WEADY TO DIG IN!!
UM, HAYATE? DOES SHE SEEM... OFF TO YOU?
I'D HAVE TO SAY YES.
I NOTICED EARLIER...
...SOME-THING SEEMED A LITTLE ODD...

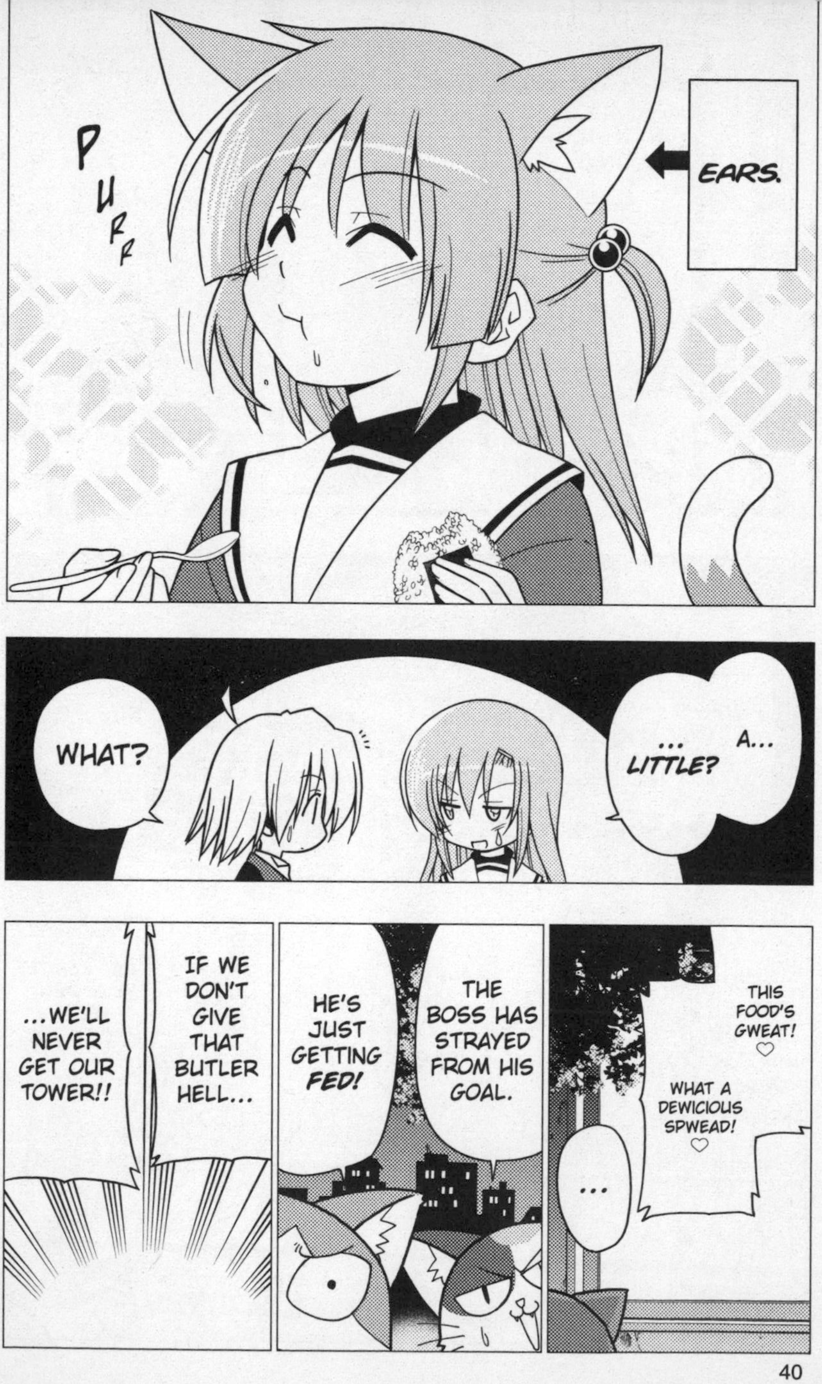
EARS.
PURR
A... ...LITTLE?
WHAT?
THIS FOOD'S GWEAT! ♡
WHAT A DEWICIOUS SPWEAD! ♡
...
THE BOSS HAS STRAYED FROM HIS GOAL.
HE'S JUST GETTING FED!
IF WE DON'T GIVE THAT BUTLER HELL...
...WE'LL NEVER GET OUR TOWER!!

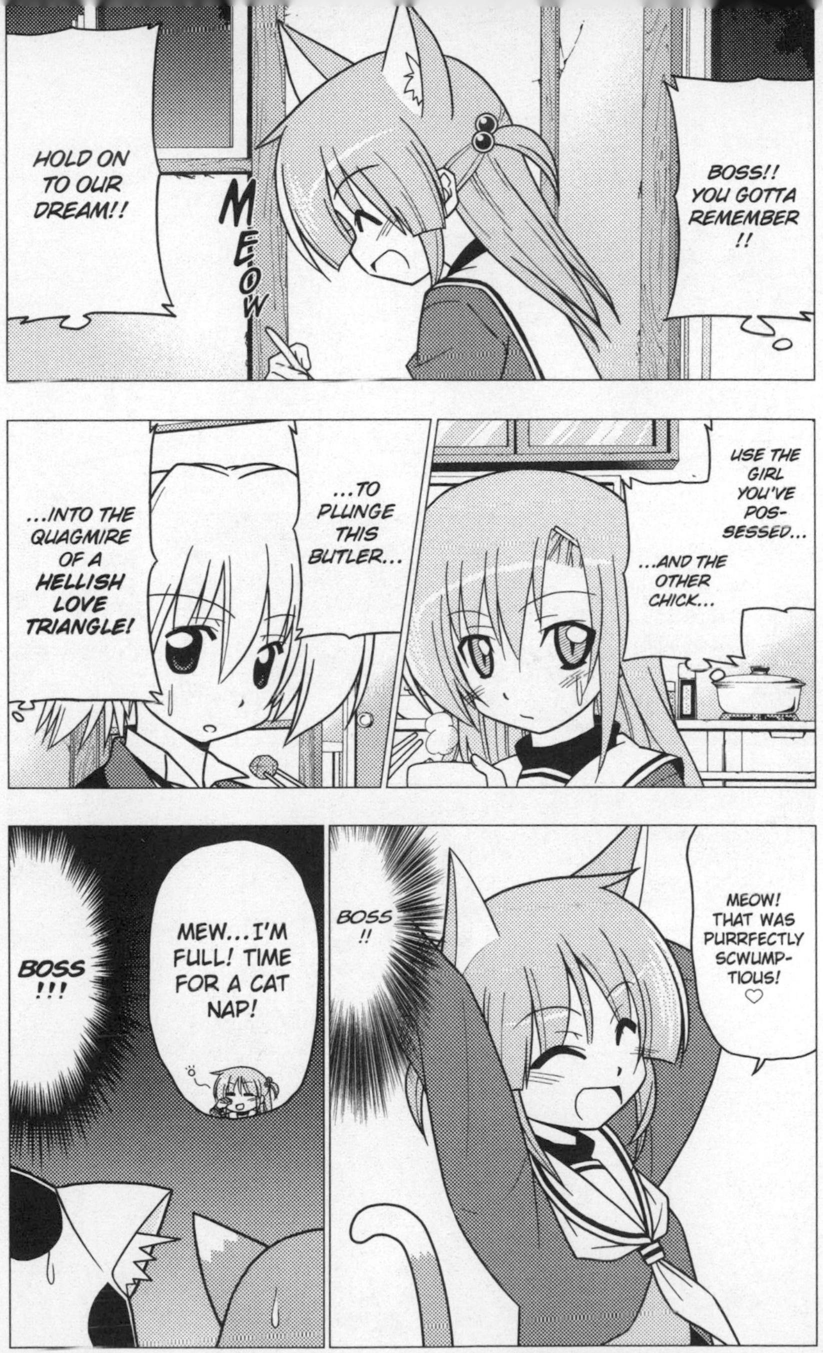
BOSS!! YOU GOTTA REMEMBER !!
MEOW
HOLD ON TO OUR DREAM!!
USE THE GIRL YOU'VE POS-SESSED...
...AND THE OTHER CHICK...
...TO PLUNGE THIS BUTLER...
...INTO THE QUAGMIRE OF A HELLISH LOVE TRIANGLE!
MEOW! THAT WAS PURRFECTLY SCWUMP-TIOUS! ♡
BOSS !!
MEW...I'M FULL! TIME FOR A CAT NAP!
BOSS !!!

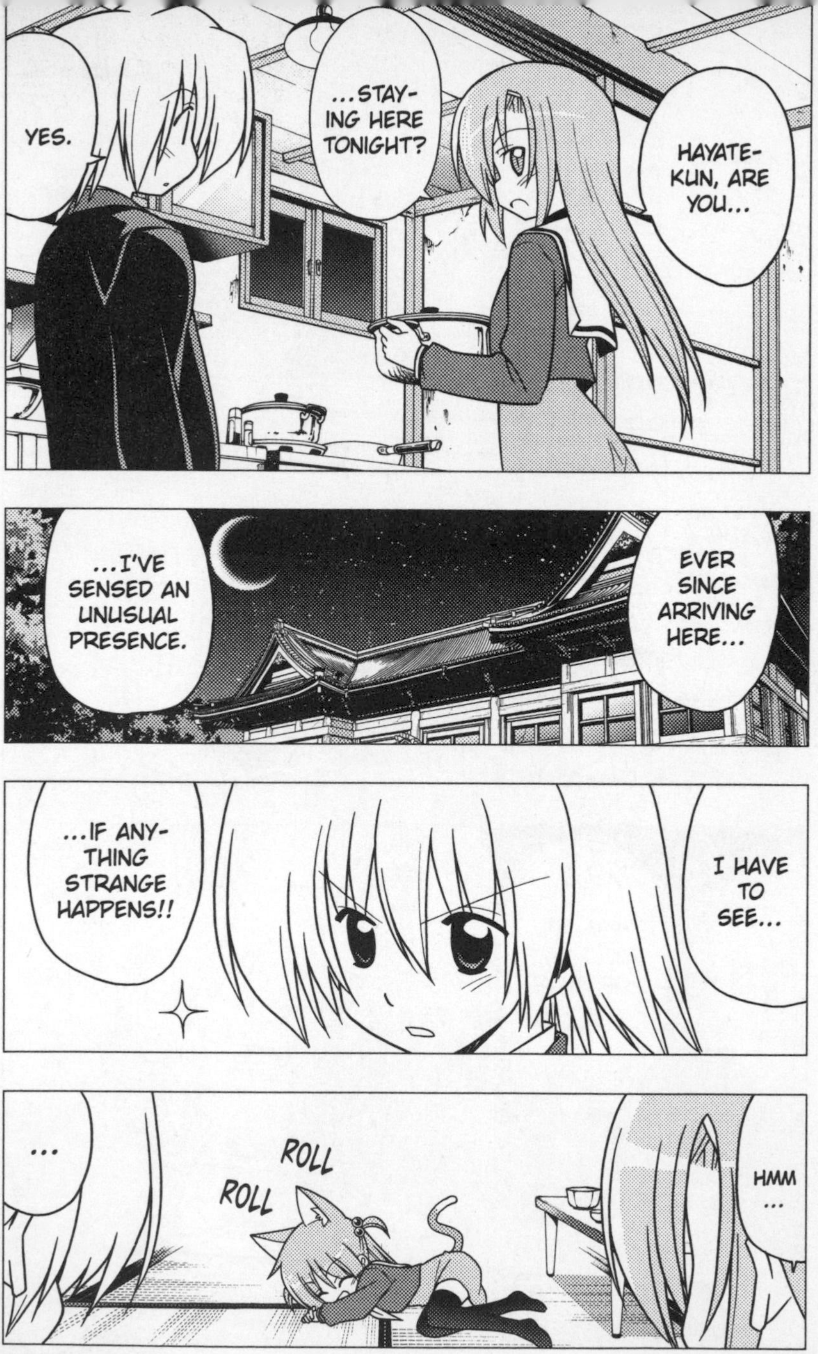
HAYATE-KUN, ARE YOU...
...STAYING HERE TONIGHT?
YES.
EVER SINCE ARRIVING HERE...
...I'VE SENSED AN UNUSUAL PRESENCE.
I HAVE TO SEE...
...IF ANYTHING STRANGE HAPPENS!!
HMM...
ROLL
ROLL
...

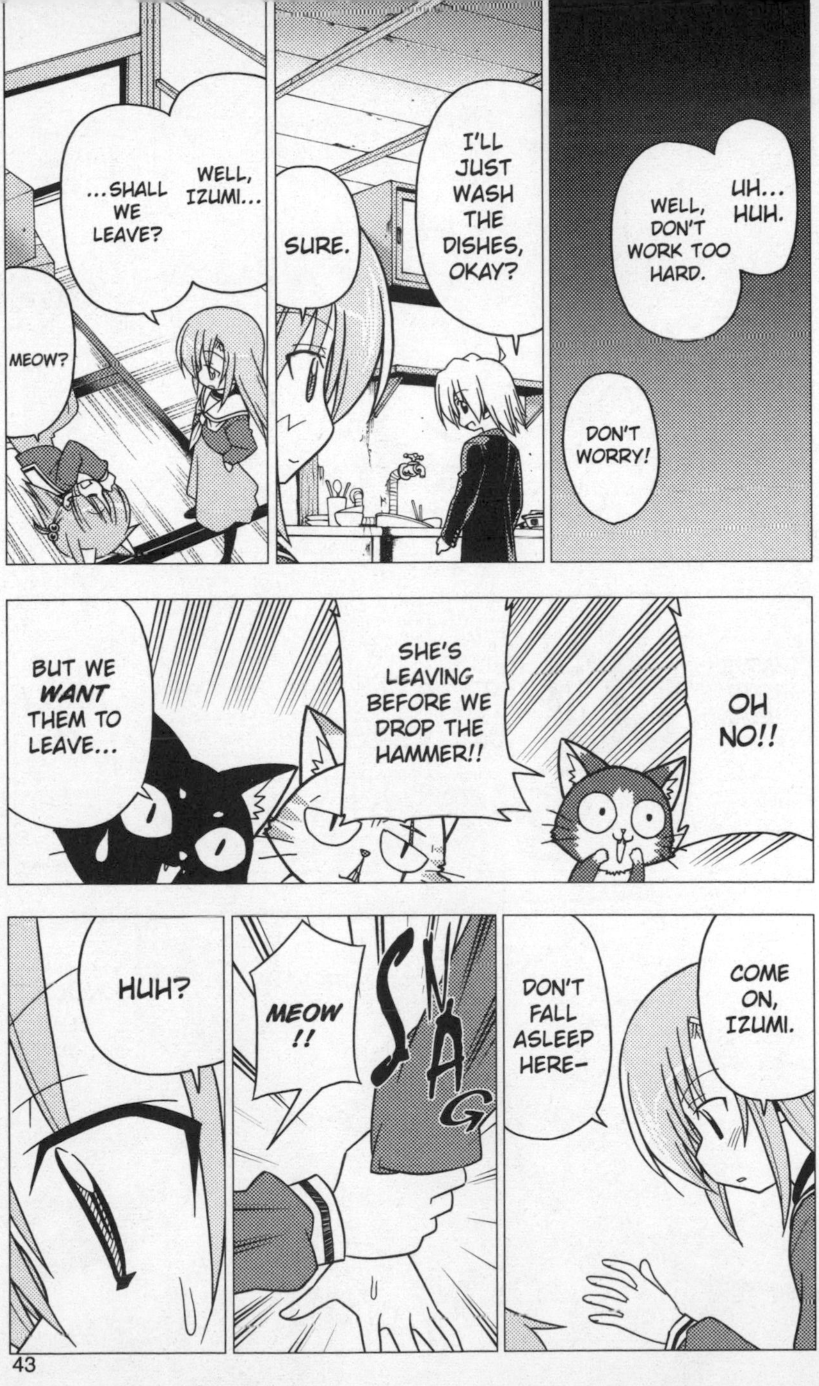
UH... HUH.
WELL, DON'T WORK TOO HARD.
DON'T WORRY!
I'LL JUST WASH THE DISHES, OKAY?
SURE.
WELL, IZUMI...
...SHALL WE LEAVE?
MEOW?
OH NO!!
SHE'S LEAVING BEFORE WE DROP THE HAMMER!!
BUT WE *WANT* THEM TO LEAVE...
COME ON, IZUMI.
DON'T FALL ASLEEP HERE-
SNAG
MEOW!!
HUH?

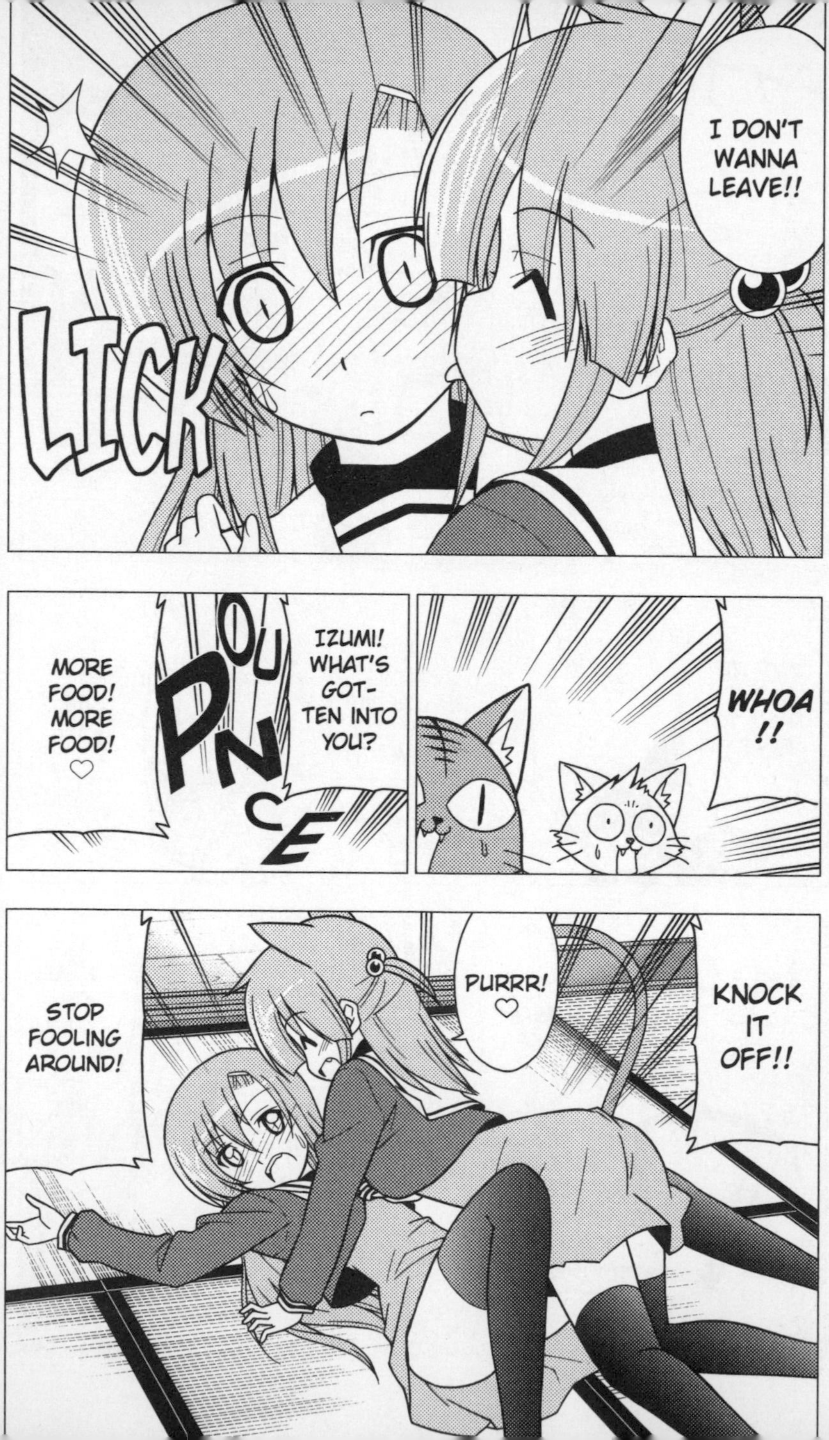
I DON'T WANNA LEAVE!!
LICK
WHOA!!
IZUMI! WHAT'S GOT-TEN INTO YOU?
POUNCE
MORE FOOD! MORE FOOD! ♡
KNOCK IT OFF!!
PURRR! ♡
STOP FOOLING AROUND!

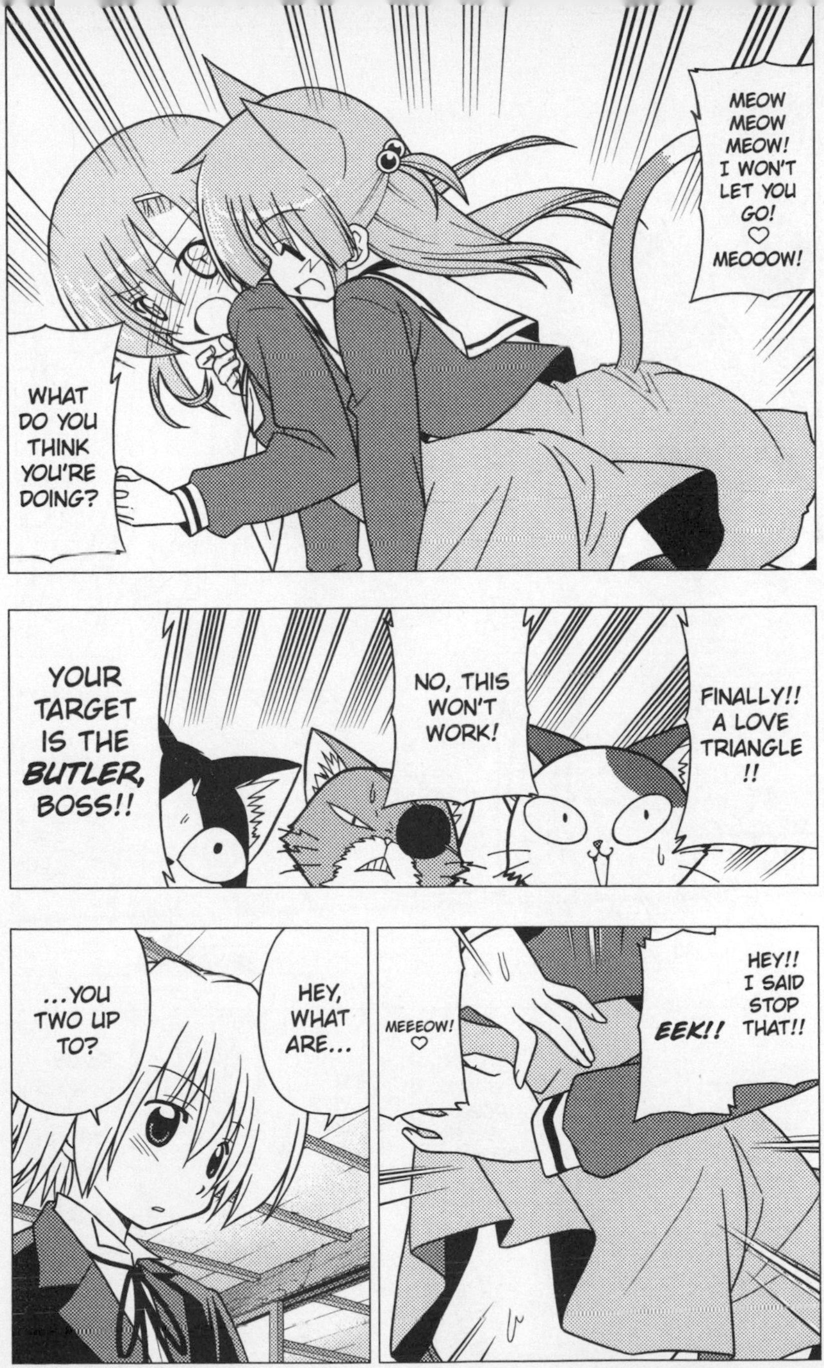
MEOW MEOW MEOW! I WON'T LET YOU GO! ♡ MEOOOW!
WHAT DO YOU THINK YOU'RE DOING?
FINALLY!! A LOVE TRIANGLE !!
NO, THIS WON'T WORK!
YOUR TARGET IS THE BUTLER, BOSS!!
HEY!! I SAID STOP THAT!!
EEK!!
MEEEOW! ♡
HEY, WHAT ARE...
...YOU TWO UP TO?

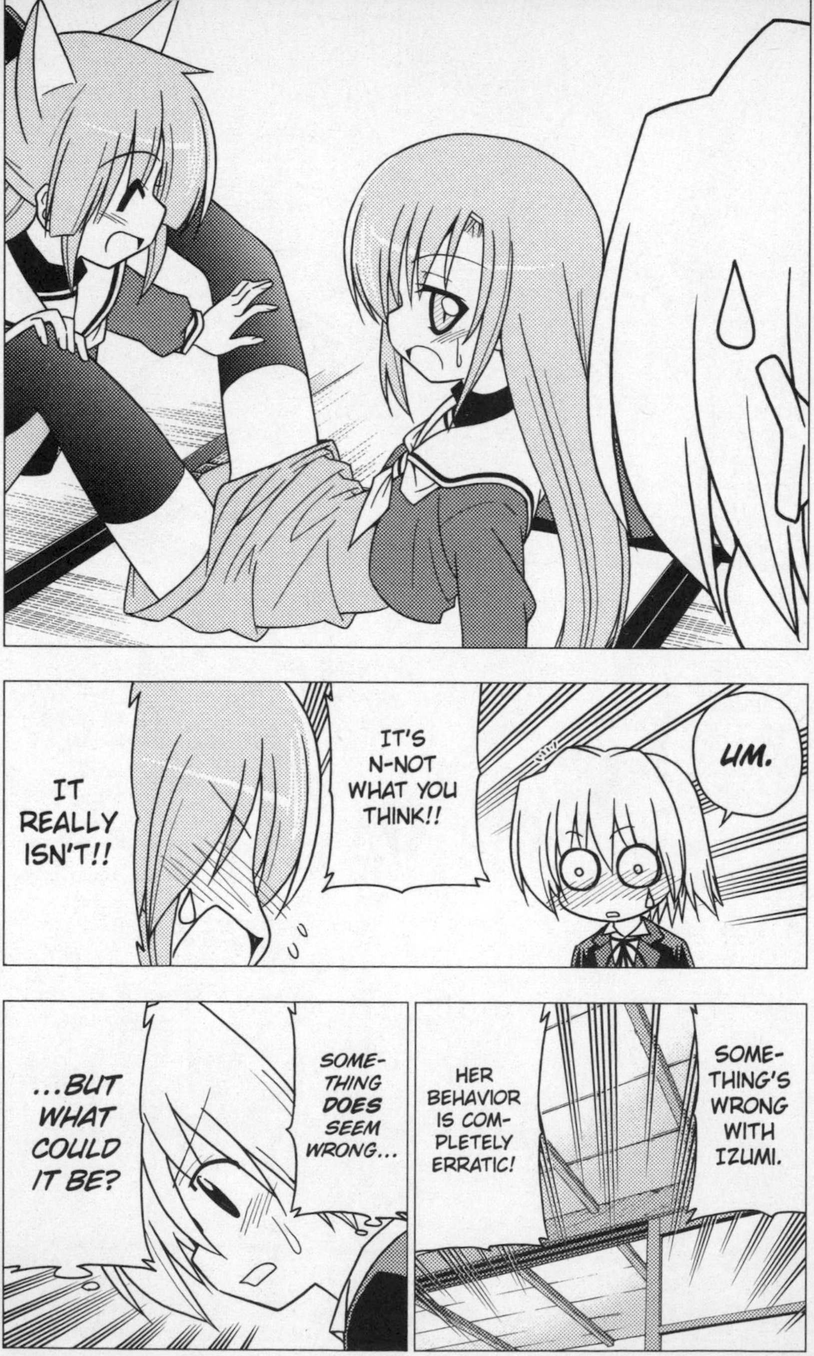
UM.
IT'S N-NOT WHAT YOU THINK!!
IT REALLY ISN'T!!
SOME-THING'S WRONG WITH IZUMI.
HER BEHAVIOR IS COM-PLETELY ERRATIC!
SOME-THING DOES SEEM WRONG...
...BUT WHAT COULD IT BE?

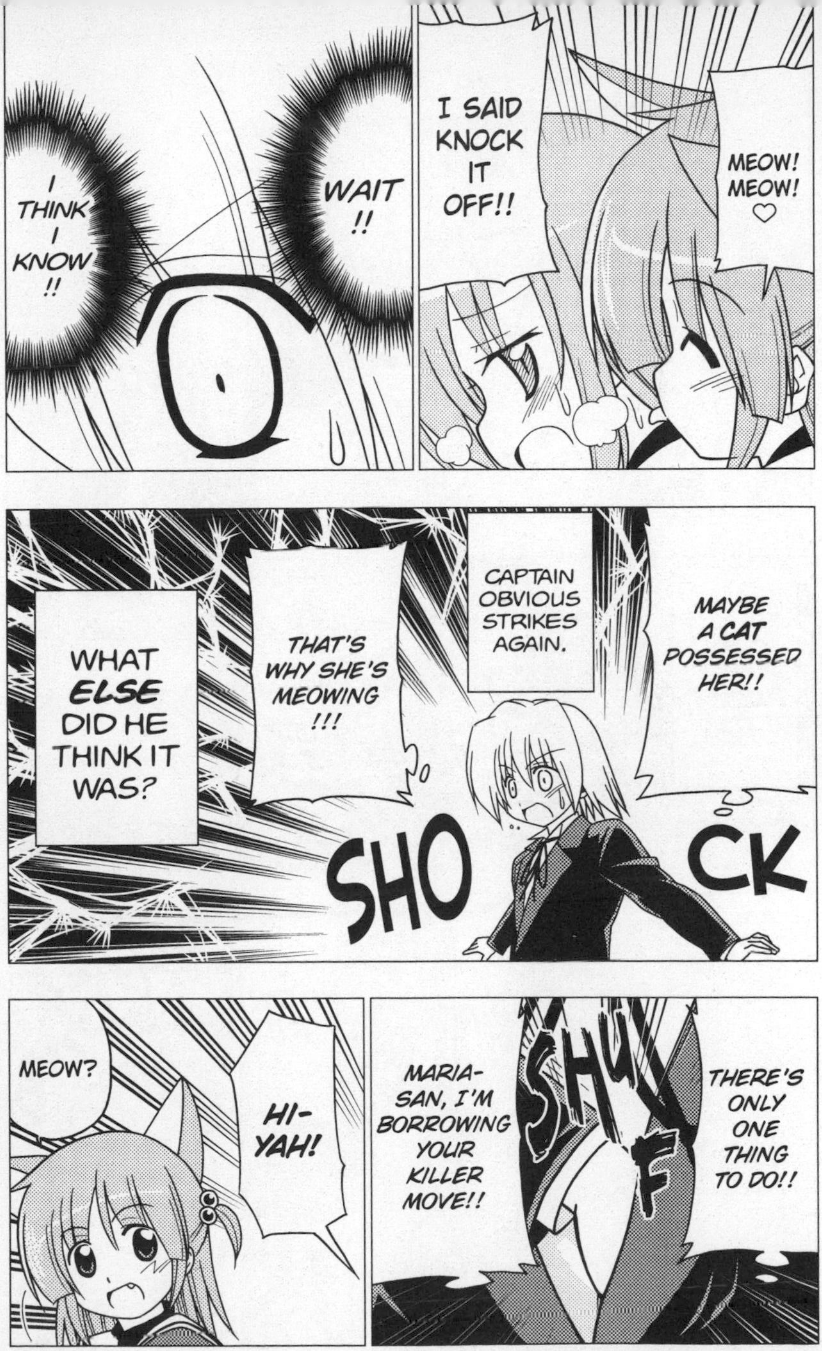
MEOW! MEOW! ♡
I SAID KNOCK IT OFF!!
WAIT!!
I THINK I KNOW!!
MAYBE A CAT POSSESSED HER!!
CAPTAIN OBVIOUS STRIKES AGAIN.
SHOCK
THAT'S WHY SHE'S MEOWING!!!
WHAT ELSE DID HE THINK IT WAS?
THERE'S ONLY ONE THING TO DO!!
SHUFF
MARIA-SAN, I'M BORROWING YOUR KILLER MOVE!!
HI-YAH!
MEOW?

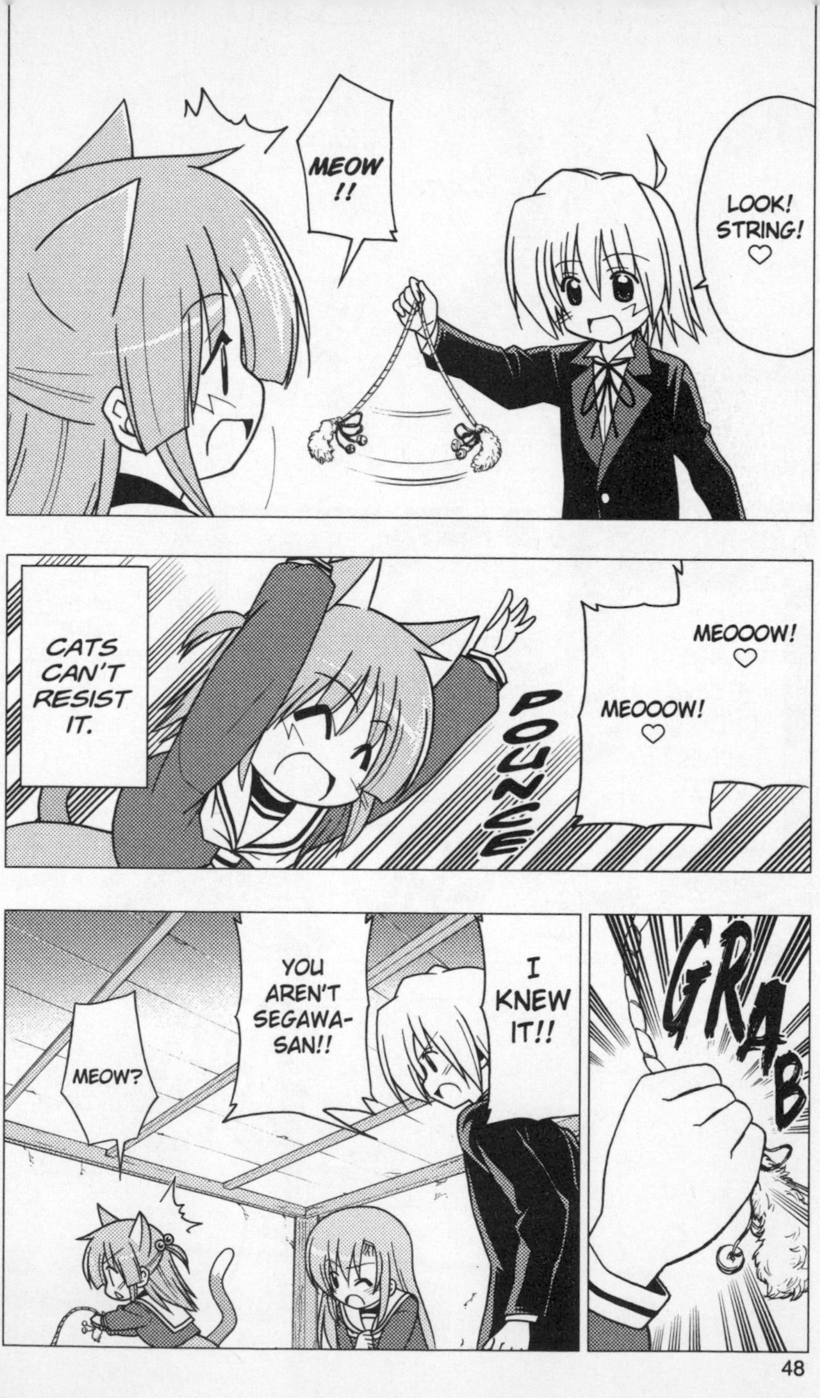
LOOK! STRING! ♡
MEOW!!
MEOOOW! ♡
MEOOOW! ♡
POUNCE
CATS CAN'T RESIST IT.
GRAB
I KNEW IT!!
YOU AREN'T SEGAWA-SAN!!
MEOW?

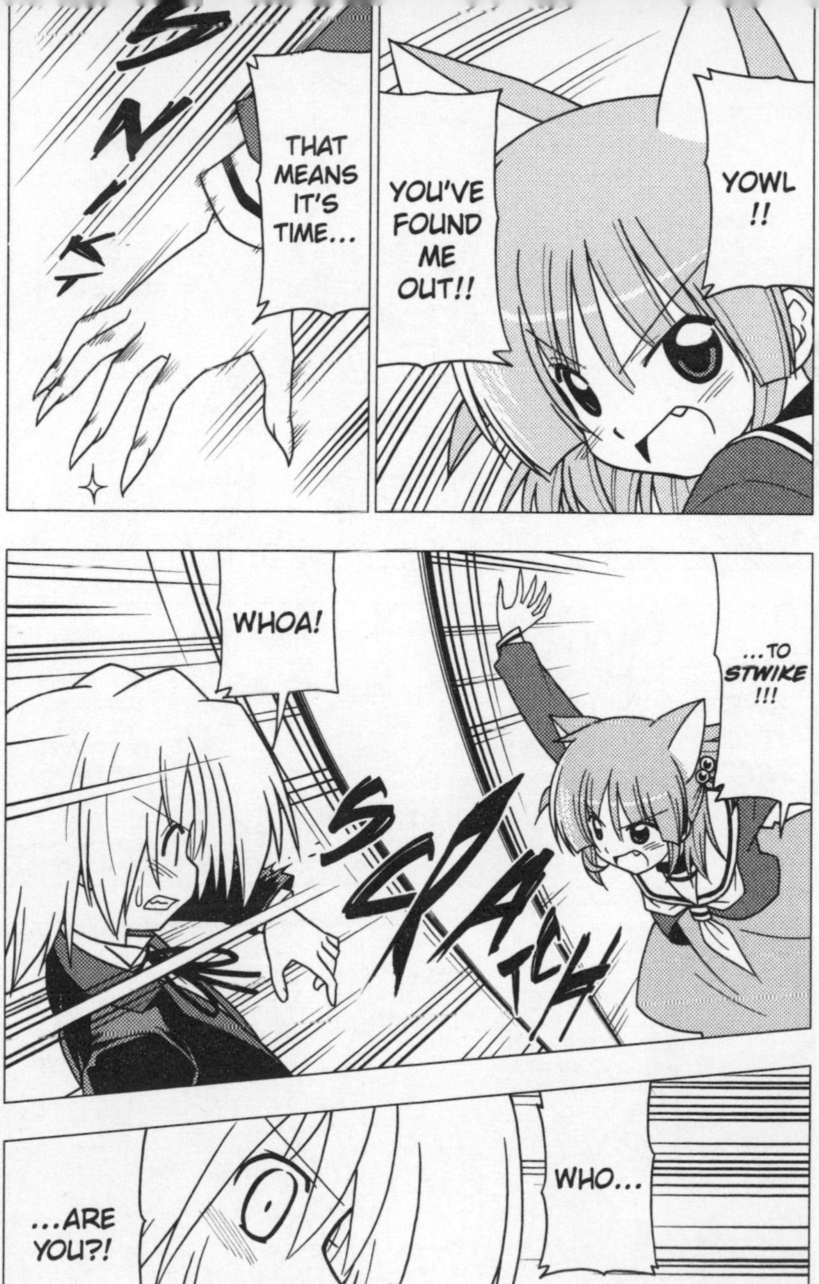
YOWL !!
YOU'VE FOUND ME OUT!!
THAT MEANS IT'S TIME...
SNIKT
...TO STWIKE !!!
WHOA!
SCRATCH
WHO...
...ARE YOU?!

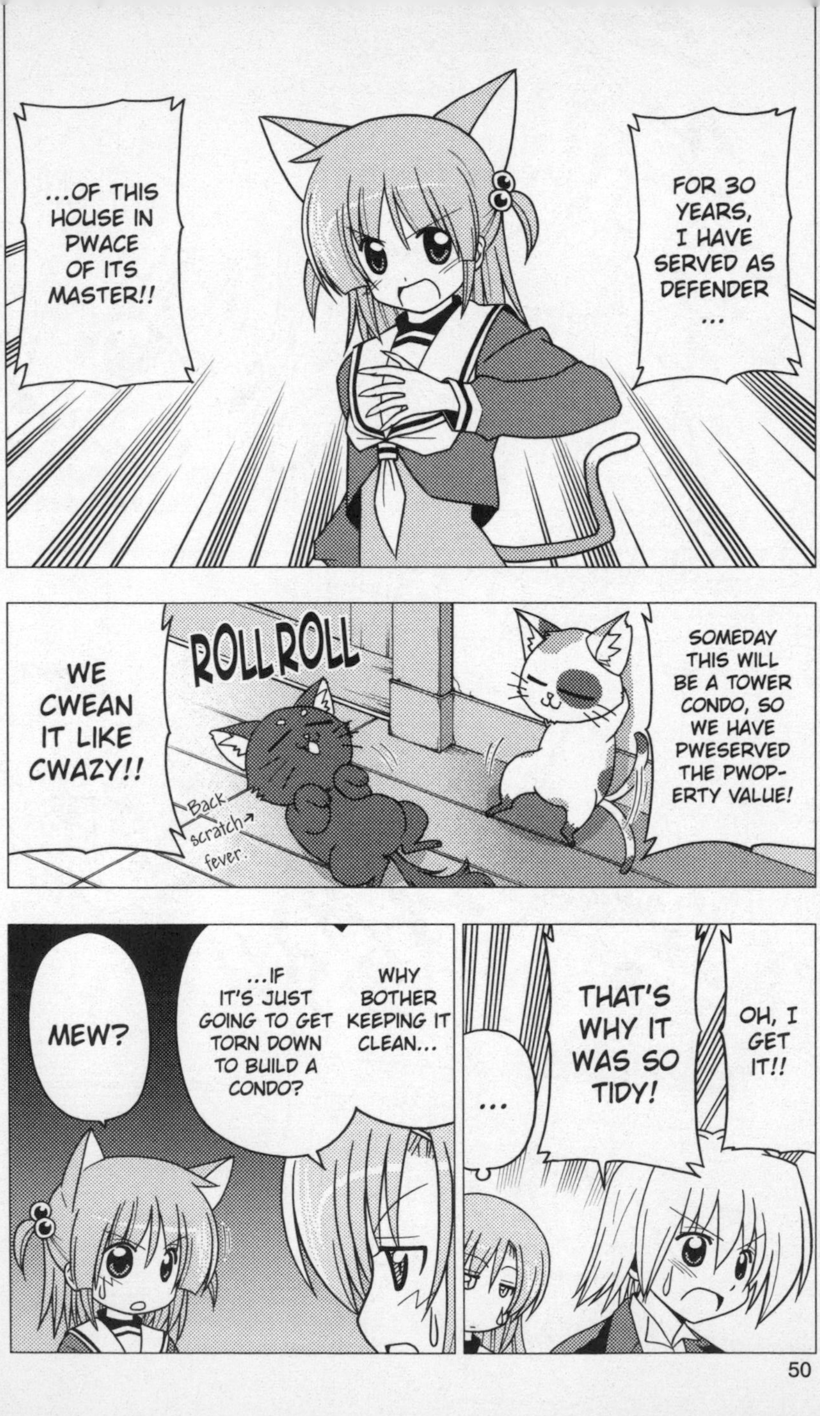
FOR 30 YEARS, I HAVE SERVED AS DEFENDER ...
...OF THIS HOUSE IN PWACE OF ITS MASTER!!
SOMEDAY THIS WILL BE A TOWER CONDO, SO WE HAVE PWESERVED THE PWOP-ERTY VALUE!
ROLL ROLL
WE CWEAN IT LIKE CWAZY!!
Back scratch fever.
OH, I GET IT!!
THAT'S WHY IT WAS SO TIDY!
...
WHY BOTHER KEEPING IT CLEAN...
...IF IT'S JUST GOING TO GET TORN DOWN TO BUILD A CONDO?
MEW?

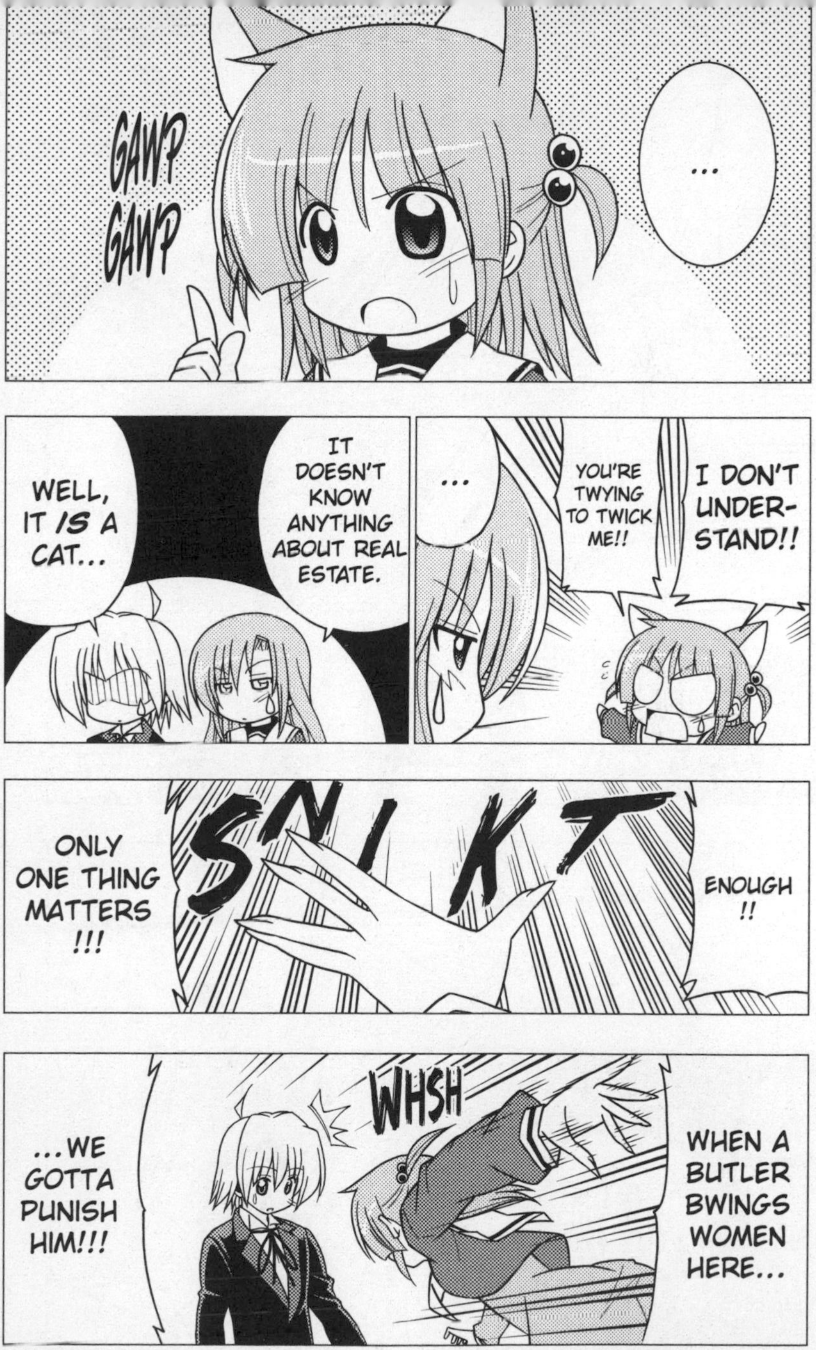
...
GAWP GAWP
I DON'T UNDERSTAND!!
YOU'RE TWYING TO TWICK ME!!
...
IT DOESN'T KNOW ANYTHING ABOUT REAL ESTATE.
WELL, IT *IS* A CAT...
ENOUGH !!
SNIKT
ONLY ONE THING MATTERS !!!
WHEN A BUTLER BWINGS WOMEN HERE...
WHSH
...WE GOTTA PUNISH HIM!!!

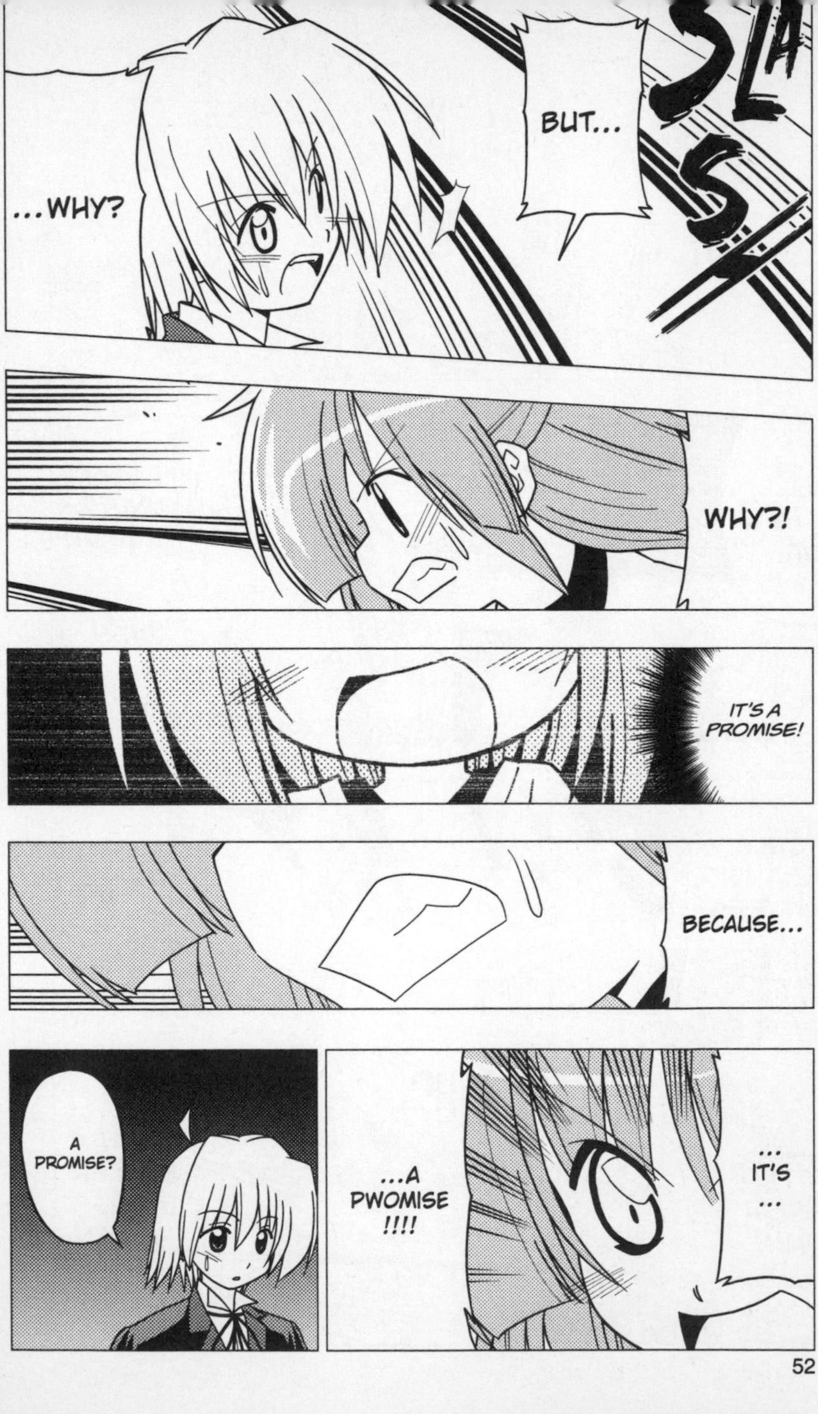
SLASH
BUT...
...WHY?
WHY?!
IT'S A PROMISE!
BECAUSE...
...IT'S...
...A PWOMISE!!!!
A PROMISE?

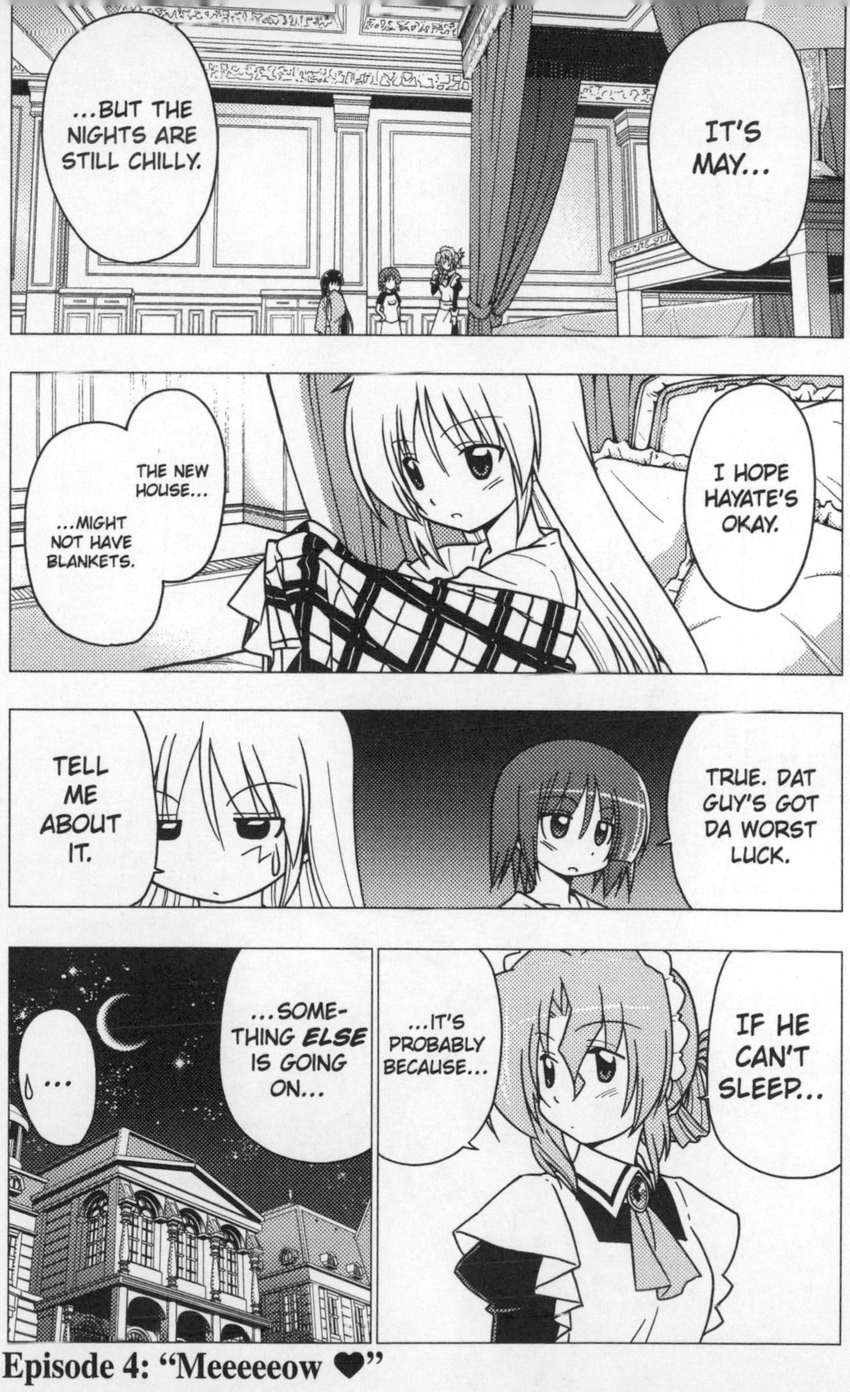
IT'S MAY...
...BUT THE NIGHTS ARE STILL CHILLY.
I HOPE HAYATE'S OKAY.
THE NEW HOUSE...
...MIGHT NOT HAVE BLANKETS.
TRUE. DAT GUY'S GOT DA WORST LUCK.
TELL ME ABOUT IT.
IF HE CAN'T SLEEP...
...IT'S PROBABLY BECAUSE...
...SOME-THING *ELSE* IS GOING ON...
...

Episode 4: "Meeeeeow ♥"

Episode 4:
"Meeeeeow ♥"

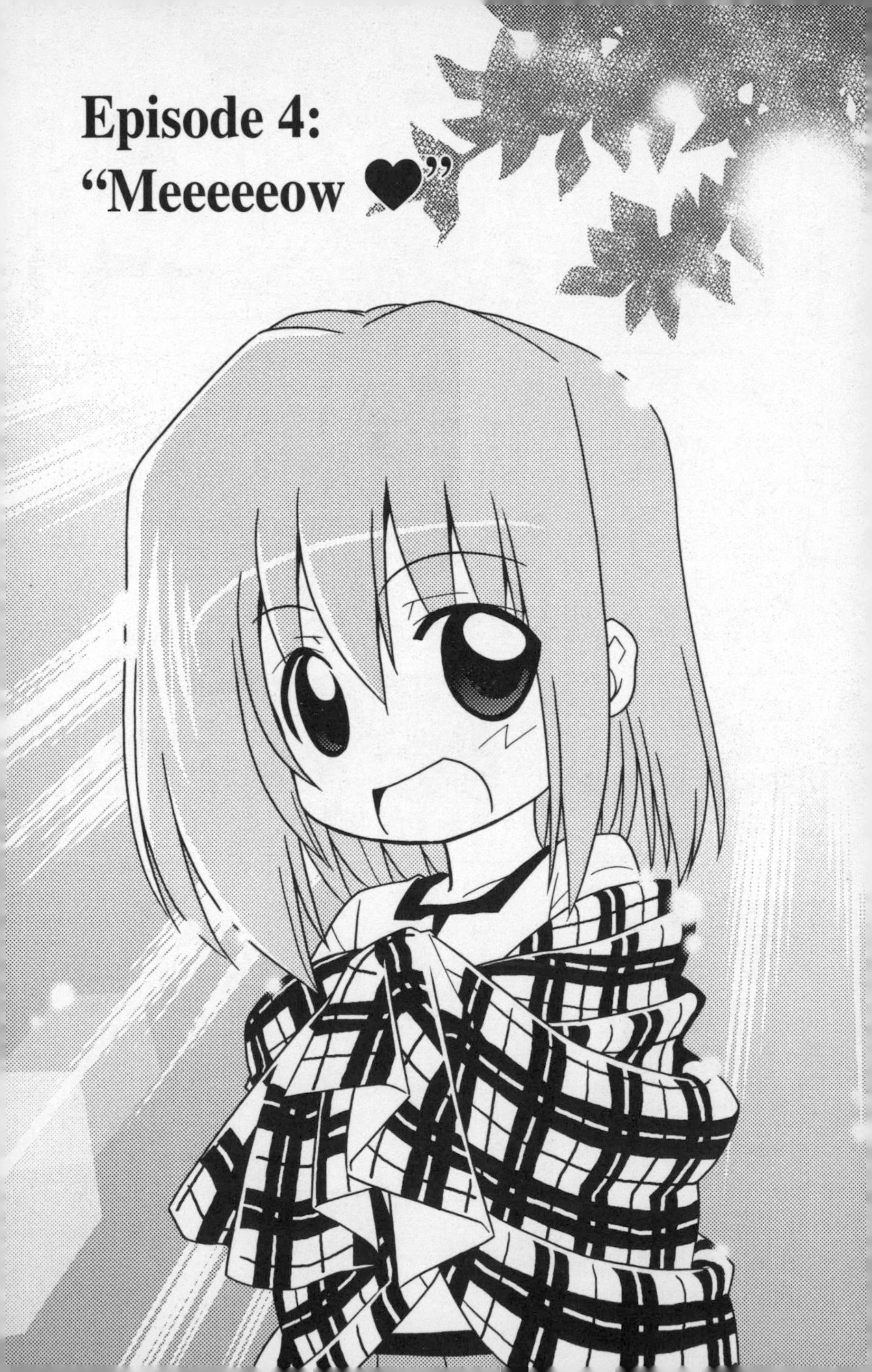

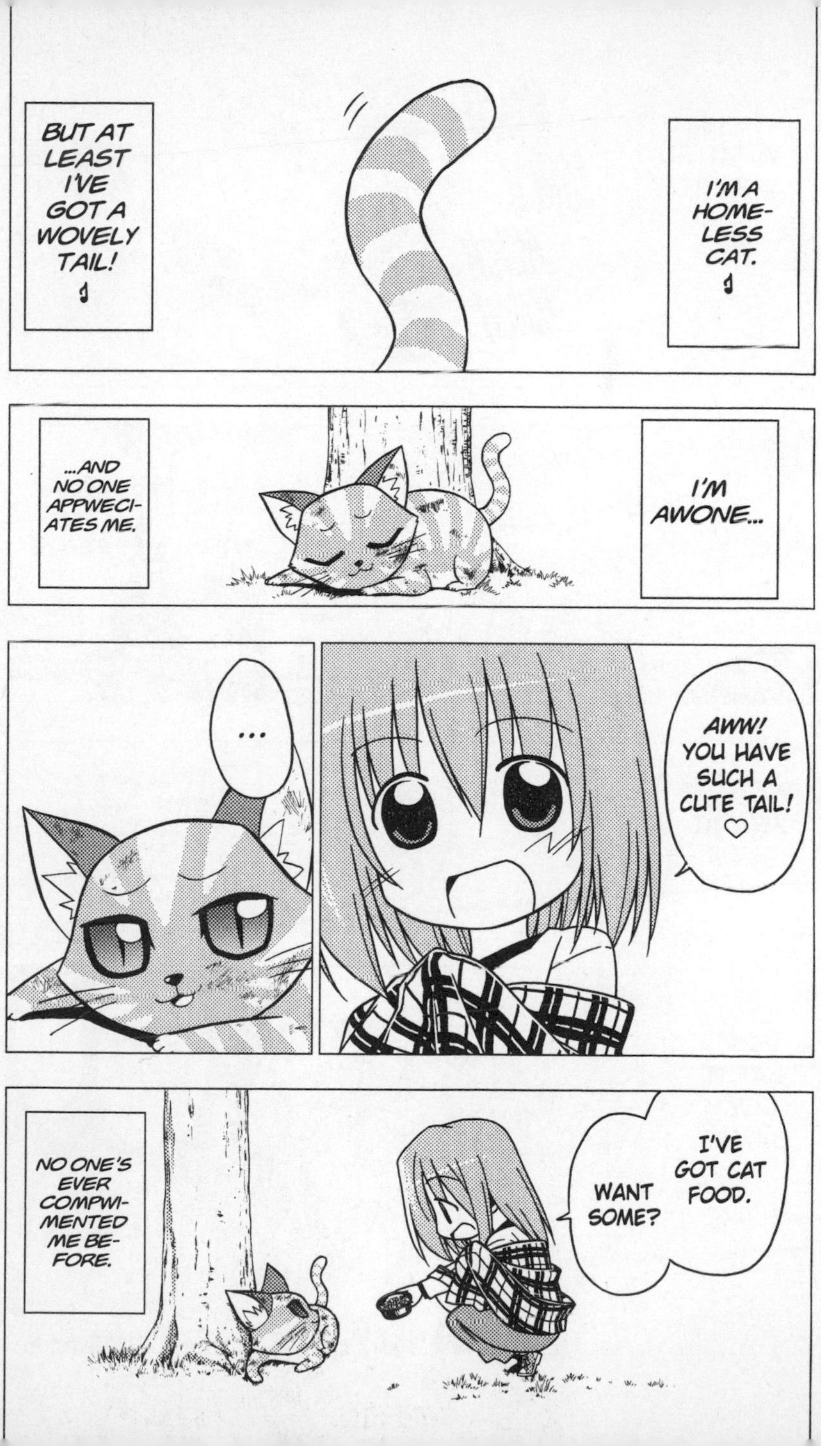
I'M A HOME-LESS CAT. ♪
BUT AT LEAST I'VE GOT A WOVELY TAIL! ♪
I'M AWONE...
...AND NO ONE APPWECI-ATES ME.
AWW! YOU HAVE SUCH A CUTE TAIL! ♡
...
I'VE GOT CAT FOOD.
WANT SOME?
NO ONE'S EVER COMPWI-MENTED ME BE-FORE.

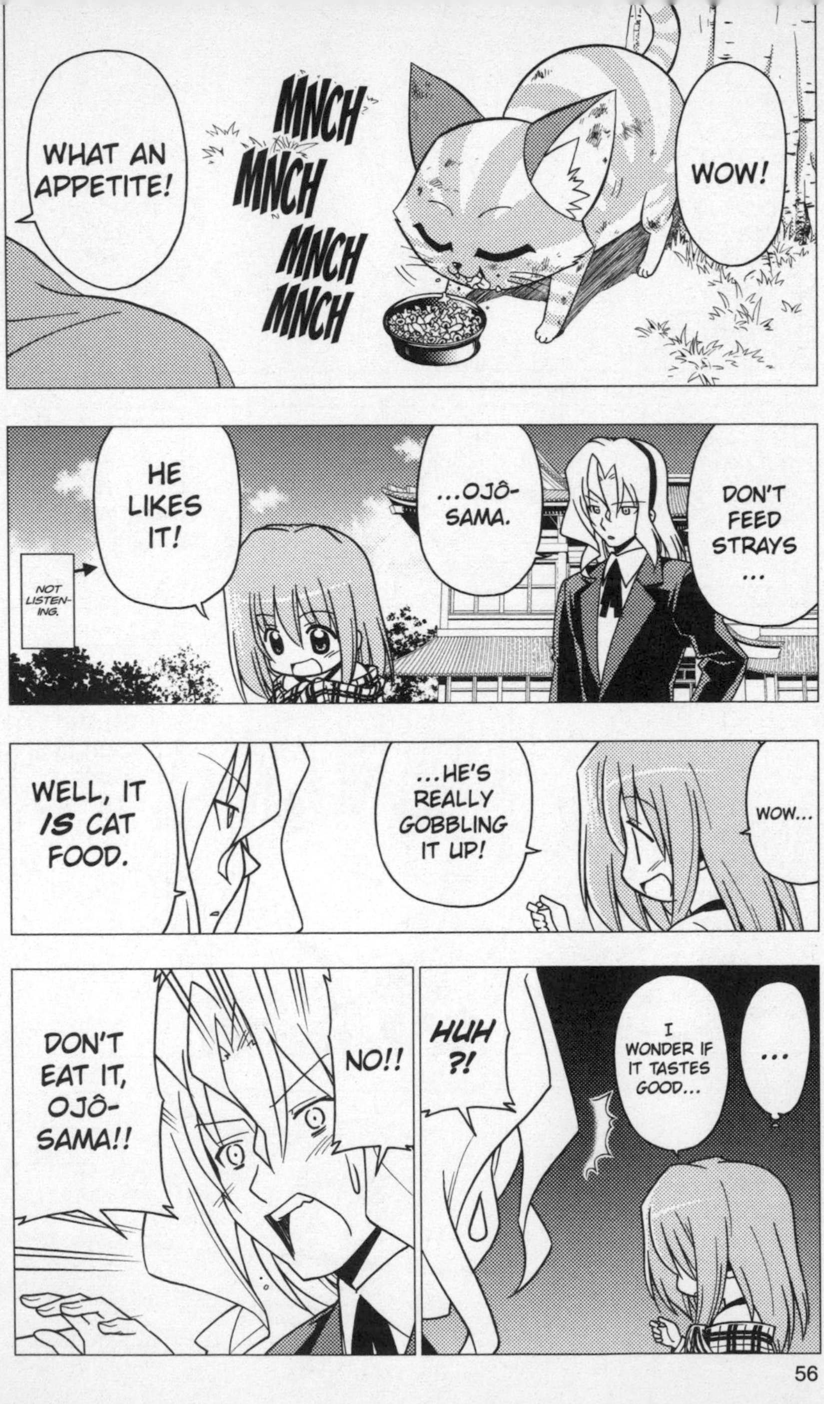
WOW!
MNCH MNCH MNCH MNCH
WHAT AN APPETITE!
DON'T FEED STRAYS...
...OJÔ-SAMA.
HE LIKES IT!
NOT LISTENING.
WOW...
...HE'S REALLY GOBBLING IT UP!
WELL, IT IS CAT FOOD.
...
I WONDER IF IT TASTES GOOD...
HUH?!
NO!!
DON'T EAT IT, OJÔ-SAMA!!

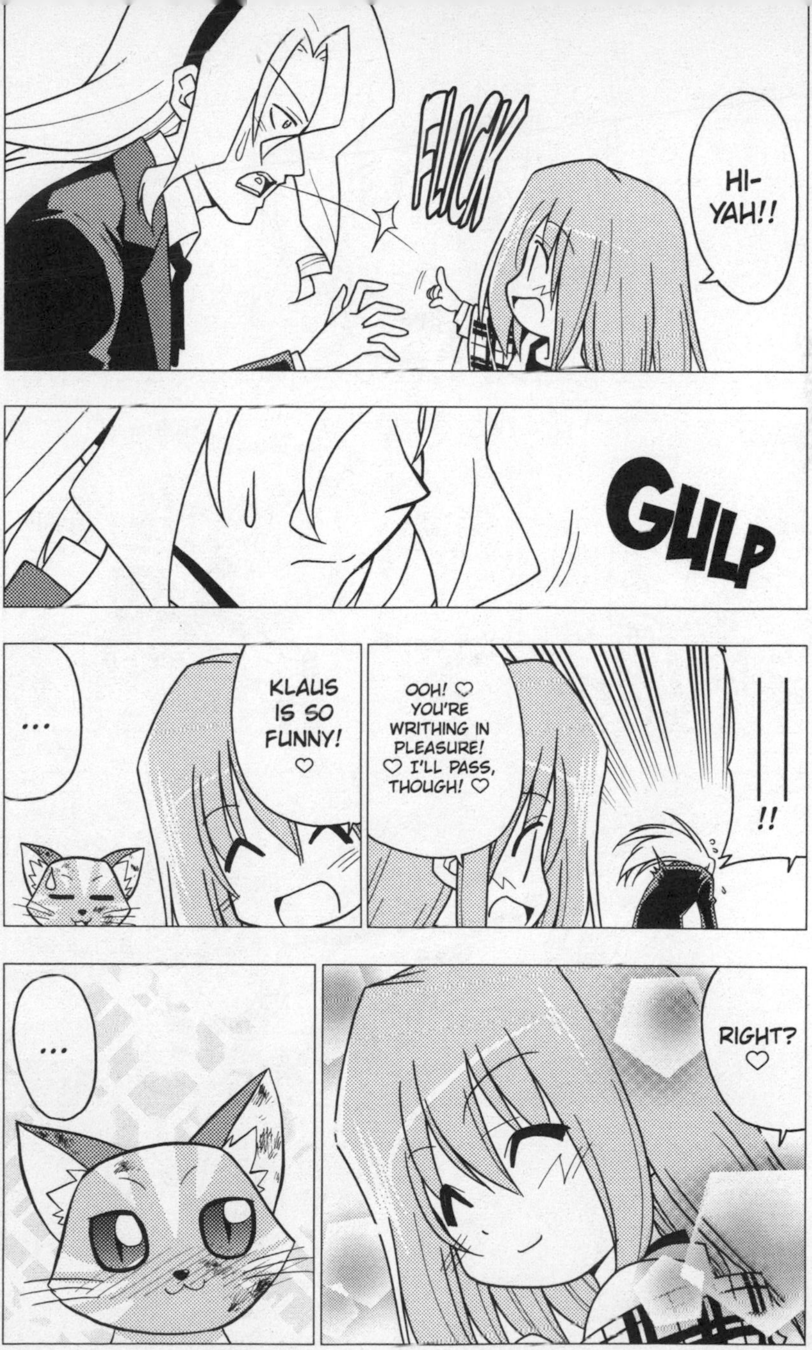
HI-
YAH!!
FLICK
GULP
!!
OOH! ♡ YOU'RE WRITHING IN PLEASURE! ♡ I'LL PASS, THOUGH! ♡
KLAUS IS SO FUNNY! ♡
...
RIGHT? ♡
...

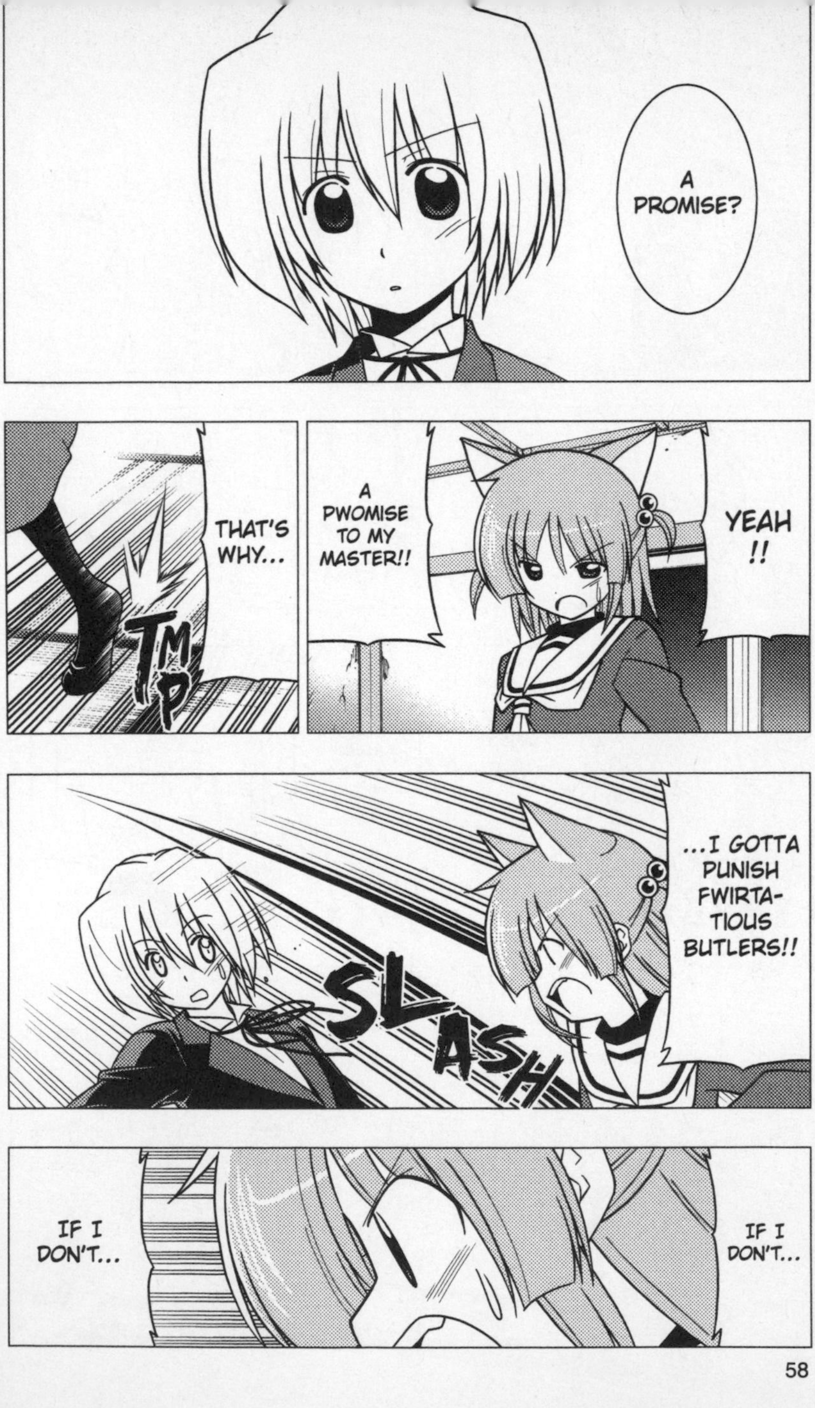
A PROMISE?
YEAH!!
A PWOMISE TO MY MASTER!!
THAT'S WHY...
TMP
...I GOTTA PUNISH FWIRTA-TIOUS BUTLERS!!
SLASH
IF I DON'T...
IF I DON'T...

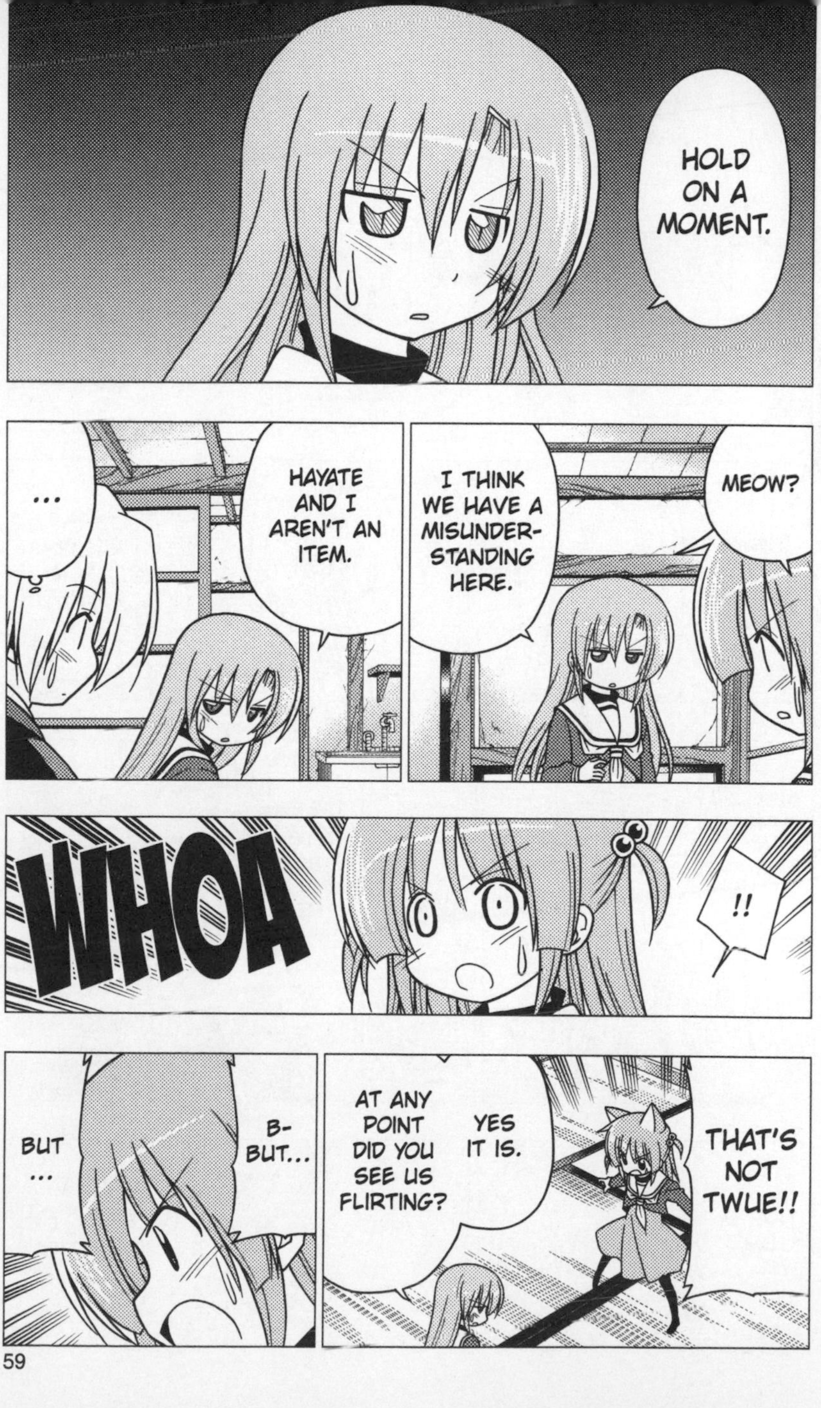
HOLD ON A MOMENT.
MEOW?
I THINK WE HAVE A MISUNDER-STANDING HERE.
HAYATE AND I AREN'T AN ITEM.
...
!!
WHOA
THAT'S NOT TWUE!!
YES IT IS.
AT ANY POINT DID YOU SEE US FLIRTING?
B-BUT...
BUT ...

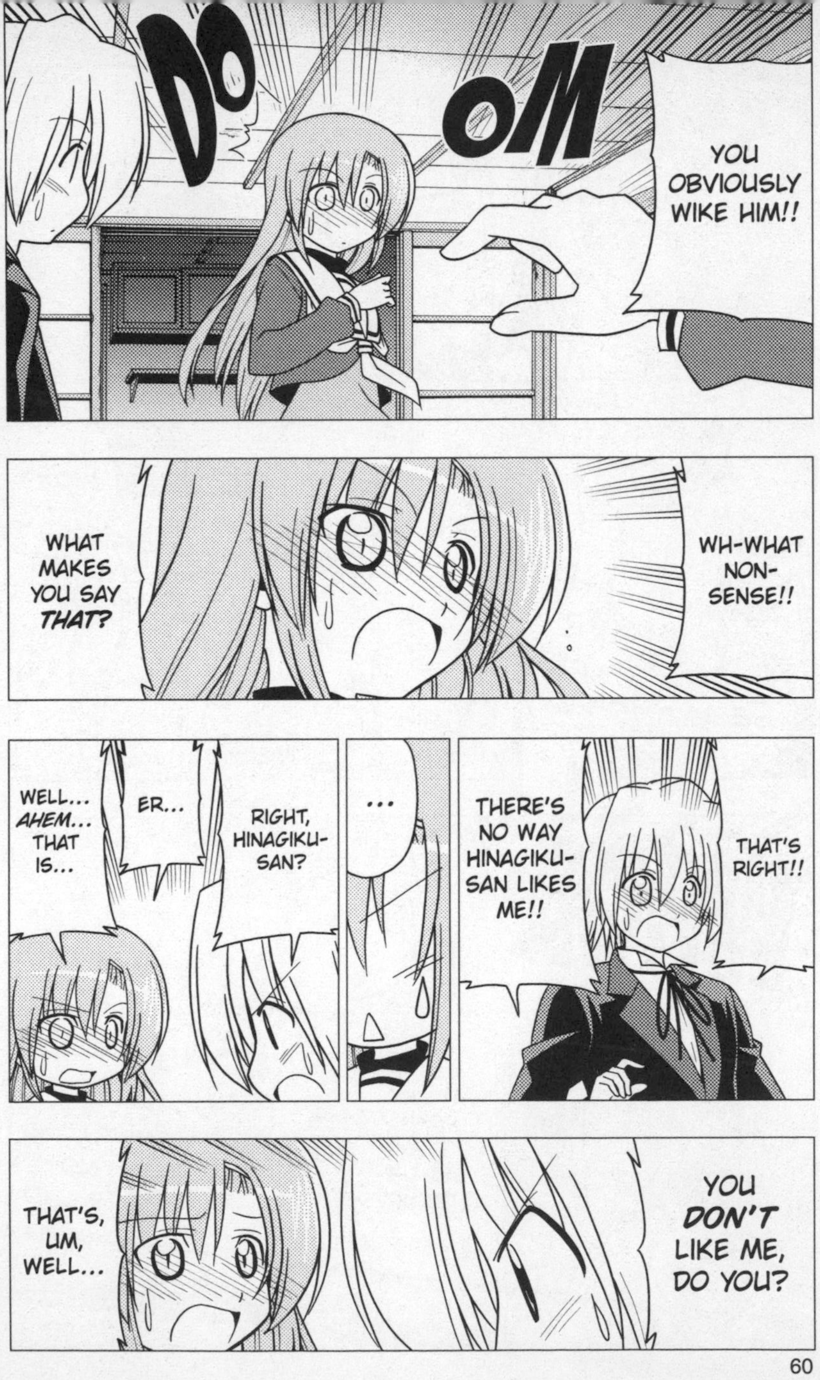
DOOM
YOU OBVIOUSLY WIKE HIM!!
WH-WHAT NON-SENSE!!
WHAT MAKES YOU SAY *THAT?*
THAT'S RIGHT!!
THERE'S NO WAY HINAGIKU-SAN LIKES ME!!
...
RIGHT, HINAGIKU-SAN?
ER...
WELL... *AHEM...* THAT IS...
YOU *DON'T* LIKE ME, DO YOU?
THAT'S, UM, WELL...

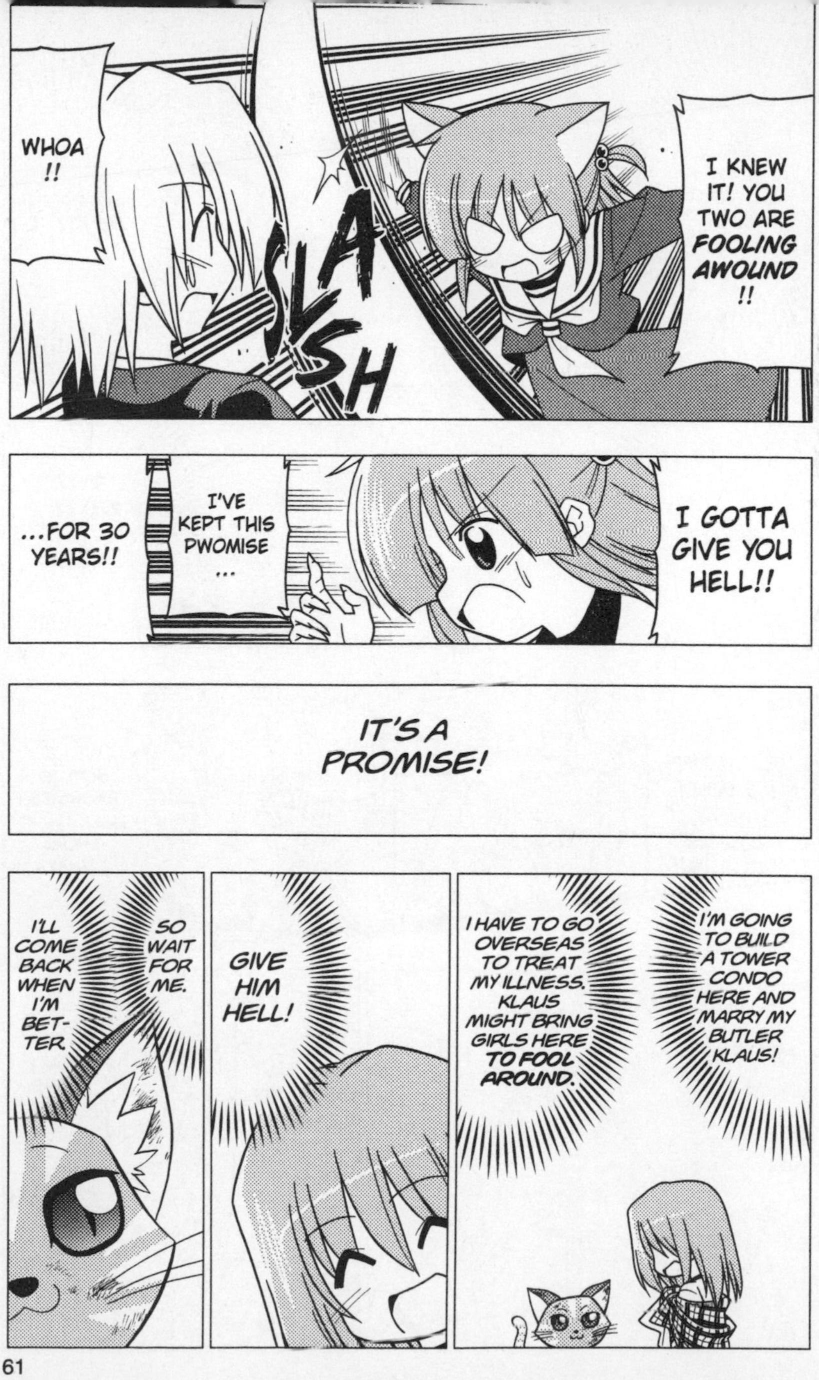
I KNEW IT! YOU TWO ARE FOOLING AWOUND!!
SLASH
WHOA!!
I GOTTA GIVE YOU HELL!!
I'VE KEPT THIS PWOMISE...
...FOR 30 YEARS!!
IT'S A PROMISE!
I'M GOING TO BUILD A TOWER CONDO HERE AND MARRY MY BUTLER KLAUS!
I HAVE TO GO OVERSEAS TO TREAT MY ILLNESS. KLAUS MIGHT BRING GIRLS HERE TO FOOL AROUND.
GIVE HIM HELL!
SO WAIT FOR ME.
I'LL COME BACK WHEN I'M BET-TER.

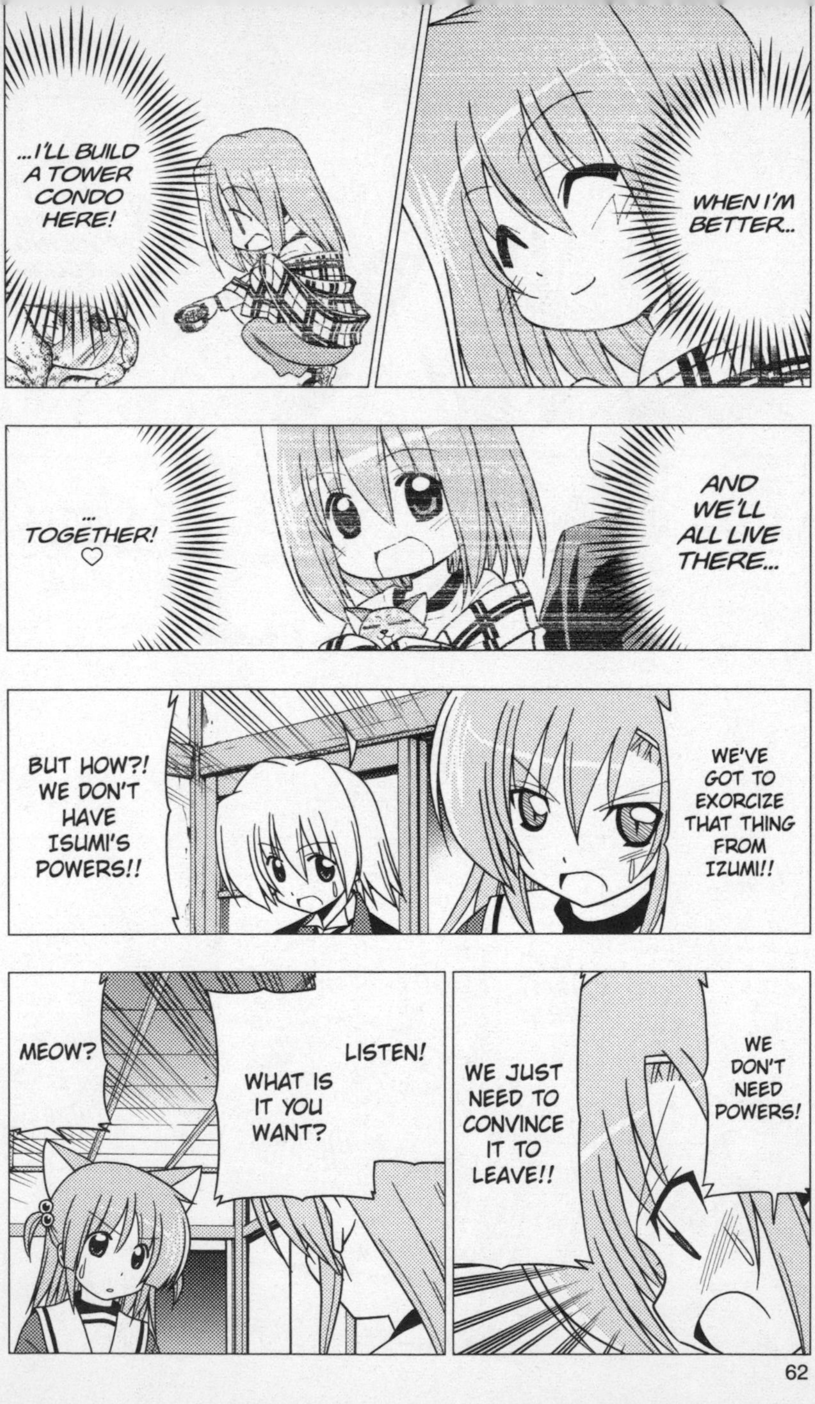
WHEN I'M BETTER...
...I'LL BUILD A TOWER CONDO HERE!
AND WE'LL ALL LIVE THERE...
... TOGETHER! ♡
WE'VE GOT TO EXORCIZE THAT THING FROM IZUMI!!
BUT HOW?! WE DON'T HAVE ISUMI'S POWERS!!
WE DON'T NEED POWERS!
WE JUST NEED TO CONVINCE IT TO LEAVE!!
LISTEN!
WHAT IS IT YOU WANT?
MEOW?

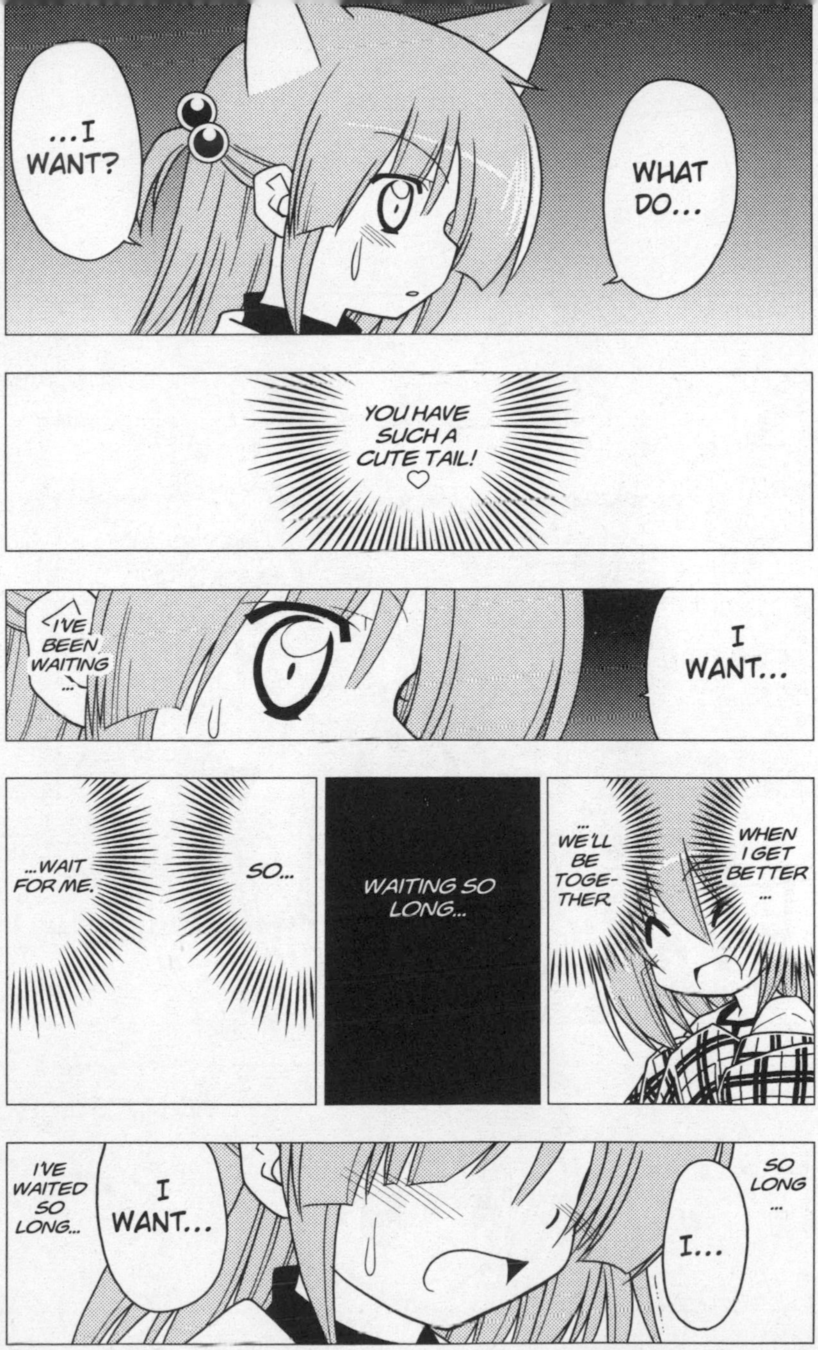
WHAT DO...
...I WANT?
YOU HAVE SUCH A CUTE TAIL! ♡
I WANT...
I'VE BEEN WAITING ...
WHEN I GET BETTER ...
... WE'LL BE TOGETHER.
WAITING SO LONG...
SO...
...WAIT FOR ME.
SO LONG ...
I...
I WANT...
I'VE WAITED SO LONG...

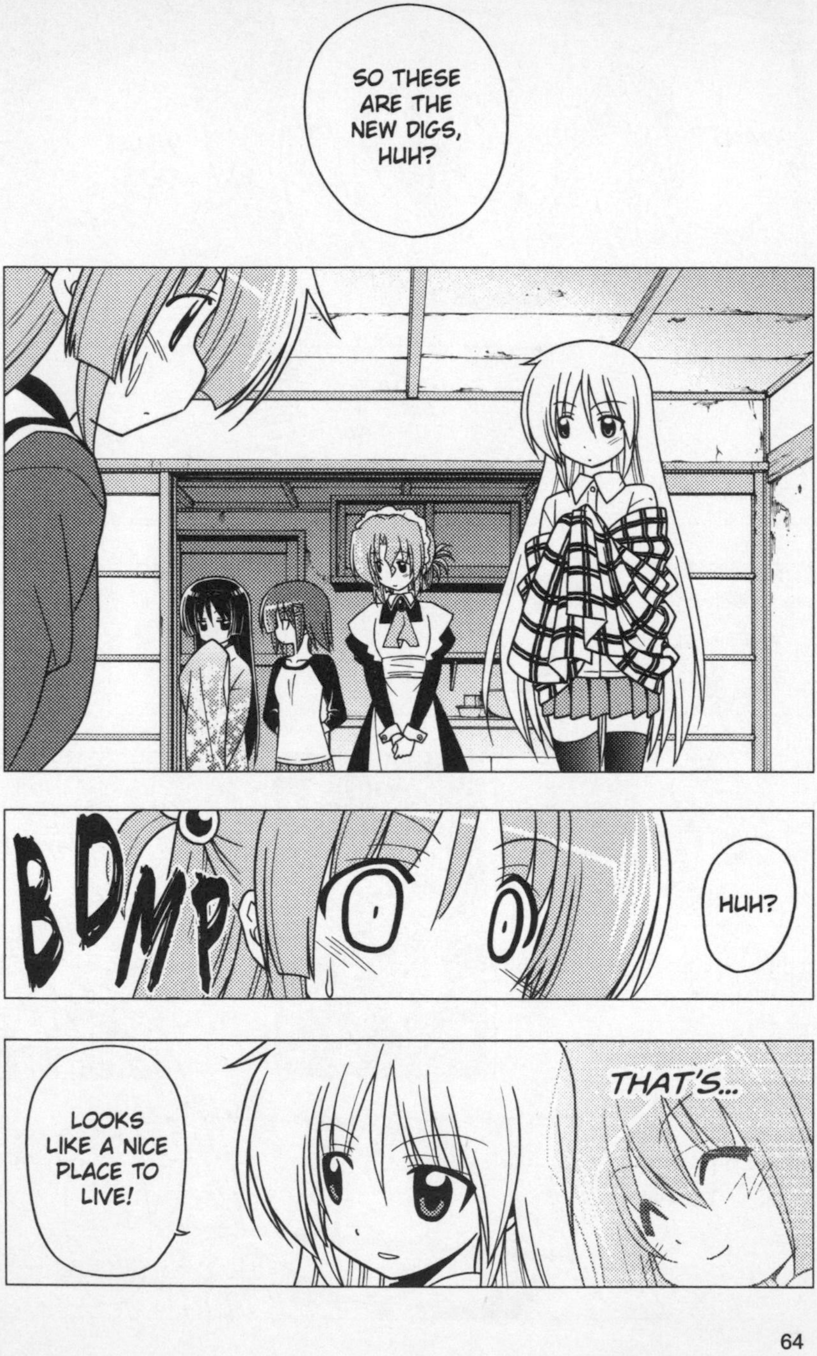
SO THESE ARE THE NEW DIGS, HUH?
HUH?
BDMP
THAT'S...
LOOKS LIKE A NICE PLACE TO LIVE!

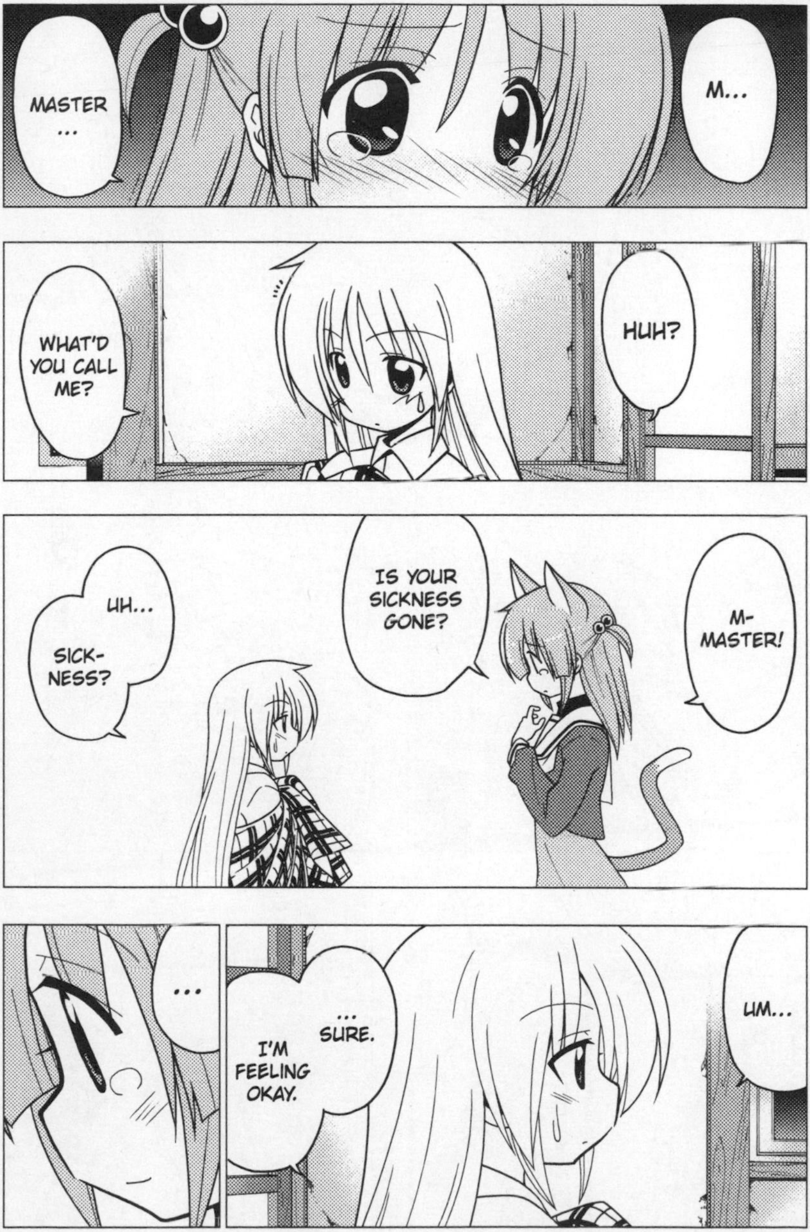
M...
MASTER ...
HUH?
WHAT'D YOU CALL ME?
M- MASTER!
IS YOUR SICKNESS GONE?
UH... SICK- NESS?
UM...
... SURE. I'M FEELING OKAY.
...

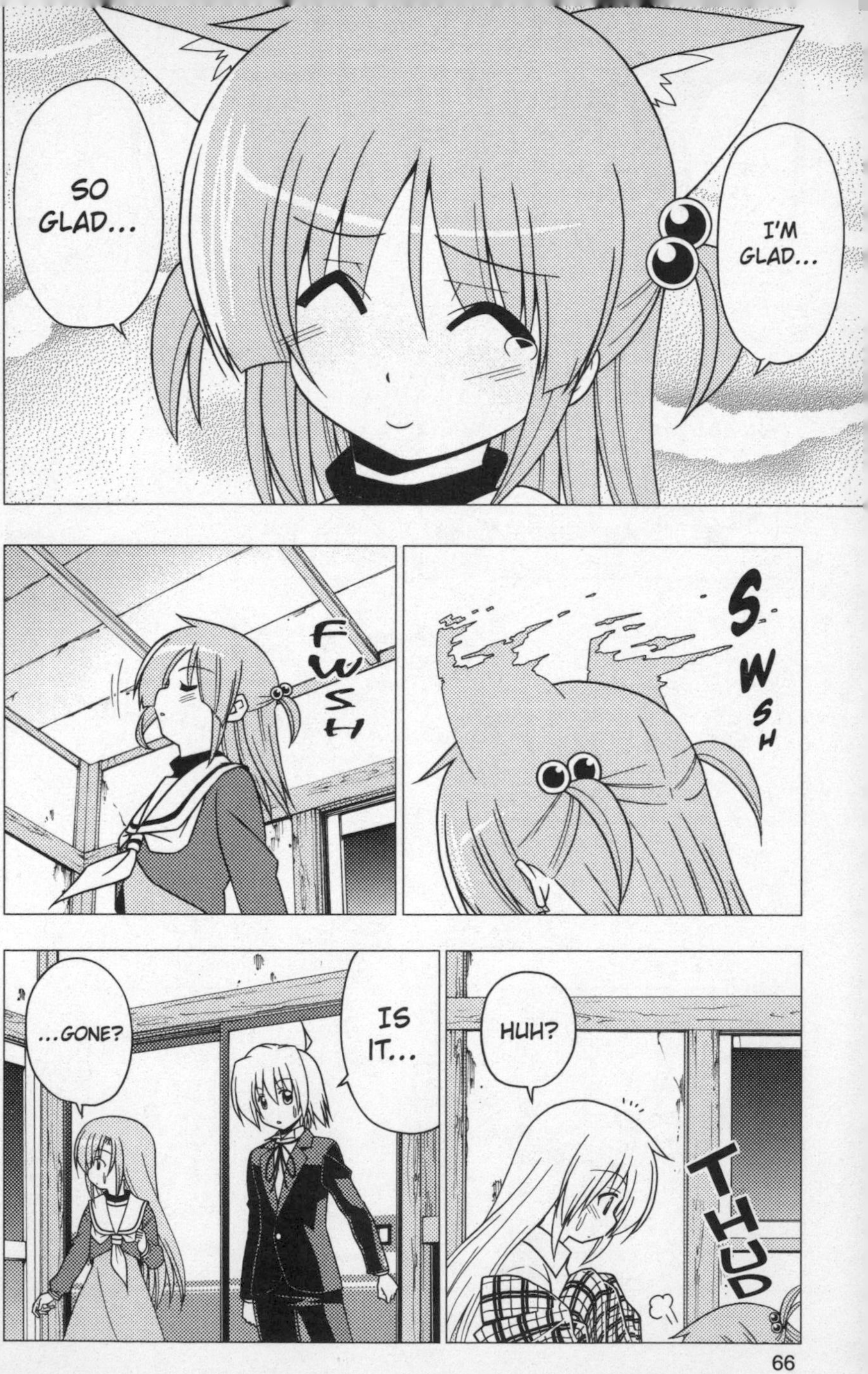
I'M GLAD...
SO GLAD...
SWSH
FWSH
HUH?
THUD
IS IT...
...GONE?

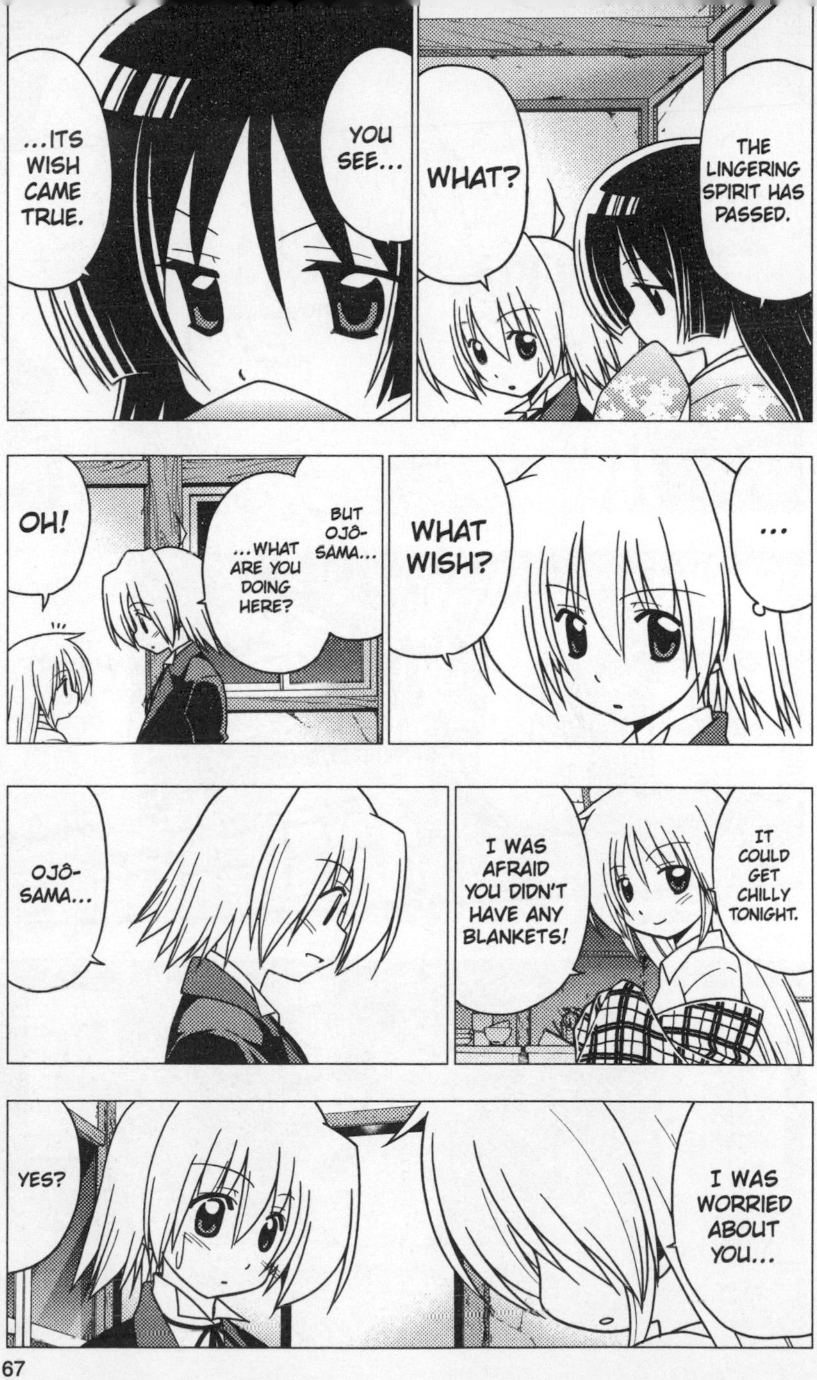
THE LINGERING SPIRIT HAS PASSED.
WHAT?
YOU SEE...
...ITS WISH CAME TRUE.
...
WHAT WISH?
BUT OJÔ-SAMA...
...WHAT ARE YOU DOING HERE?
OH!
IT COULD GET CHILLY TONIGHT.
I WAS AFRAID YOU DIDN'T HAVE ANY BLANKETS!
OJÔ-SAMA...
I WAS WORRIED ABOUT YOU...
YES?

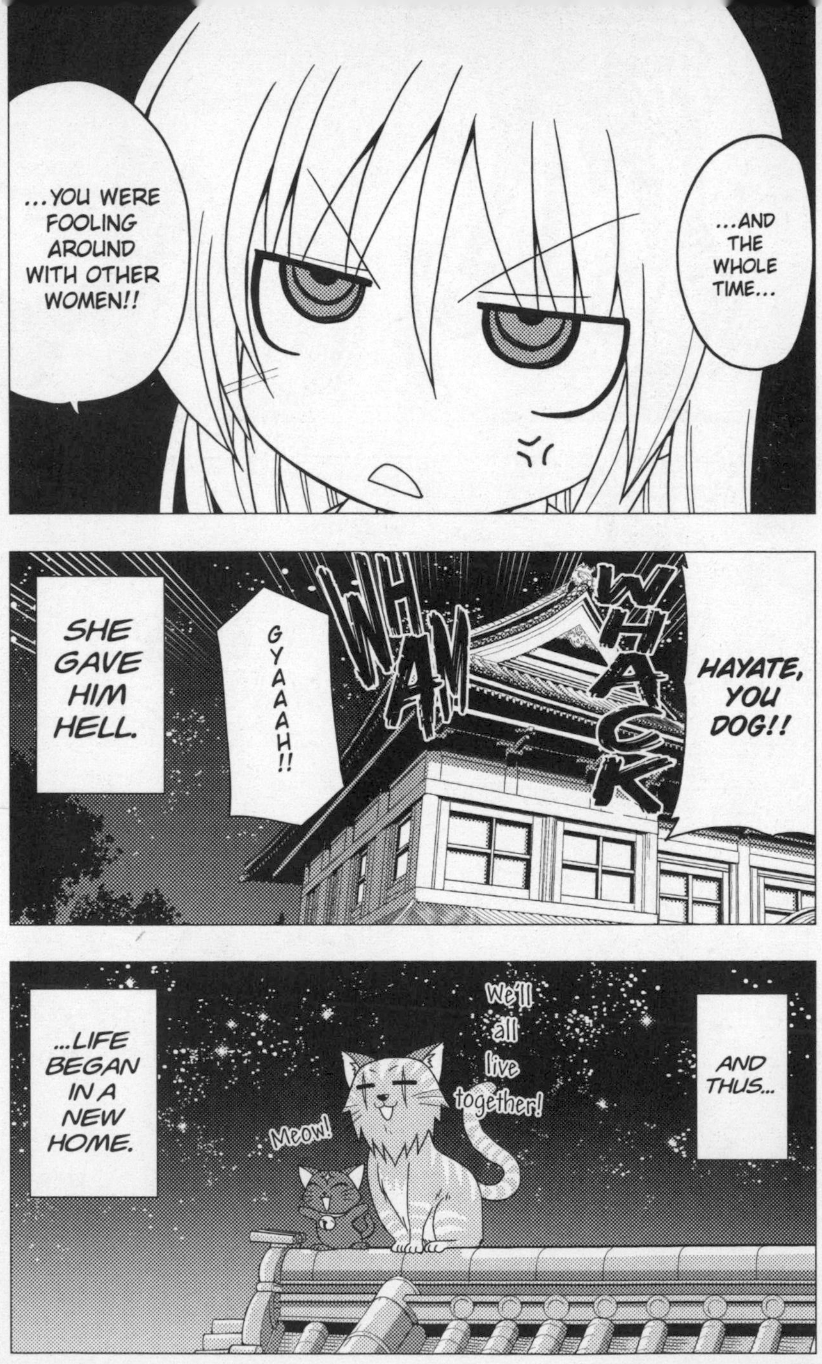
...AND THE WHOLE TIME...
...YOU WERE FOOLING AROUND WITH OTHER WOMEN!!
HAYATE, YOU DOG!!
WHACK
WHAM
GYAAAH!!
SHE GAVE HIM HELL.
AND THUS...
We'll all live together!
Meow!
...LIFE BEGAN IN A NEW HOME.

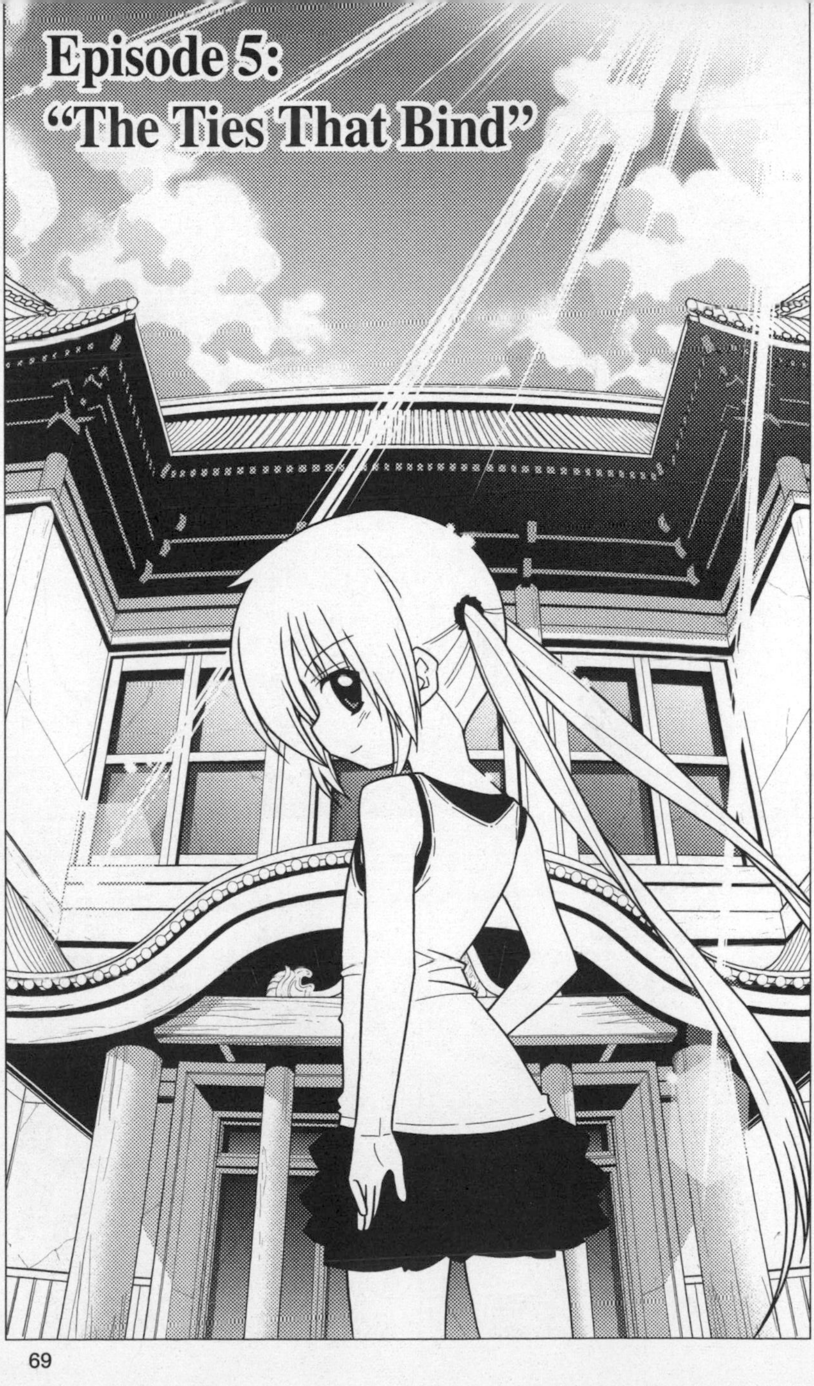
Episode 5:
"The Ties That Bind"

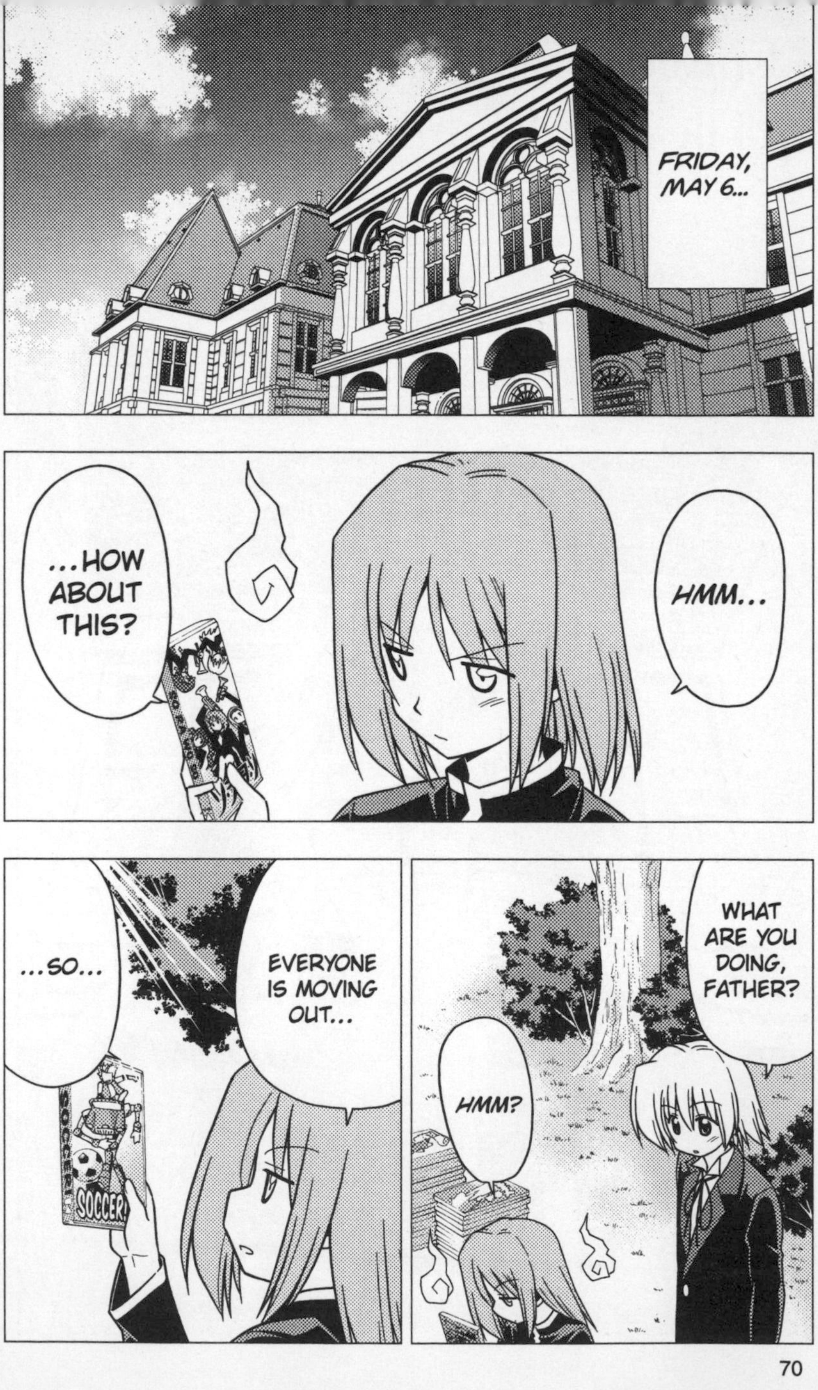
FRIDAY, MAY 6...
HMM...
...HOW ABOUT THIS?
WHAT ARE YOU DOING, FATHER?
HMM?
EVERYONE IS MOVING OUT...
...SO...
SOCCER!

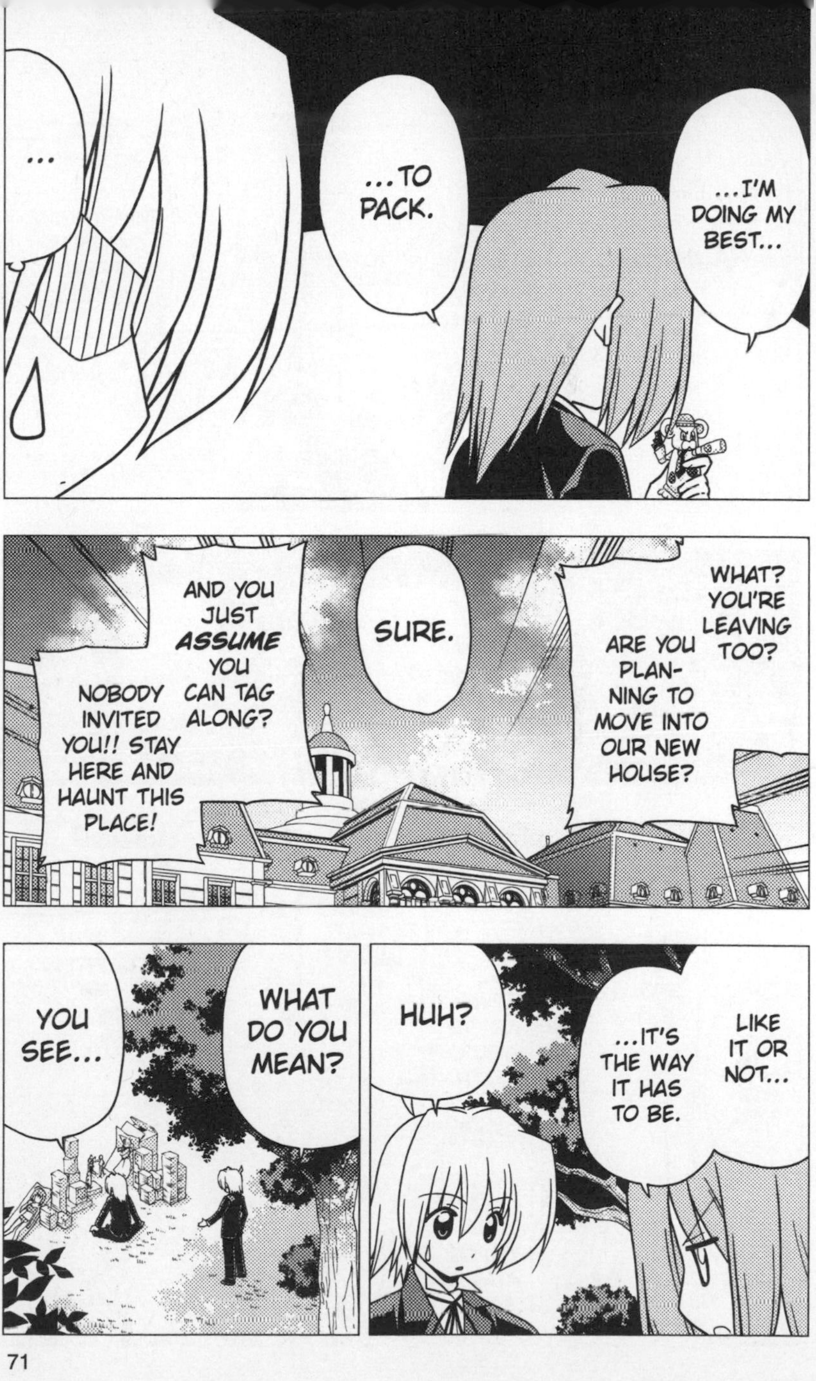
...I'M DOING MY BEST...
...TO PACK.
...
WHAT? YOU'RE LEAVING TOO?
ARE YOU PLAN-NING TO MOVE INTO OUR NEW HOUSE?
SURE.
AND YOU JUST ASSUME YOU CAN TAG ALONG?
NOBODY INVITED YOU!! STAY HERE AND HAUNT THIS PLACE!
LIKE IT OR NOT...
...IT'S THE WAY IT HAS TO BE.
HUH?
WHAT DO YOU MEAN?
YOU SEE...

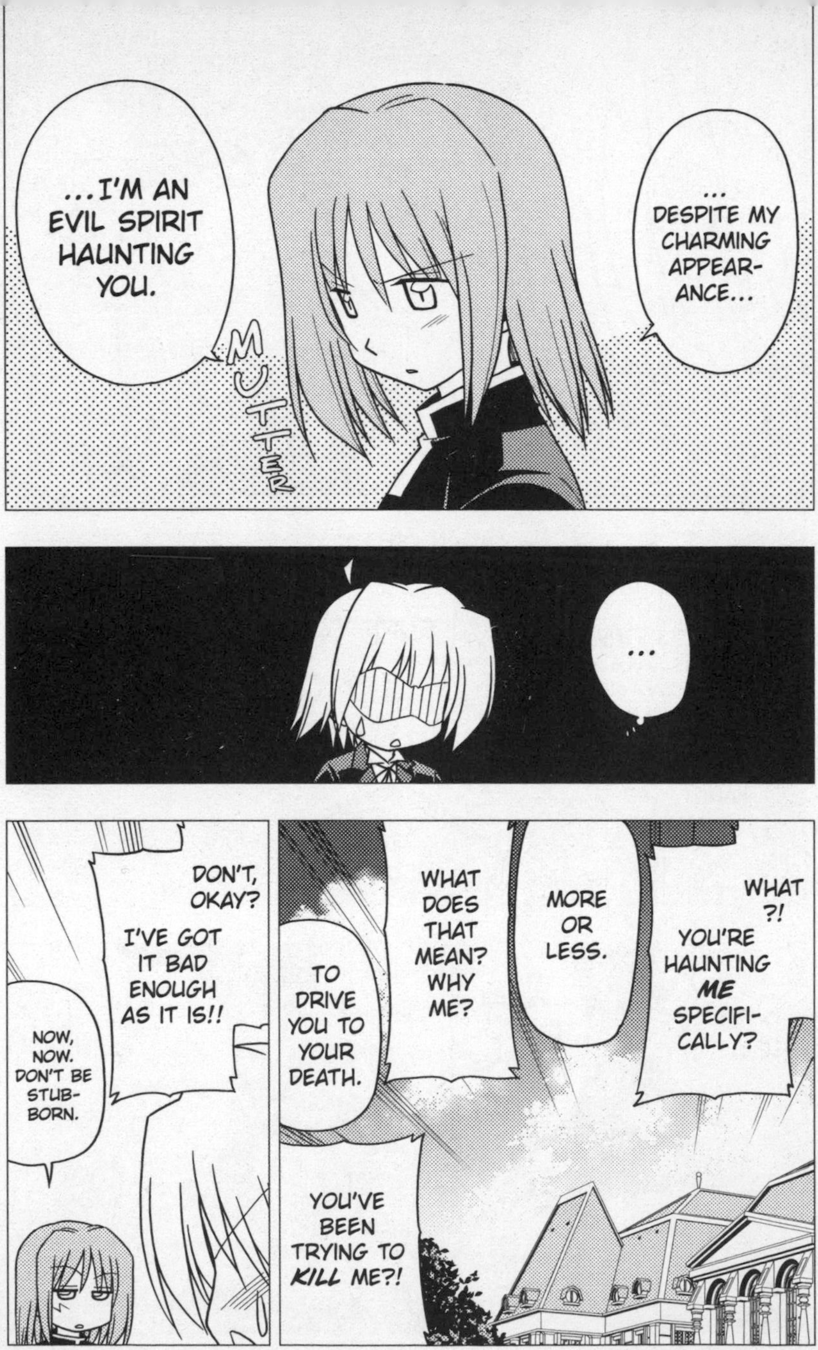
...DESPITE MY CHARMING APPEARANCE...
...I'M AN EVIL SPIRIT HAUNTING YOU.
MUTTER
...
WHAT?! YOU'RE HAUNTING *ME* SPECIFICALLY?
MORE OR LESS.
WHAT DOES THAT MEAN? WHY ME?
TO DRIVE YOU TO YOUR DEATH.
YOU'VE BEEN TRYING TO *KILL* ME?!
DON'T, OKAY? I'VE GOT IT BAD ENOUGH AS IT IS!!
NOW, NOW. DON'T BE STUBBORN.

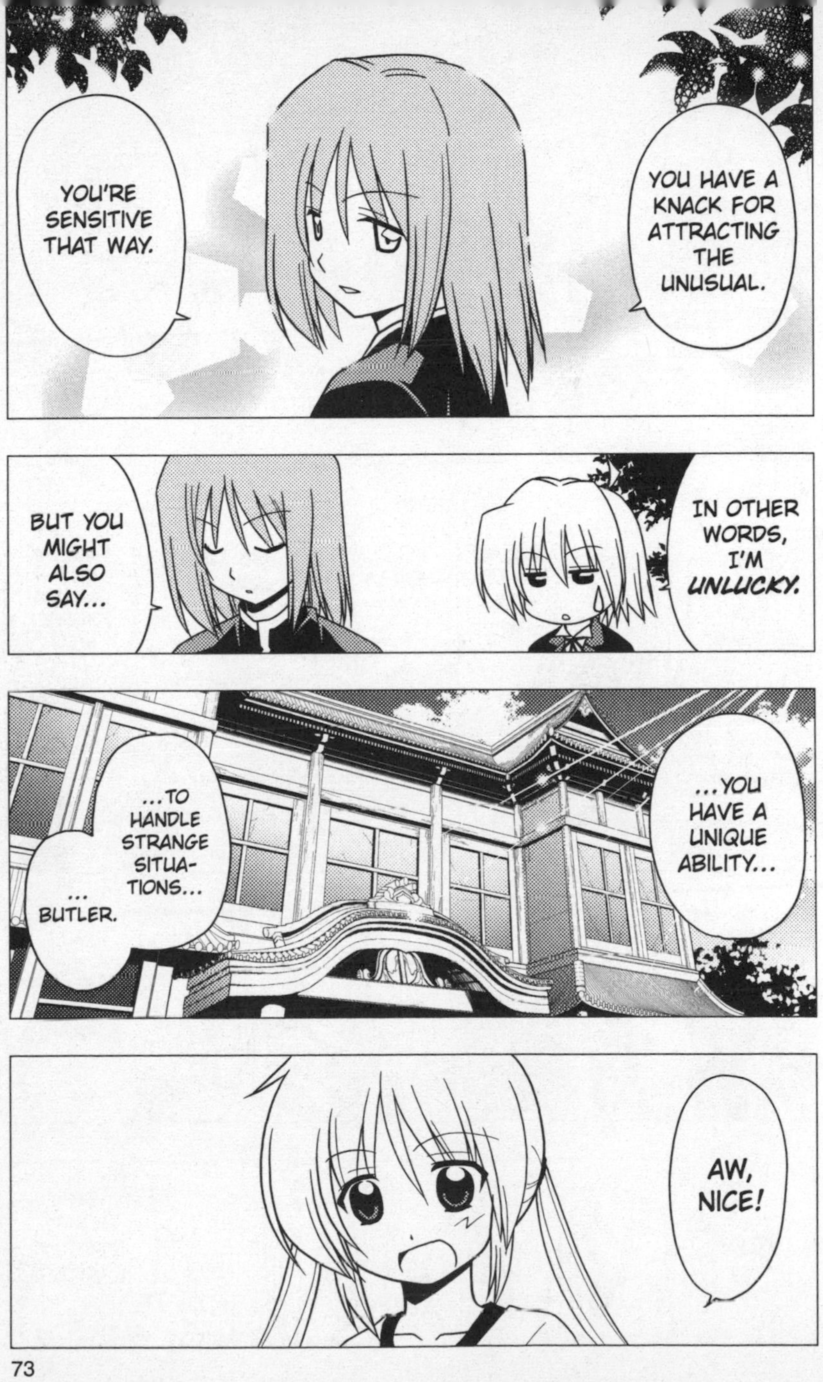
YOU HAVE A KNACK FOR ATTRACTING THE UNUSUAL.
YOU'RE SENSITIVE THAT WAY.
IN OTHER WORDS, I'M *UNLUCKY.*
BUT YOU MIGHT ALSO SAY...
...YOU HAVE A UNIQUE ABILITY...
...TO HANDLE STRANGE SITUA-TIONS...
... BUTLER.
AW, NICE!

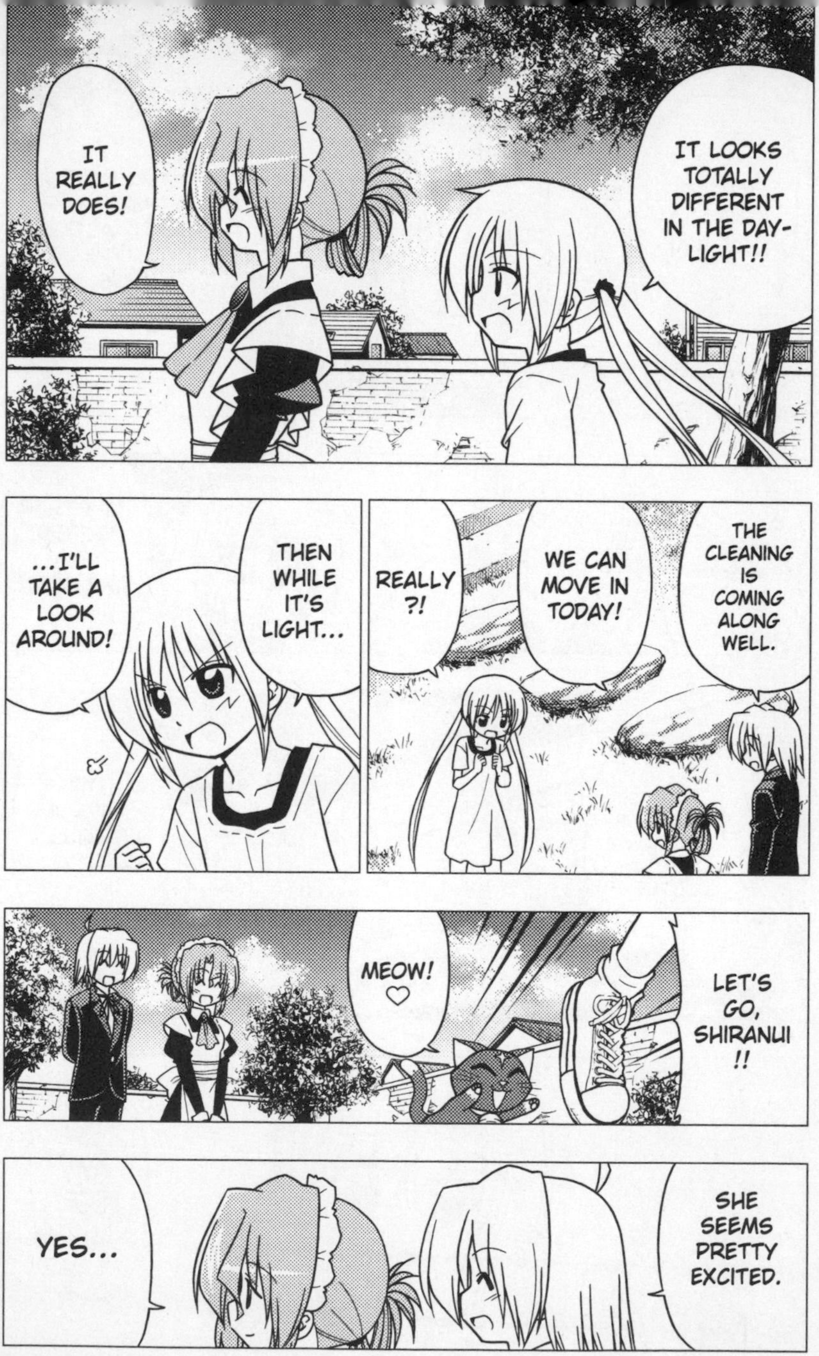
IT LOOKS TOTALLY DIFFERENT IN THE DAY-LIGHT!!
IT REALLY DOES!
THE CLEANING IS COMING ALONG WELL.
WE CAN MOVE IN TODAY!
REALLY?!
THEN WHILE IT'S LIGHT...
...I'LL TAKE A LOOK AROUND!
LET'S GO, SHIRANUI!!
MEOW! ♡
SHE SEEMS PRETTY EXCITED.
YES...

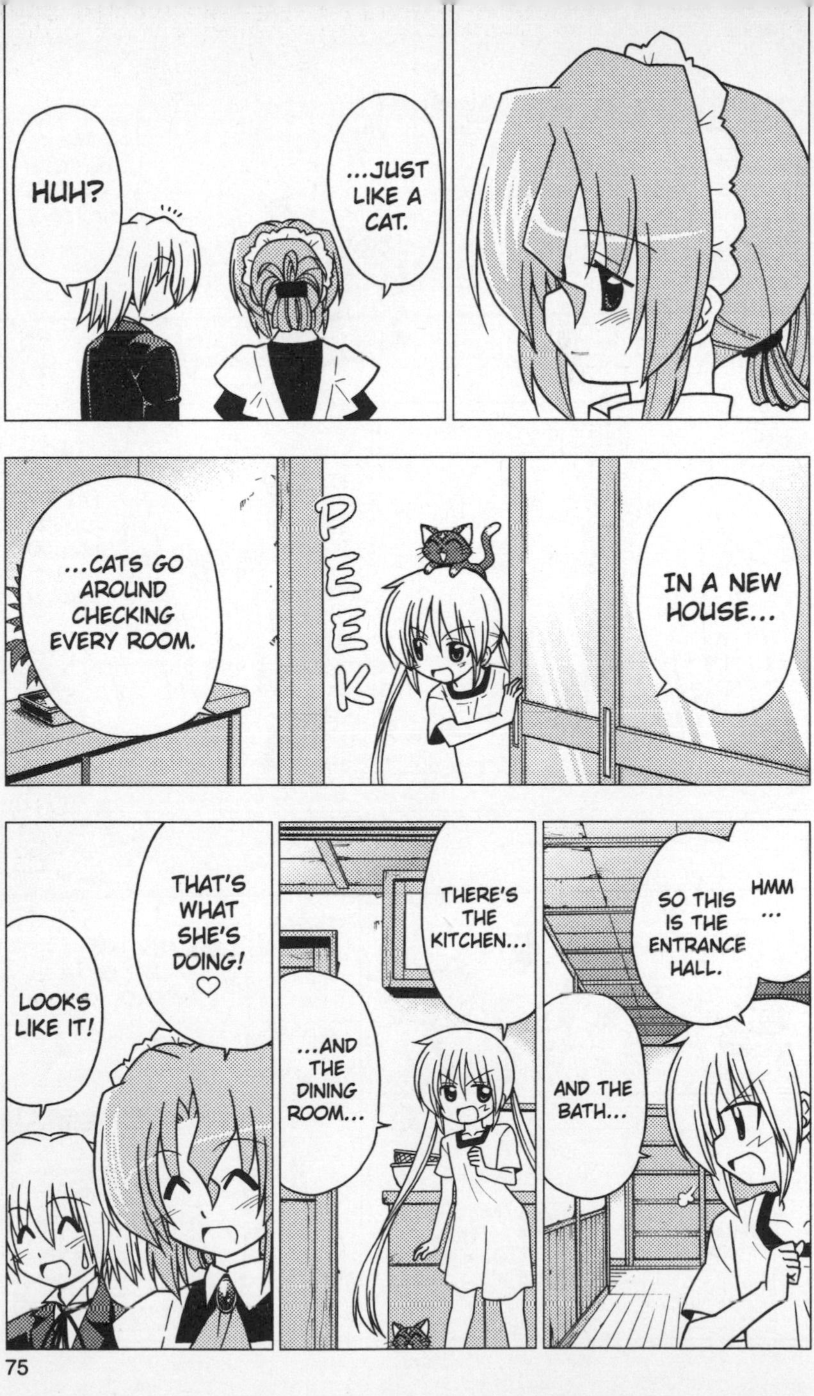
...JUST LIKE A CAT.
HUH?
IN A NEW HOUSE...
PEEK
...CATS GO AROUND CHECKING EVERY ROOM.
HMM ...
SO THIS IS THE ENTRANCE HALL.
AND THE BATH...
THERE'S THE KITCHEN...
...AND THE DINING ROOM...
THAT'S WHAT SHE'S DOING! ♡
LOOKS LIKE IT!

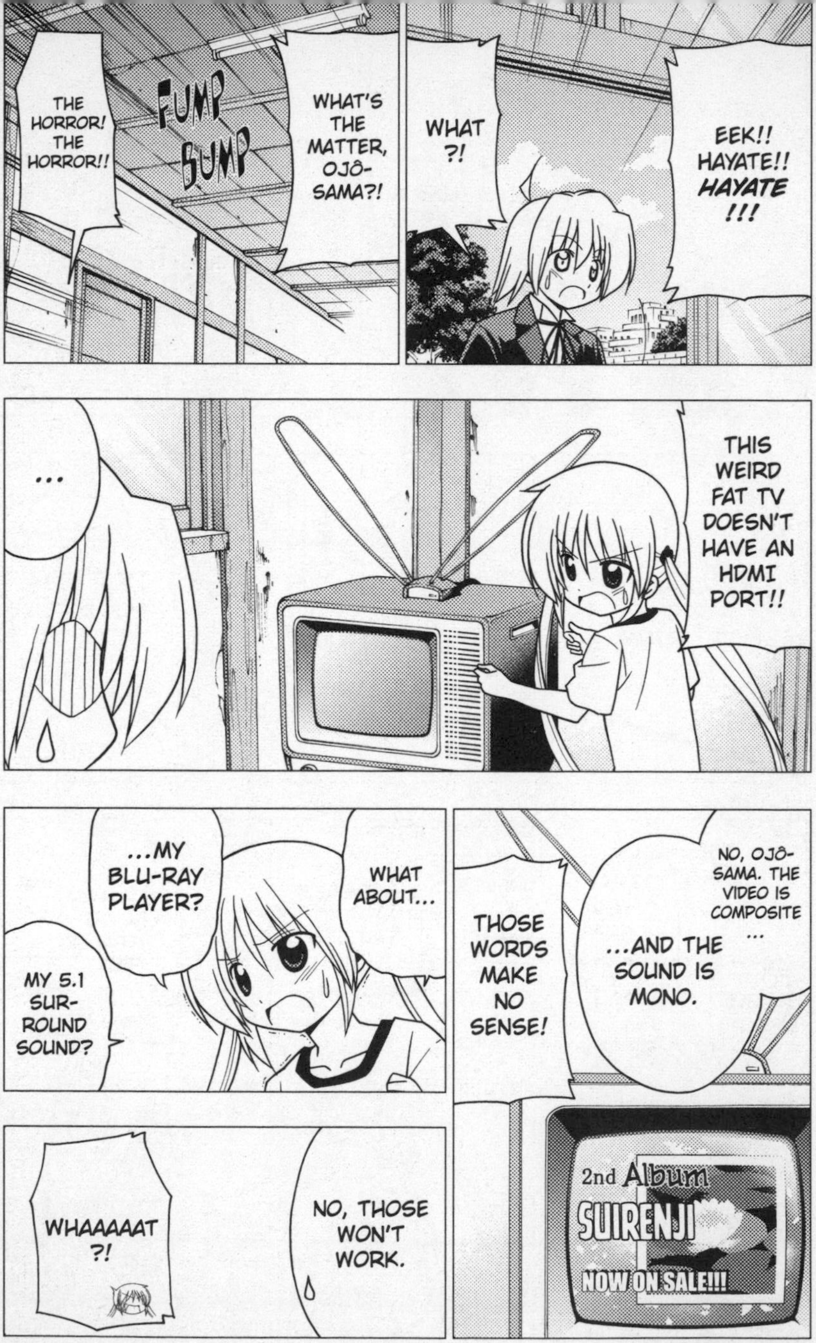
EEK!! HAYATE!! HAYATE!!!
WHAT?!
WHAT'S THE MATTER, OJÔ-SAMA?!
FUMP BUMP
THE HORROR! THE HORROR!!
THIS WEIRD FAT TV DOESN'T HAVE AN HDMI PORT!!
...
NO, OJÔ-SAMA. THE VIDEO IS COMPOSITE ...
...AND THE SOUND IS MONO.
THOSE WORDS MAKE NO SENSE!
2nd Album
SUIRENJI
NOW ON SALE!!!
WHAT ABOUT...
...MY BLU-RAY PLAYER?
MY 5.1 SURROUND SOUND?
NO, THOSE WON'T WORK.
WHAAAAAT?!

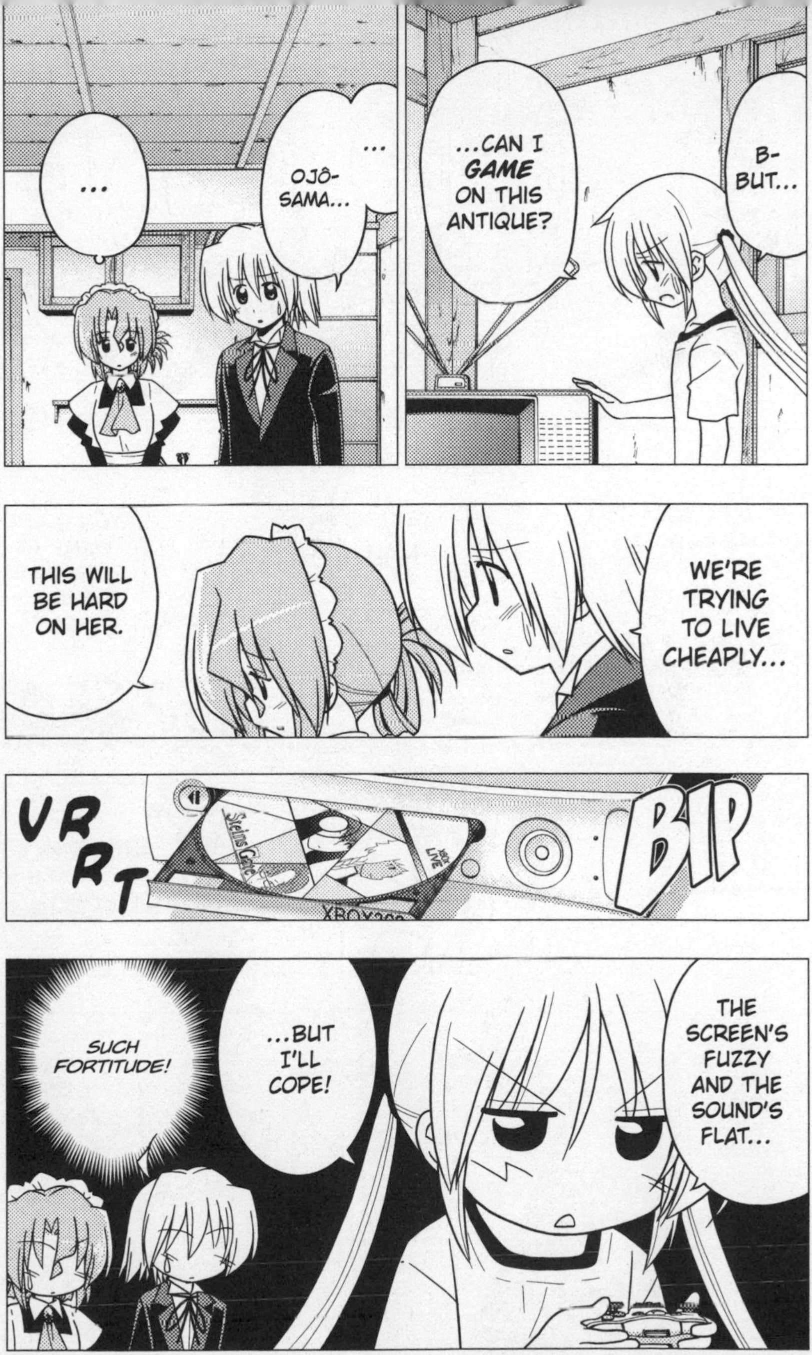
B-BUT...
...CAN I *GAME* ON THIS ANTIQUE?
... OJÔ-SAMA...
...
WE'RE TRYING TO LIVE CHEAPLY...
THIS WILL BE HARD ON HER.
BIP
VRRT
THE SCREEN'S FUZZY AND THE SOUND'S FLAT...
...BUT I'LL COPE!
SUCH FORTITUDE!

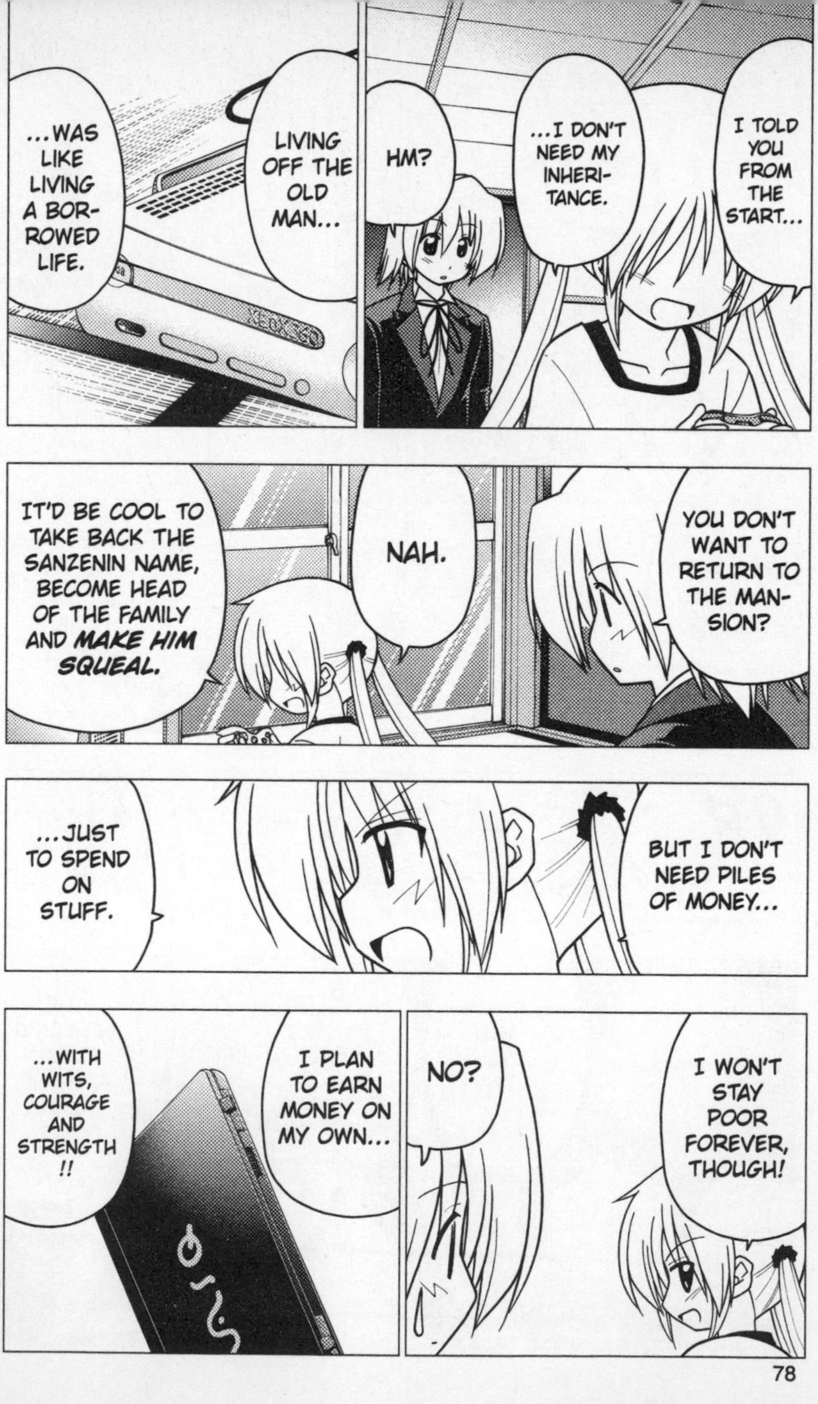
I TOLD YOU FROM THE START...
...I DON'T NEED MY INHERI-TANCE.
HM?
LIVING OFF THE OLD MAN...
...WAS LIKE LIVING A BOR-ROWED LIFE.
YOU DON'T WANT TO RETURN TO THE MAN-SION?
NAH.
IT'D BE COOL TO TAKE BACK THE SANZENIN NAME, BECOME HEAD OF THE FAMILY AND ***MAKE HIM SQUEAL.***
BUT I DON'T NEED PILES OF MONEY...
...JUST TO SPEND ON STUFF.
I WON'T STAY POOR FOREVER, THOUGH!
NO?
I PLAN TO EARN MONEY ON MY OWN...
...WITH WITS, COURAGE AND STRENGTH !!

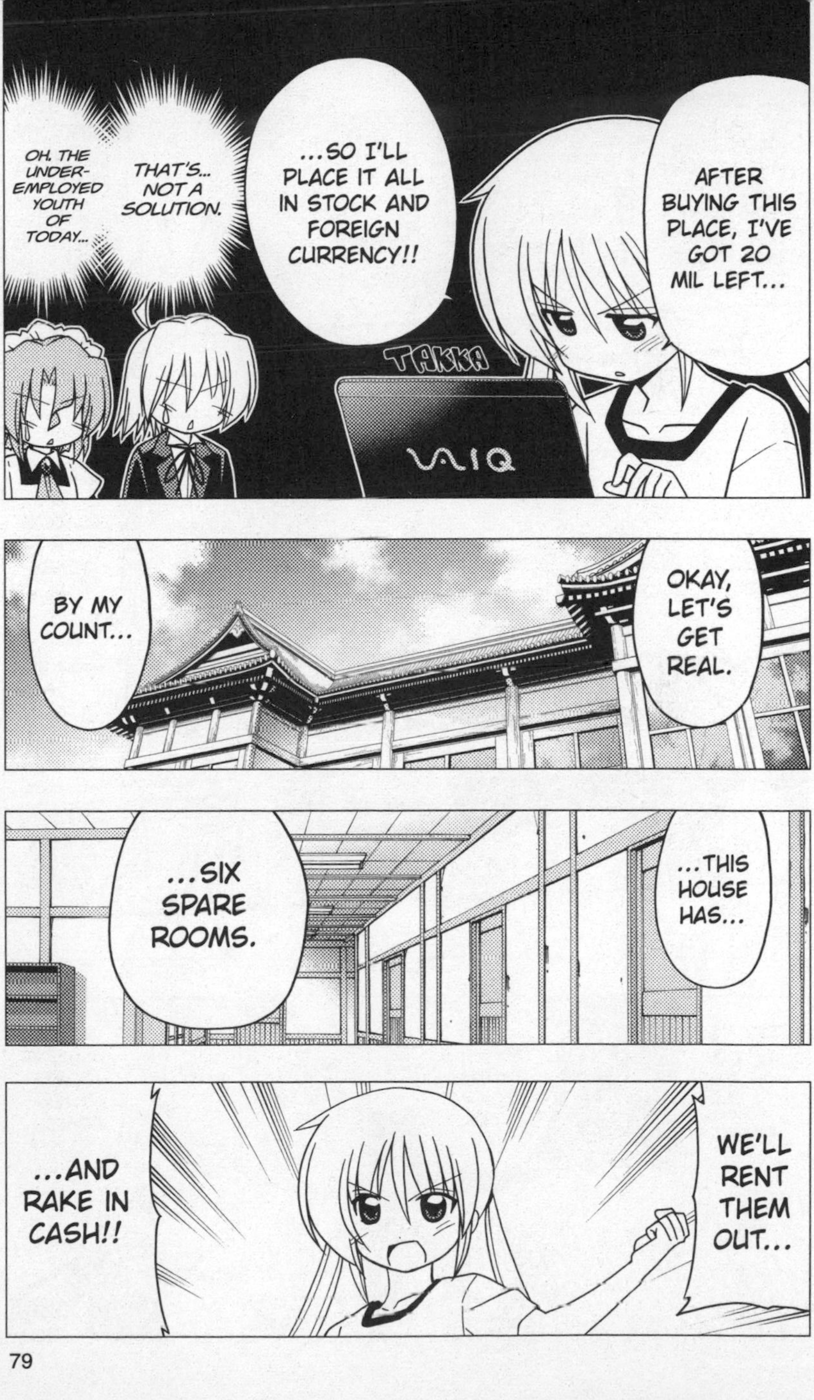
AFTER BUYING THIS PLACE, I'VE GOT 20 MIL LEFT...
...SO I'LL PLACE IT ALL IN STOCK AND FOREIGN CURRENCY!!
TAKKA
VAIQ
THAT'S... NOT A SOLUTION.
OH. THE UNDER-EMPLOYED YOUTH OF TODAY...
OKAY, LET'S GET REAL.
BY MY COUNT...
...THIS HOUSE HAS...
...SIX SPARE ROOMS.
WE'LL RENT THEM OUT...
...AND RAKE IN CASH!!

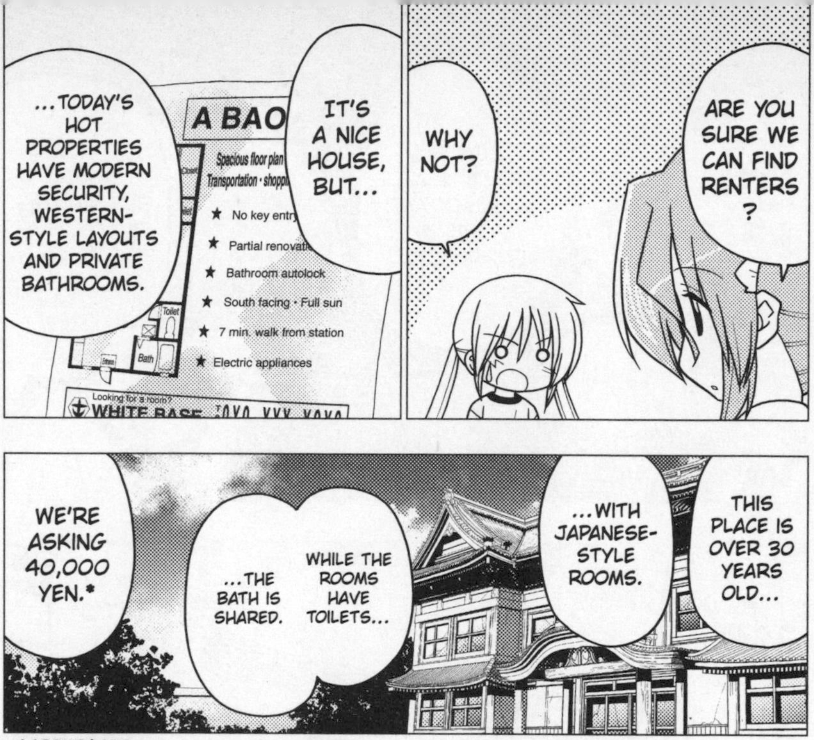
ARE YOU SURE WE CAN FIND RENTERS ?
WHY NOT?
IT'S A NICE HOUSE, BUT...
...TODAY'S HOT PROPERTIES HAVE MODERN SECURITY, WESTERN-STYLE LAYOUTS AND PRIVATE BATHROOMS.
A BAO
Spacious floor plan
Transportation · shoppi
No key entr
Partial renovat
Bathroom autolock
South facing · Full sun
7 min. walk from station
Electric appliances
Toilet
Bath
Looking for a room?
THIS PLACE IS OVER 30 YEARS OLD...
...WITH JAPANESE-STYLE ROOMS.
WHILE THE ROOMS HAVE TOILETS...
...THE BATH IS SHARED.
WE'RE ASKING 40,000 YEN.*

*ABOUT $400.

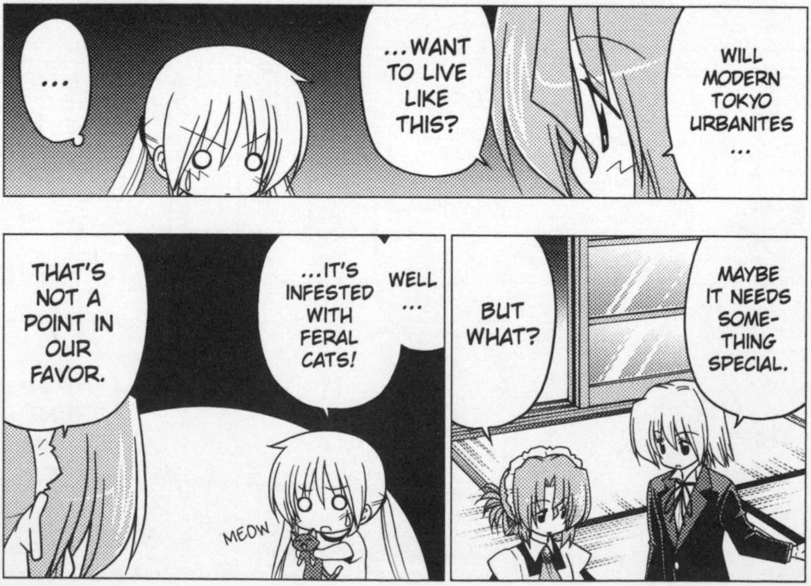
WILL MODERN TOKYO URBANITES ...
...WANT TO LIVE LIKE THIS?
...
MAYBE IT NEEDS SOME-THING SPECIAL.
BUT WHAT?
WELL ...
...IT'S INFESTED WITH FERAL CATS!
MEOW
THAT'S NOT A POINT IN OUR FAVOR.

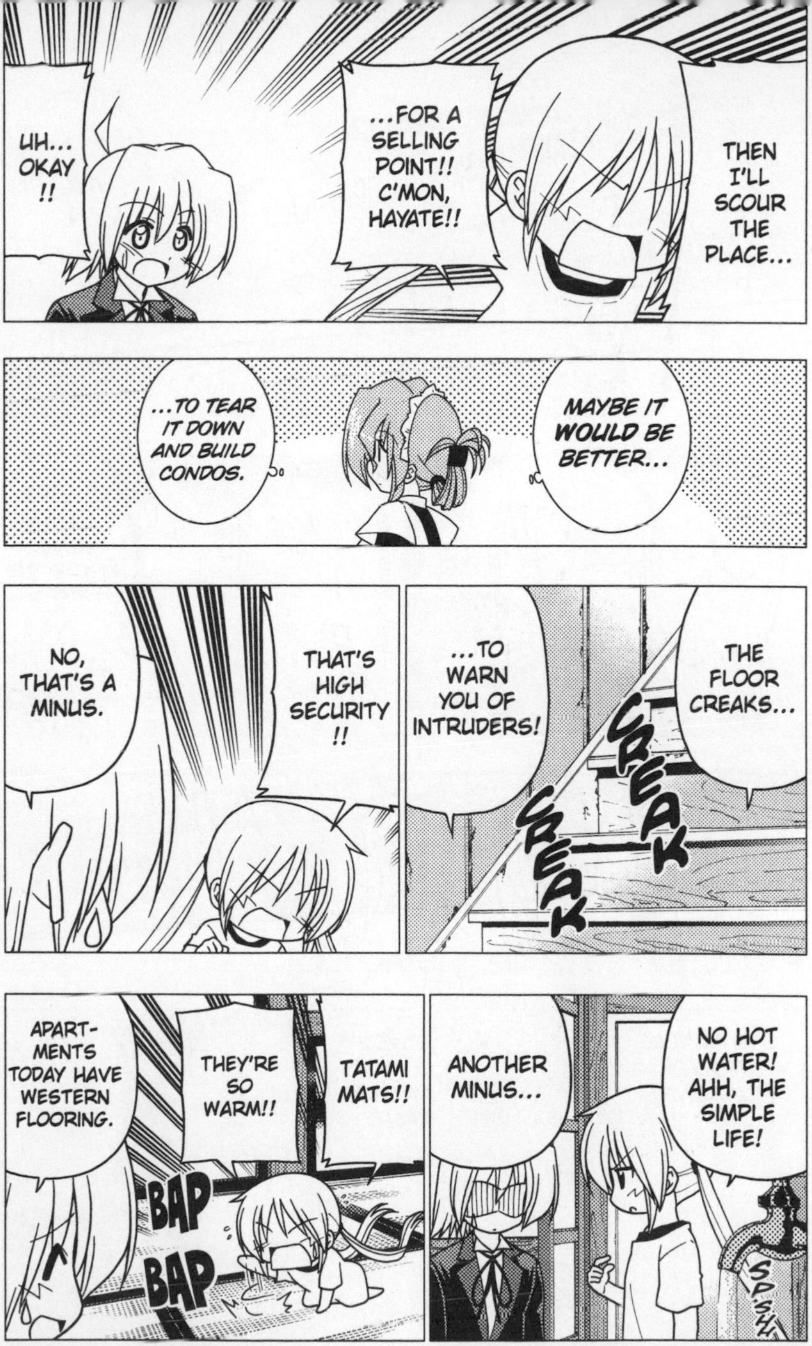
THEN I'LL SCOUR THE PLACE...
...FOR A SELLING POINT!! C'MON, HAYATE!!
UH... OKAY !!
MAYBE IT WOULD BE BETTER...
...TO TEAR IT DOWN AND BUILD CONDOS.
THE FLOOR CREAKS...
CREAK
CREAK
...TO WARN YOU OF INTRUDERS!
THAT'S HIGH SECURITY !!
NO, THAT'S A MINUS.
NO HOT WATER! AHH, THE SIMPLE LIFE!
SPSH
ANOTHER MINUS...
TATAMI MATS!!
THEY'RE SO WARM!!
BAP
BAP
APARTMENTS TODAY HAVE WESTERN FLOORING.

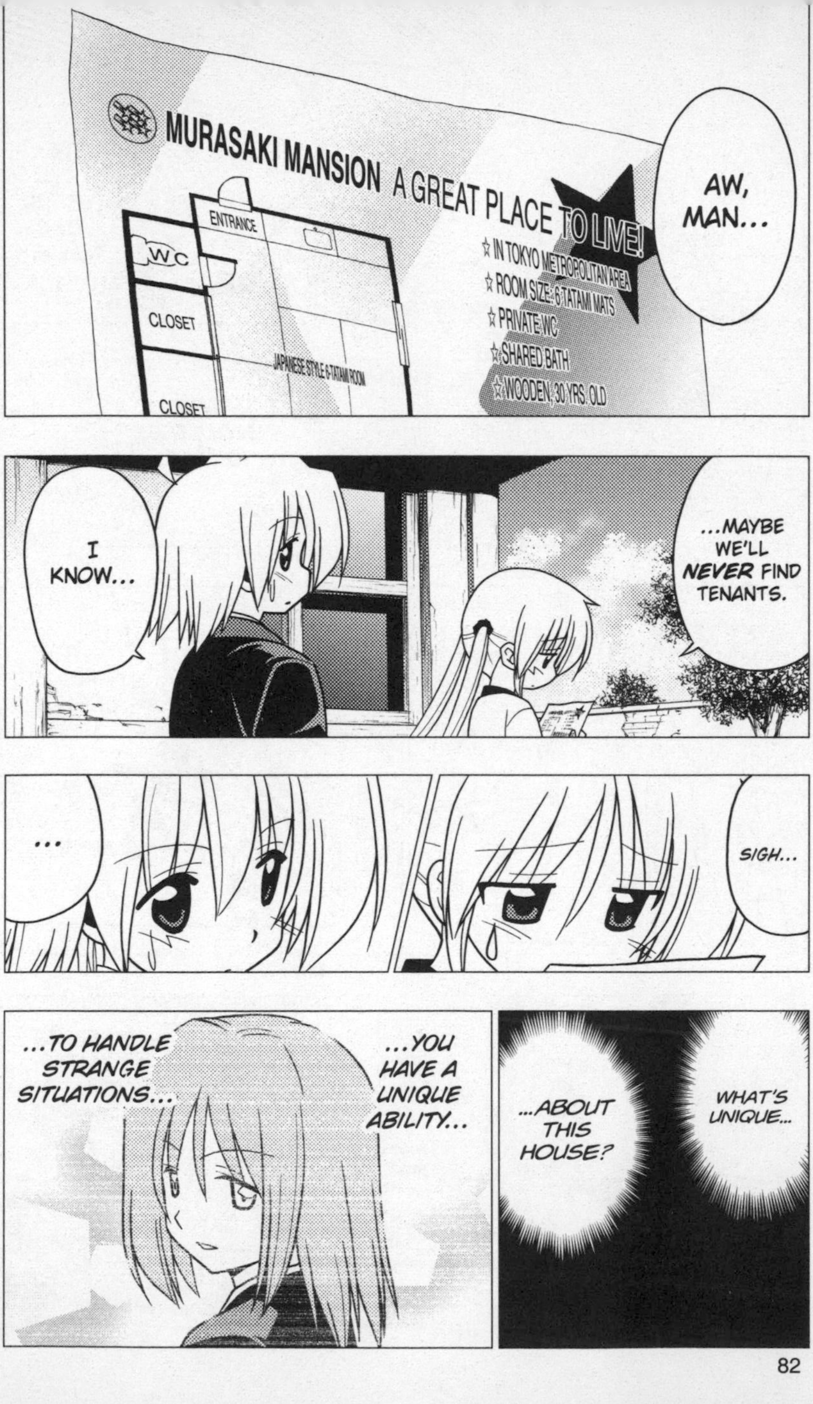
AW, MAN...
MURASAKI MANSION A GREAT PLACE TO LIVE!
☆ IN TOKYO METROPOLITAN AREA
☆ ROOM SIZE: 6 TATAMI MATS
☆ PRIVATE WC
☆ SHARED BATH
☆ WOODEN, 30 YRS. OLD
ENTRANCE
WC
CLOSET
JAPANESE STYLE 6-TATAMI ROOM
CLOSET
...MAYBE WE'LL NEVER FIND TENANTS.
I KNOW...
SIGH...
...
WHAT'S UNIQUE...
...ABOUT THIS HOUSE?
...YOU HAVE A UNIQUE ABILITY...
...TO HANDLE STRANGE SITUATIONS...

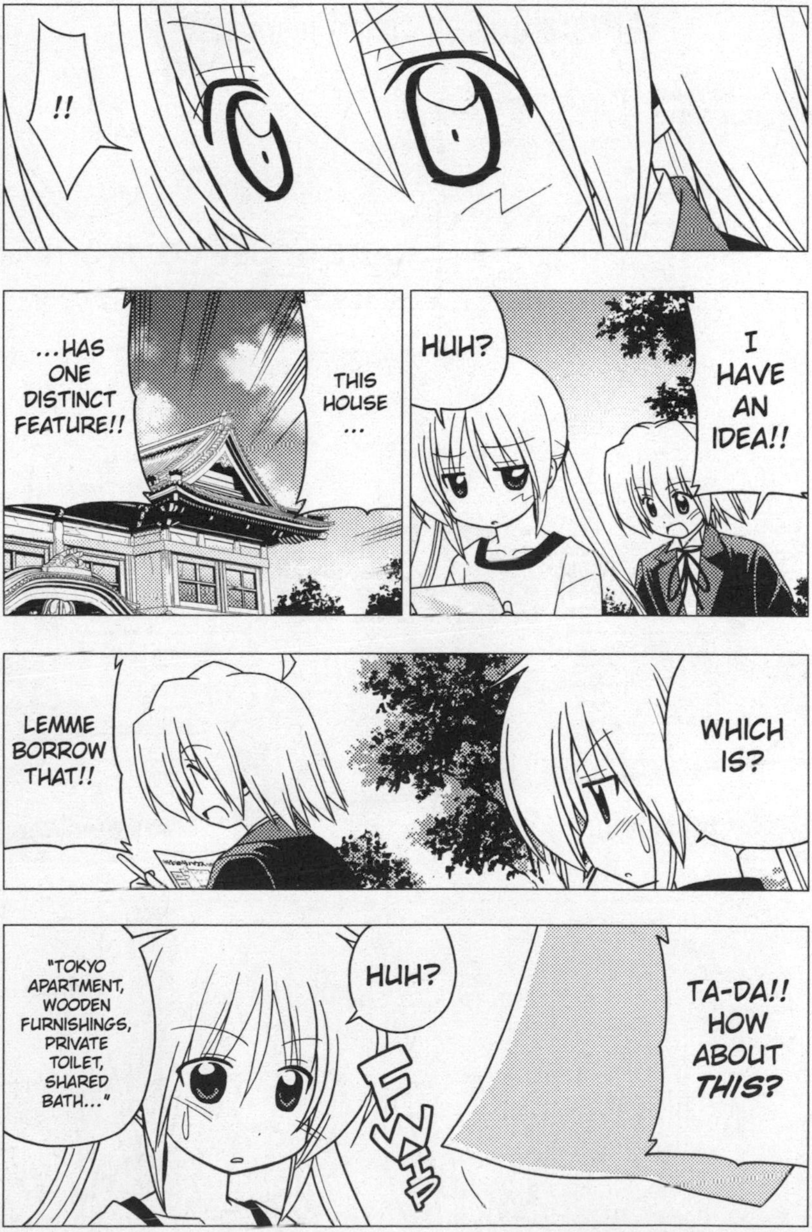
!!
I HAVE AN IDEA!!
HUH?
THIS HOUSE...
...HAS ONE DISTINCT FEATURE!!
WHICH IS?
LEMME BORROW THAT!!
TA-DA!! HOW ABOUT *THIS?*
HUH?
FWAP
"TOKYO APARTMENT, WOODEN FURNISHINGS, PRIVATE TOILET, SHARED BATH..."

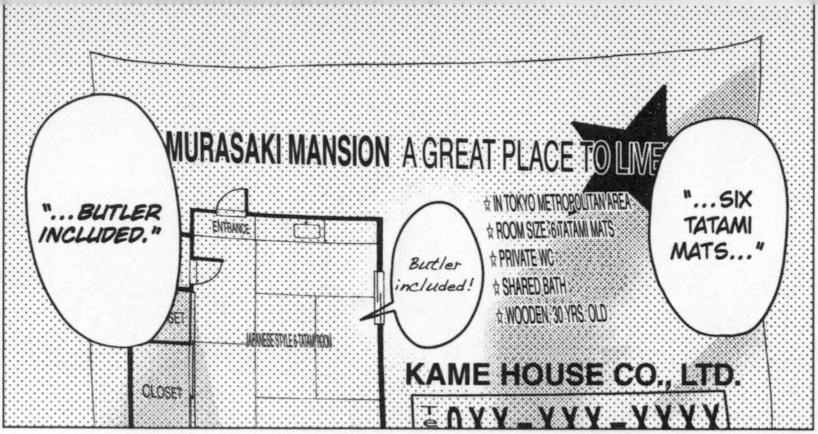
"...SIX TATAMI MATS..."
MURASAKI MANSION A GREAT PLACE TO LIVE
☆ IN TOKYO METROPOLITAN AREA
☆ ROOM SIZE: 6 TATAMI MATS
☆ PRIVATE WC
☆ SHARED BATH
☆ WOODEN, 30 YRS. OLD
KAME HOUSE CO., LTD.
ENTRANCE
JAPANESE STYLE 6-TATAMI ROOM
CLOSET
Butler included!
"...BUTLER INCLUDED."

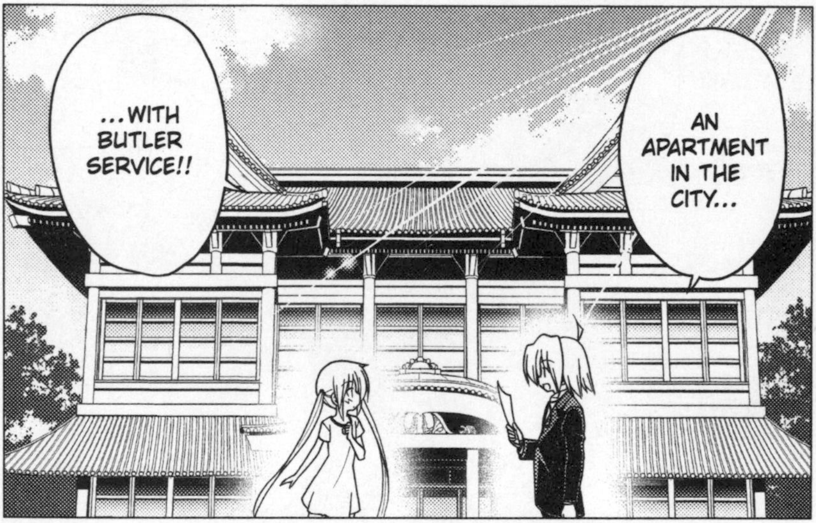
AN APARTMENT IN THE CITY...
...WITH BUTLER SERVICE!!

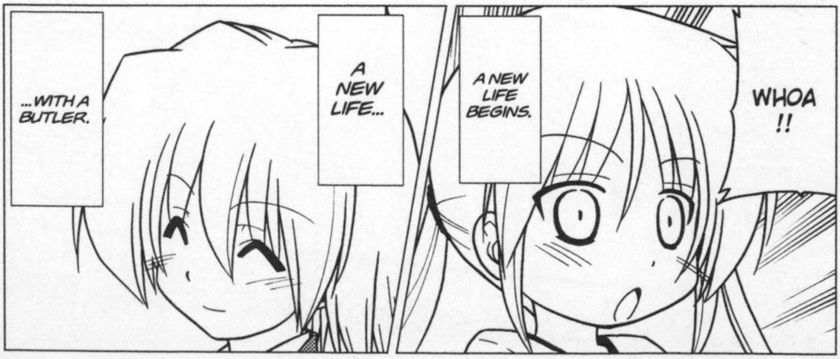
WHOA!!
A NEW LIFE BEGINS.
A NEW LIFE...
...WITH A BUTLER.

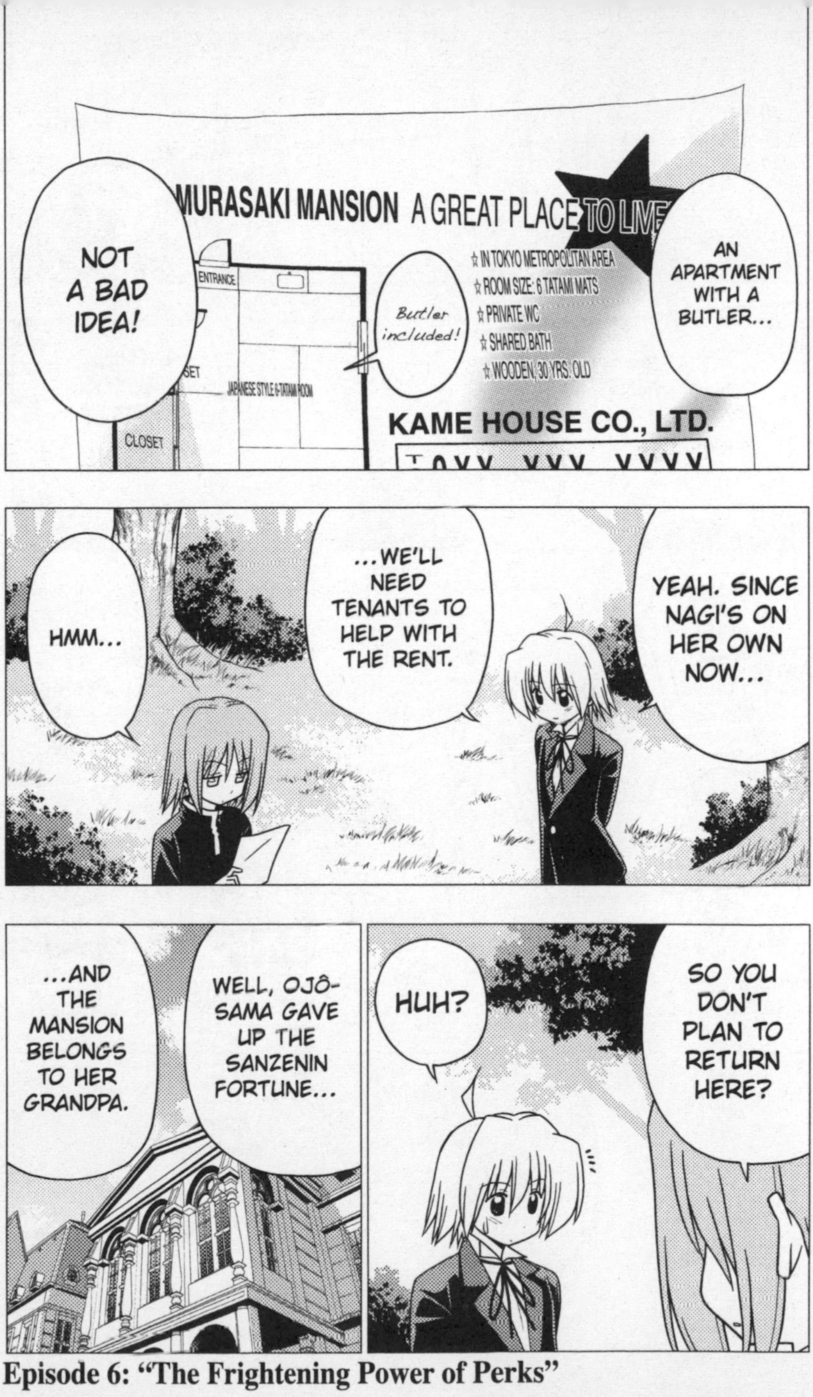
AN APARTMENT WITH A BUTLER...
MURASAKI MANSION A GREAT PLACE TO LIVE
☆ IN TOKYO METROPOLITAN AREA
☆ ROOM SIZE: 6 TATAMI MATS
☆ PRIVATE WC
☆ SHARED BATH
☆ WOODEN, 30 YRS. OLD
Butler included!
ENTRANCE
JAPANESE STYLE 6-TATAMI ROOM
CLOSET
KAME HOUSE CO., LTD.
NOT A BAD IDEA!
YEAH. SINCE NAGI'S ON HER OWN NOW...
...WE'LL NEED TENANTS TO HELP WITH THE RENT.
HMM...
SO YOU DON'T PLAN TO RETURN HERE?
HUH?
WELL, OJÔ-SAMA GAVE UP THE SANZENIN FORTUNE...
...AND THE MANSION BELONGS TO HER GRANDPA.

Episode 6: "The Frightening Power of Perks"

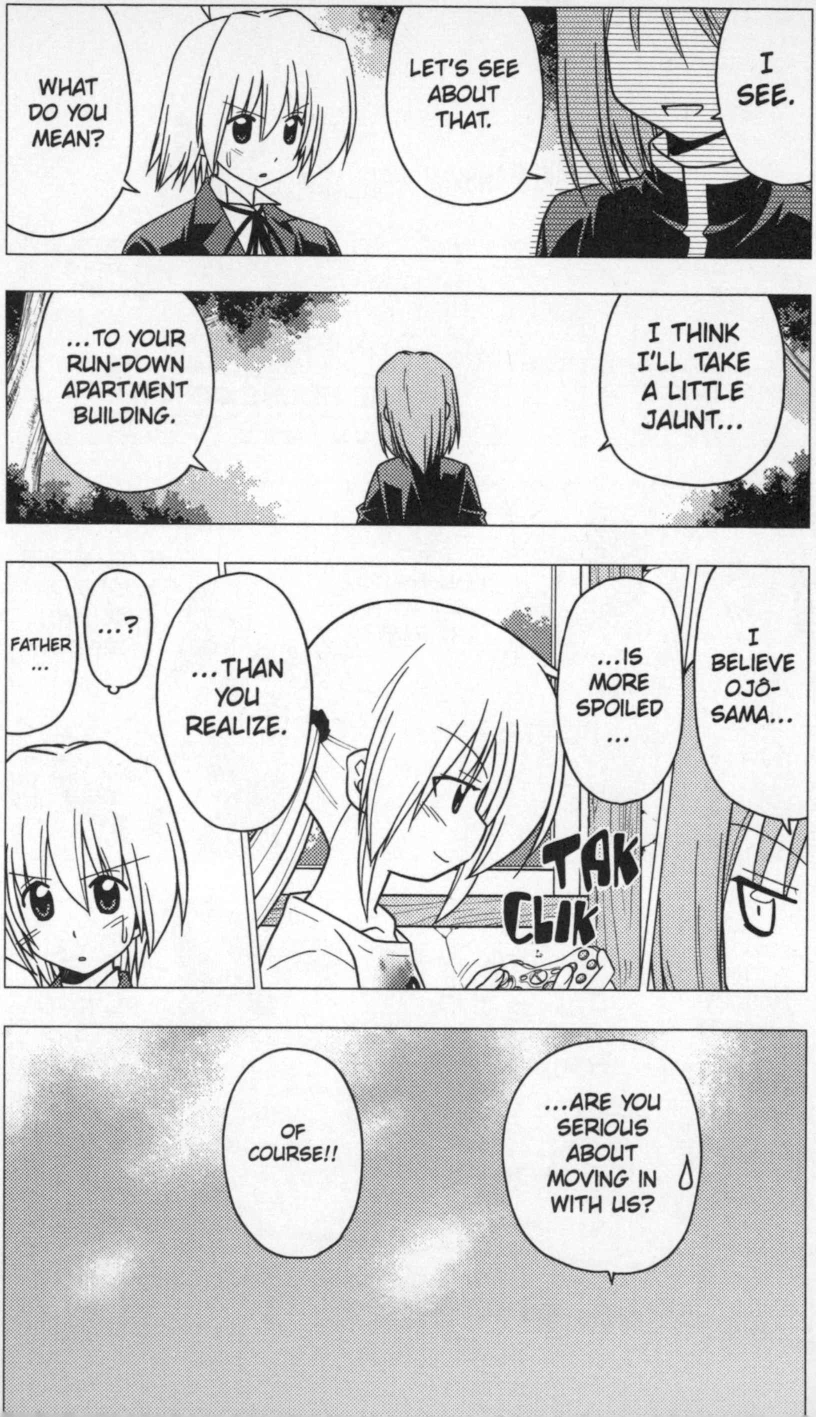
I SEE.
LET'S SEE ABOUT THAT.
WHAT DO YOU MEAN?
I THINK I'LL TAKE A LITTLE JAUNT...
...TO YOUR RUN-DOWN APARTMENT BUILDING.
I BELIEVE OJÔ-SAMA...
...IS MORE SPOILED...
TAK
CLIK
...THAN YOU REALIZE.
...?
FATHER...
...ARE YOU SERIOUS ABOUT MOVING IN WITH US?
OF COURSE!!

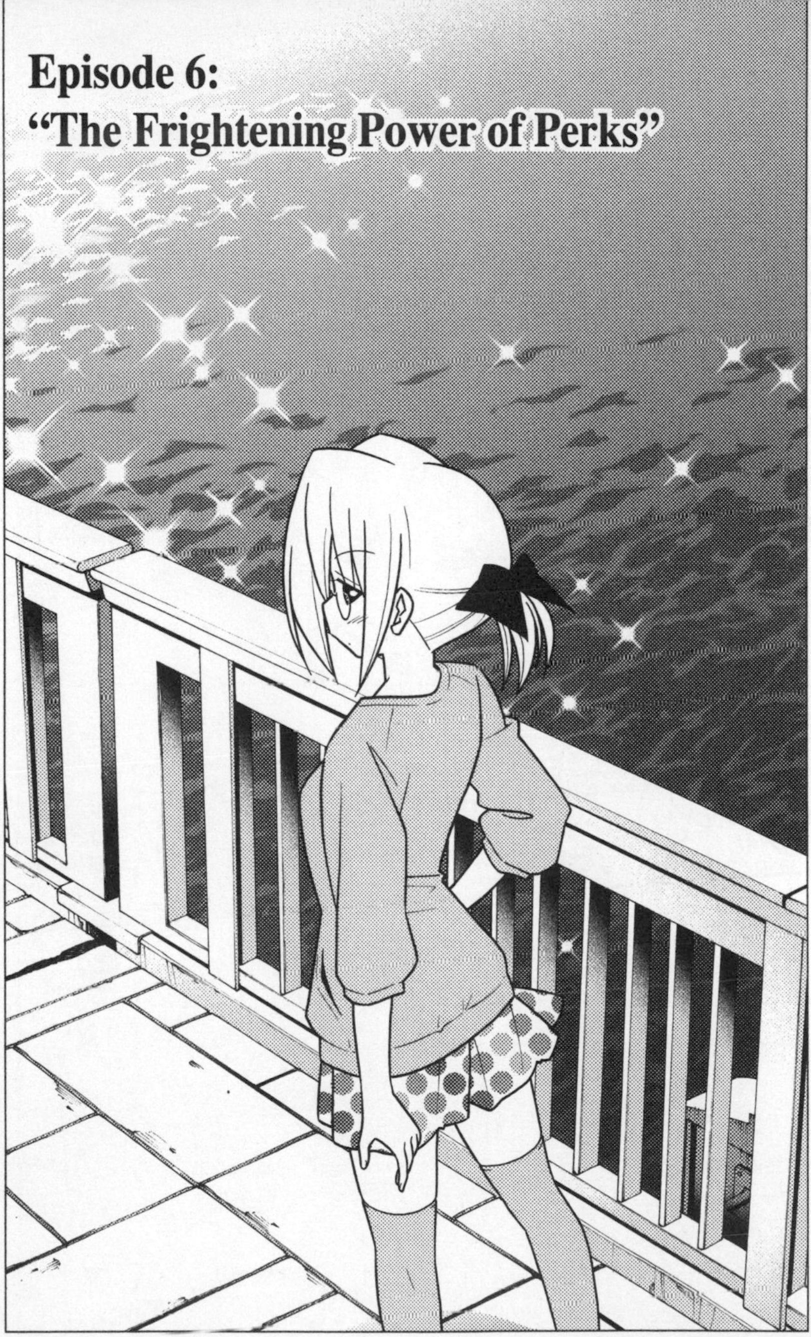
Episode 6:
"The Frightening Power of Perks"

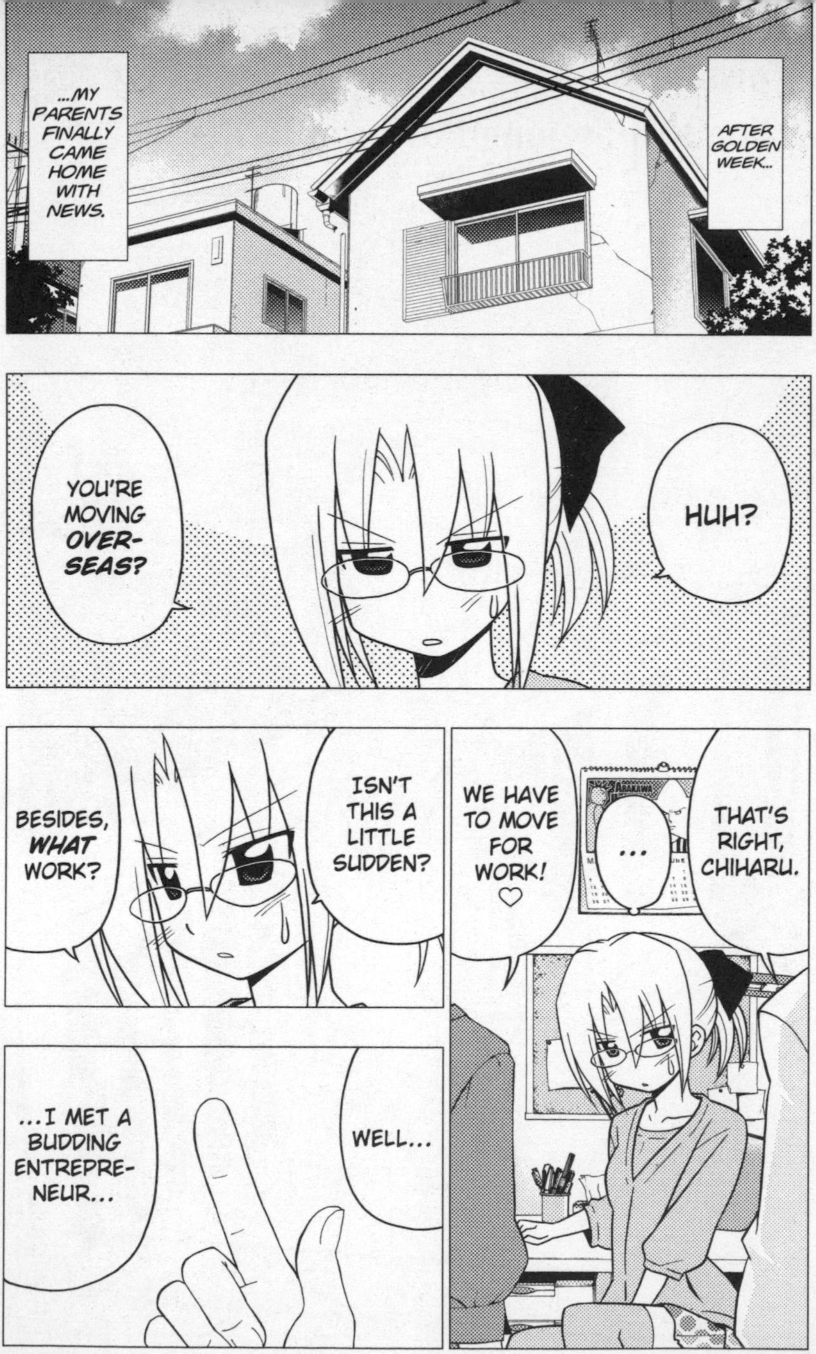
AFTER GOLDEN WEEK...
...MY PARENTS FINALLY CAME HOME WITH NEWS.
HUH?
YOU'RE MOVING *OVERSEAS?*
THAT'S RIGHT, CHIHARU.
...
WE HAVE TO MOVE FOR WORK! ♡
ISN'T THIS A LITTLE SUDDEN?
BESIDES, *WHAT* WORK?
WELL...
...I MET A BUDDING ENTREPRENEUR...

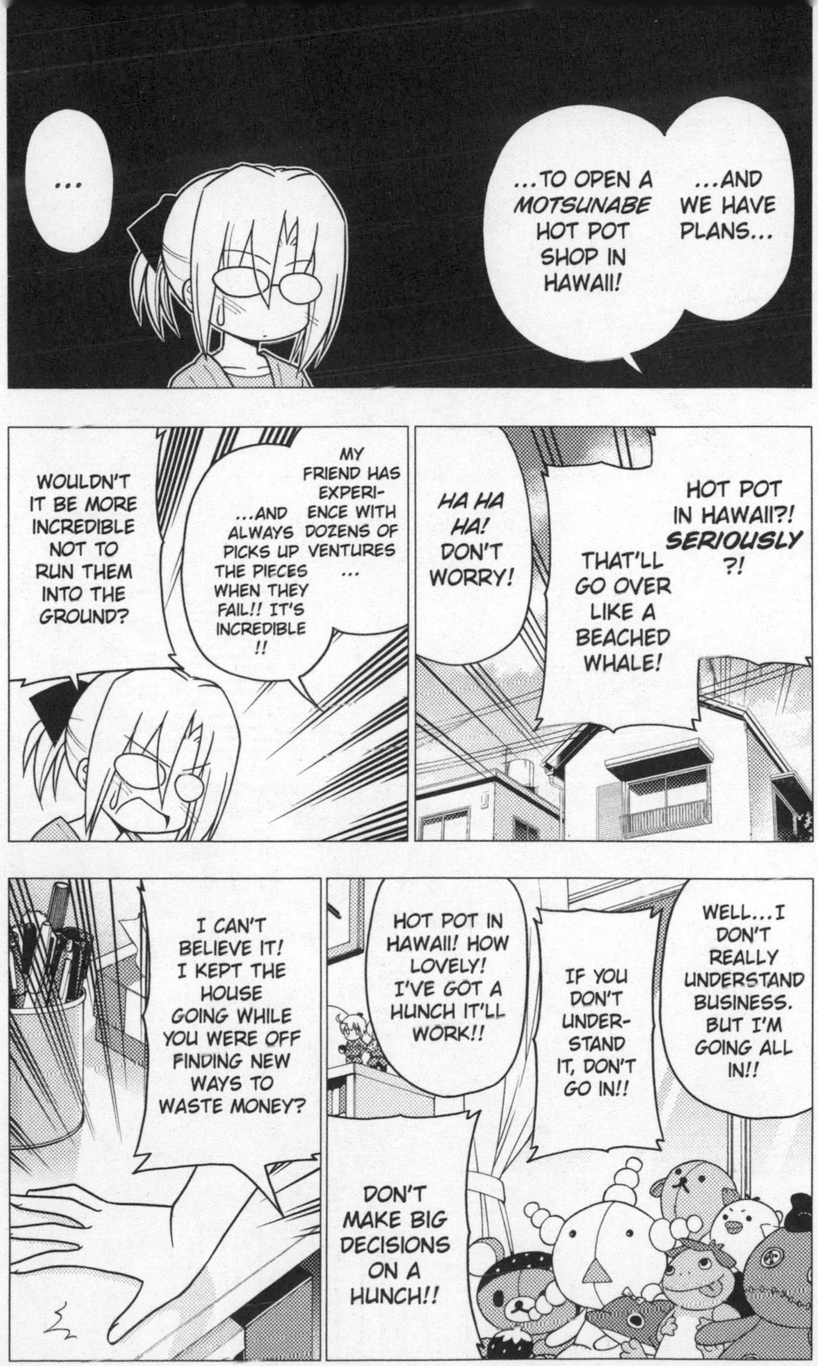
...AND WE HAVE PLANS...
...TO OPEN A *MOTSUNABE* HOT POT SHOP IN HAWAII!
...
HOT POT IN HAWAII?! ***SERIOUSLY***?!
THAT'LL GO OVER LIKE A BEACHED WHALE!
HA HA HA! DON'T WORRY!
MY FRIEND HAS EXPERIENCE WITH DOZENS OF VENTURES...
...AND ALWAYS PICKS UP THE PIECES WHEN THEY FAIL!! IT'S INCREDIBLE!!
WOULDN'T IT BE MORE INCREDIBLE NOT TO RUN THEM INTO THE GROUND?
WELL...I DON'T REALLY UNDERSTAND BUSINESS. BUT I'M GOING ALL IN!!
IF YOU DON'T UNDERSTAND IT, DON'T GO IN!!
HOT POT IN HAWAII! HOW LOVELY! I'VE GOT A HUNCH IT'LL WORK!!
DON'T MAKE BIG DECISIONS ON A HUNCH!!
I CAN'T BELIEVE IT! I KEPT THE HOUSE GOING WHILE YOU WERE OFF FINDING NEW WAYS TO WASTE MONEY?

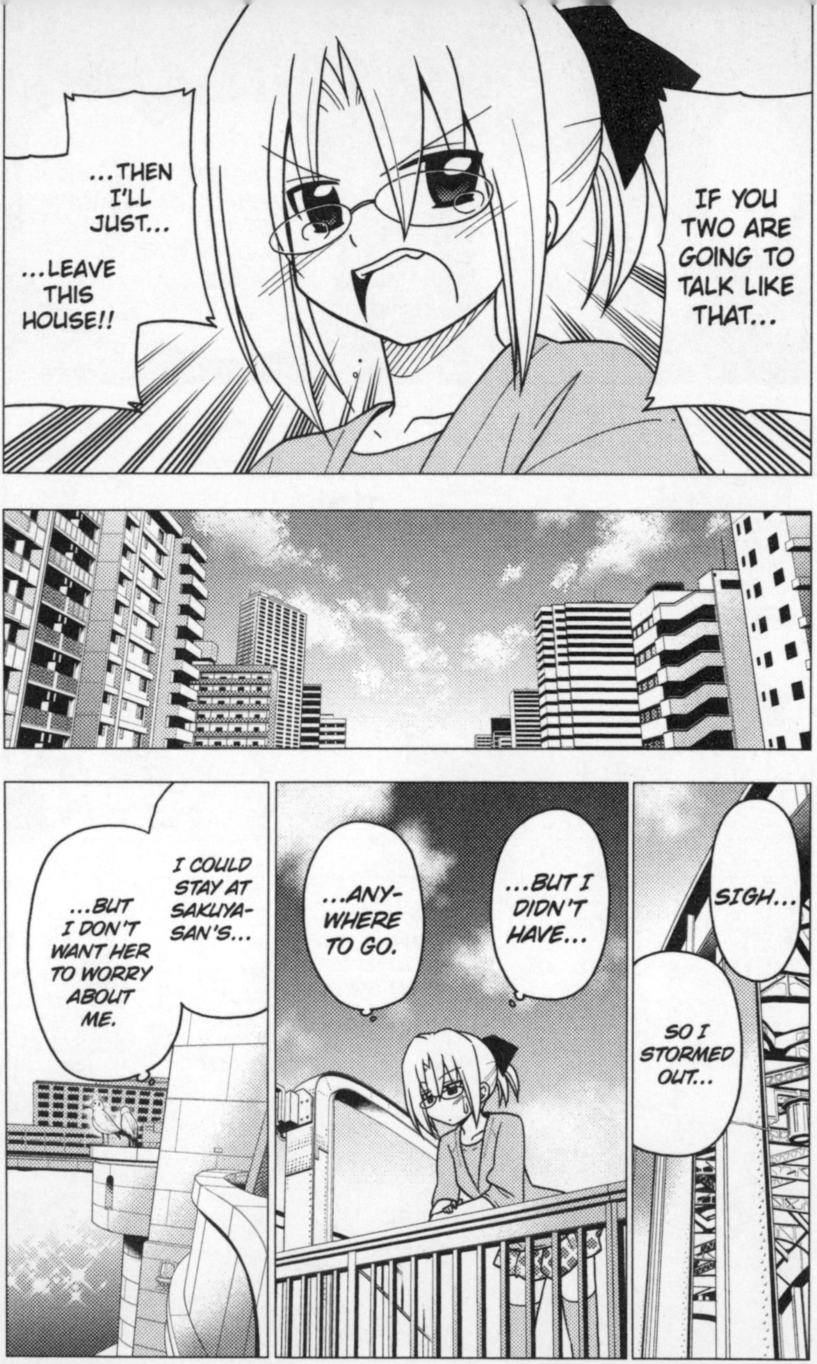
IF YOU TWO ARE GOING TO TALK LIKE THAT...
...THEN I'LL JUST...
...LEAVE THIS HOUSE!!
SIGH...
SO I STORMED OUT...
...BUT I DIDN'T HAVE...
...ANYWHERE TO GO.
I COULD STAY AT SAKUYA-SAN'S...
...BUT I DON'T WANT HER TO WORRY ABOUT ME.

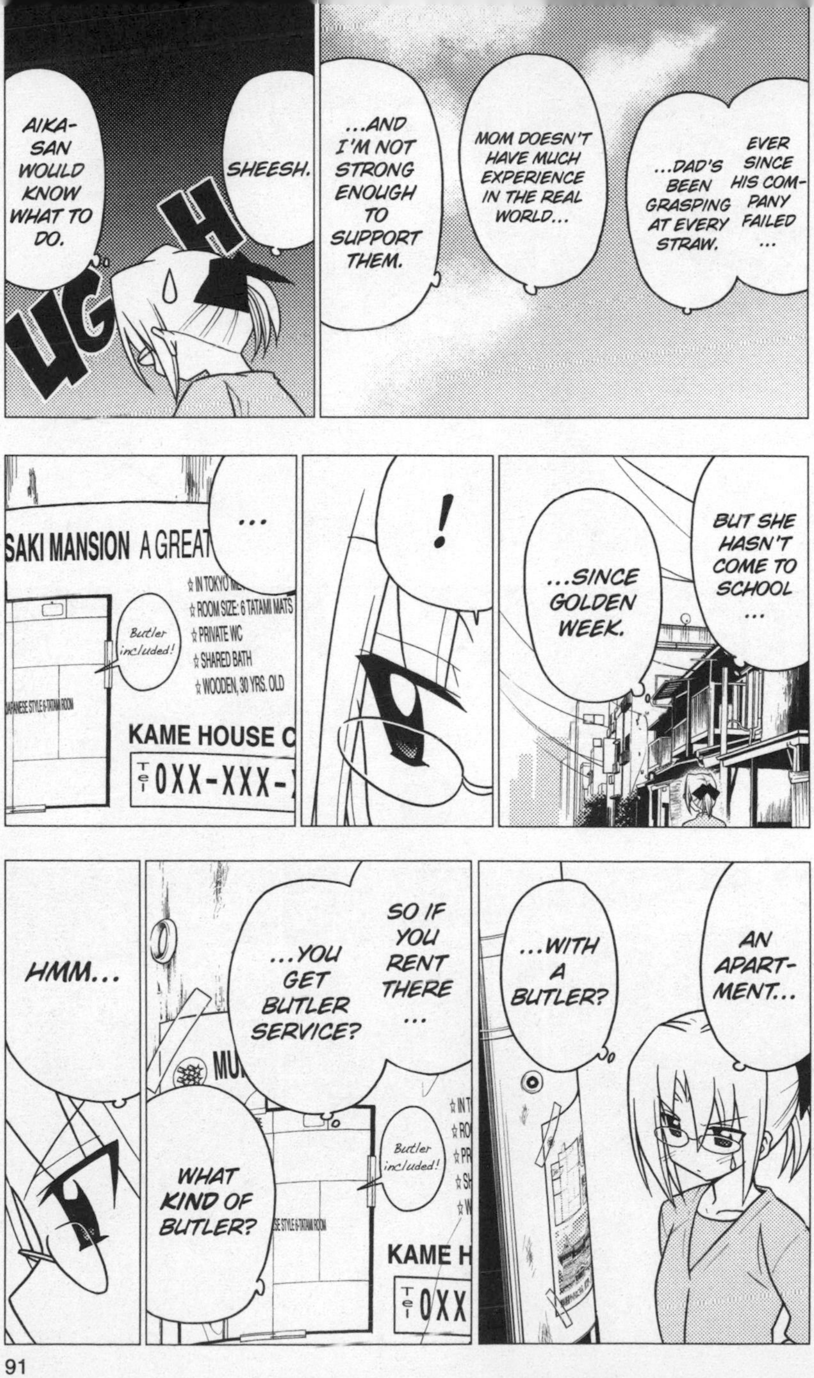
EVER SINCE HIS COMPANY FAILED...
...DAD'S BEEN GRASPING AT EVERY STRAW.
MOM DOESN'T HAVE MUCH EXPERIENCE IN THE REAL WORLD...
...AND I'M NOT STRONG ENOUGH TO SUPPORT THEM.
SHEESH.
AIKA-SAN WOULD KNOW WHAT TO DO.
UGH
BUT SHE HASN'T COME TO SCHOOL...
...SINCE GOLDEN WEEK.
!
...
SAKI MANSION A GREAT
☆ ROOM SIZE: 6 TATAMI MATS
☆ PRIVATE WC
☆ SHARED BATH
☆ WOODEN, 30 YRS. OLD
Butler included!
KAME HOUSE C
Tel 0XX-XXX-
AN APARTMENT...
...WITH A BUTLER?
SO IF YOU RENT THERE...
...YOU GET BUTLER SERVICE?
WHAT KIND OF BUTLER?
Butler included!
KAME H
Tel 0XX
HMM...

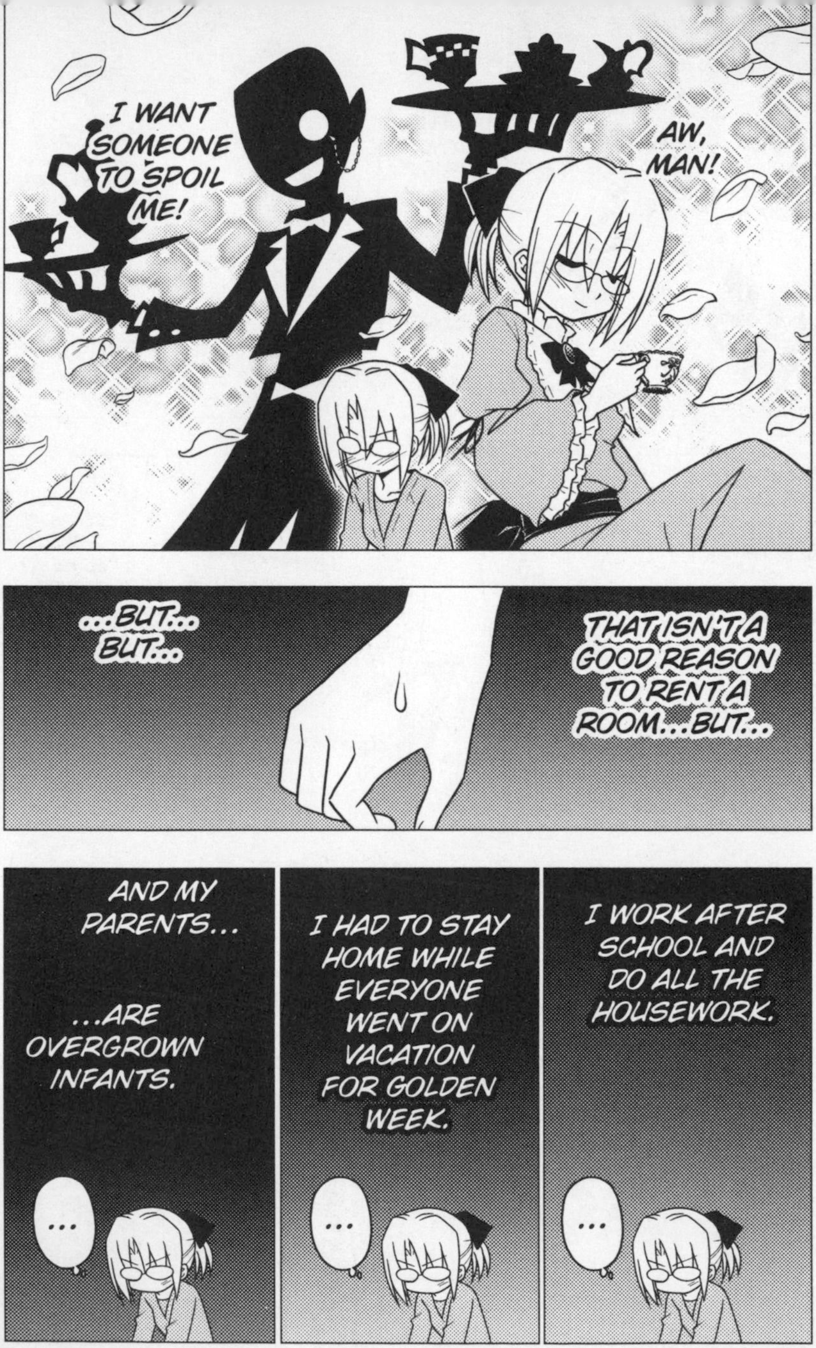
AW, MAN!
I WANT SOMEONE TO SPOIL ME!
THAT ISN'T A GOOD REASON TO RENT A ROOM...BUT...
...BUT... BUT...
I WORK AFTER SCHOOL AND DO ALL THE HOUSEWORK.
...
I HAD TO STAY HOME WHILE EVERYONE WENT ON VACATION FOR GOLDEN WEEK.
...
AND MY PARENTS...
...ARE OVERGROWN INFANTS.
...

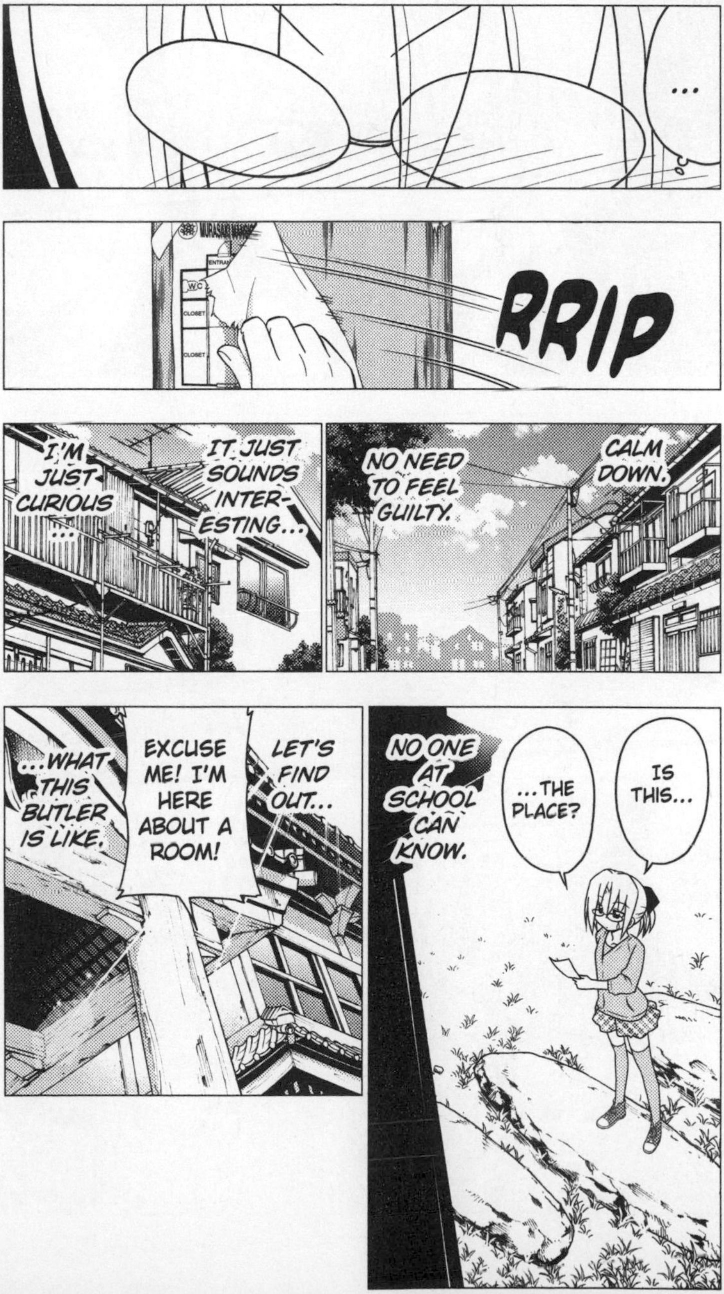
...
RRIP
W.C
CLOSET
CLOSET
CALM DOWN.
NO NEED TO FEEL GUILTY.
IT JUST SOUNDS INTERESTING...
I'M JUST CURIOUS...
IS THIS...
...THE PLACE?
NO ONE AT SCHOOL CAN KNOW.
LET'S FIND OUT...
...WHAT THIS BUTLER IS LIKE.
EXCUSE ME! I'M HERE ABOUT A ROOM!

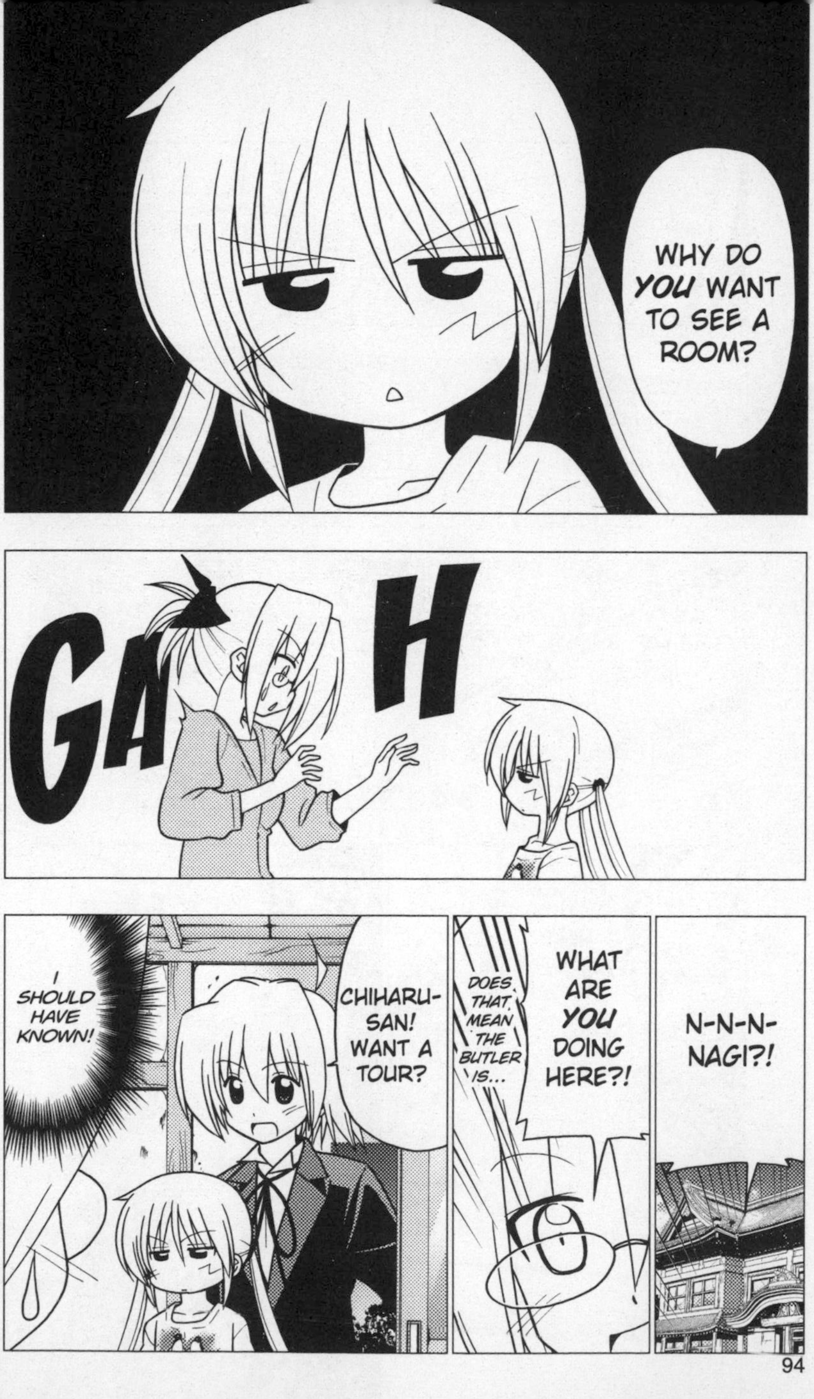
WHY DO YOU WANT TO SEE A ROOM?
GAH
N-N-N-NAGI?!
WHAT ARE YOU DOING HERE?!
DOES THAT MEAN THE BUTLER IS...
CHIHARU-SAN! WANT A TOUR?
I SHOULD HAVE KNOWN!

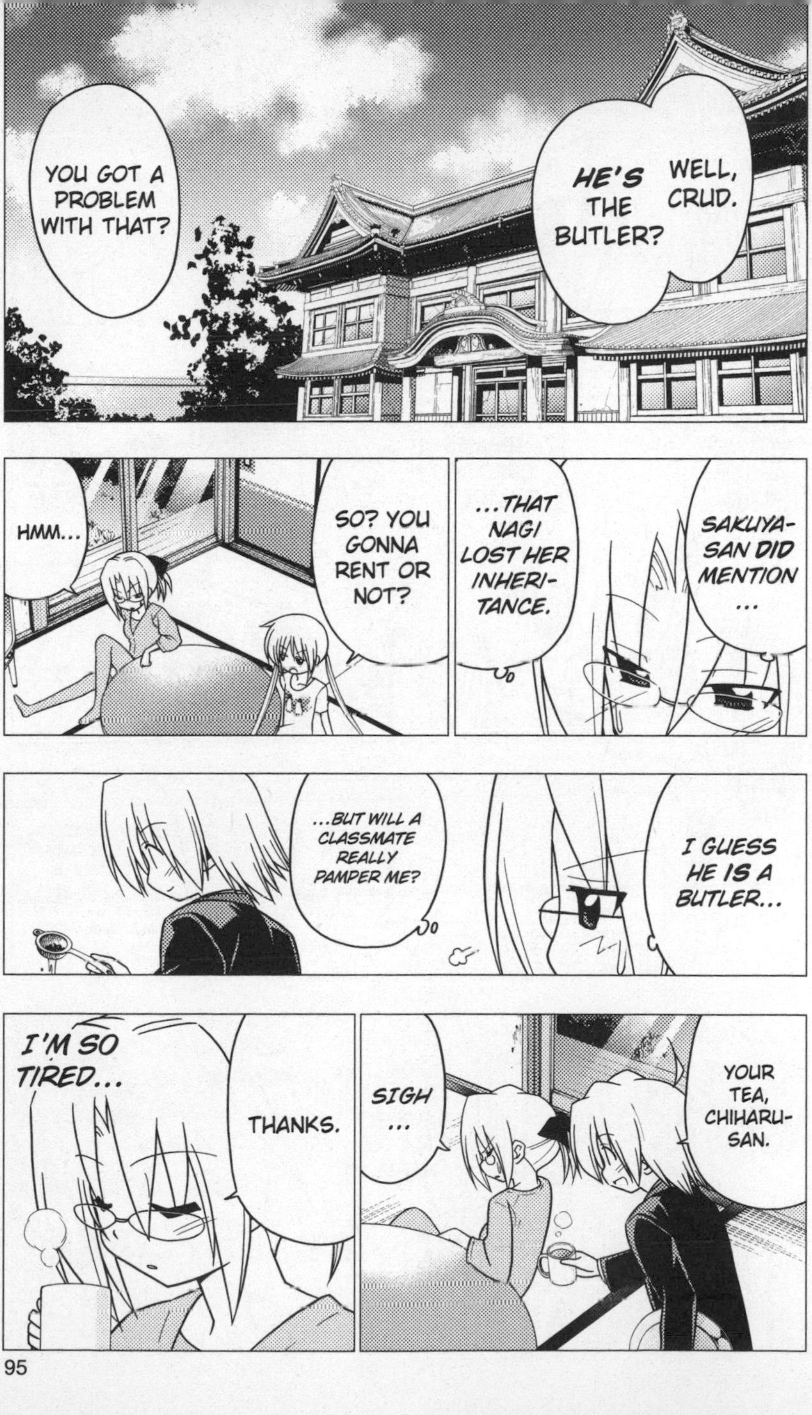
WELL, CRUD.
HE'S THE BUTLER?
YOU GOT A PROBLEM WITH THAT?
SAKUYA-SAN DID MENTION...
...THAT NAGI LOST HER INHERITANCE.
SO? YOU GONNA RENT OR NOT?
HMM...
I GUESS HE IS A BUTLER...
...BUT WILL A CLASSMATE REALLY PAMPER ME?
YOUR TEA, CHIHARU-SAN.
SIGH...
THANKS.
I'M SO TIRED...

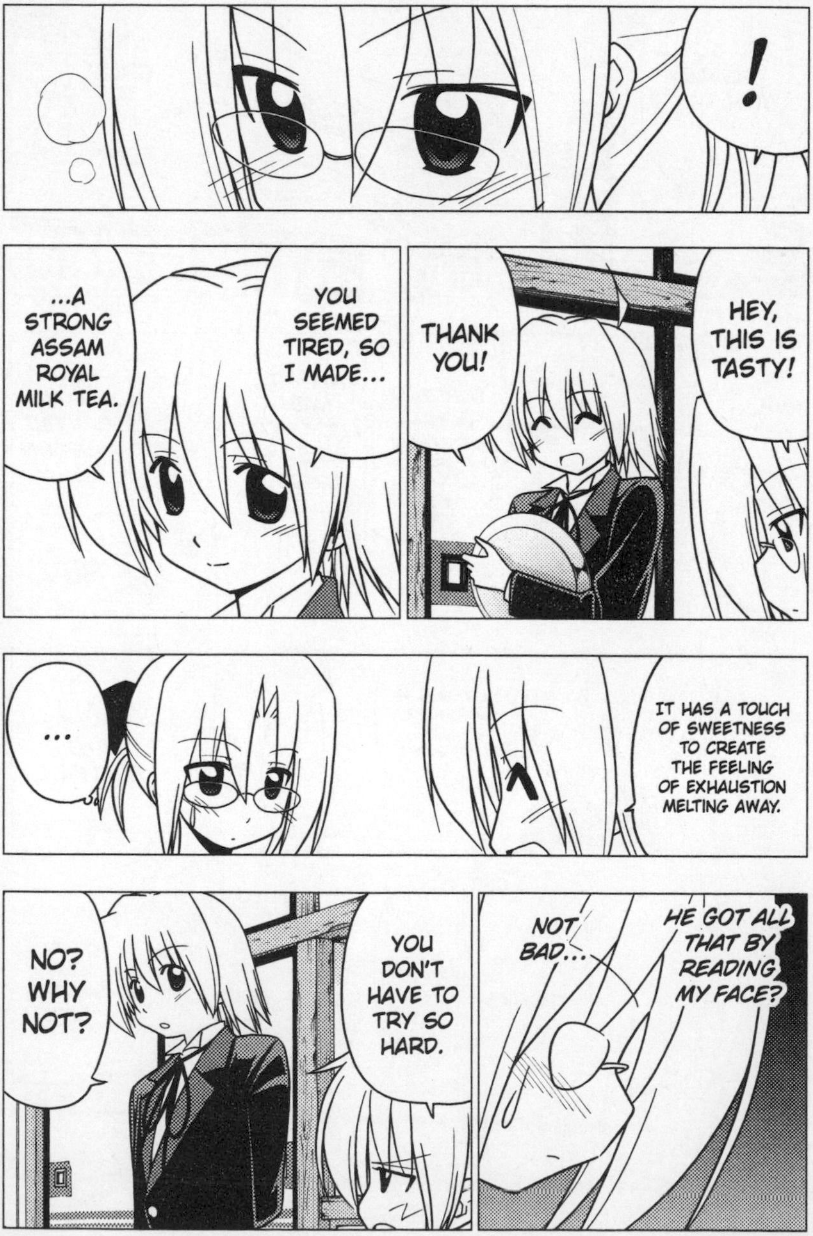
!
HEY, THIS IS TASTY!
THANK YOU!
YOU SEEMED TIRED, SO I MADE...
...A STRONG ASSAM ROYAL MILK TEA.
IT HAS A TOUCH OF SWEETNESS TO CREATE THE FEELING OF EXHAUSTION MELTING AWAY.
...
HE GOT ALL THAT BY READING MY FACE?
NOT BAD...
YOU DON'T HAVE TO TRY SO HARD.
NO? WHY NOT?

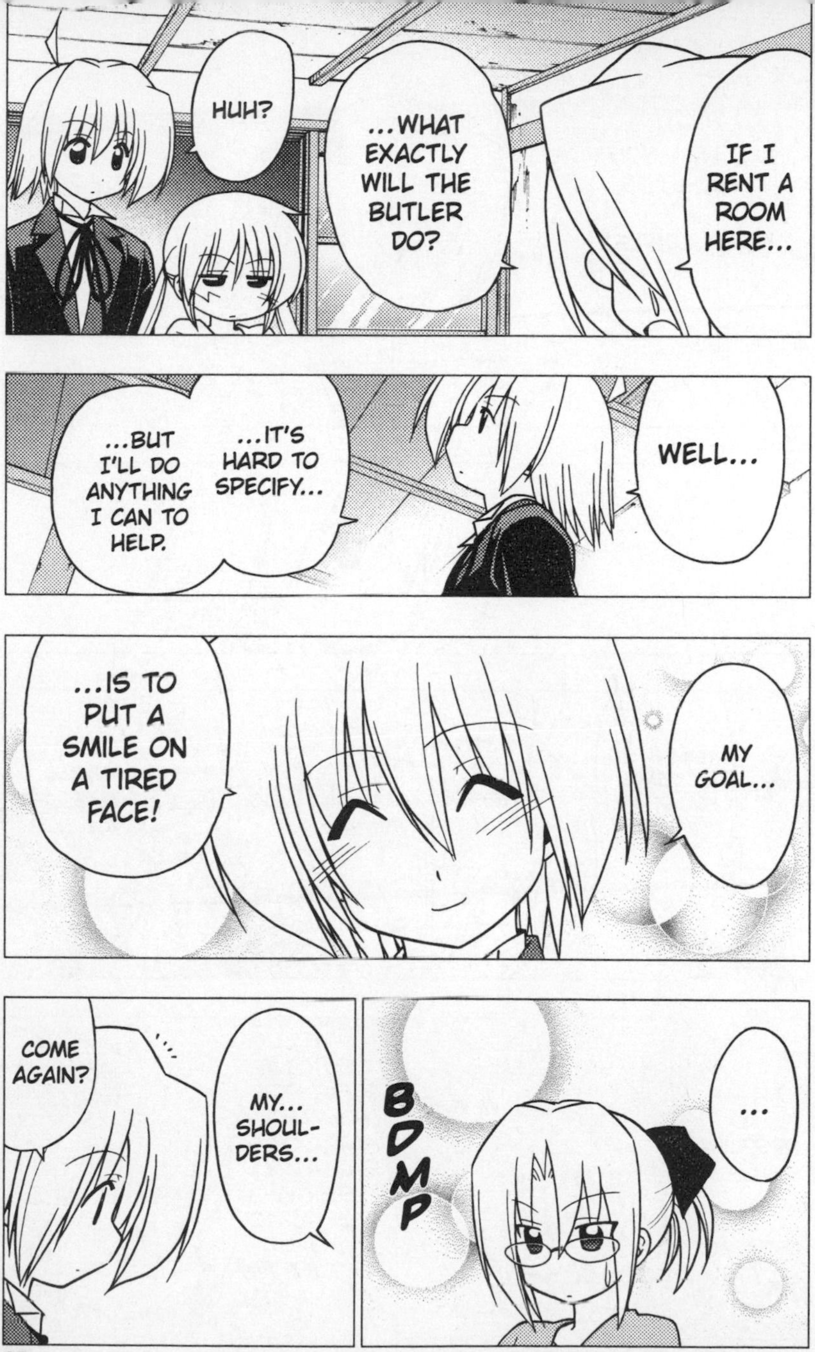
IF I RENT A ROOM HERE...
...WHAT EXACTLY WILL THE BUTLER DO?
HUH?
WELL...
...IT'S HARD TO SPECIFY...
...BUT I'LL DO ANYTHING I CAN TO HELP.
MY GOAL...
...IS TO PUT A SMILE ON A TIRED FACE!
...
BDMP
MY... SHOULDERS...
COME AGAIN?

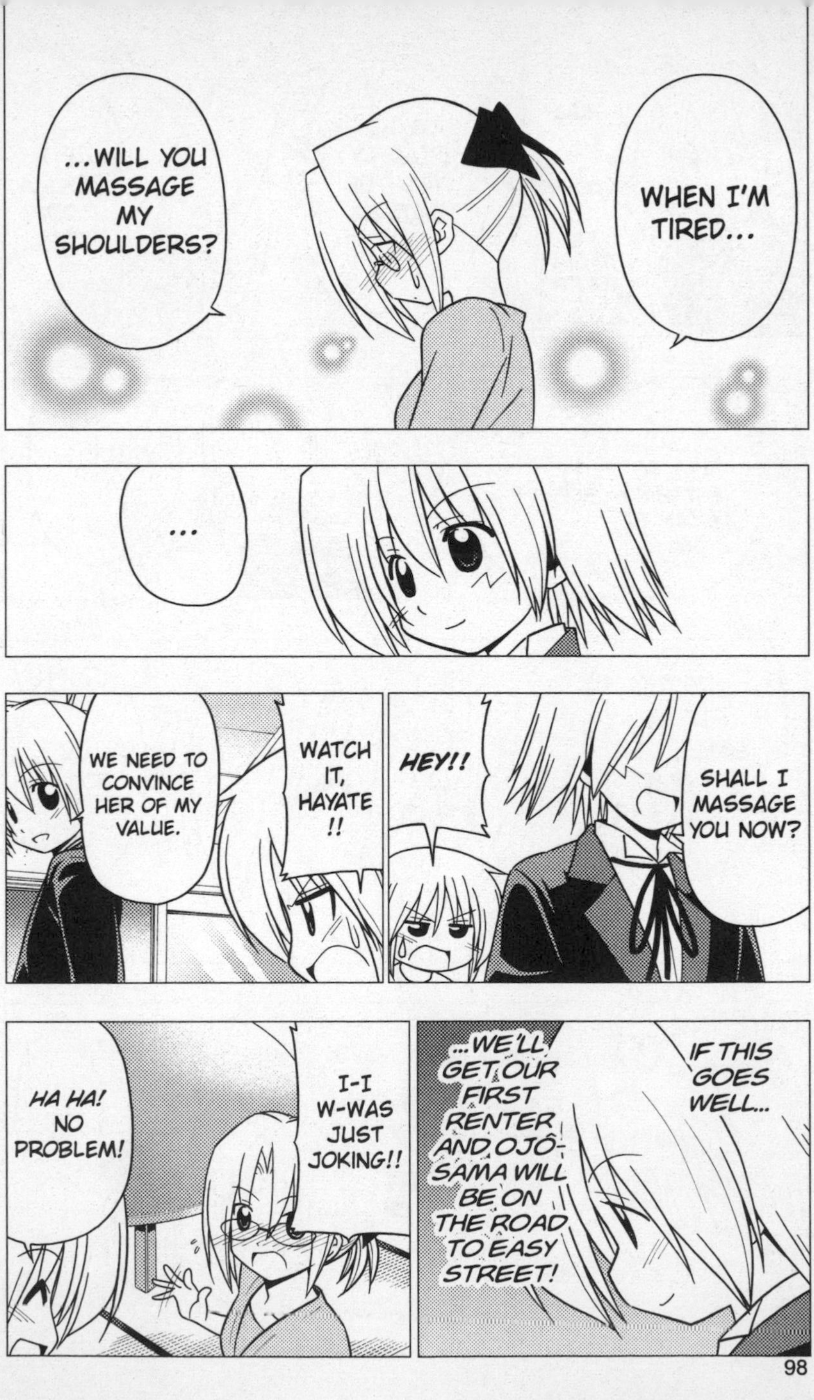
WHEN I'M TIRED...
...WILL YOU MASSAGE MY SHOULDERS?
...
SHALL I MASSAGE YOU NOW?
HEY!!
WATCH IT, HAYATE!!
WE NEED TO CONVINCE HER OF MY VALUE.
IF THIS GOES WELL...
...WE'LL GET OUR FIRST RENTER AND OJŌ-SAMA WILL BE ON THE ROAD TO EASY STREET!
I-I W-WAS JUST JOKING!!
HA HA! NO PROBLEM!

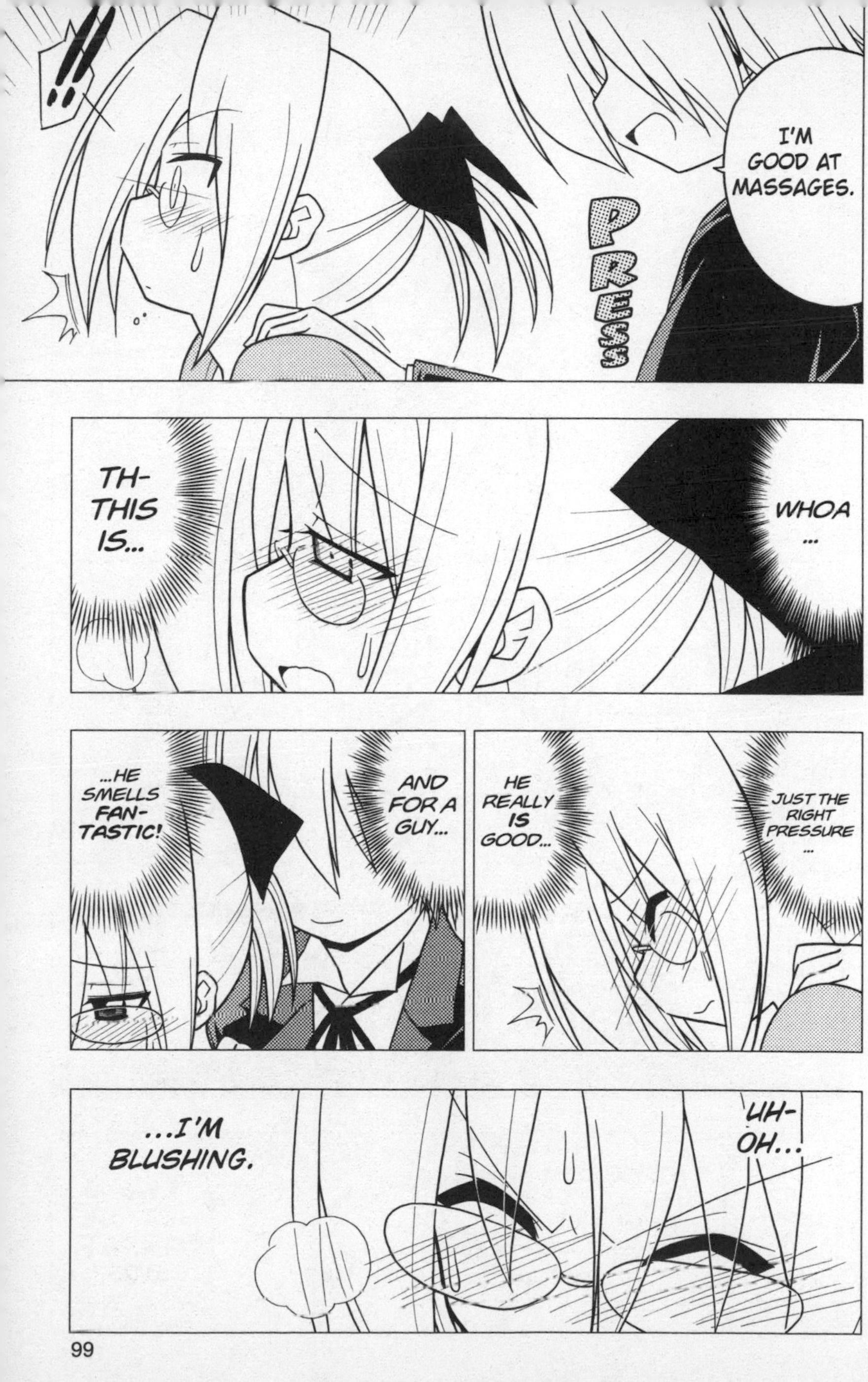
I'M GOOD AT MASSAGES.
PRESS
!!
WHOA ...
TH- THIS IS...
JUST THE RIGHT PRESSURE ...
HE REALLY IS GOOD...
AND FOR A GUY...
...HE SMELLS FAN-TASTIC!
UH- OH...
...I'M BLUSHING.

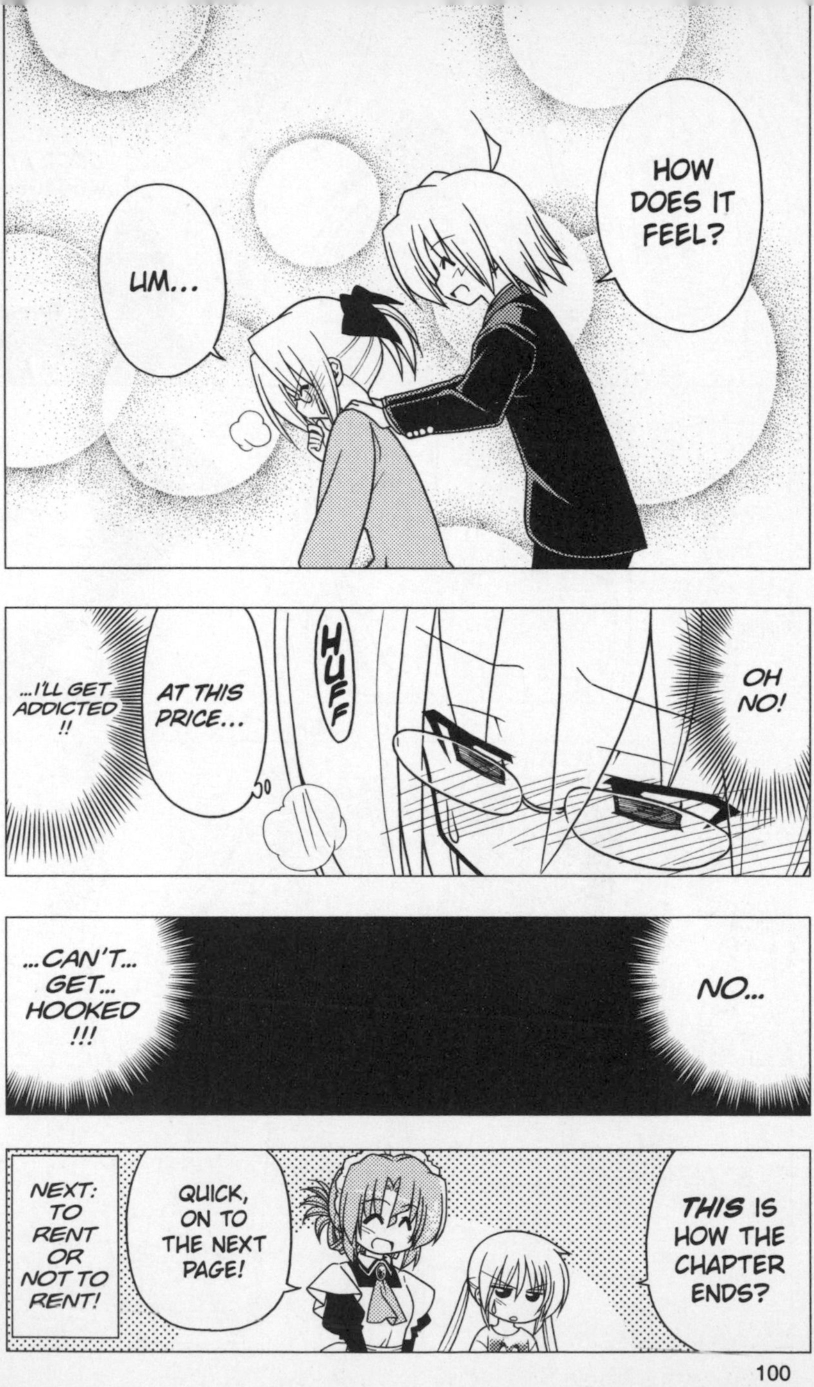
HOW DOES IT FEEL?
UM...
OH NO!
HUFF
AT THIS PRICE...
...I'LL GET ADDICTED !!
NO...
...CAN'T... GET... HOOKED !!!
THIS IS HOW THE CHAPTER ENDS?
QUICK, ON TO THE NEXT PAGE!
NEXT: TO RENT OR NOT TO RENT!

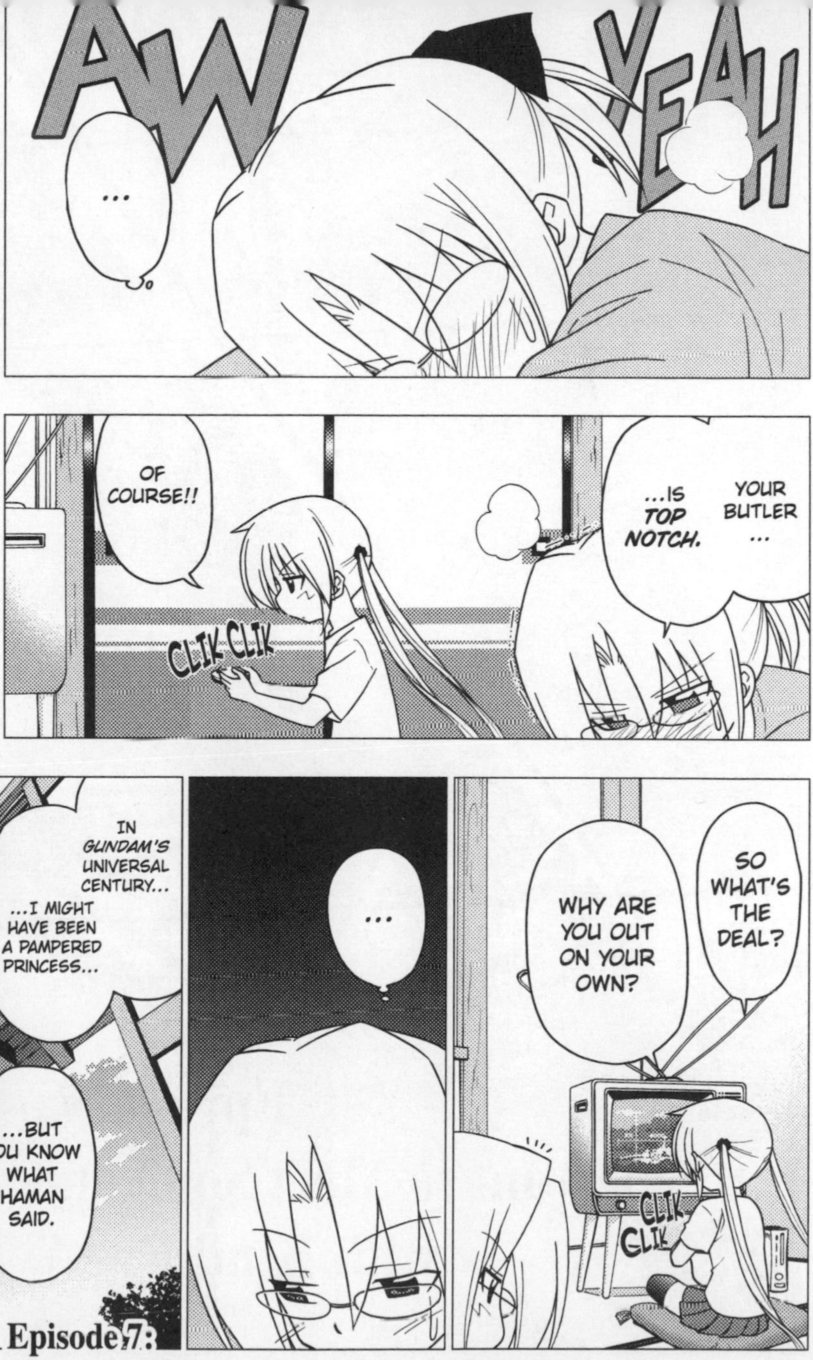
AW YEAH
...
YOUR BUTLER...
...IS TOP NOTCH.
OF COURSE!!
CLIK CLIK
SO WHAT'S THE DEAL?
WHY ARE YOU OUT ON YOUR OWN?
CLIK CLIK
...
IN GUNDAM'S UNIVERSAL CENTURY...
...I MIGHT HAVE BEEN A PAMPERED PRINCESS...
...BUT YOU KNOW WHAT HAMAN SAID.

Episode 7:
"I Want to Meet Someone with Kind Eyes"

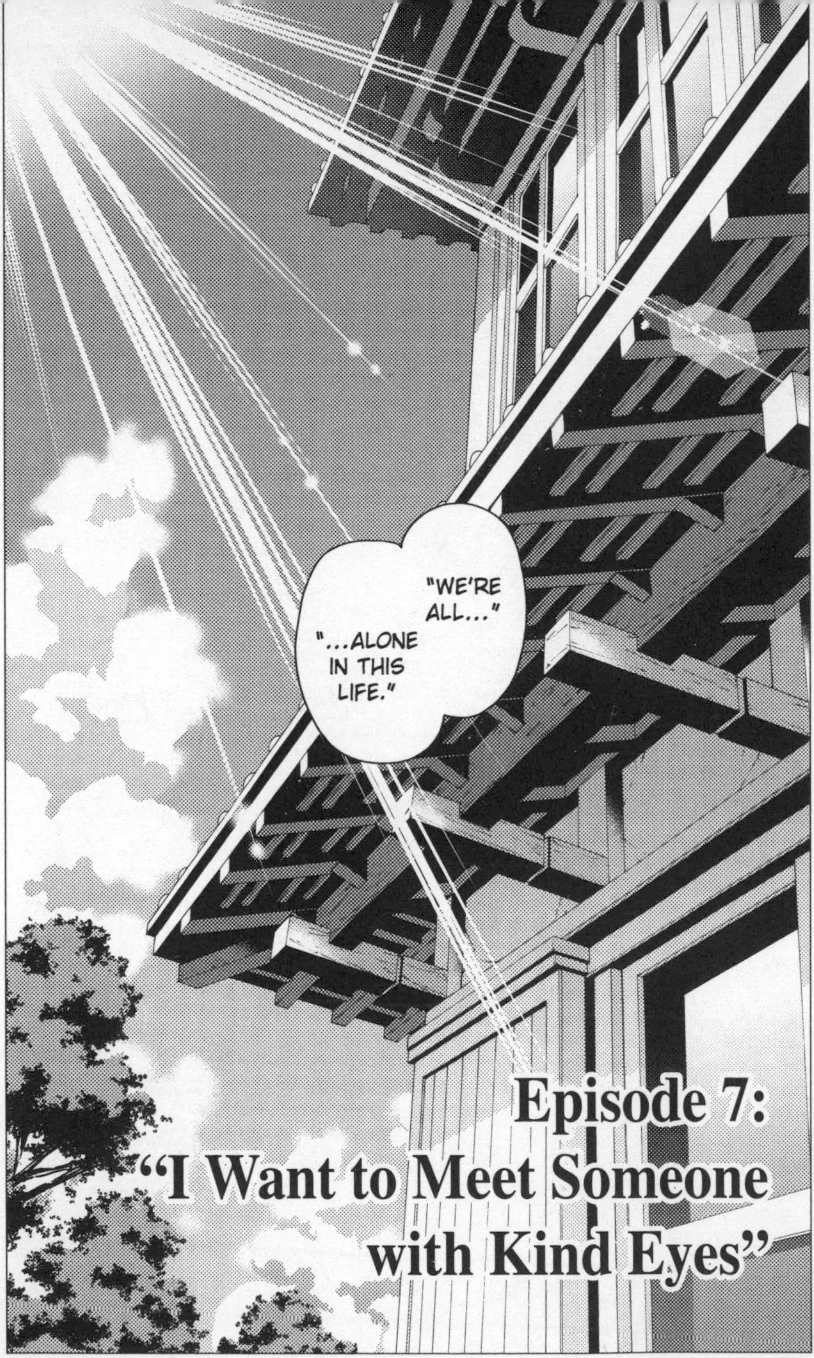
"WE'RE ALL..."
"...ALONE IN THIS LIFE."

Episode 7: "I Want to Meet Someone with Kind Eyes"

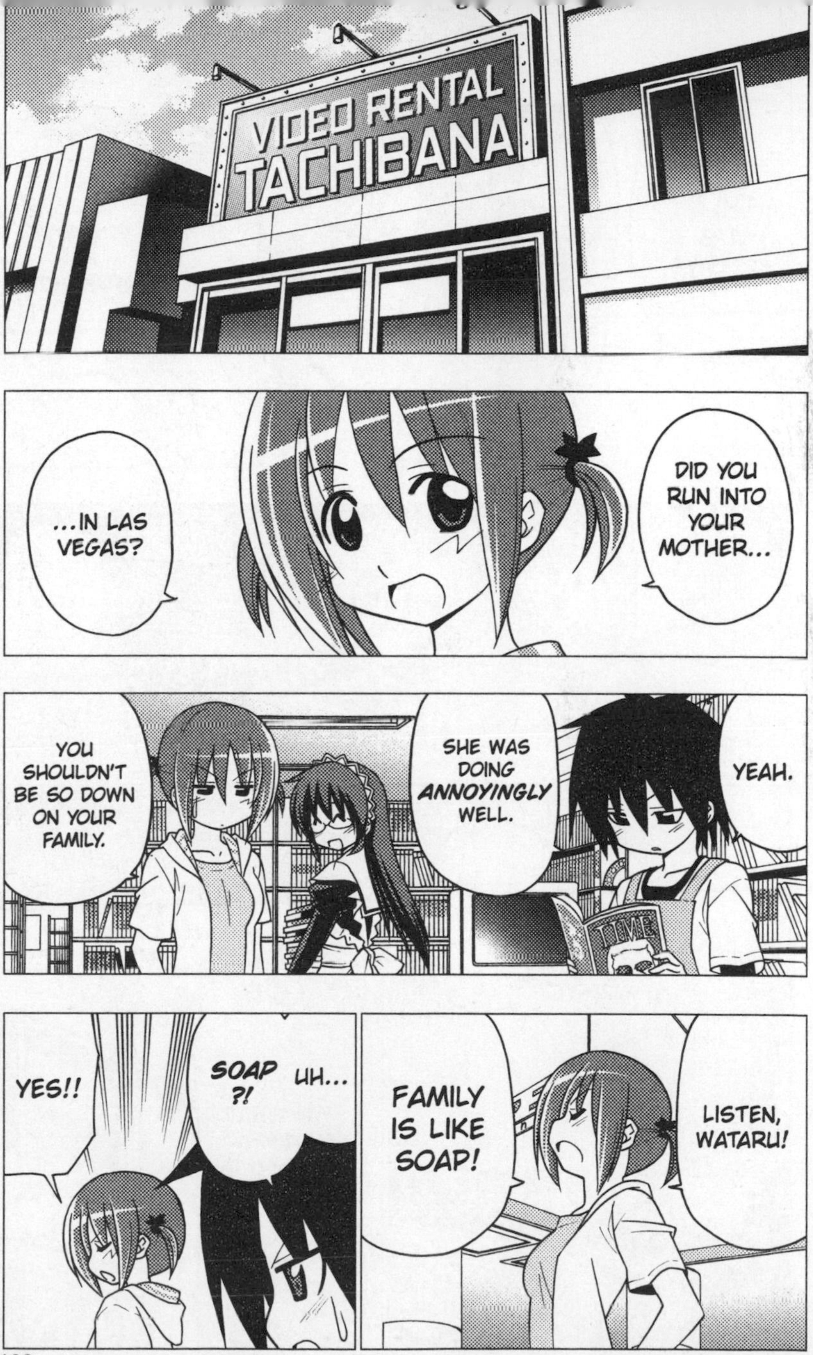
VIDEO RENTAL TACHIBANA
DID YOU RUN INTO YOUR MOTHER...
...IN LAS VEGAS?
YEAH.
SHE WAS DOING *ANNOYINGLY* WELL.
YOU SHOULDN'T BE SO DOWN ON YOUR FAMILY.
LISTEN, WATARU!
FAMILY IS LIKE SOAP!
UH...
SOAP ?!
YES!!

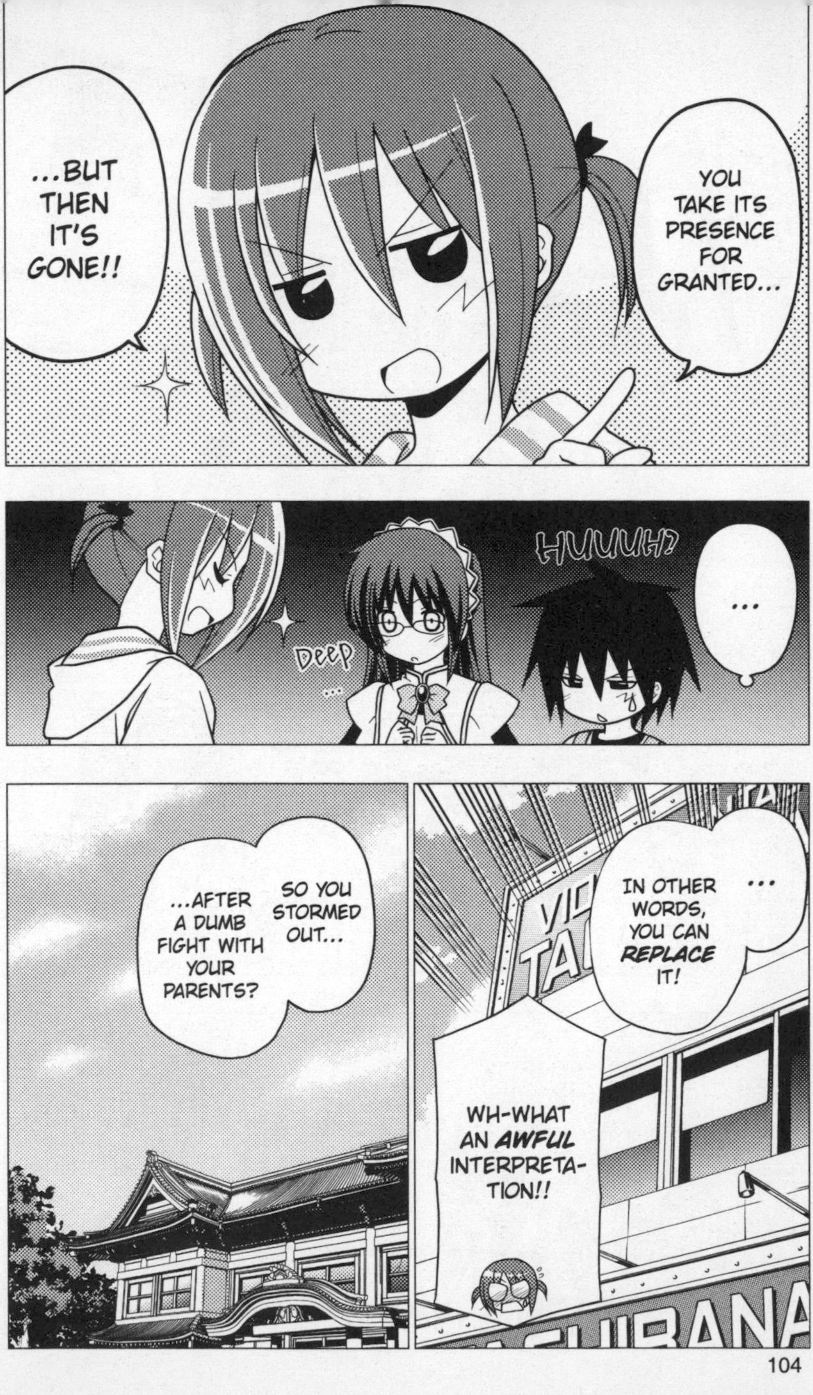

YOU TAKE ITS PRESENCE FOR GRANTED...
...BUT THEN IT'S GONE!!
...
HUUUH?
Deep...
...
IN OTHER WORDS, YOU CAN REPLACE IT!
WH-WHAT AN AWFUL INTERPRETATION!!
SO YOU STORMED OUT...
...AFTER A DUMB FIGHT WITH YOUR PARENTS?

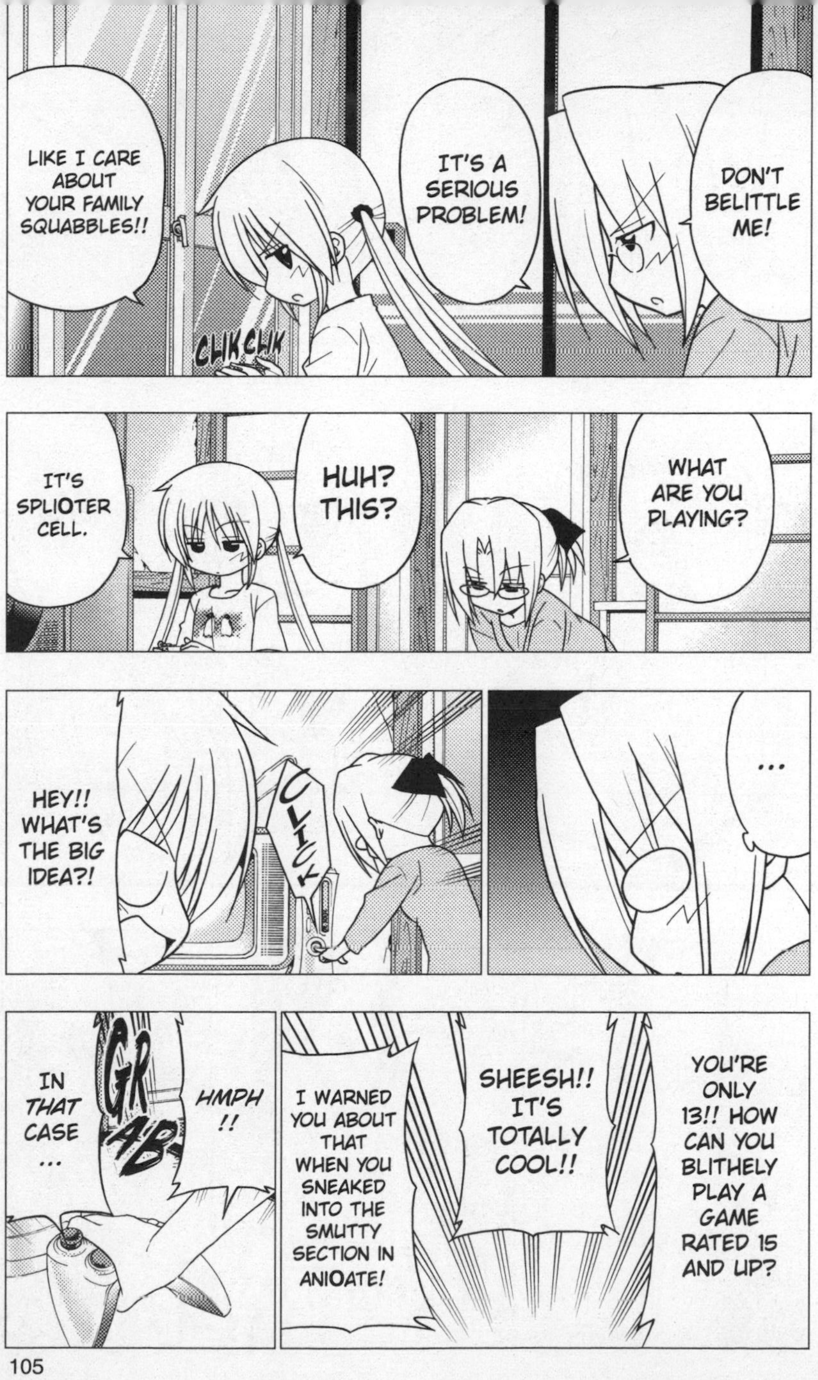
DON'T BELITTLE ME!
IT'S A SERIOUS PROBLEM!
LIKE I CARE ABOUT YOUR FAMILY SQUABBLES!!
CLIKCLIK
WHAT ARE YOU PLAYING?
HUH? THIS?
IT'S SPLIOTER CELL.
...
CLICK
HEY!! WHAT'S THE BIG IDEA?!
YOU'RE ONLY 13!! HOW CAN YOU BLITHELY PLAY A GAME RATED 15 AND UP?
SHEESH!! IT'S TOTALLY COOL!!
I WARNED YOU ABOUT THAT WHEN YOU SNEAKED INTO THE SMUTTY SECTION IN ANIOATE!
HMPH!!
GRAB
IN THAT CASE...

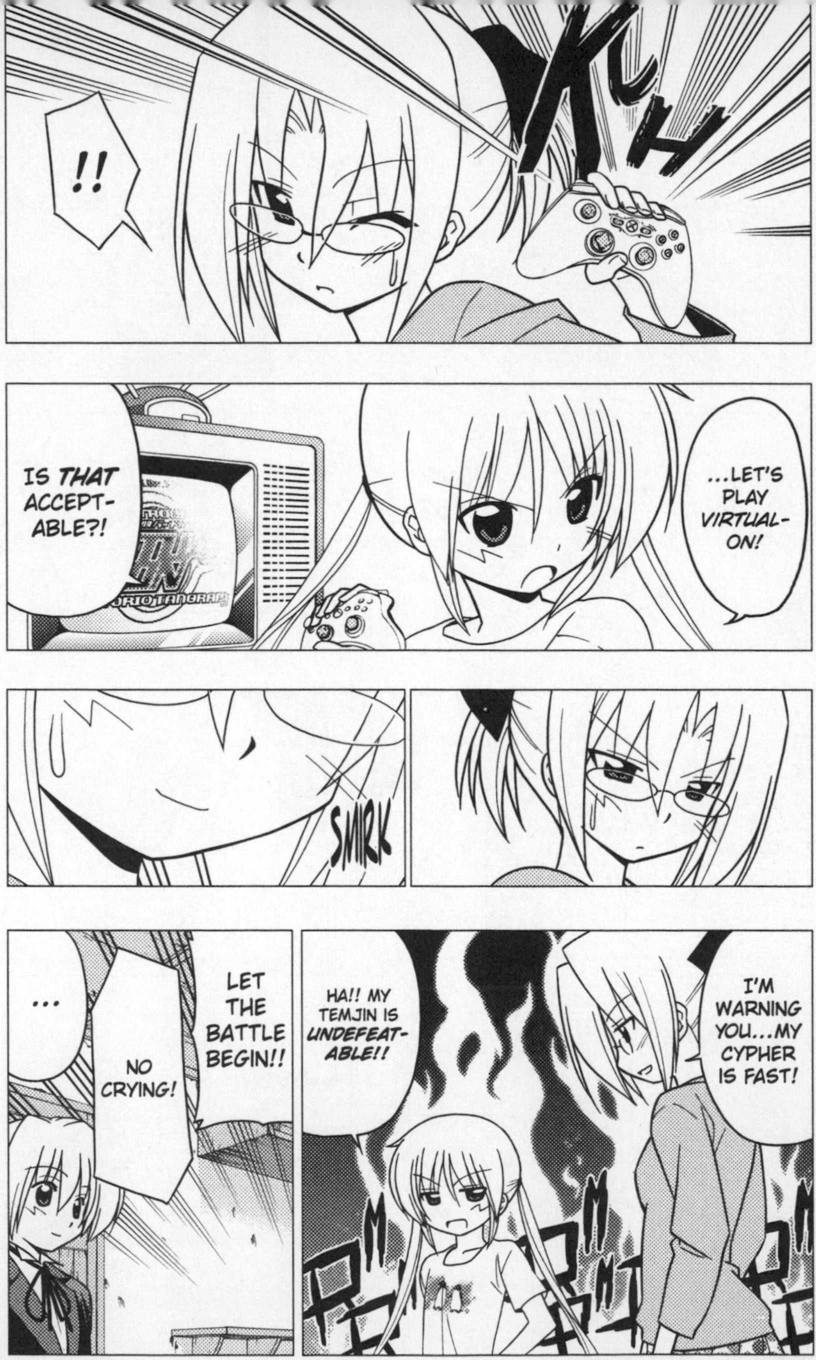
!!
...LET'S PLAY VIRTUAL-ON!
IS THAT ACCEPTABLE?!
SMIRK
I'M WARNING YOU...MY CYPHER IS FAST!
HA!! MY TEMJIN IS UNDEFEATABLE!!
LET THE BATTLE BEGIN!!
NO CRYING!
...

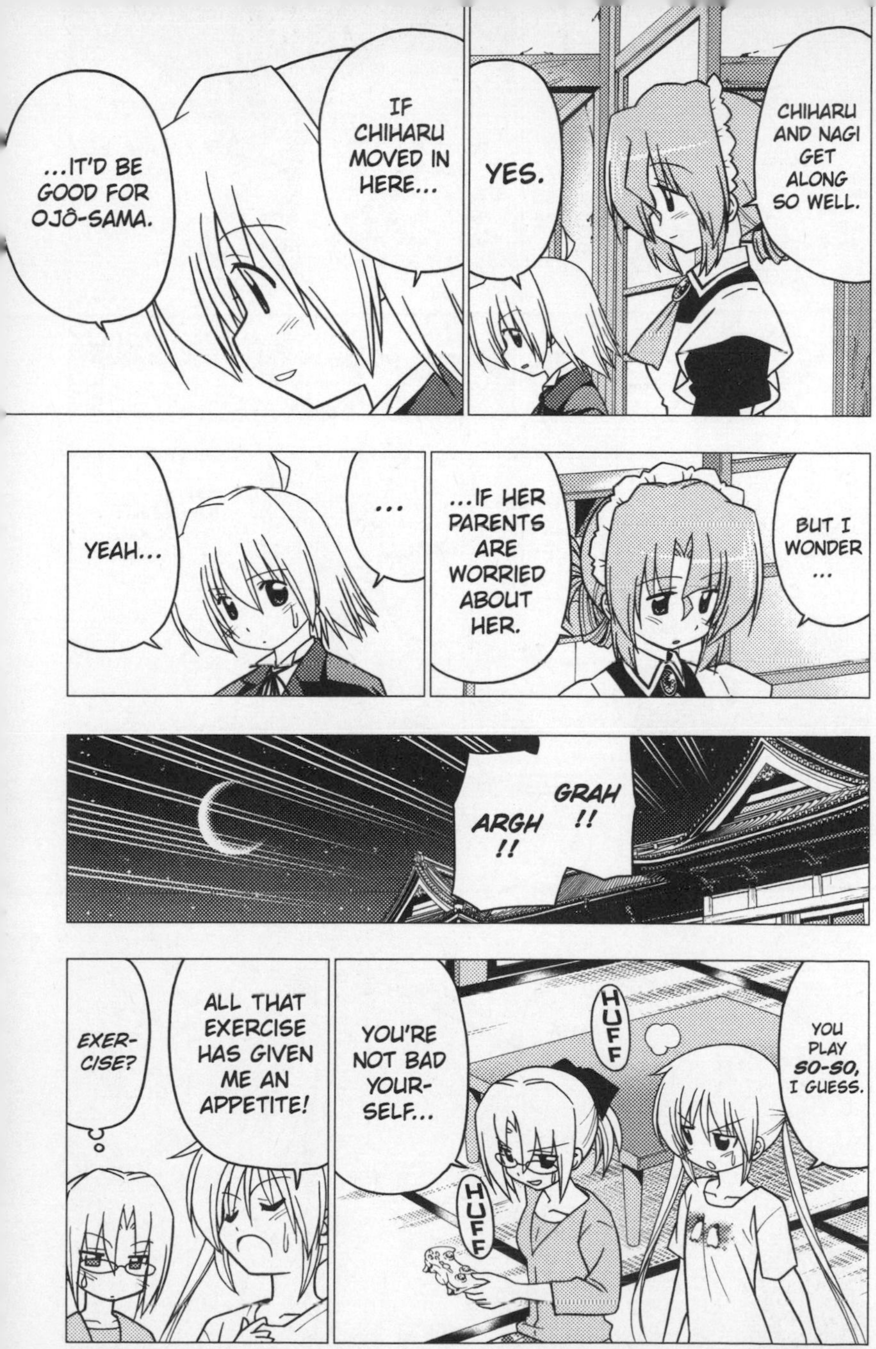
CHIHARU AND NAGI GET ALONG SO WELL.
YES.
IF CHIHARU MOVED IN HERE...
...IT'D BE GOOD FOR OJÔ-SAMA.
BUT I WONDER ...
...IF HER PARENTS ARE WORRIED ABOUT HER.
...
YEAH...
GRAH !!
ARGH !!
YOU PLAY SO-SO, I GUESS.
HUFF
YOU'RE NOT BAD YOUR-SELF...
HUFF
ALL THAT EXERCISE HAS GIVEN ME AN APPETITE!
EXER-CISE?

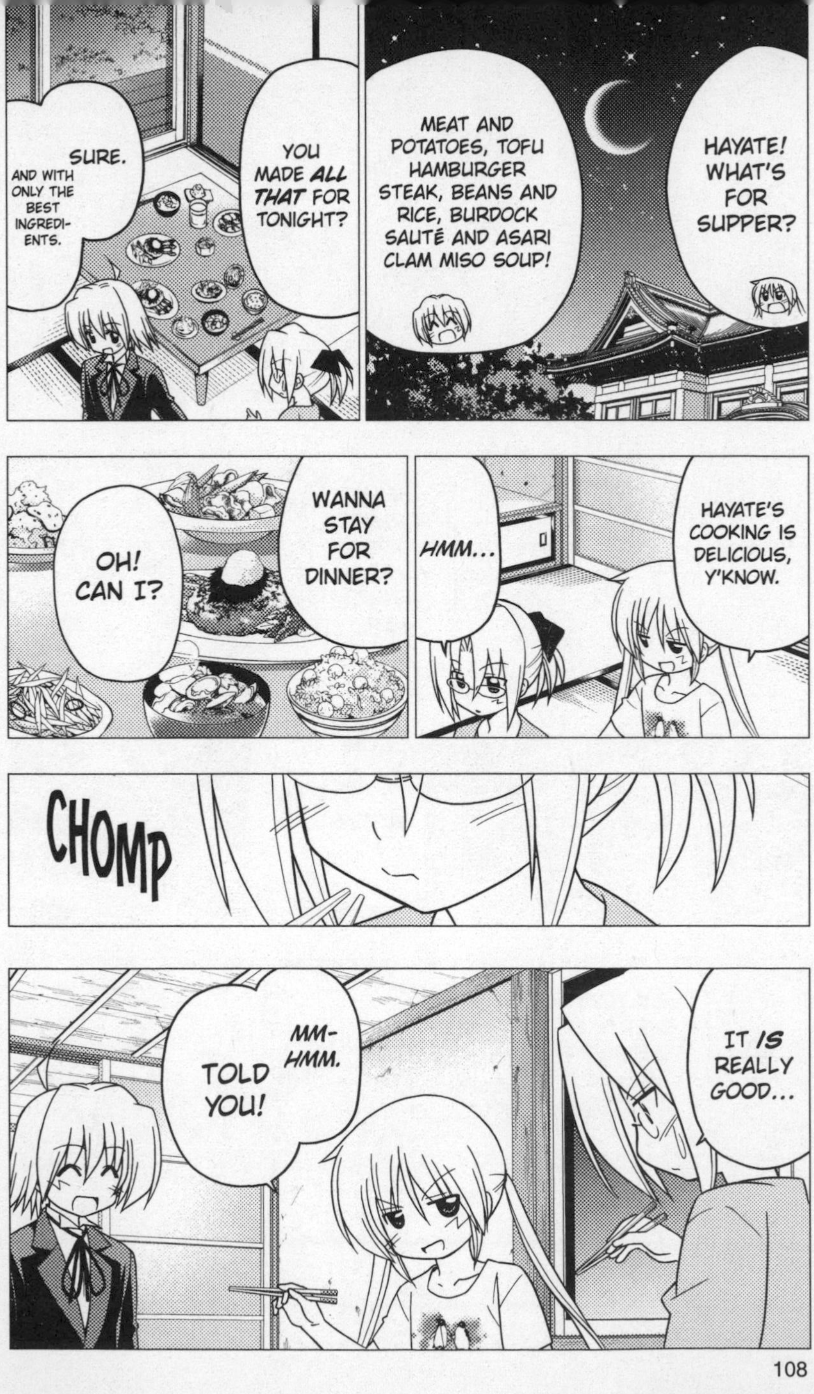
HAYATE! WHAT'S FOR SUPPER?
MEAT AND POTATOES, TOFU HAMBURGER STEAK, BEANS AND RICE, BURDOCK SAUTÉ AND ASARI CLAM MISO SOUP!
YOU MADE ALL THAT FOR TONIGHT?
SURE.
AND WITH ONLY THE BEST INGREDIENTS.
HAYATE'S COOKING IS DELICIOUS, Y'KNOW.
HMM...
WANNA STAY FOR DINNER?
OH! CAN I?
CHOMP
IT IS REALLY GOOD...
MM-HMM.
TOLD YOU!

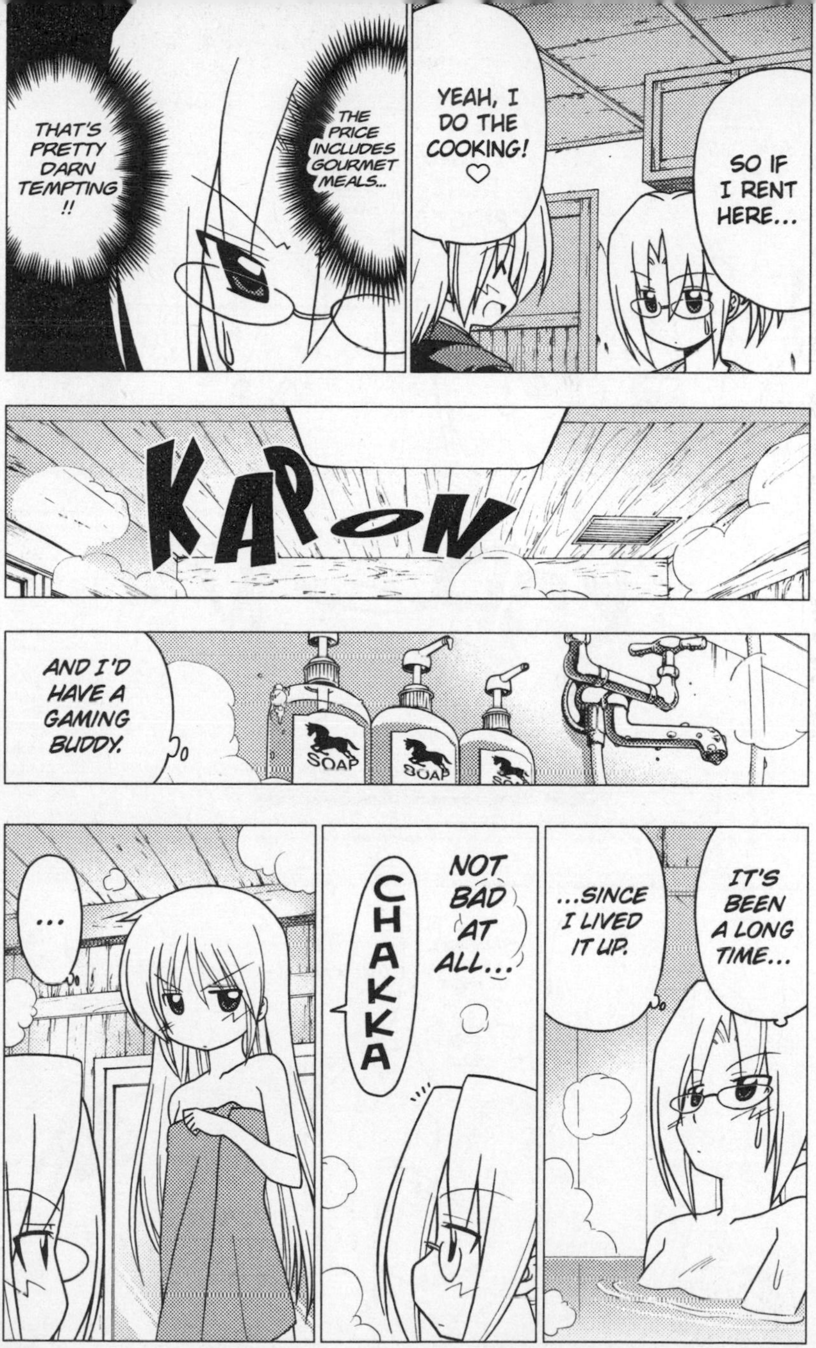
SO IF I RENT HERE...
YEAH, I DO THE COOKING! ♡
THE PRICE INCLUDES GOURMET MEALS...
THAT'S PRETTY DARN TEMPTING !!
KAPON
AND I'D HAVE A GAMING BUDDY.
IT'S BEEN A LONG TIME...
...SINCE I LIVED IT UP.
NOT BAD AT ALL...
CHAKKA
...

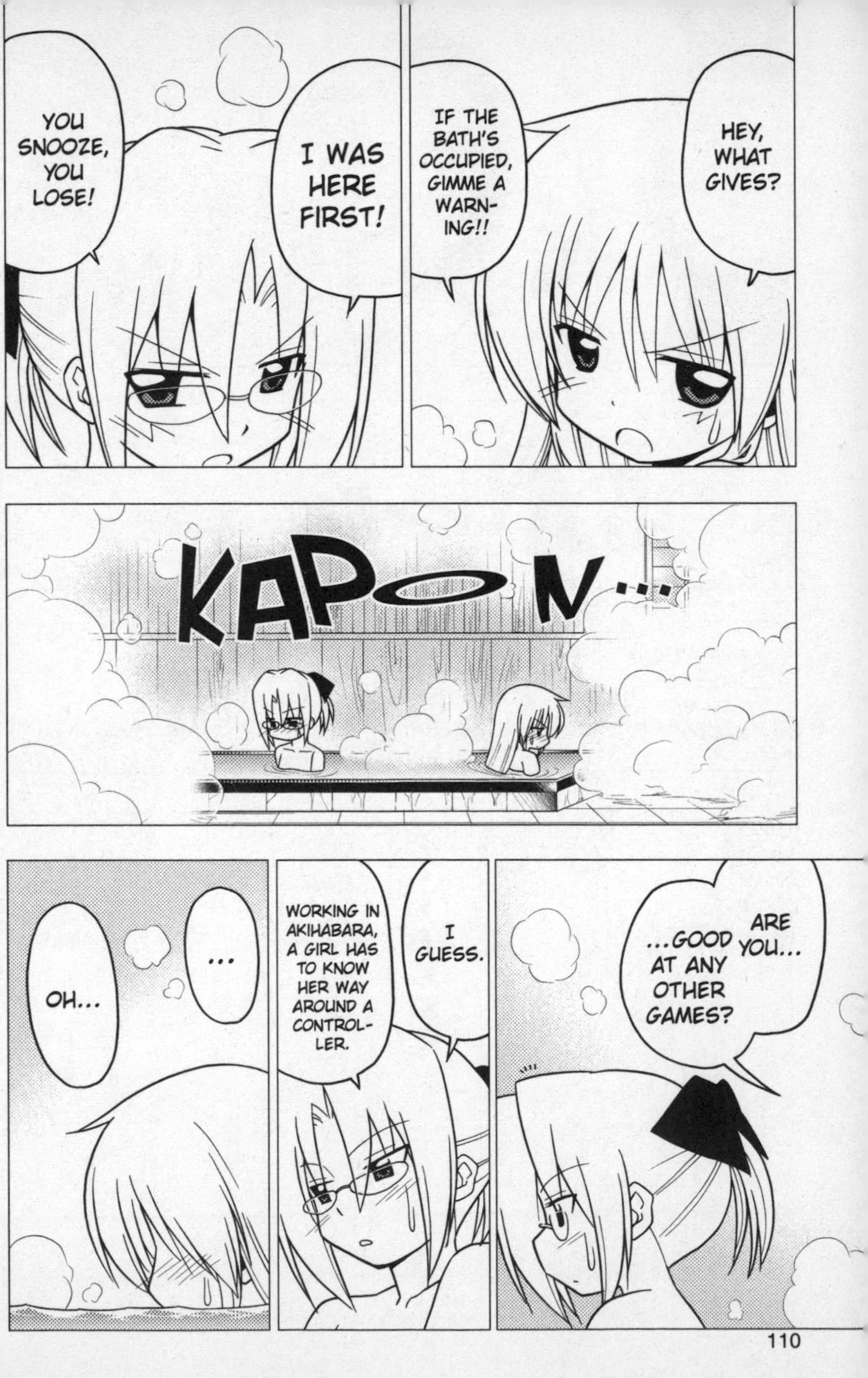
HEY, WHAT GIVES?
IF THE BATH'S OCCUPIED, GIMME A WARNING!!
I WAS HERE FIRST!
YOU SNOOZE, YOU LOSE!
KAPON...
ARE YOU...
...GOOD AT ANY OTHER GAMES?
I GUESS.
WORKING IN AKIHABARA, A GIRL HAS TO KNOW HER WAY AROUND A CONTROLLER.
...
OH...

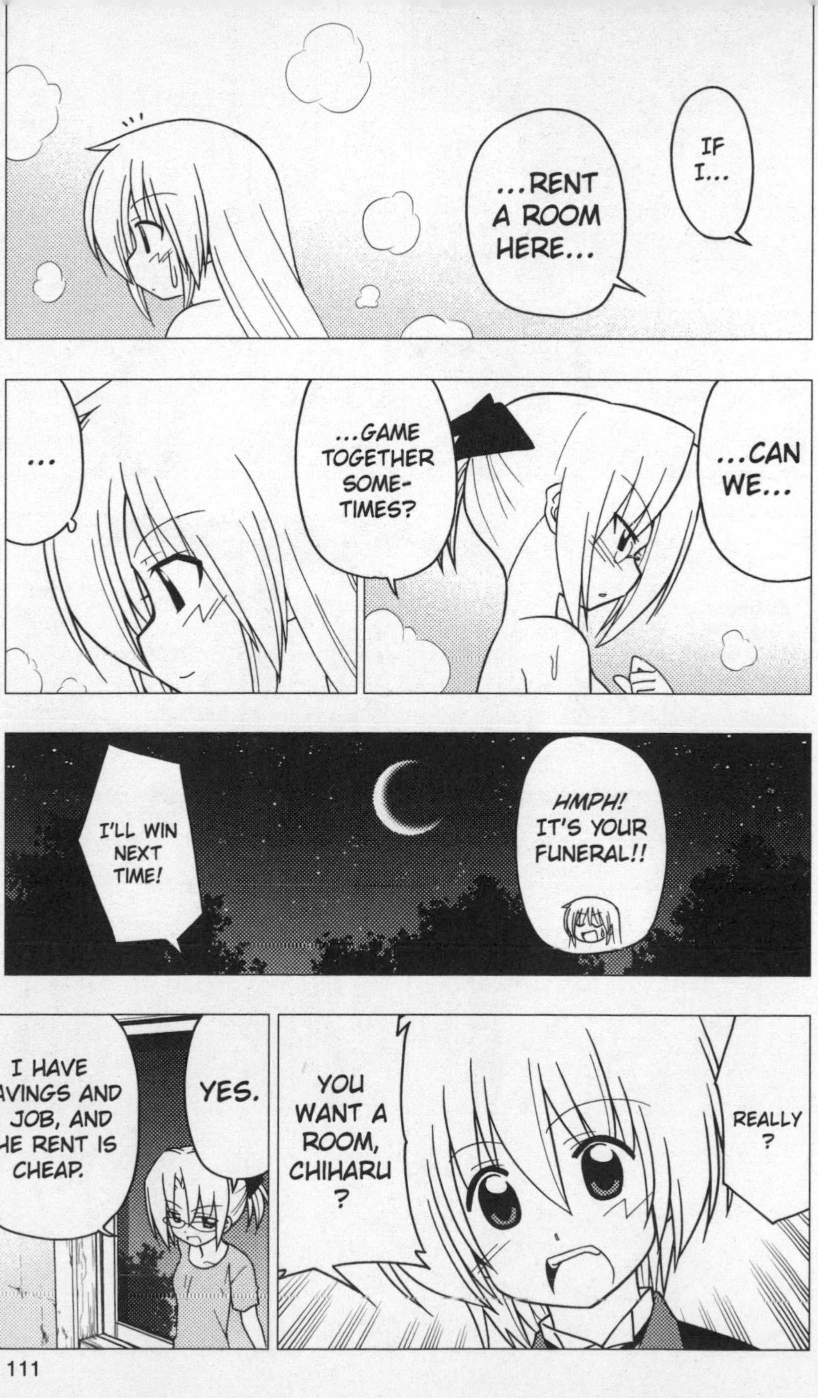
IF I...
...RENT A ROOM HERE...
...CAN WE...
...GAME TOGETHER SOME-TIMES?
...
HMPH! IT'S YOUR FUNERAL!!
I'LL WIN NEXT TIME!
REALLY?
YOU WANT A ROOM, CHIHARU?
YES.
I HAVE SAVINGS AND A JOB, AND THE RENT IS CHEAP.

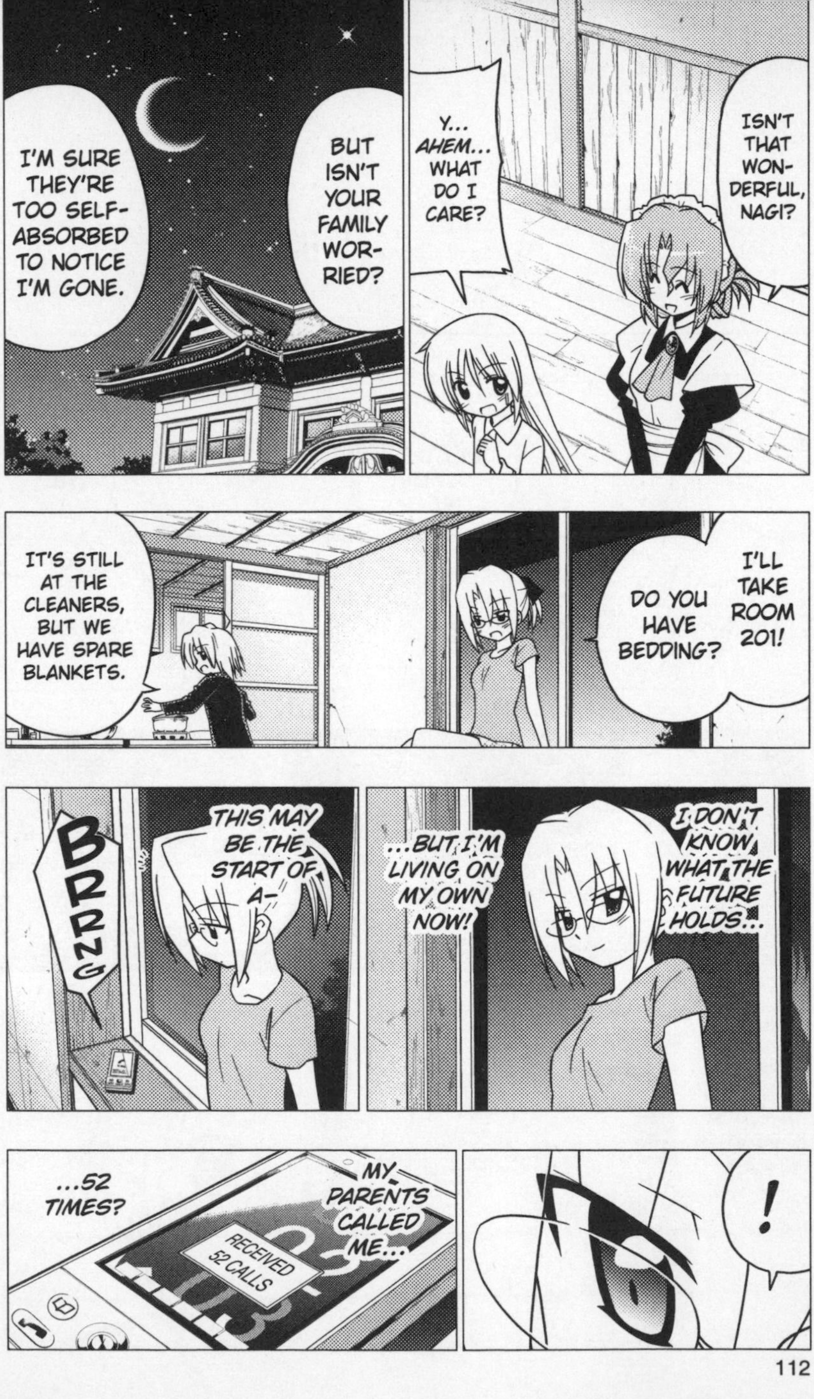
ISN'T THAT WONDERFUL, NAGI?
Y... AHEM... WHAT DO I CARE?
BUT ISN'T YOUR FAMILY WORRIED?
I'M SURE THEY'RE TOO SELF-ABSORBED TO NOTICE I'M GONE.
I'LL TAKE ROOM 201!
DO YOU HAVE BEDDING?
IT'S STILL AT THE CLEANERS, BUT WE HAVE SPARE BLANKETS.
I DON'T KNOW WHAT THE FUTURE HOLDS...
...BUT I'M LIVING ON MY OWN NOW!
THIS MAY BE THE START OF A-
BRRRNG
!
MY PARENTS CALLED ME...
RECEIVED 52 CALLS
...52 TIMES?

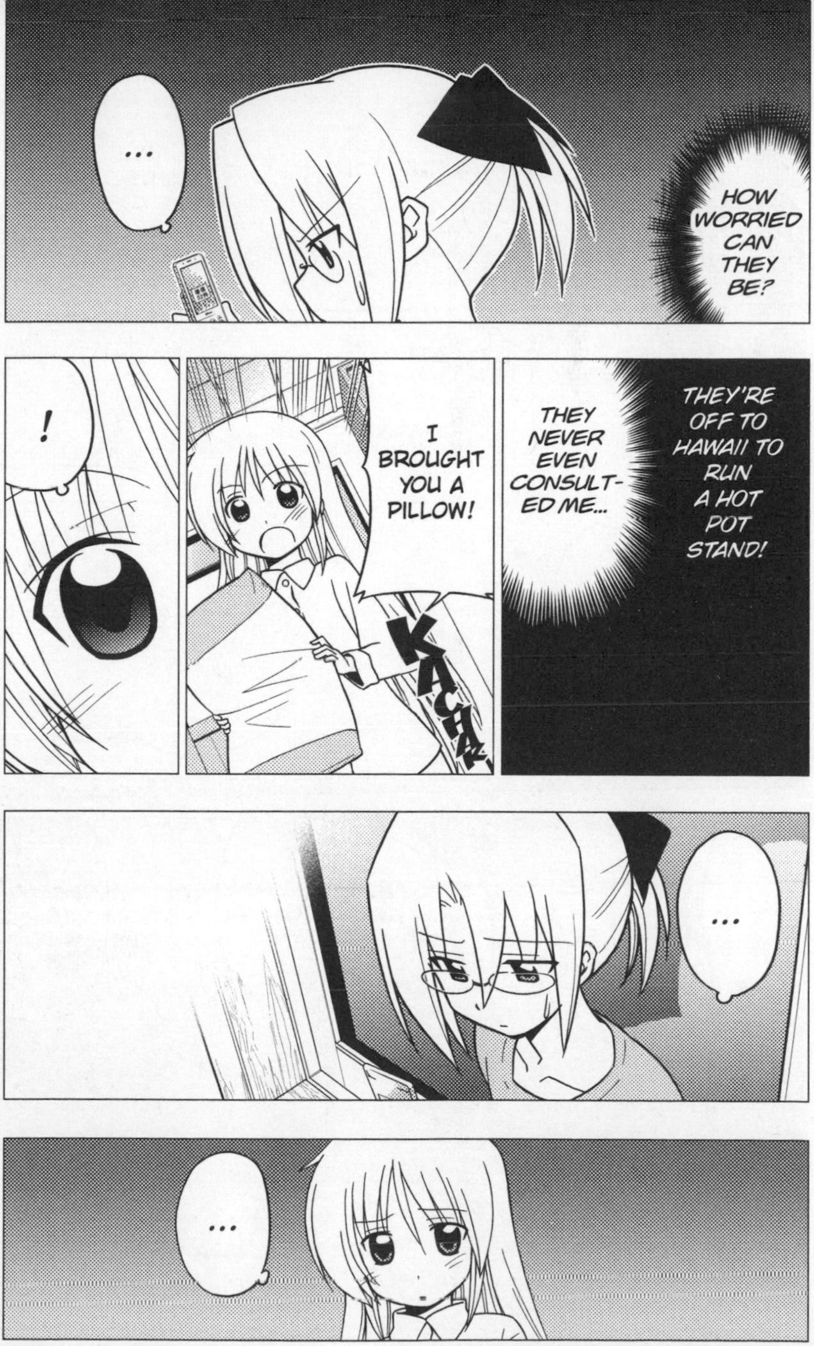

HOW WORRIED CAN THEY BE?
...
THEY'RE OFF TO HAWAII TO RUN A HOT POT STAND!
THEY NEVER EVEN CONSULT-ED ME...
I BROUGHT YOU A PILLOW!
KACHA
!
...
...

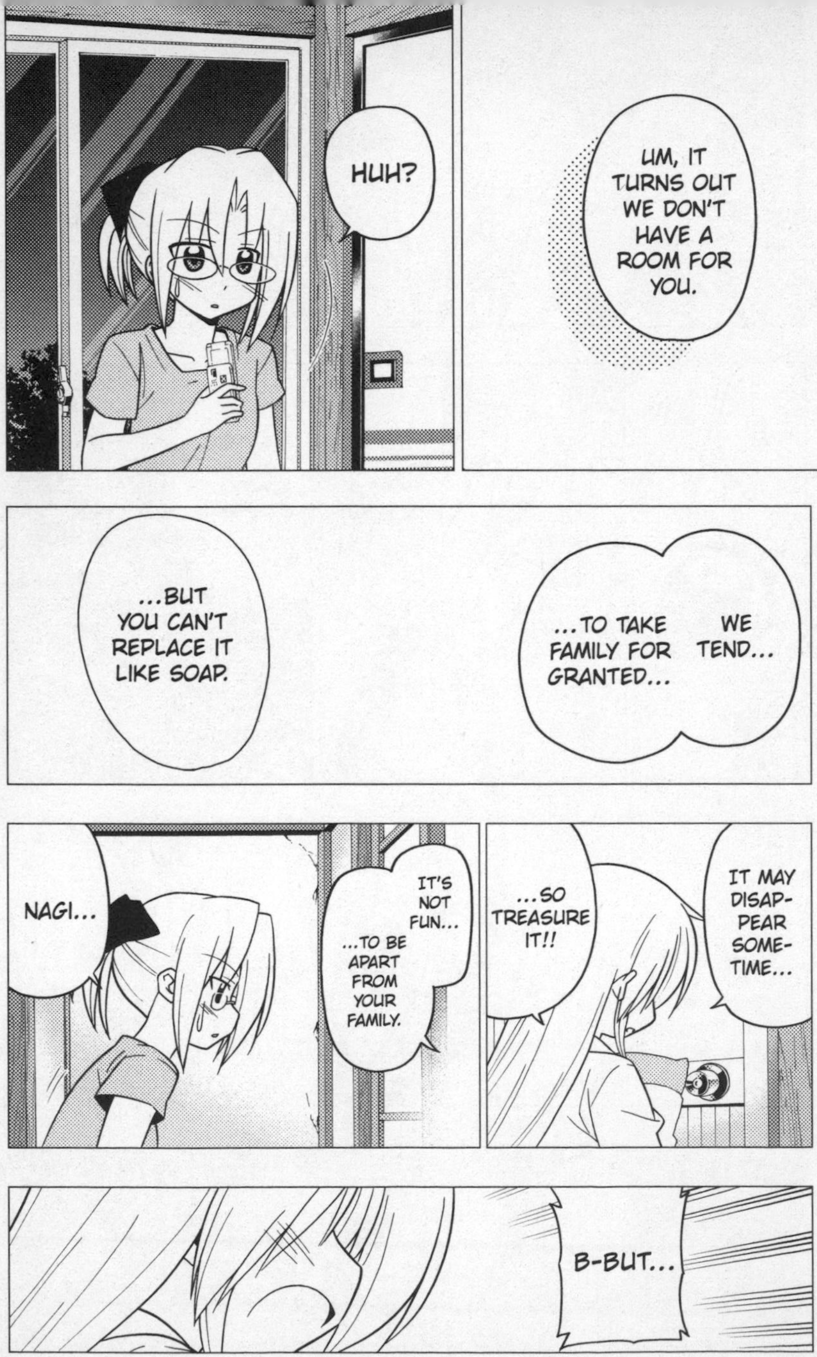
UM, IT TURNS OUT WE DON'T HAVE A ROOM FOR YOU.
HUH?
WE TEND...
...TO TAKE FAMILY FOR GRANTED...
...BUT YOU CAN'T REPLACE IT LIKE SOAP.
IT MAY DISAP-PEAR SOME-TIME...
...SO TREASURE IT!!
IT'S NOT FUN...
...TO BE APART FROM YOUR FAMILY.
NAGI...
B-BUT...

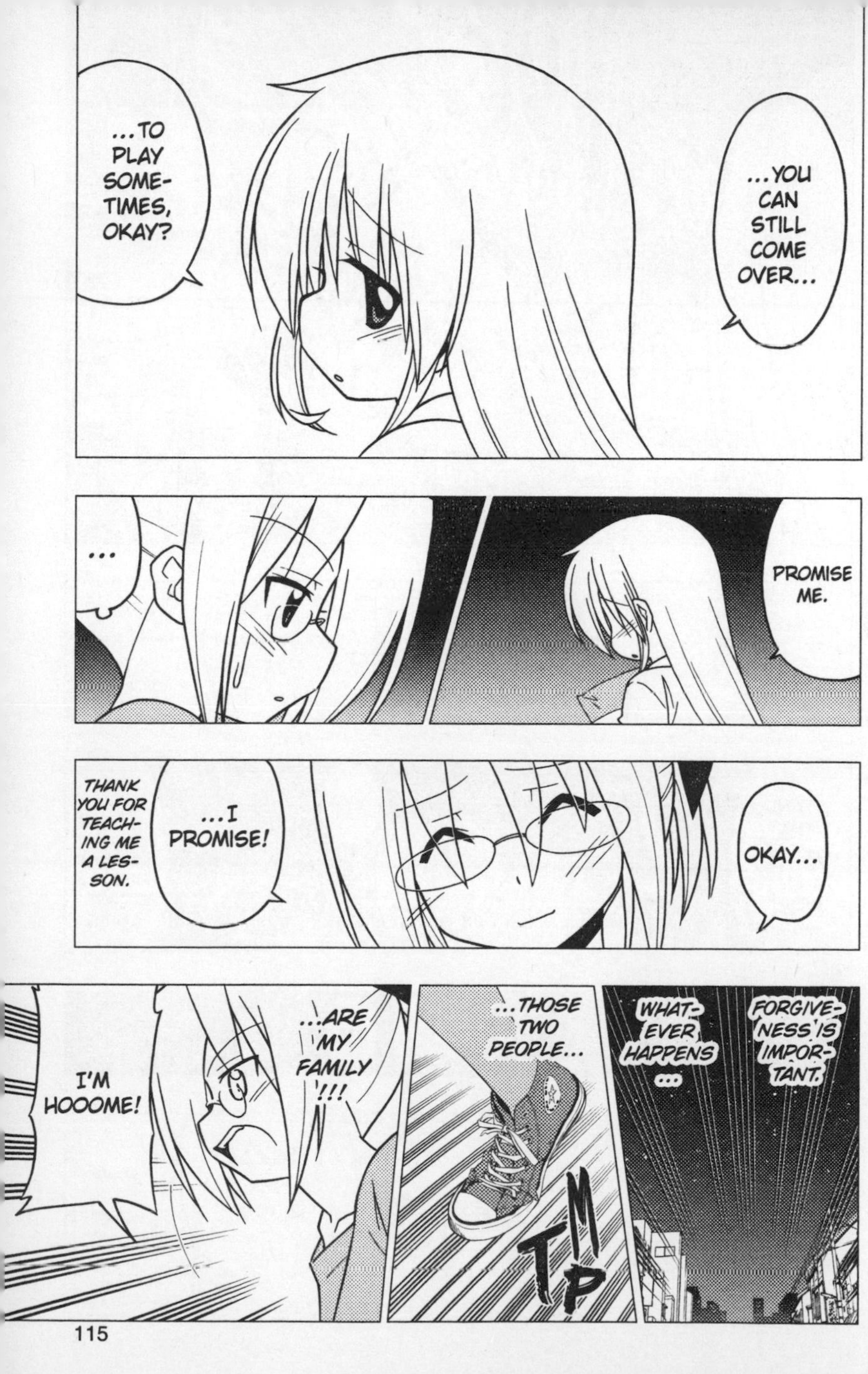
...YOU CAN STILL COME OVER...
...TO PLAY SOME-TIMES, OKAY?
PROMISE ME.
...
OKAY...
...I PROMISE!
THANK YOU FOR TEACHING ME A LES-SON.
FORGIVE-NESS IS IMPOR-TANT.
WHAT-EVER HAPPENS...
...THOSE TWO PEOPLE...
TMP
...ARE MY FAMILY!!!
I'M HOOOME!

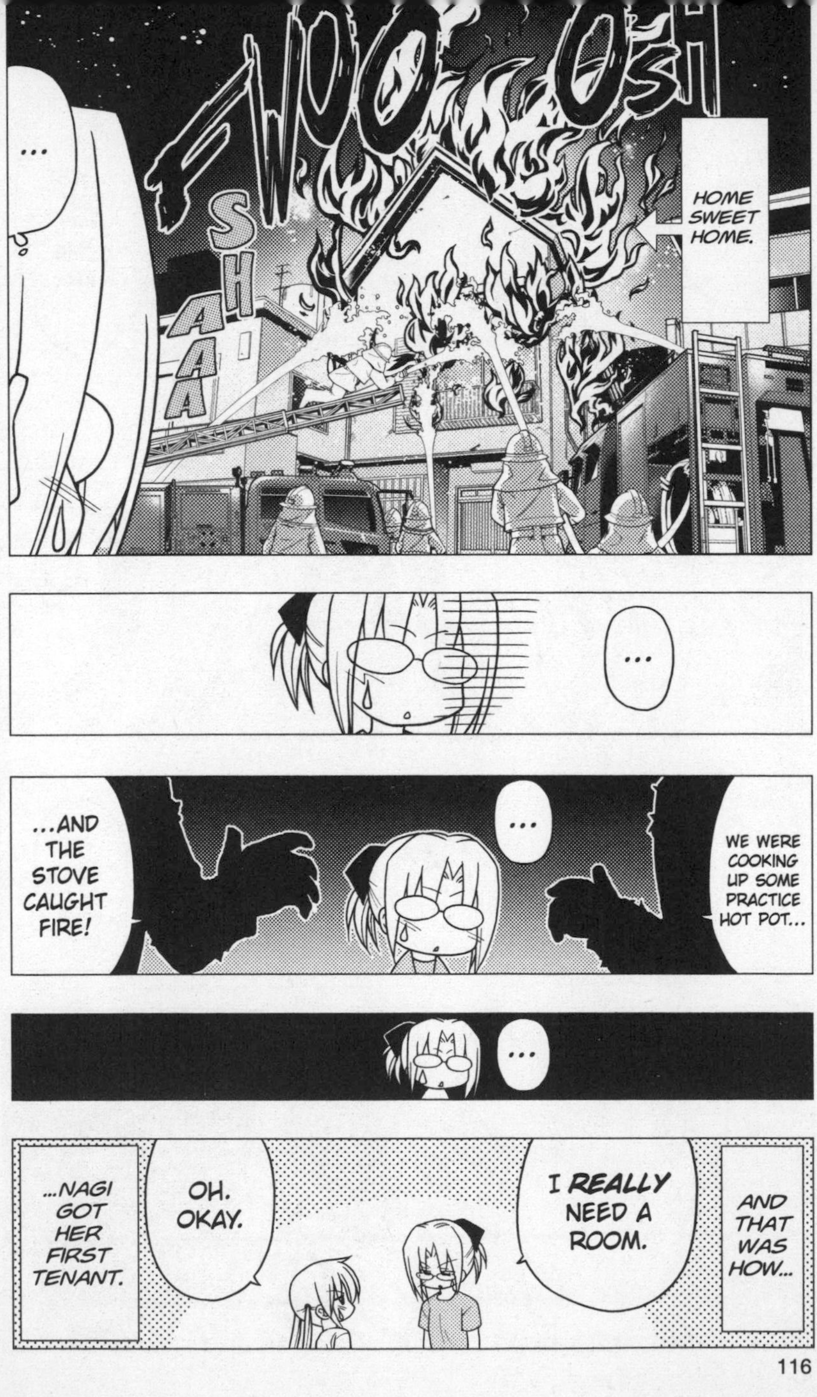
HOME SWEET HOME.
FWOOOSH
SHAAAA
...
...
WE WERE COOKING UP SOME PRACTICE HOT POT...
...
...AND THE STOVE CAUGHT FIRE!
...
AND THAT WAS HOW...
I REALLY NEED A ROOM.
OH. OKAY.
...NAGI GOT HER FIRST TENANT.

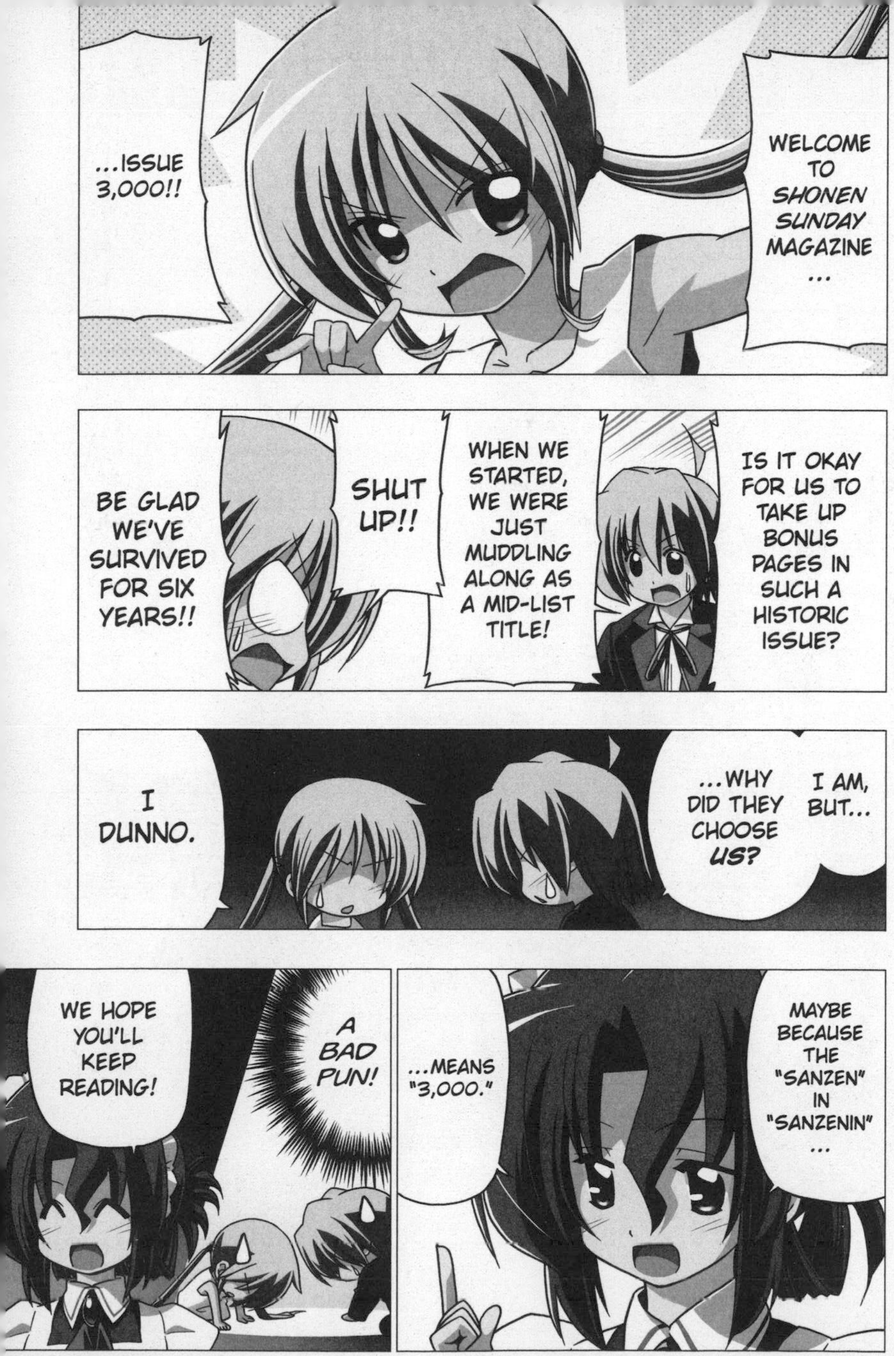
WELCOME TO SHONEN SUNDAY MAGAZINE ...
...ISSUE 3,000!!
IS IT OKAY FOR US TO TAKE UP BONUS PAGES IN SUCH A HISTORIC ISSUE?
WHEN WE STARTED, WE WERE JUST MUDDLING ALONG AS A MID-LIST TITLE!
SHUT UP!!
BE GLAD WE'VE SURVIVED FOR SIX YEARS!!
I AM, BUT...
...WHY DID THEY CHOOSE *US*?
I DUNNO.
MAYBE BECAUSE THE "SANZEN" IN "SANZENIN" ...
...MEANS "3,000."
A BAD PUN!
WE HOPE YOU'LL KEEP READING!

Episode 8: "It's Destiny"

Episode 8:
"It's Destiny"

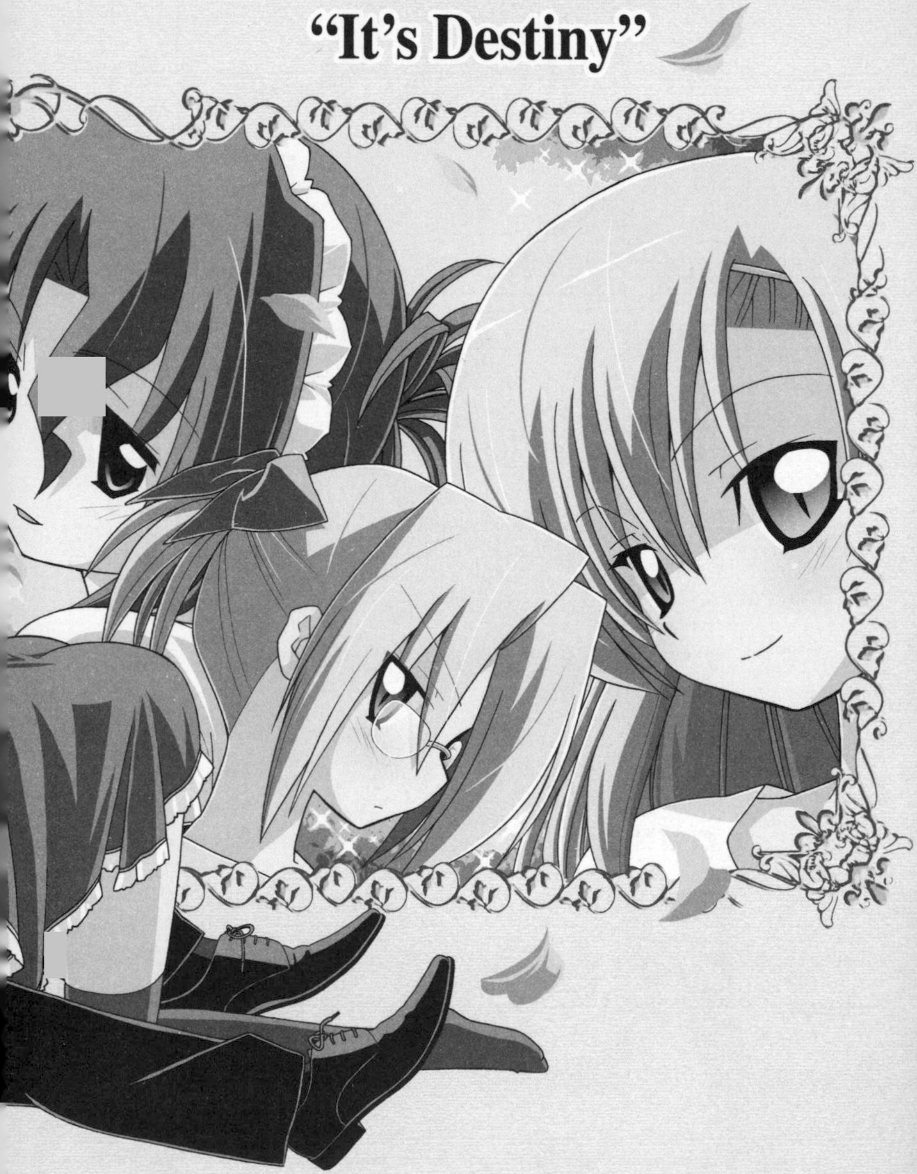

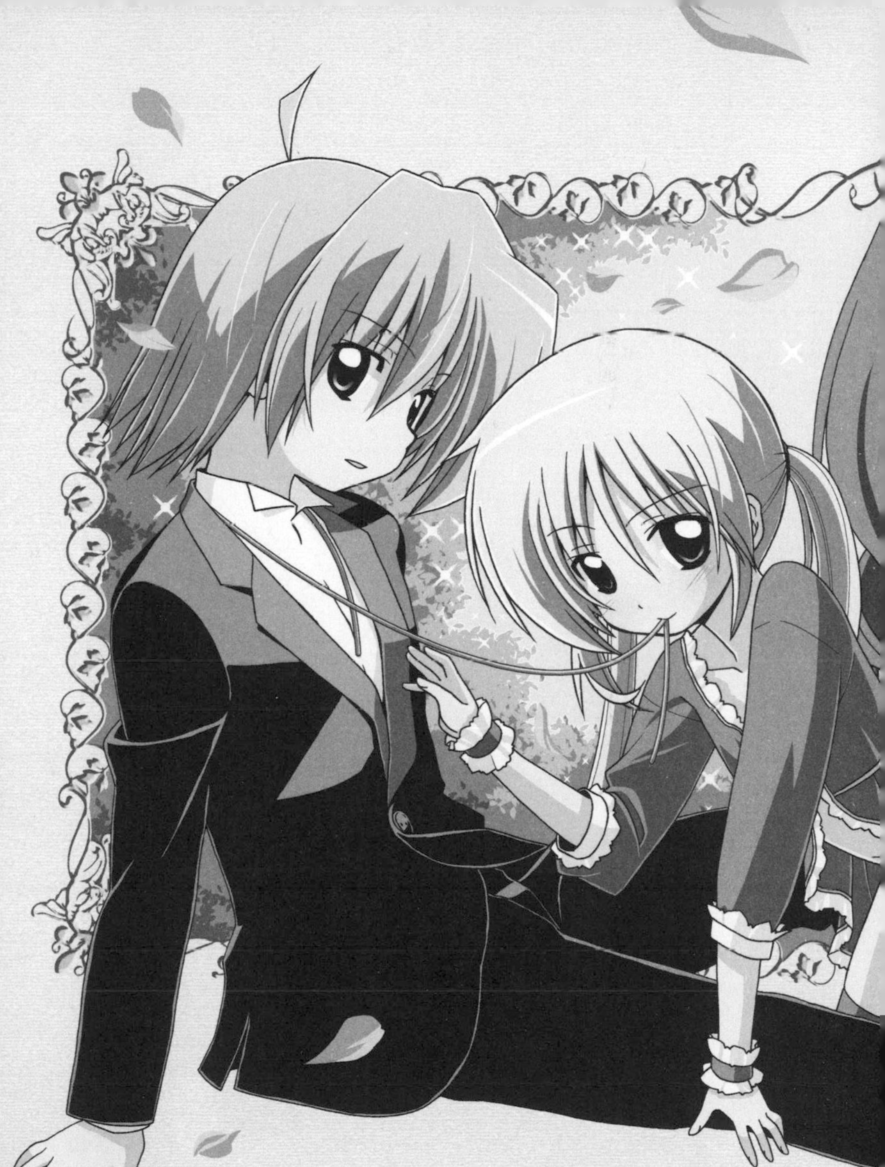

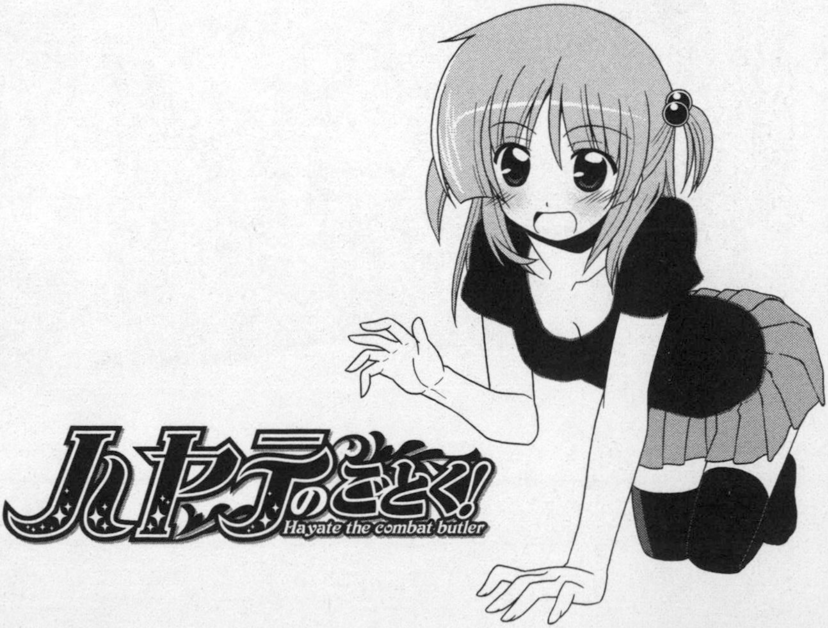
ハヤテのごとく!
Hayate the combat butler

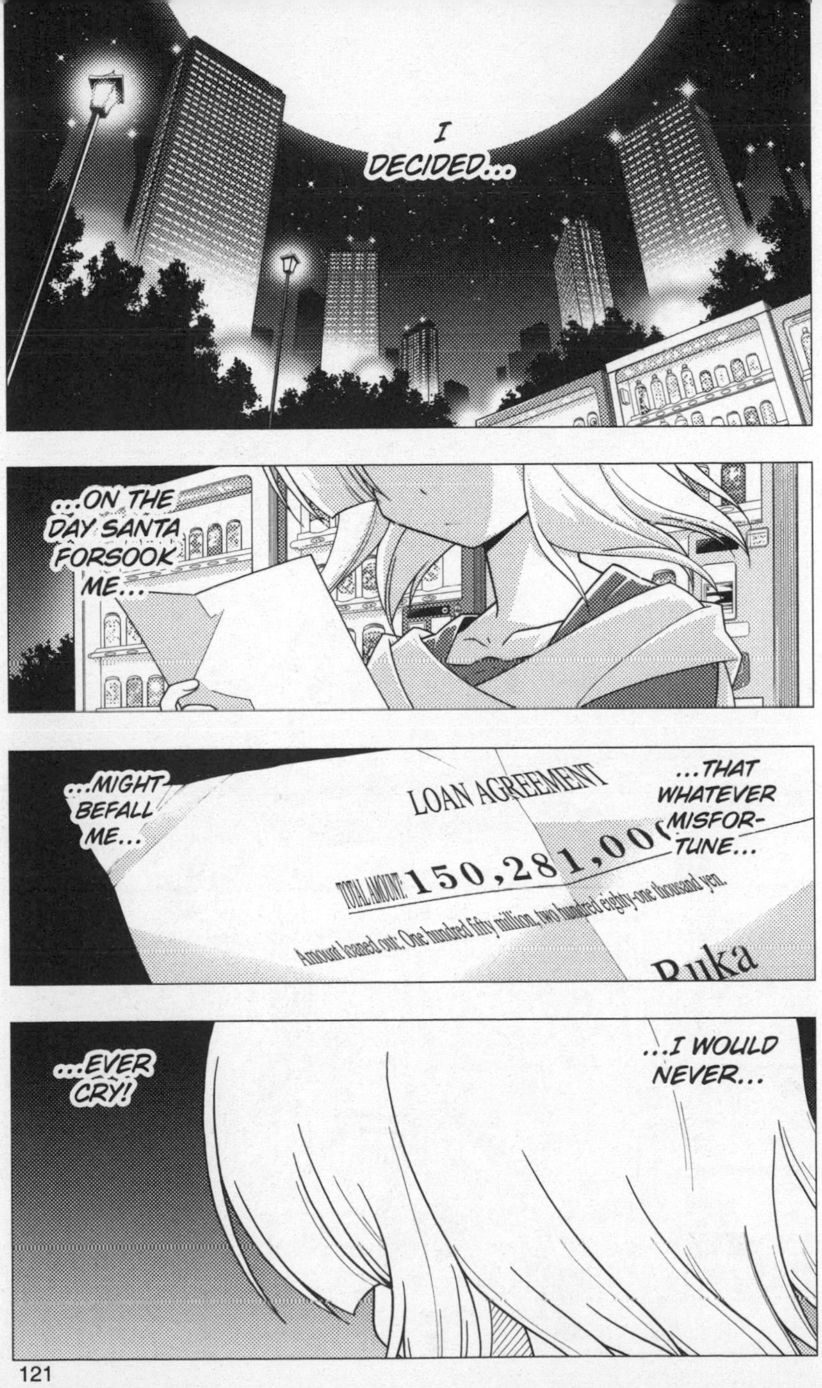
I DECIDED...
...ON THE DAY SANTA FORSOOK ME...
...THAT WHATEVER MISFOR-TUNE...
LOAN AGREEMENT
TOTAL AMOUNT: 150,281,00
Amount loaned out: One hundred fifty million, two hundred eighty-one thousand yen.
...MIGHT BEFALL ME...
...I WOULD NEVER...
...EVER CRY!

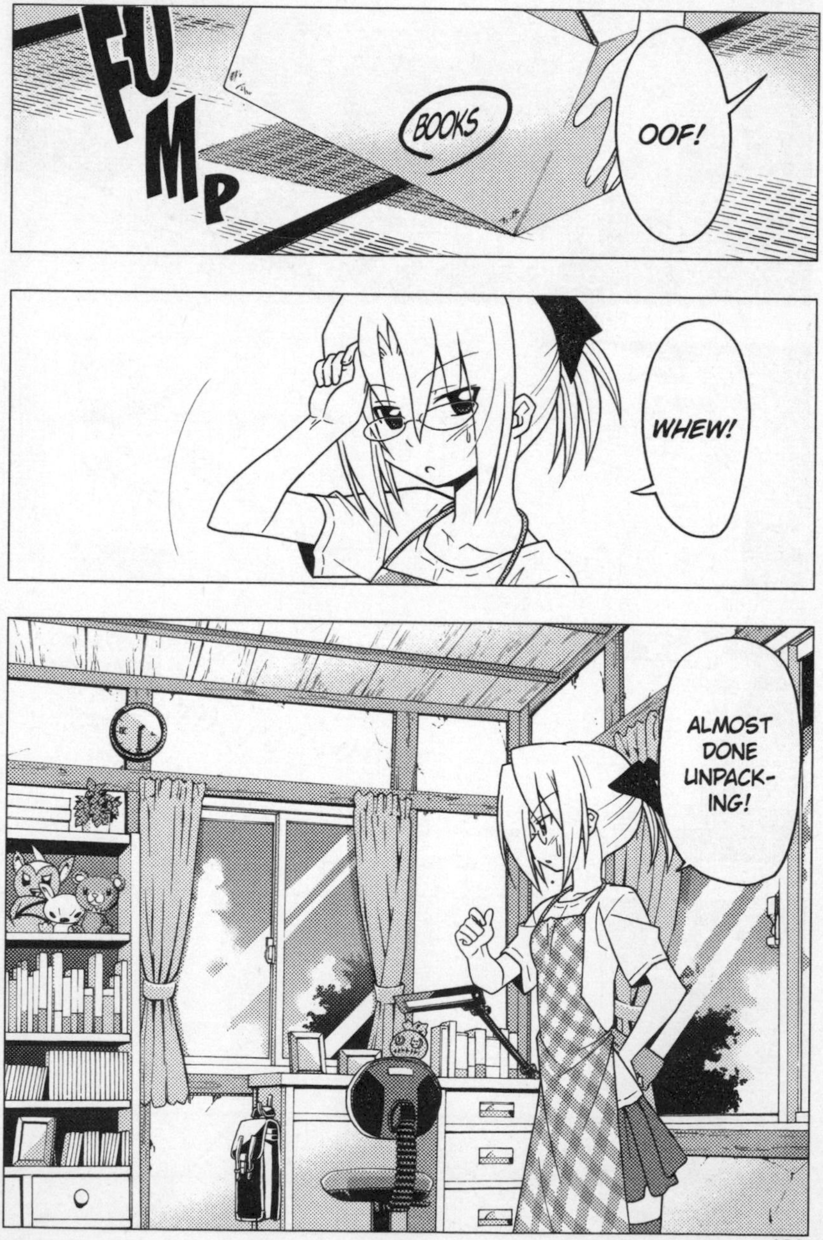
OOF!
BOOKS
FUMP
WHEW!
ALMOST DONE UNPACK-ING!

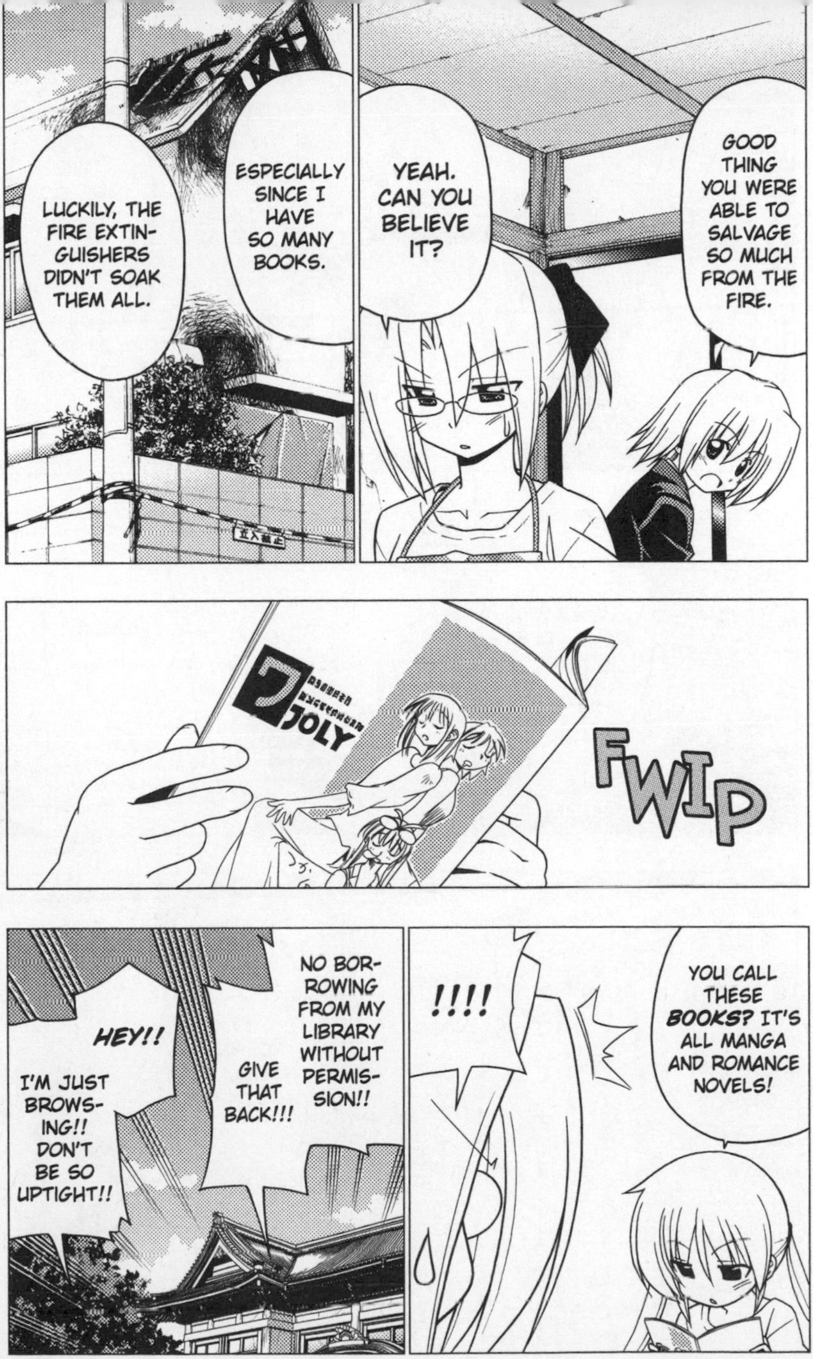

GOOD THING YOU WERE ABLE TO SALVAGE SO MUCH FROM THE FIRE.
YEAH. CAN YOU BELIEVE IT?
ESPECIALLY SINCE I HAVE SO MANY BOOKS.
LUCKILY, THE FIRE EXTINGUISHERS DIDN'T SOAK THEM ALL.
FWIP
JOLY
YOU CALL THESE *BOOKS?* IT'S ALL MANGA AND ROMANCE NOVELS!
!!!!
NO BORROWING FROM MY LIBRARY WITHOUT PERMISSION!!
GIVE THAT BACK!!!
HEY!!
I'M JUST BROWSING!! DON'T BE SO UPTIGHT!!

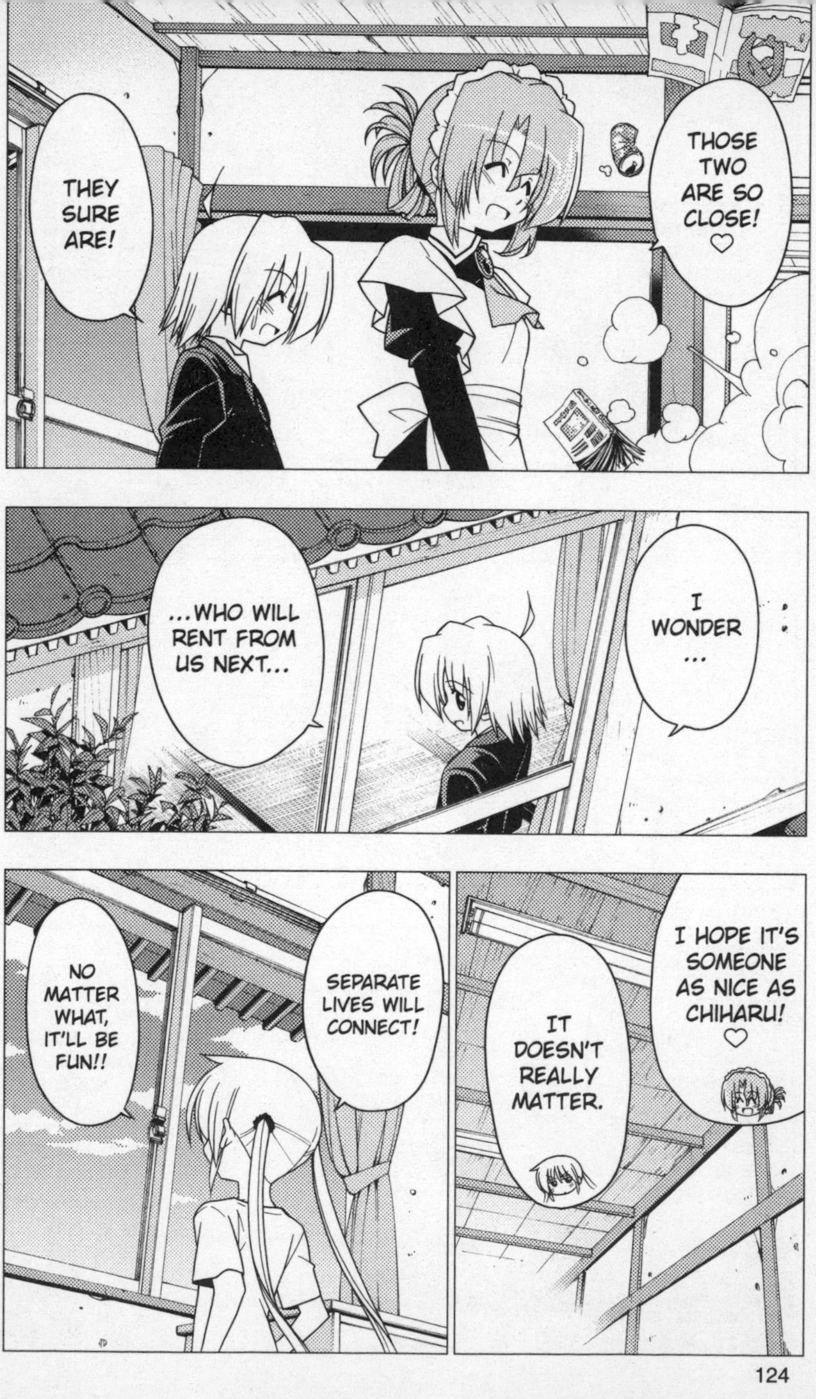
THOSE TWO ARE SO CLOSE! ♡
THEY SURE ARE!
I WONDER...
...WHO WILL RENT FROM US NEXT...
I HOPE IT'S SOMEONE AS NICE AS CHIHARU! ♡
IT DOESN'T REALLY MATTER.
SEPARATE LIVES WILL CONNECT!
NO MATTER WHAT, IT'LL BE FUN!!

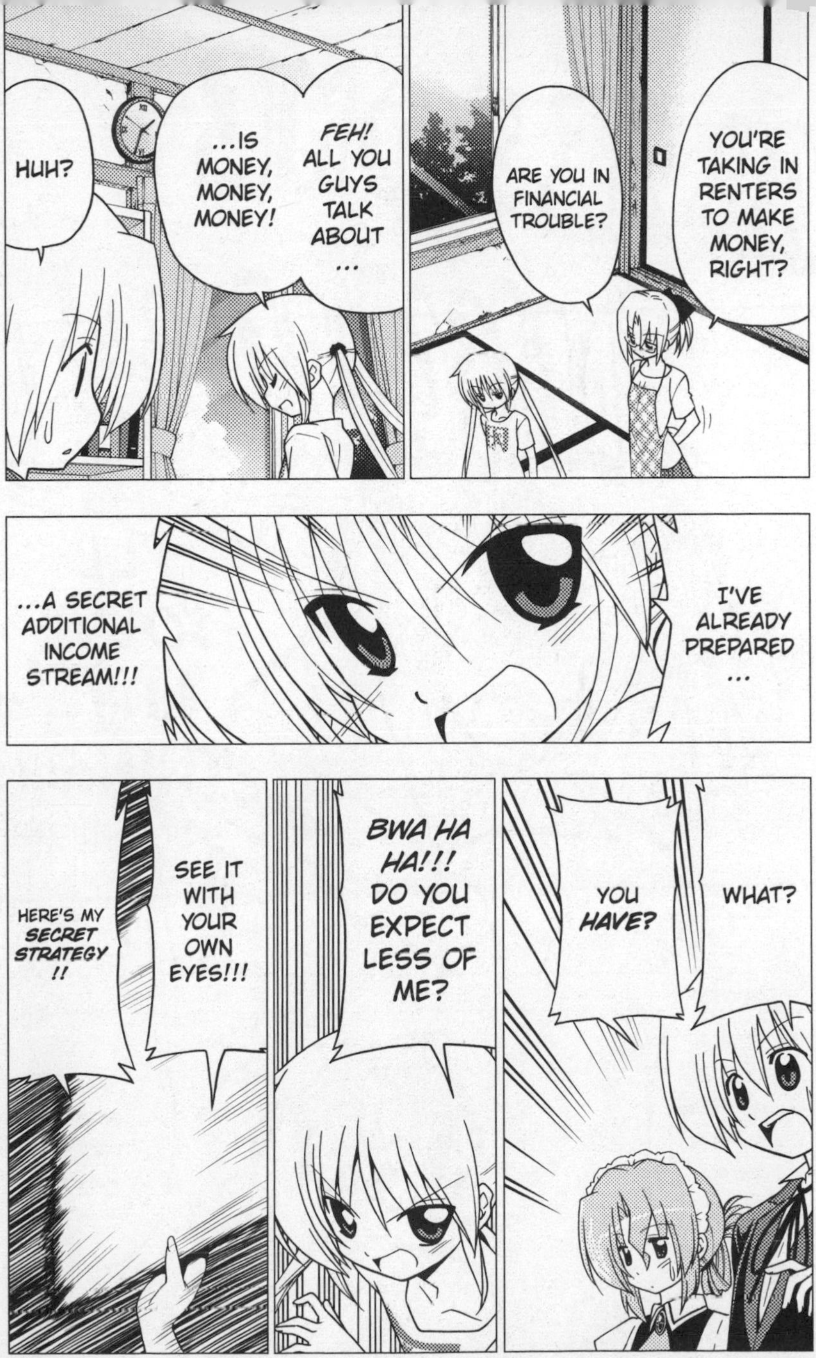
YOU'RE TAKING IN RENTERS TO MAKE MONEY, RIGHT?
ARE YOU IN FINANCIAL TROUBLE?
FEH! ALL YOU GUYS TALK ABOUT ...
...IS MONEY, MONEY, MONEY!
HUH?
I'VE ALREADY PREPARED ...
...A SECRET ADDITIONAL INCOME STREAM!!!
WHAT?
YOU *HAVE?*
BWA HA HA!!! DO YOU EXPECT LESS OF ME?
SEE IT WITH YOUR OWN EYES!!!
HERE'S MY *SECRET STRATEGY* !!

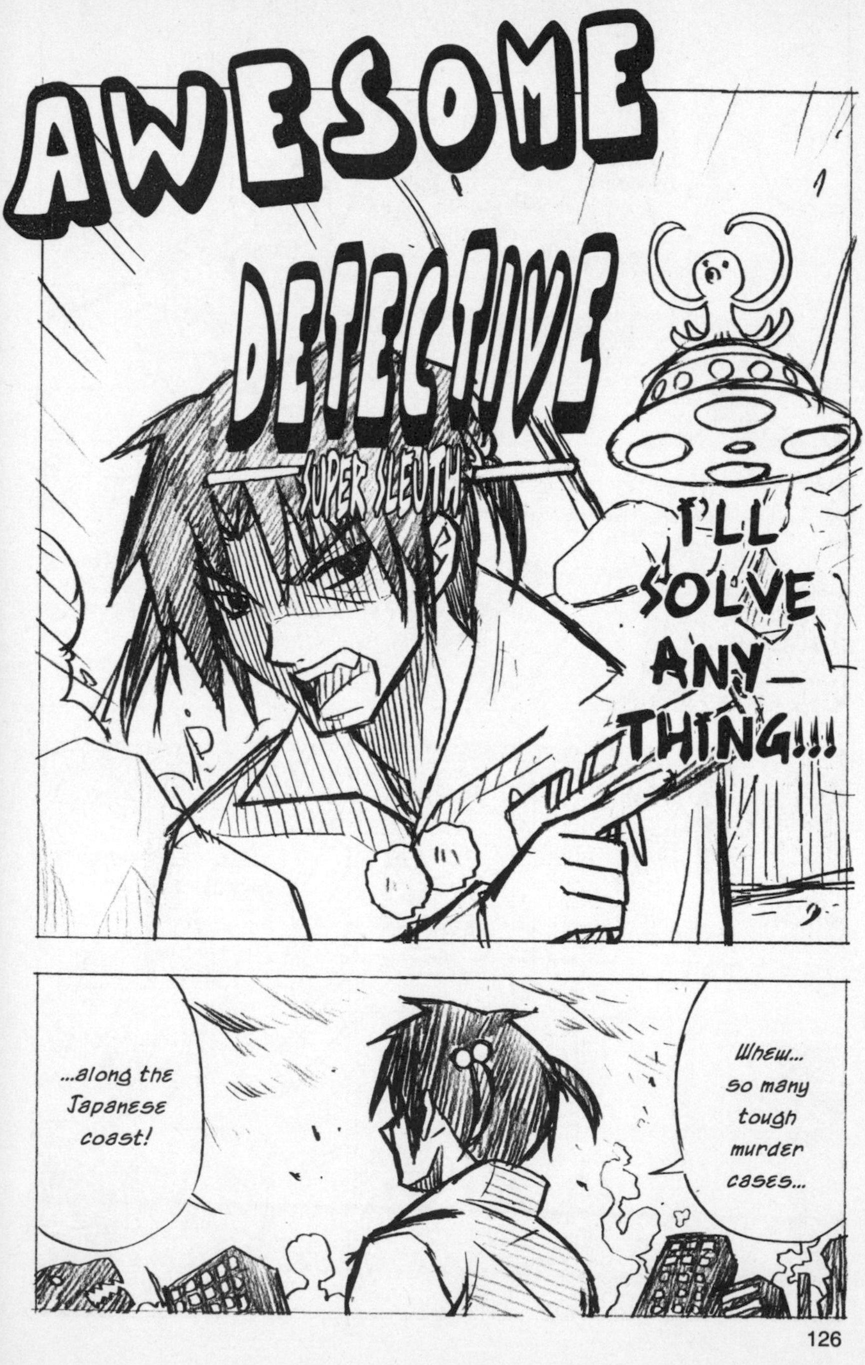
AWESOME
DETECTIVE
SUPER SLEUTH
I'LL SOLVE ANY-THING!!!
Whew... so many tough murder cases...
...along the Japanese coast!

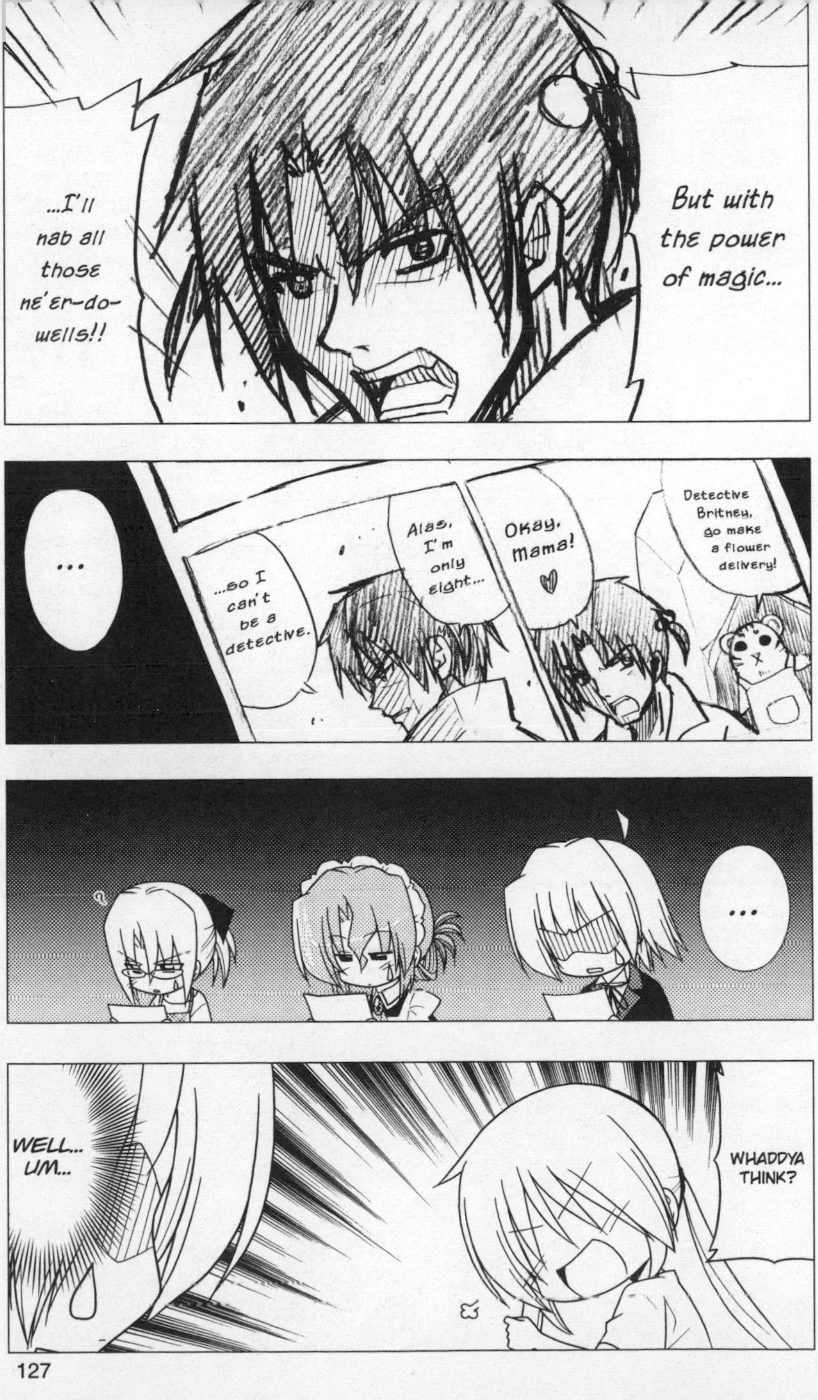
But with the power of magic...
...I'll nab all those ne'er-do-wells!!
Detective Britney, go make a flower delivery!
Okay, Mama!
Alas, I'm only eight...
...so I can't be a detective.
...
...
WHADDYA THINK?
WELL... UM...

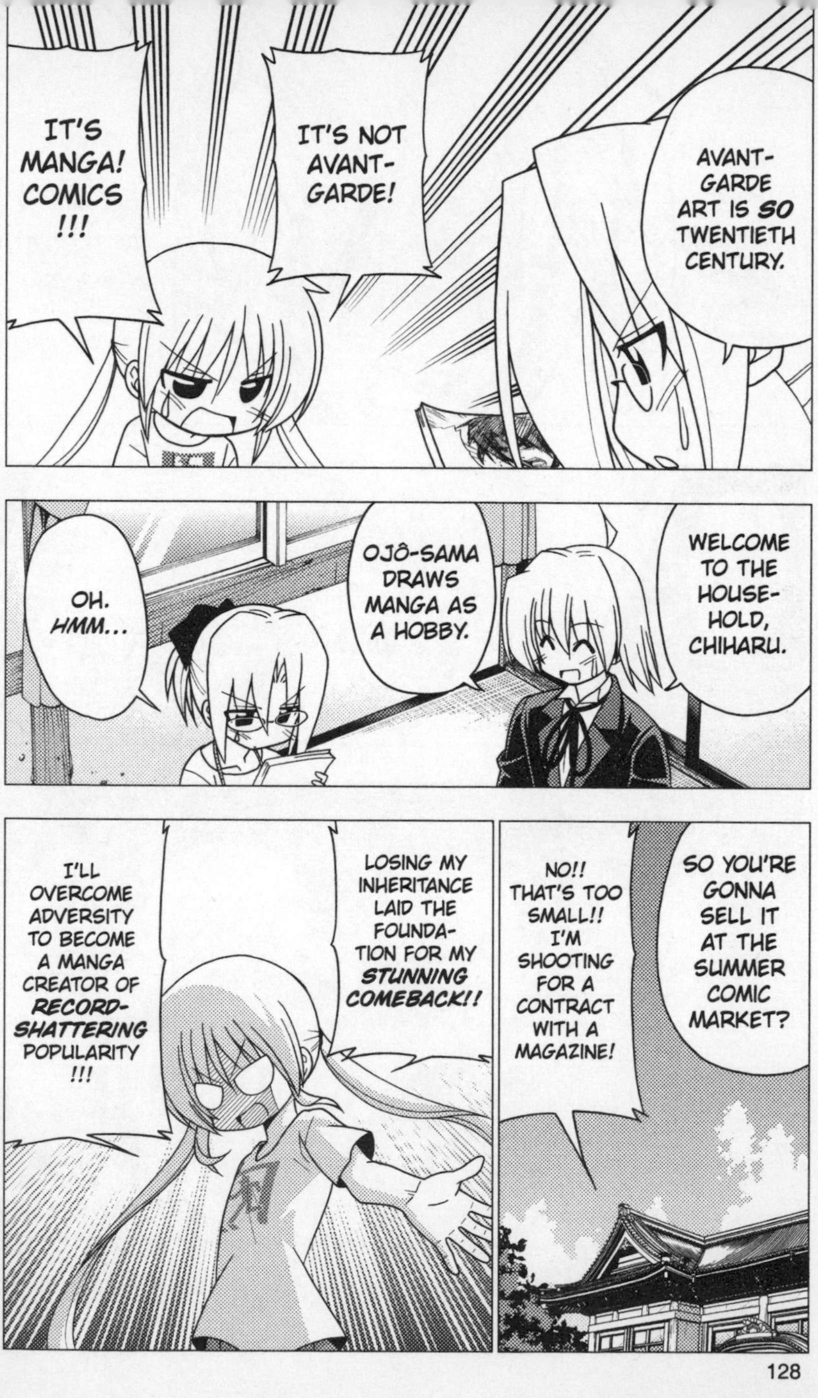
AVANT-GARDE ART IS SO TWENTIETH CENTURY.
IT'S NOT AVANT-GARDE!
IT'S MANGA! COMICS!!!
WELCOME TO THE HOUSEHOLD, CHIHARU.
OJÔ-SAMA DRAWS MANGA AS A HOBBY.
OH. HMM...
SO YOU'RE GONNA SELL IT AT THE SUMMER COMIC MARKET?
NO!! THAT'S TOO SMALL!! I'M SHOOTING FOR A CONTRACT WITH A MAGAZINE!
LOSING MY INHERITANCE LAID THE FOUNDATION FOR MY STUNNING COMEBACK!!
I'LL OVERCOME ADVERSITY TO BECOME A MANGA CREATOR OF RECORD-SHATTERING POPULARITY!!!

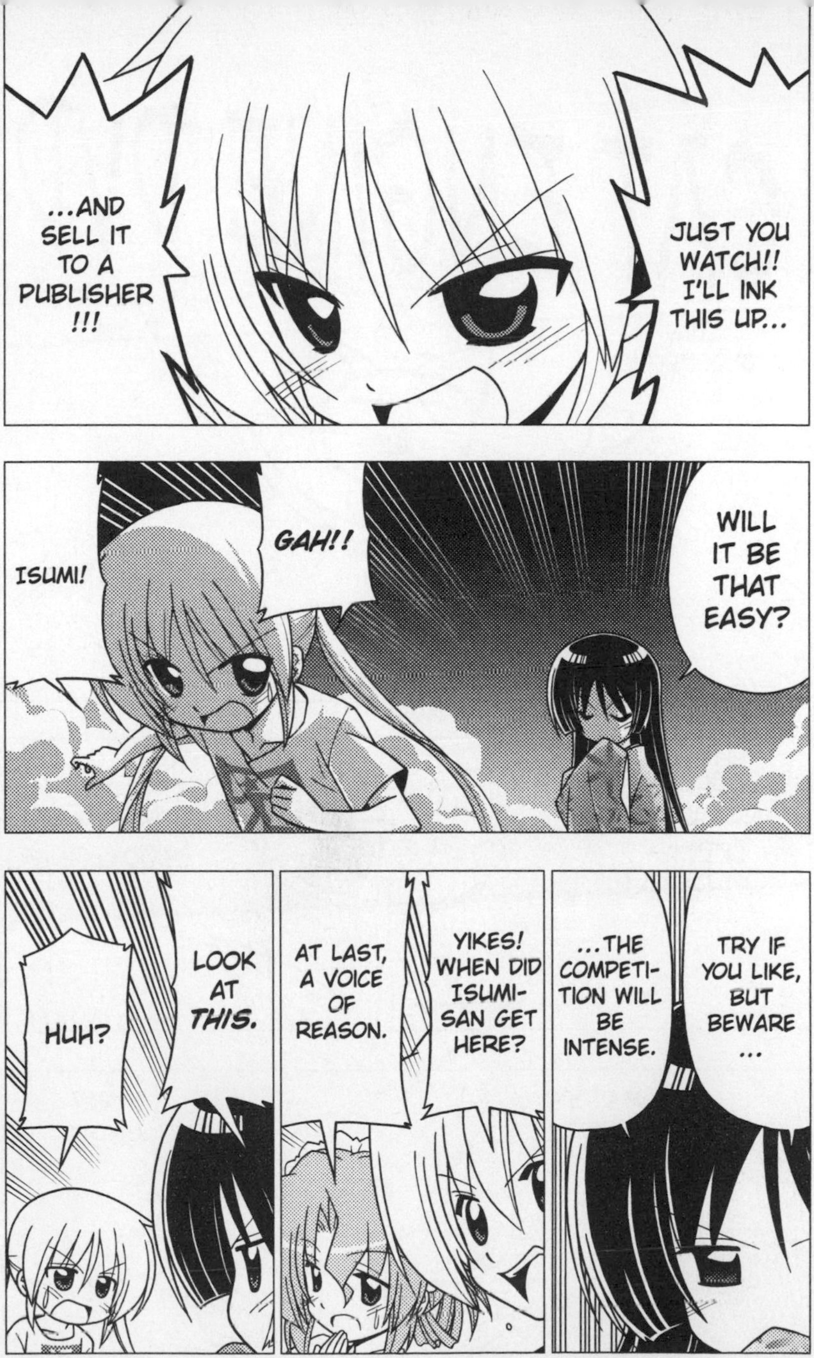
JUST YOU WATCH!! I'LL INK THIS UP...
...AND SELL IT TO A PUBLISHER !!!
WILL IT BE THAT EASY?
GAH!!
ISUMI!
TRY IF YOU LIKE, BUT BEWARE ...
...THE COMPETI- TION WILL BE INTENSE.
YIKES! WHEN DID ISUMI- SAN GET HERE?
AT LAST, A VOICE OF REASON.
LOOK AT *THIS.*
HUH?

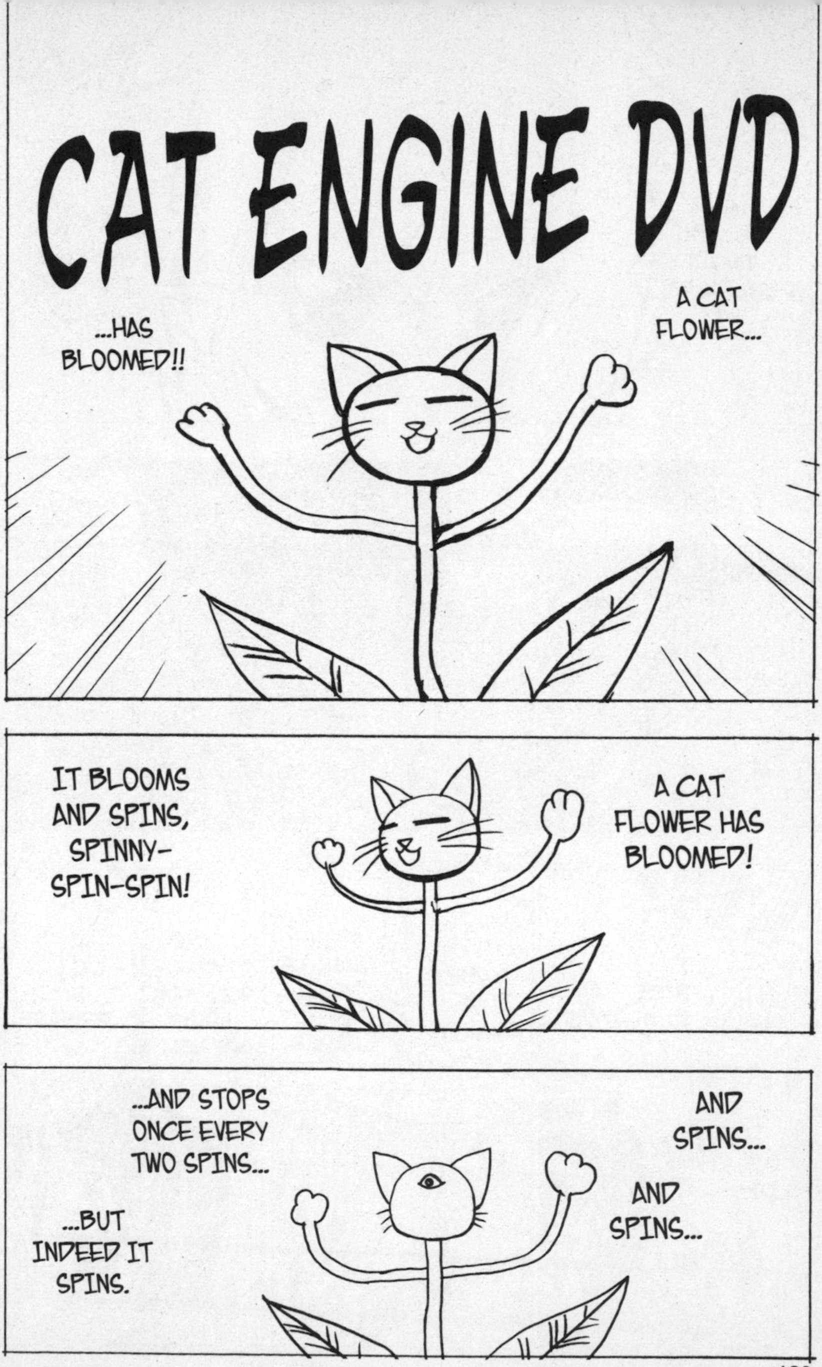
CAT ENGINE DVD
A CAT FLOWER...
...HAS BLOOMED!!
A CAT FLOWER HAS BLOOMED!
IT BLOOMS AND SPINS, SPINNY-SPIN-SPIN!
AND SPINS...
AND SPINS...
...AND STOPS ONCE EVERY TWO SPINS...
...BUT INDEED IT SPINS.

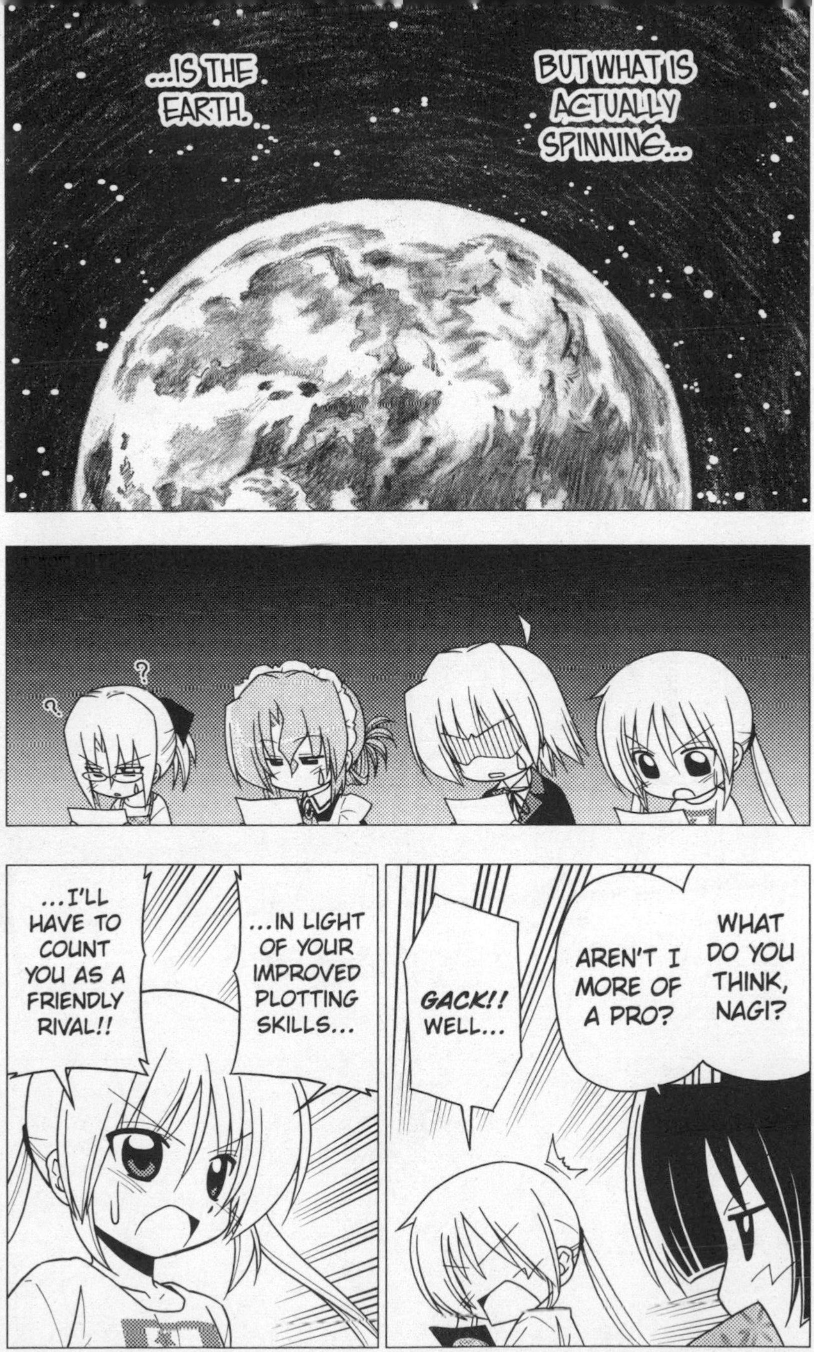

BUT WHAT IS ACTUALLY SPINNING...
...IS THE EARTH.
WHAT DO YOU THINK, NAGI?
AREN'T I MORE OF A PRO?
GACK!! WELL...
...IN LIGHT OF YOUR IMPROVED PLOTTING SKILLS...
...I'LL HAVE TO COUNT YOU AS A FRIENDLY RIVAL!!

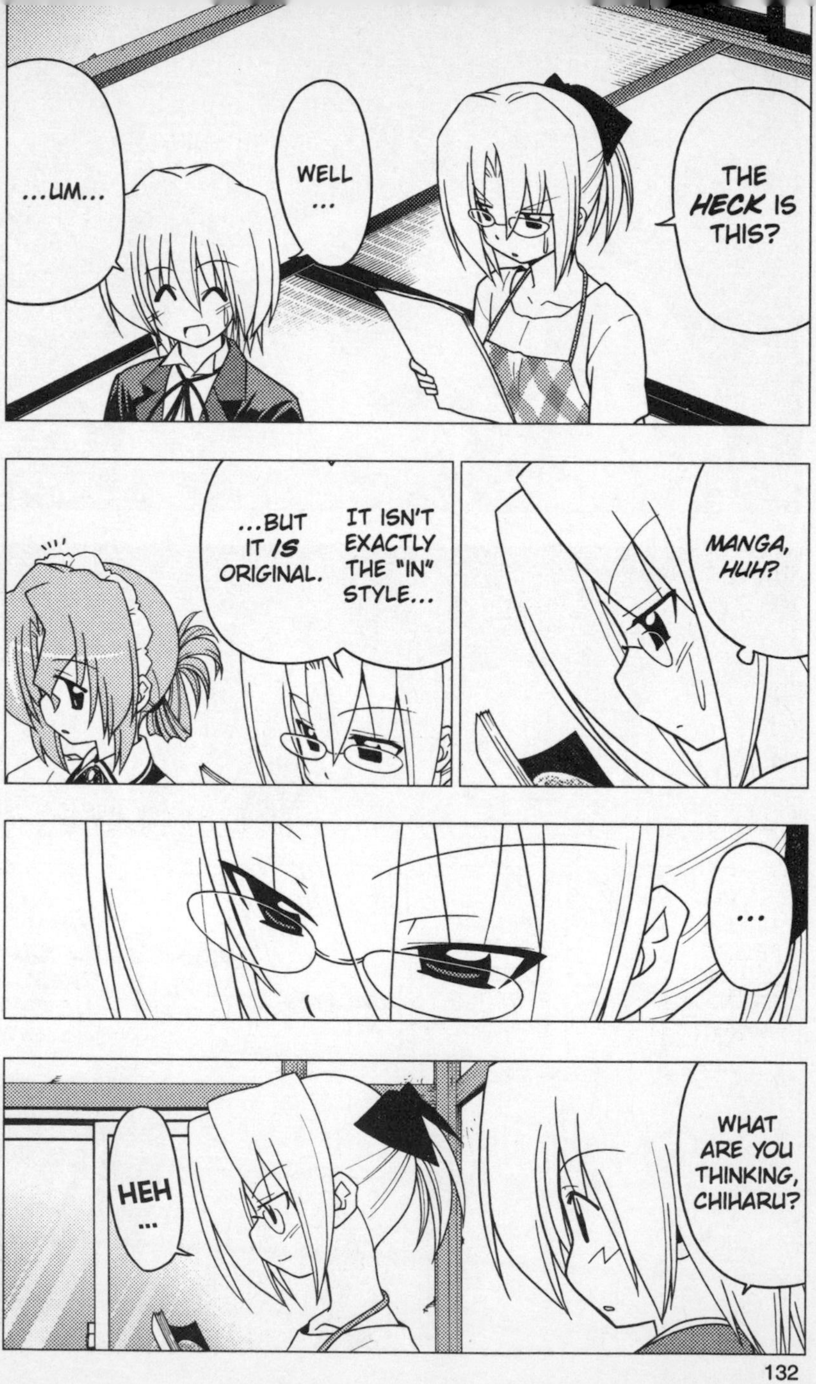
THE *HECK* IS THIS?
WELL ...
...UM...
MANGA, HUH?
IT ISN'T EXACTLY THE "IN" STYLE...
...BUT IT *IS* ORIGINAL.
...
WHAT ARE YOU THINKING, CHIHARU?
HEH ...

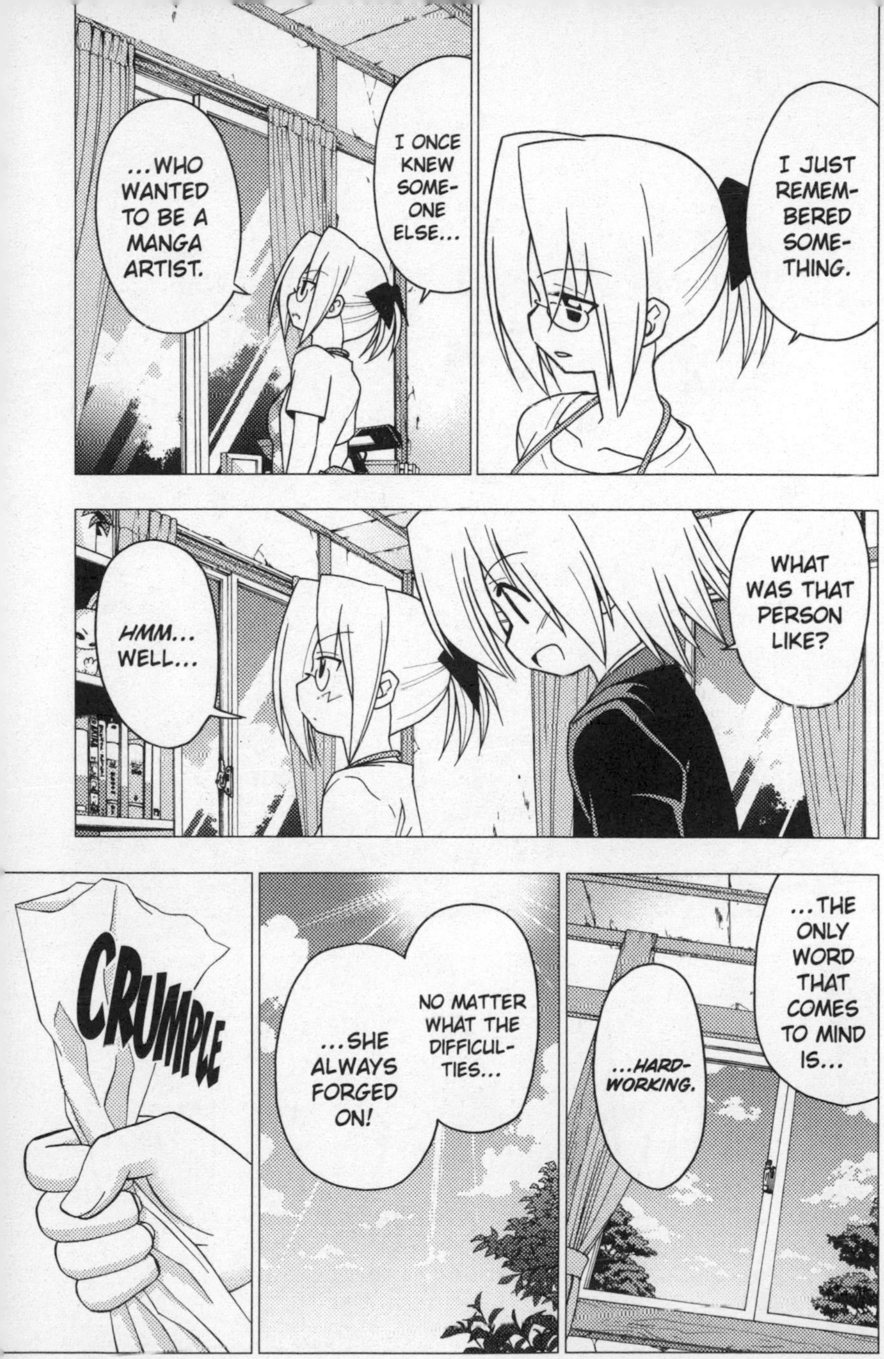
I JUST REMEM-BERED SOME-THING.
I ONCE KNEW SOME-ONE ELSE...
...WHO WANTED TO BE A MANGA ARTIST.
WHAT WAS THAT PERSON LIKE?
HMM... WELL...
...THE ONLY WORD THAT COMES TO MIND IS...
...HARD-WORKING.
NO MATTER WHAT THE DIFFICUL-TIES...
...SHE ALWAYS FORGED ON!
CRUMPLE

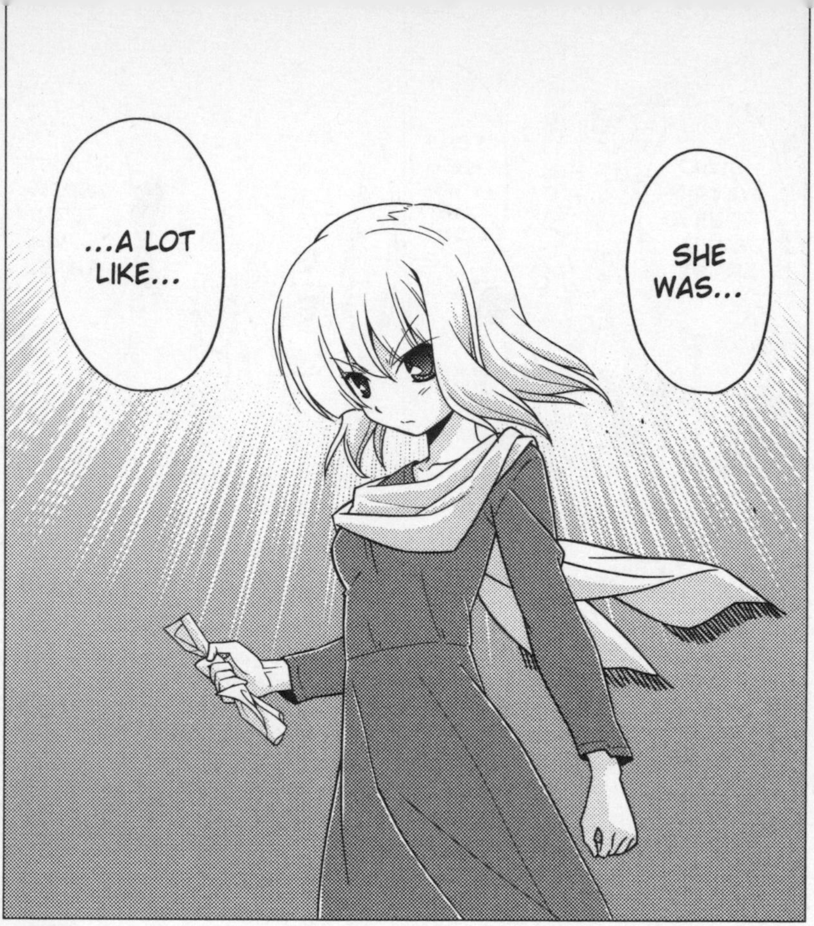
SHE WAS...
...A LOT LIKE...

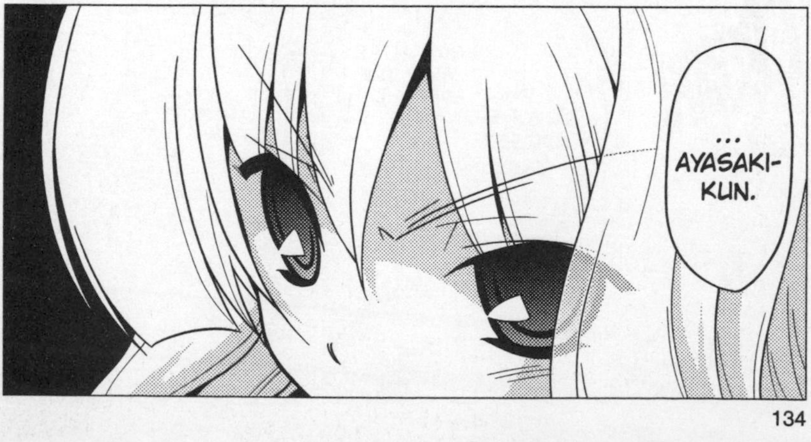
... AYASAKI-KUN.

Episode 9:
"My Birthday Is October 19. I'm a Libra."

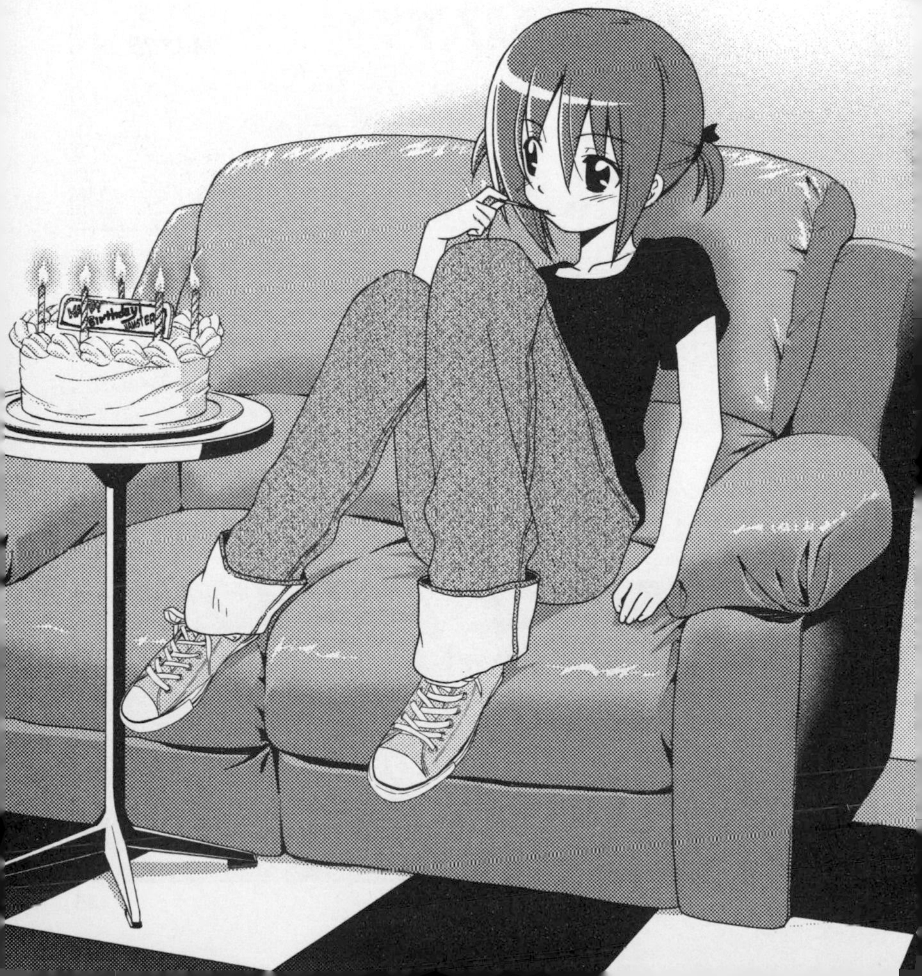

CHIRP

CHIRP

MAY

sun	mon	tue	wed	thu	fri	sat
1	2	3	4	5	6	7
8	9	10	11	12	13	14
15	16	17	18	19	20	21

IT'S MAY 15.

...17 YEARS OLD!!!

TODAY I'M...

...YOU BECOME THE STAR OF YOUR OWN LIFE.

ONCE A YEAR...

IT'S MY BIRTHDAY.

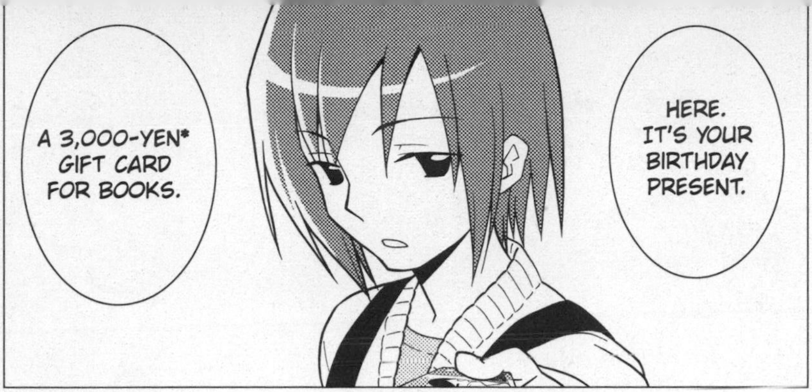
HERE. IT'S YOUR BIRTHDAY PRESENT.
A 3,000-YEN* GIFT CARD FOR BOOKS.

*ABOUT $30.

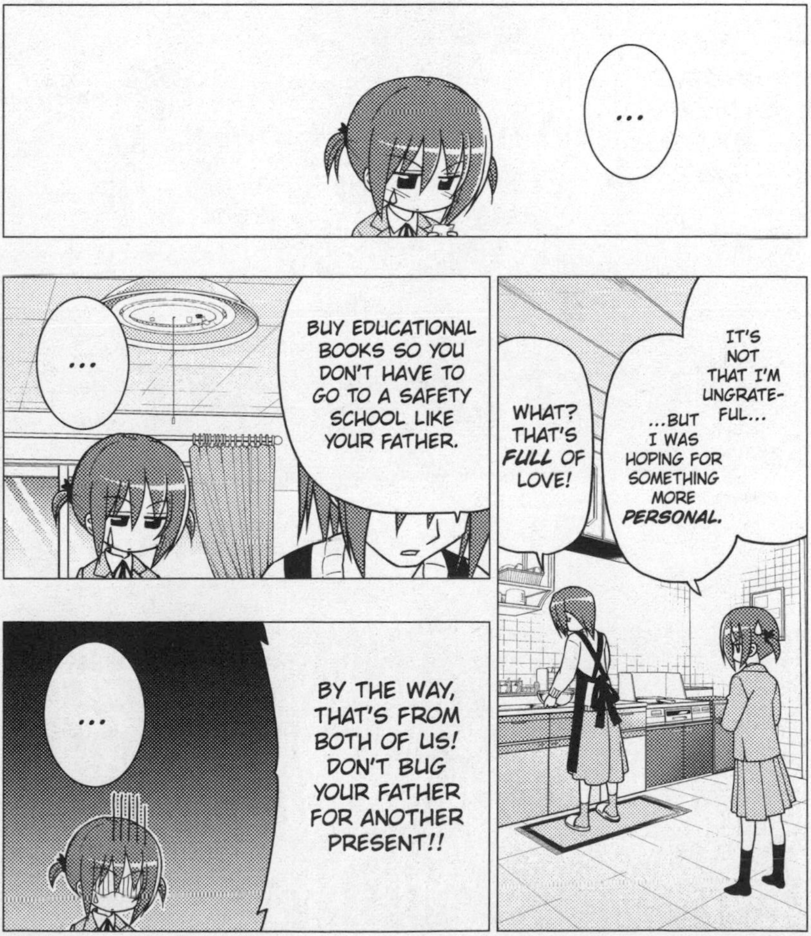
...
IT'S NOT THAT I'M UNGRATE-FUL...
...BUT I WAS HOPING FOR SOMETHING MORE PERSONAL.
WHAT? THAT'S FULL OF LOVE!
BUY EDUCATIONAL BOOKS SO YOU DON'T HAVE TO GO TO A SAFETY SCHOOL LIKE YOUR FATHER.
...
BY THE WAY, THAT'S FROM BOTH OF US! DON'T BUG YOUR FATHER FOR ANOTHER PRESENT!!
...

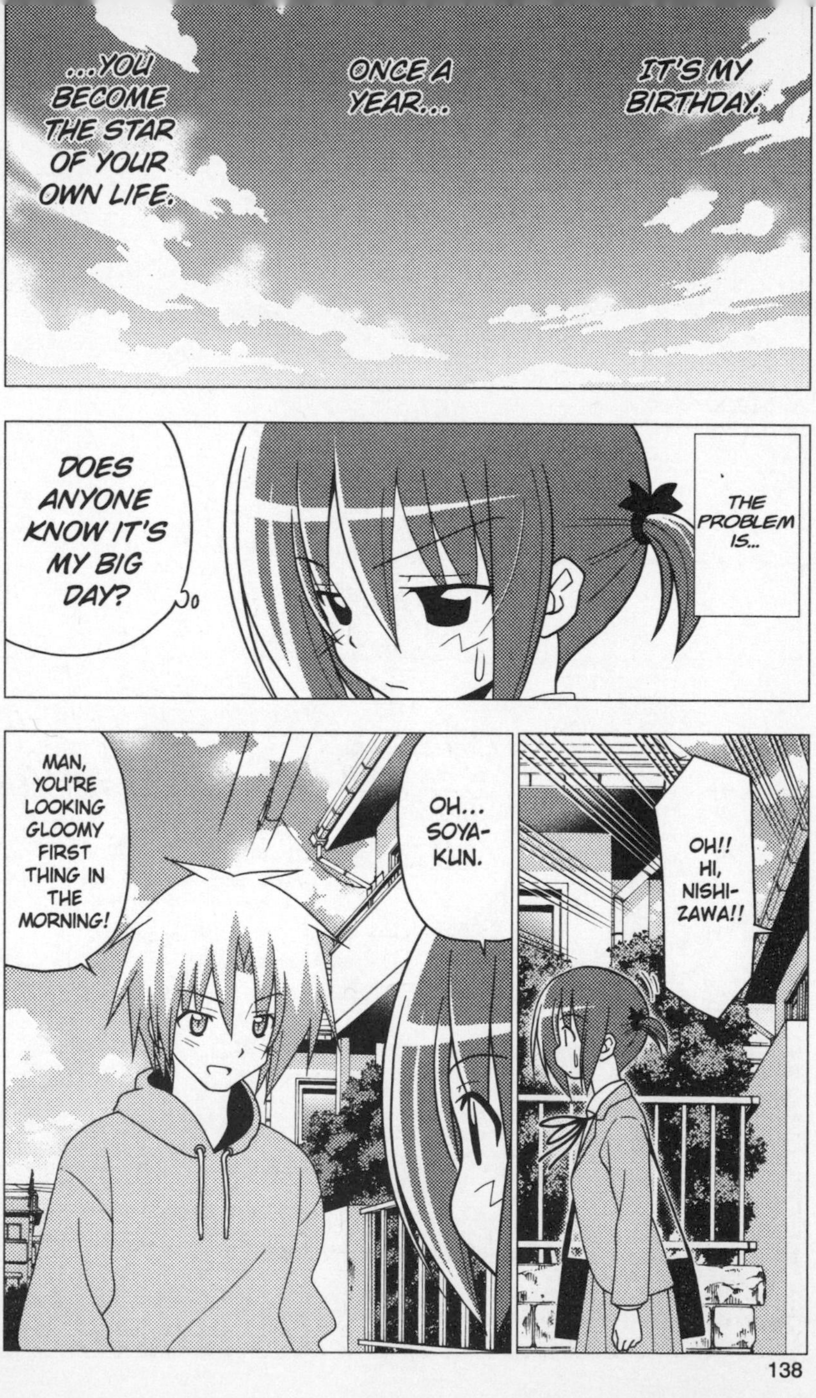
IT'S MY BIRTHDAY.
ONCE A YEAR...
...YOU BECOME THE STAR OF YOUR OWN LIFE.
THE PROBLEM IS...
DOES ANYONE KNOW IT'S MY BIG DAY?
OH!! HI, NISHIZAWA!!
OH... SOYA-KUN.
MAN, YOU'RE LOOKING GLOOMY FIRST THING IN THE MORNING!

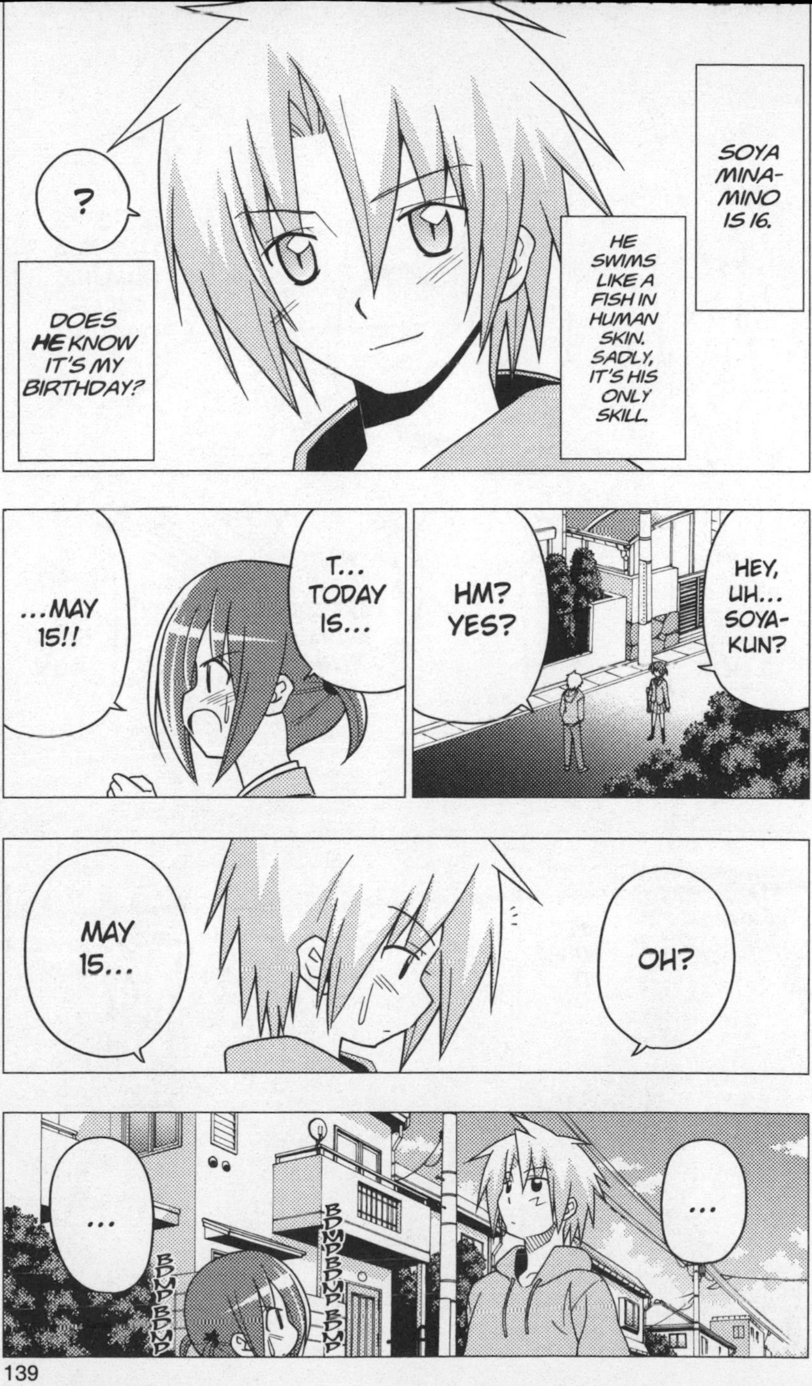
SOYA MINA-MINO IS 16.
HE SWIMS LIKE A FISH IN HUMAN SKIN. SADLY, IT'S HIS ONLY SKILL.
?
DOES HE KNOW IT'S MY BIRTHDAY?
HEY, UH... SOYA-KUN?
HM? YES?
T... TODAY IS...
...MAY 15!!
OH?
MAY 15...
...
BDMP BDMP BDMP BDMP
BDMP BDMP BDMP
...

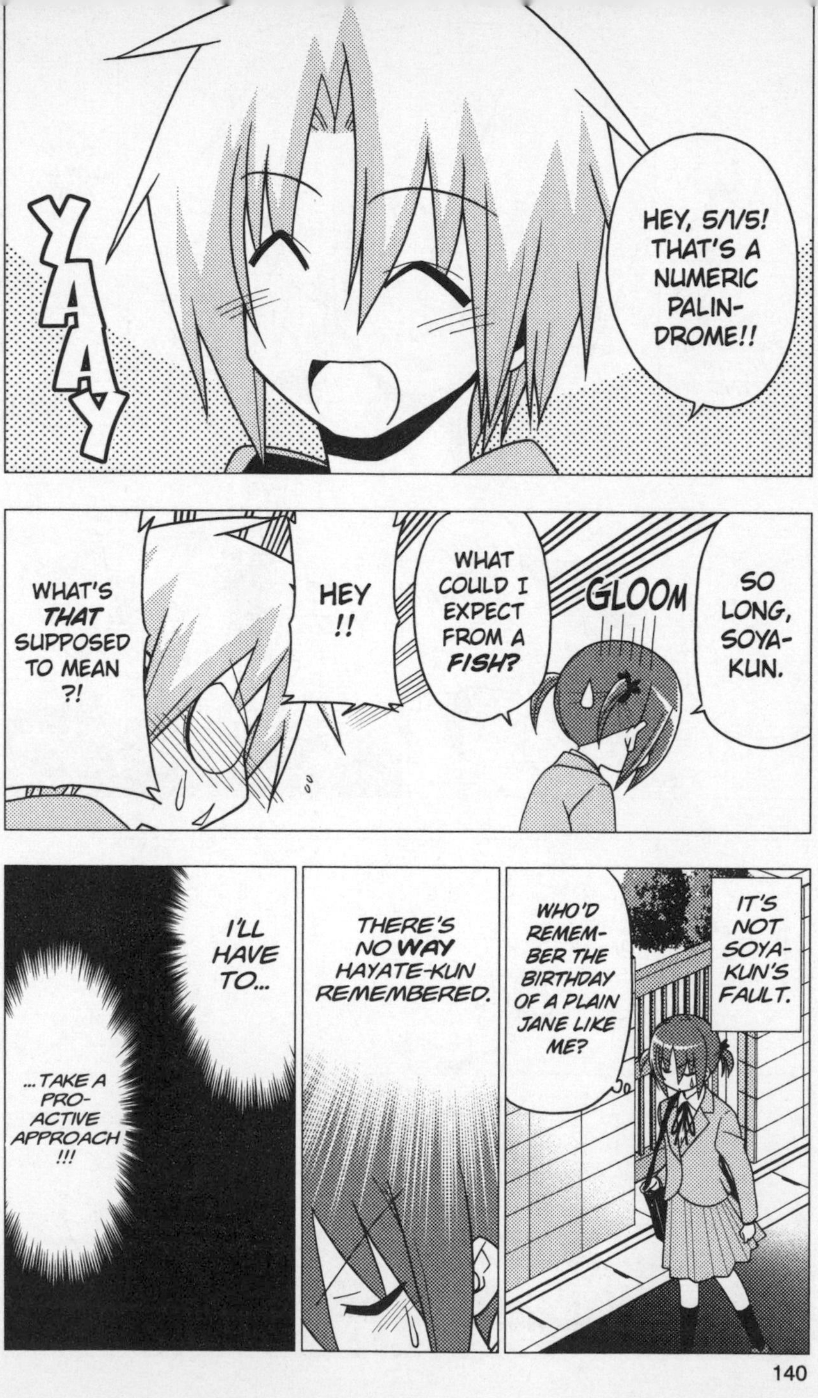
HEY, 5/1/5! THAT'S A NUMERIC PALIN-DROME!!
YAAY
SO LONG, SOYA-KUN.
GLOOM
WHAT COULD I EXPECT FROM A *FISH?*
HEY !!
WHAT'S *THAT* SUPPOSED TO MEAN ?!
IT'S NOT SOYA-KUN'S FAULT.
WHO'D REMEM-BER THE BIRTHDAY OF A PLAIN JANE LIKE ME?
THERE'S NO **WAY** HAYATE-KUN REMEMBERED.
I'LL HAVE TO...
...TAKE A PRO-ACTIVE APPROACH !!!

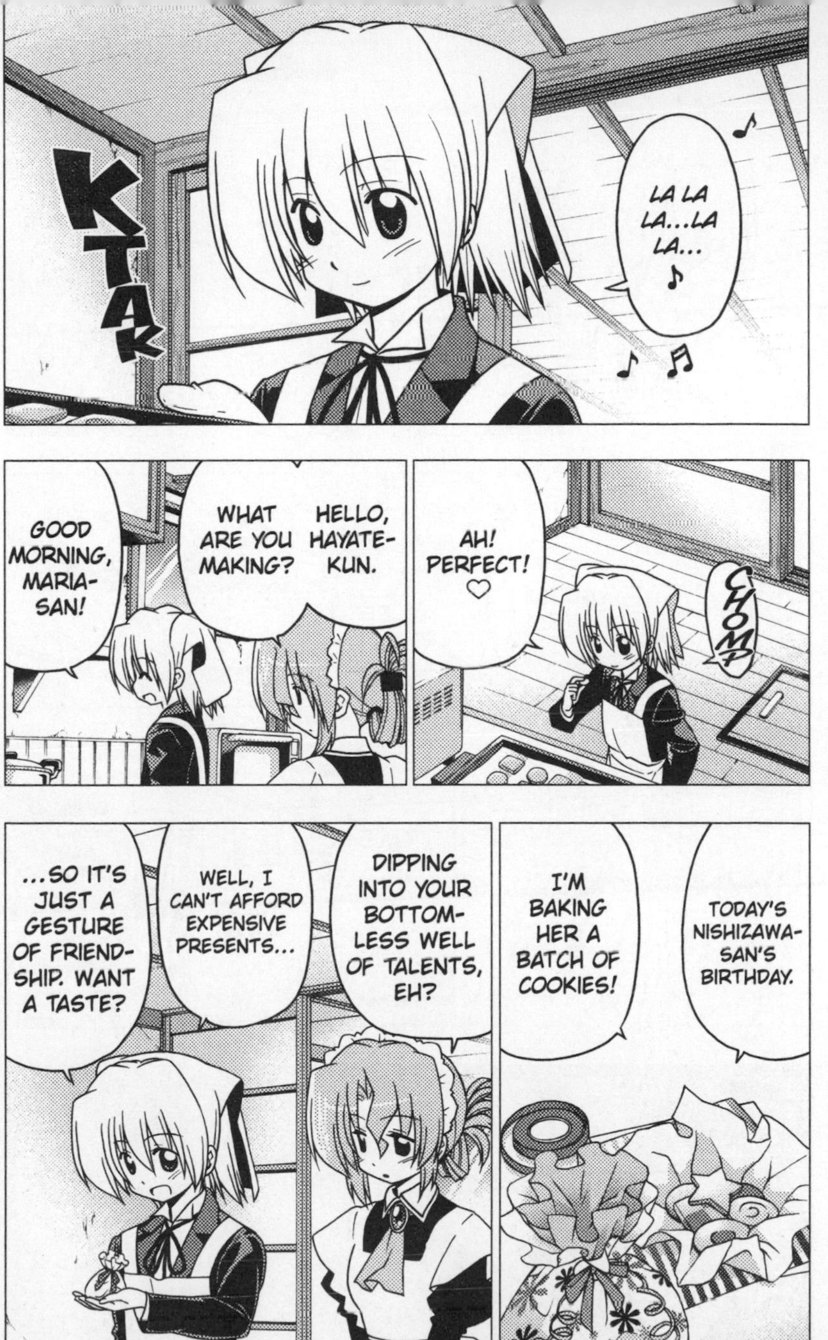
LA LA LA...LA LA...
KTAK
AH! PERFECT! ♡
CHOMP
HELLO, HAYATE-KUN.
WHAT ARE YOU MAKING?
GOOD MORNING, MARIA-SAN!
TODAY'S NISHIZAWA-SAN'S BIRTHDAY.
I'M BAKING HER A BATCH OF COOKIES!
DIPPING INTO YOUR BOTTOMLESS WELL OF TALENTS, EH?
WELL, I CAN'T AFFORD EXPENSIVE PRESENTS...
...SO IT'S JUST A GESTURE OF FRIENDSHIP. WANT A TASTE?

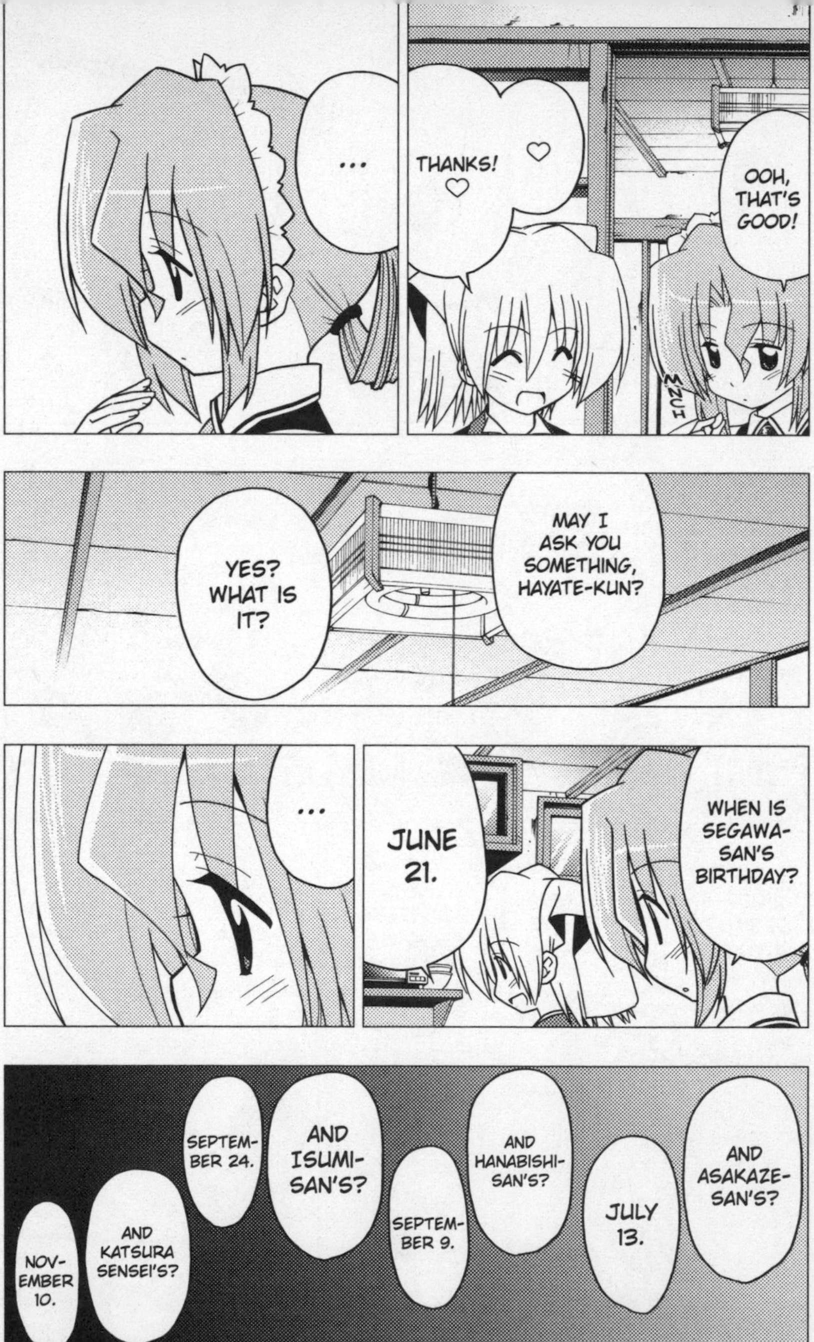
OOH, THAT'S GOOD!
MUNCH
THANKS! ♡ ♡
...
MAY I ASK YOU SOMETHING, HAYATE-KUN?
YES? WHAT IS IT?
WHEN IS SEGAWA-SAN'S BIRTHDAY?
JUNE 21.
...
AND ASAKAZE-SAN'S?
JULY 13.
AND HANABISHI-SAN'S?
SEPTEMBER 9.
AND ISUMI-SAN'S?
SEPTEMBER 24.
AND KATSURA SENSEI'S?
NOVEMBER 10.

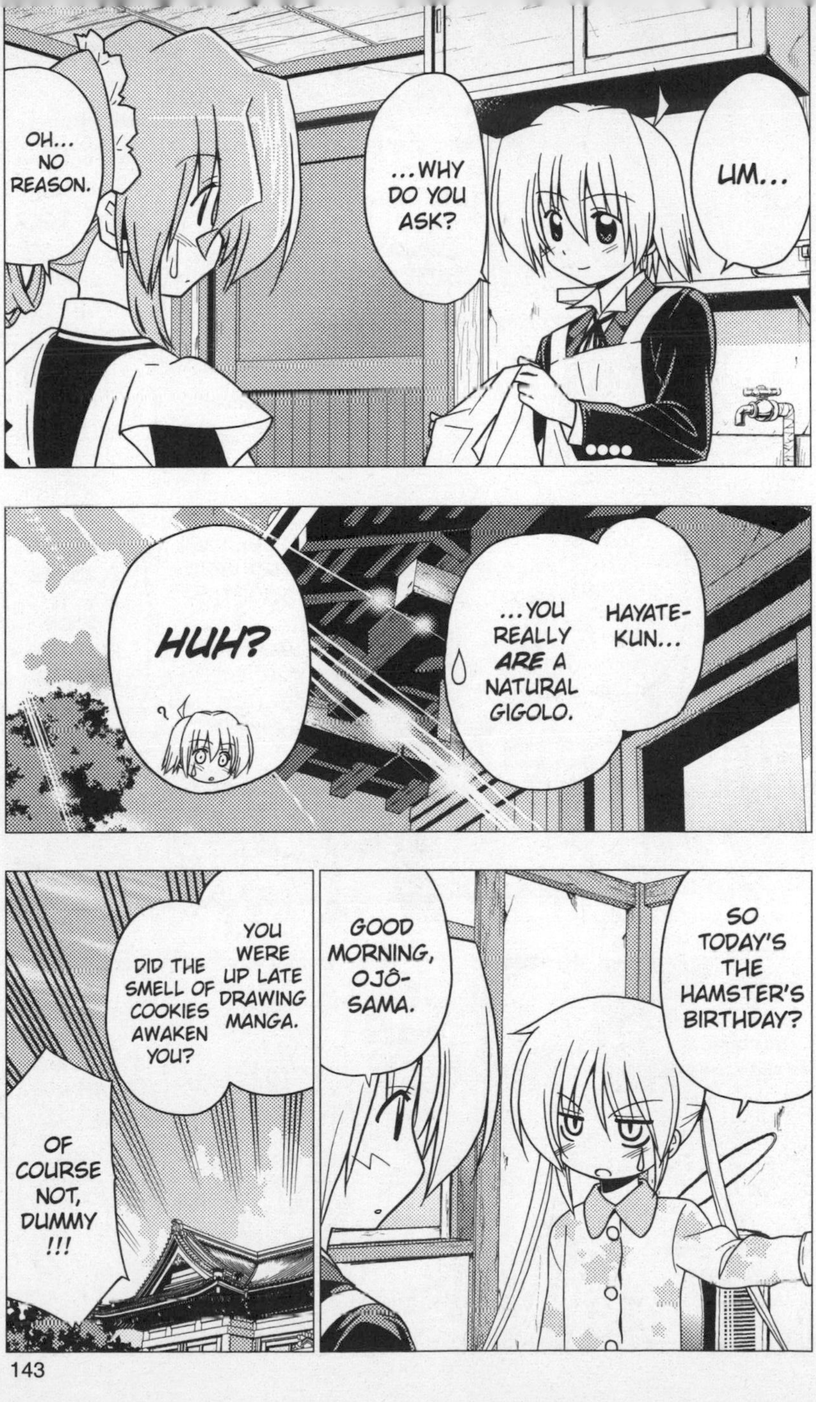
UM...
...WHY DO YOU ASK?
OH... NO REASON.
HAYATE-KUN... ...YOU REALLY ARE A NATURAL GIGOLO.
HUH?
SO TODAY'S THE HAMSTER'S BIRTHDAY?
GOOD MORNING, OJÔ-SAMA.
YOU WERE UP LATE DRAWING MANGA. DID THE SMELL OF COOKIES AWAKEN YOU?
OF COURSE NOT, DUMMY!!!

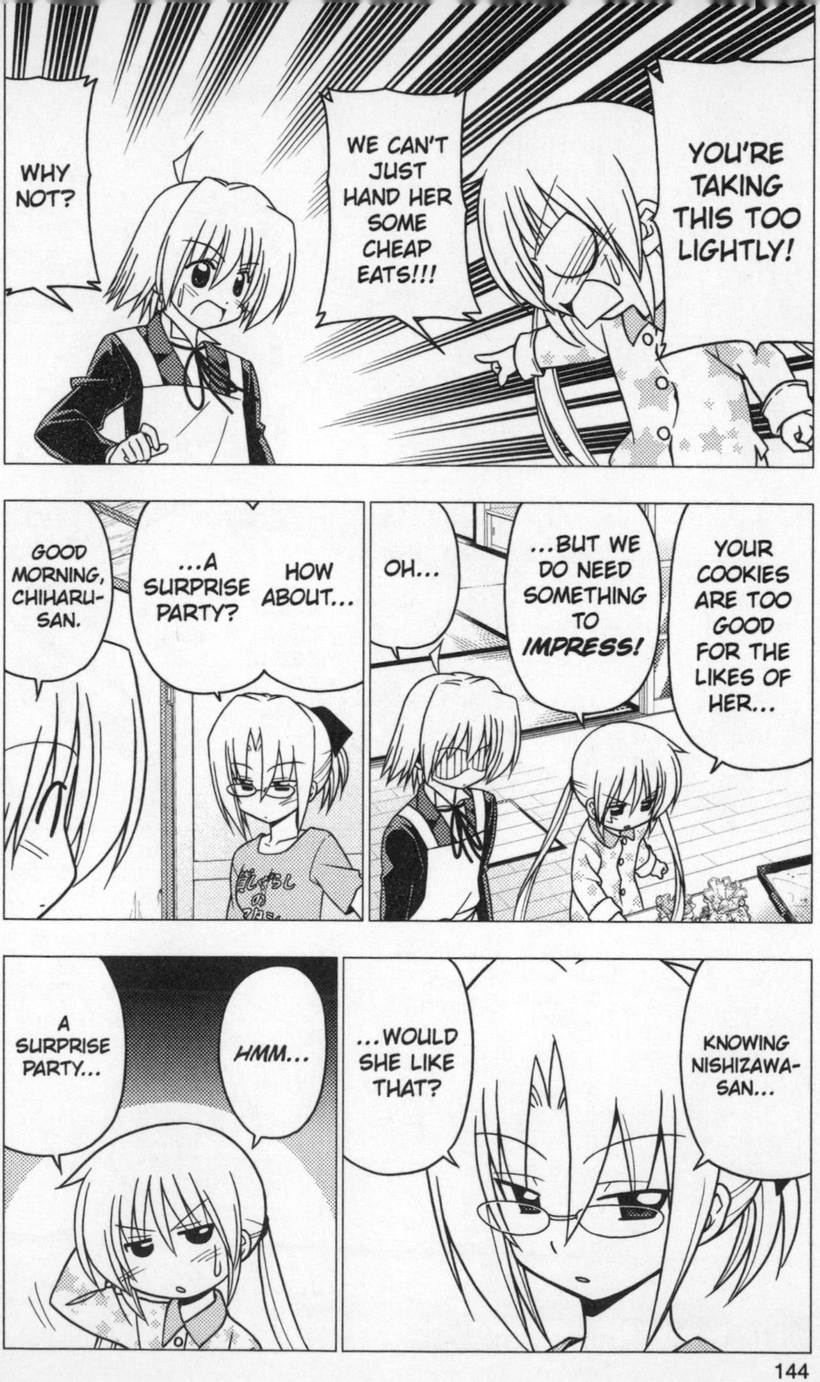
YOU'RE TAKING THIS TOO LIGHTLY!
WE CAN'T JUST HAND HER SOME CHEAP EATS!!!
WHY NOT?
YOUR COOKIES ARE TOO GOOD FOR THE LIKES OF HER...
...BUT WE DO NEED SOMETHING TO *IMPRESS!*
OH...
HOW ABOUT...
...A SURPRISE PARTY?
GOOD MORNING, CHIHARU-SAN.
KNOWING NISHIZAWA-SAN...
...WOULD SHE LIKE THAT?
HMM...
A SURPRISE PARTY...

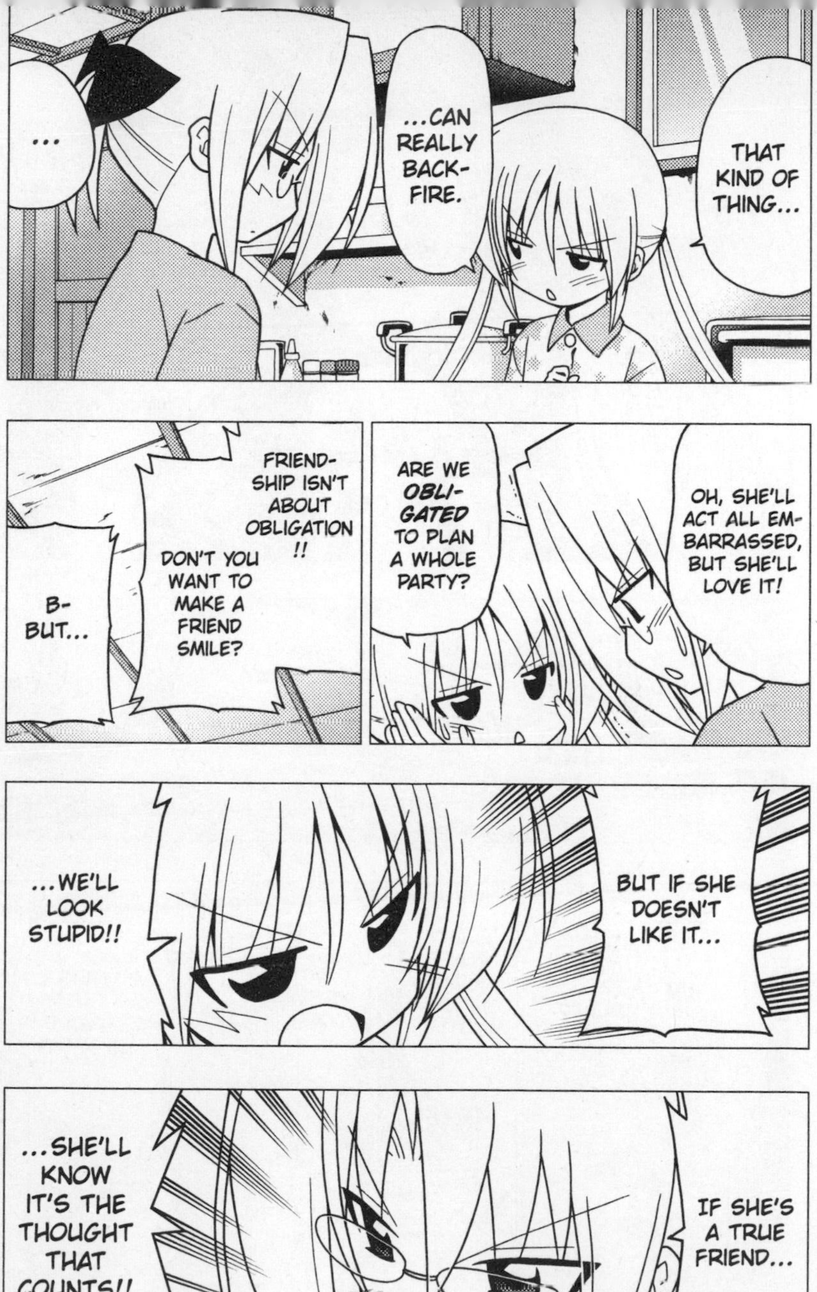
THAT KIND OF THING...
...CAN REALLY BACK-FIRE.
...
OH, SHE'LL ACT ALL EM-BARRASSED, BUT SHE'LL LOVE IT!
ARE WE *OBLI-GATED* TO PLAN A WHOLE PARTY?
FRIEND-SHIP ISN'T ABOUT OBLIGATION!!
DON'T YOU WANT TO MAKE A FRIEND SMILE?
B-BUT...
BUT IF SHE DOESN'T LIKE IT...
...WE'LL LOOK STUPID!!
IF SHE'S A TRUE FRIEND...
...SHE'LL KNOW IT'S THE THOUGHT THAT COUNTS!!

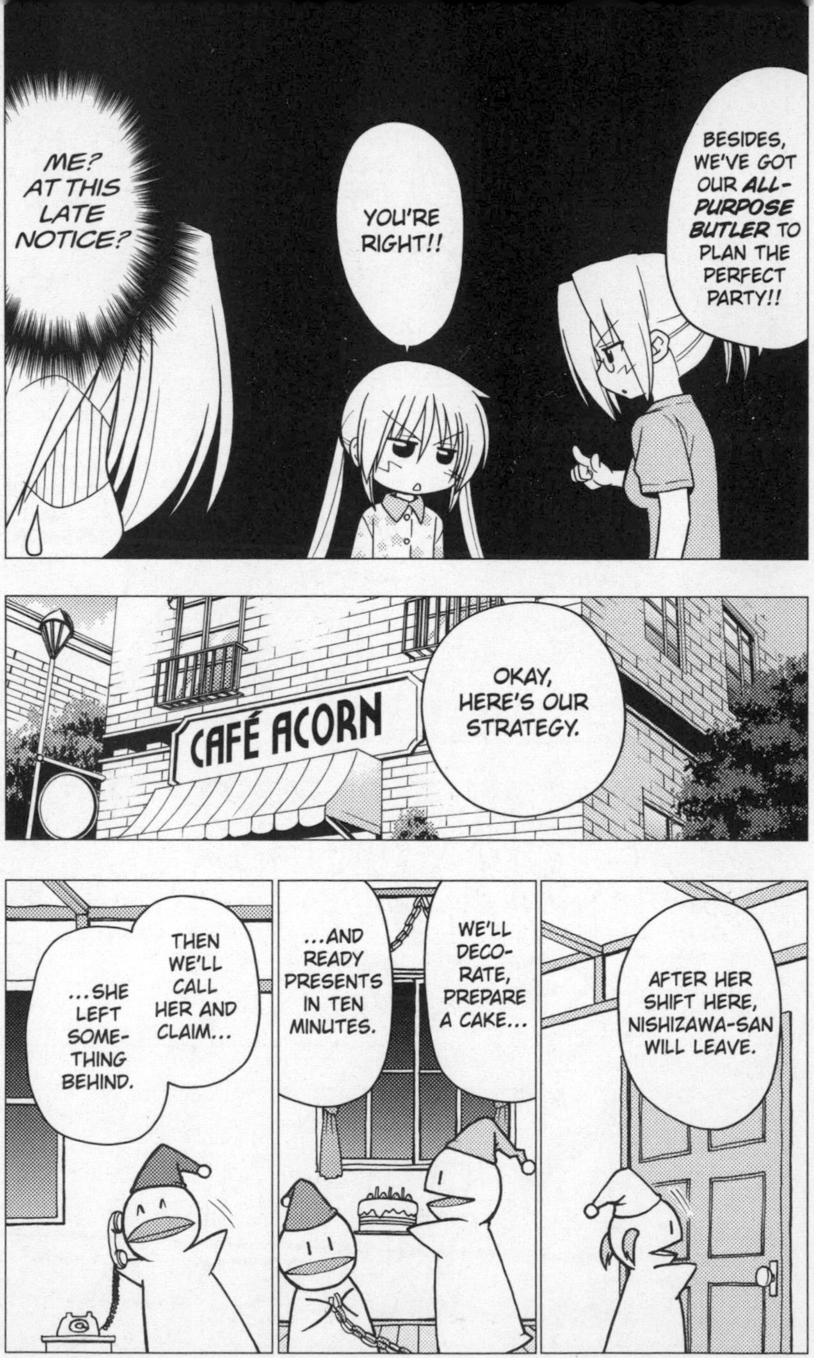
BESIDES, WE'VE GOT OUR **ALL-PURPOSE BUTLER** TO PLAN THE PERFECT PARTY!!
YOU'RE RIGHT!!
ME? AT THIS LATE NOTICE?
CAFÉ ACORN
OKAY, HERE'S OUR STRATEGY.
AFTER HER SHIFT HERE, NISHIZAWA-SAN WILL LEAVE.
WE'LL DECO-RATE, PREPARE A CAKE...
...AND READY PRESENTS IN TEN MINUTES.
THEN WE'LL CALL HER AND CLAIM...
...SHE LEFT SOME-THING BEHIND.

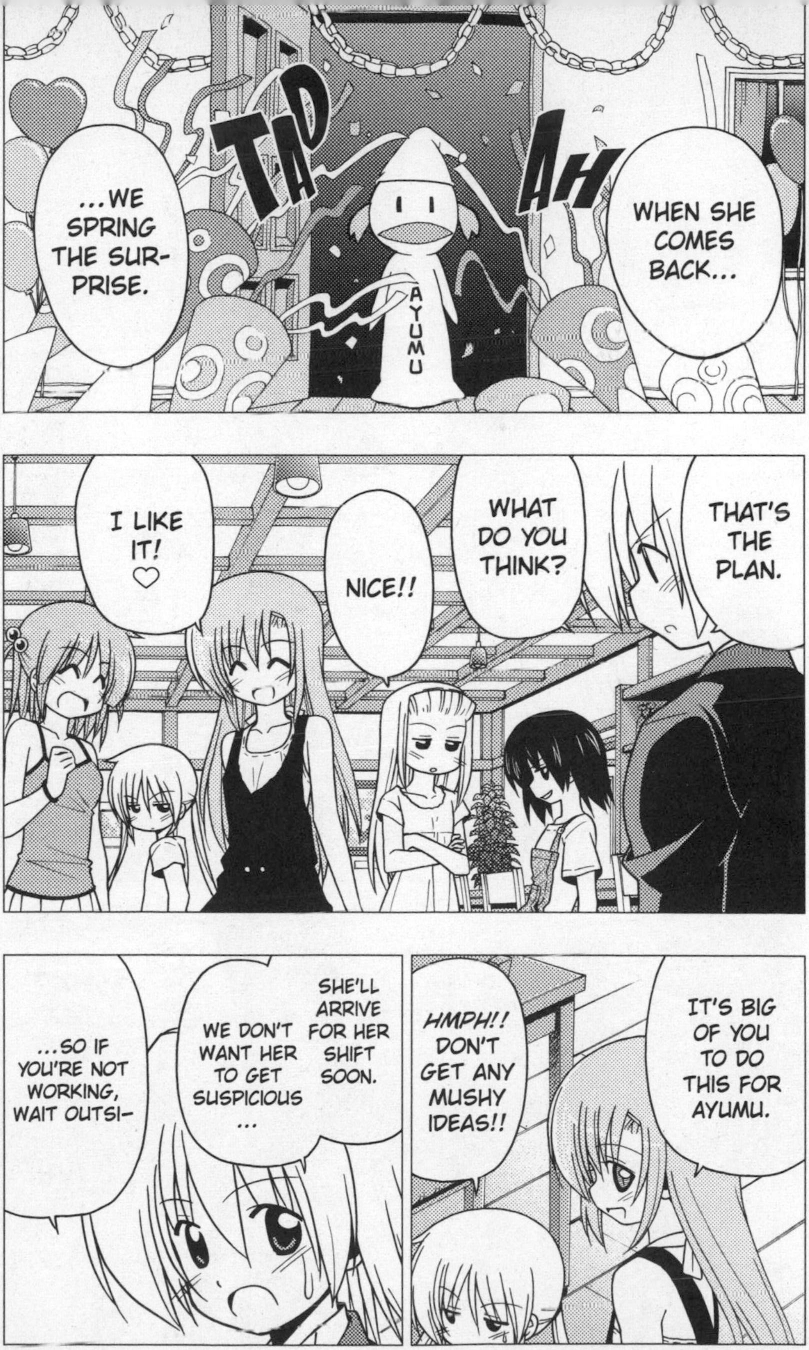
WHEN SHE COMES BACK...
TADAH
AYUMU
...WE SPRING THE SUR-PRISE.
THAT'S THE PLAN.
WHAT DO YOU THINK?
NICE!!
I LIKE IT! ♡
IT'S BIG OF YOU TO DO THIS FOR AYUMU.
HMPH!! DON'T GET ANY MUSHY IDEAS!!
SHE'LL ARRIVE FOR HER SHIFT SOON.
WE DON'T WANT HER TO GET SUSPICIOUS...
...SO IF YOU'RE NOT WORKING, WAIT OUTSI-

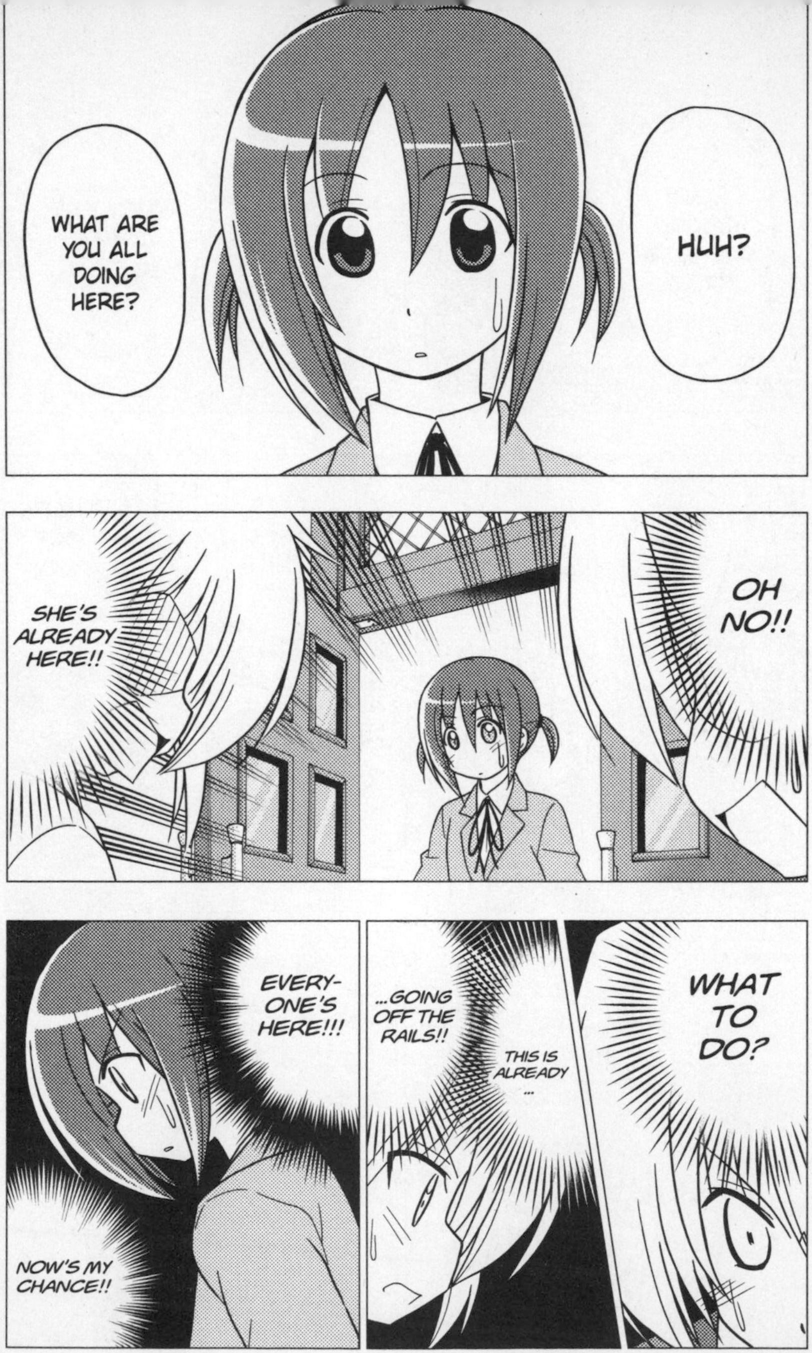
HUH?
WHAT ARE YOU ALL DOING HERE?
OH NO!!
SHE'S ALREADY HERE!!
WHAT TO DO?
THIS IS ALREADY ...
...GOING OFF THE RAILS!!
EVERY-ONE'S HERE!!!
NOW'S MY CHANCE!!

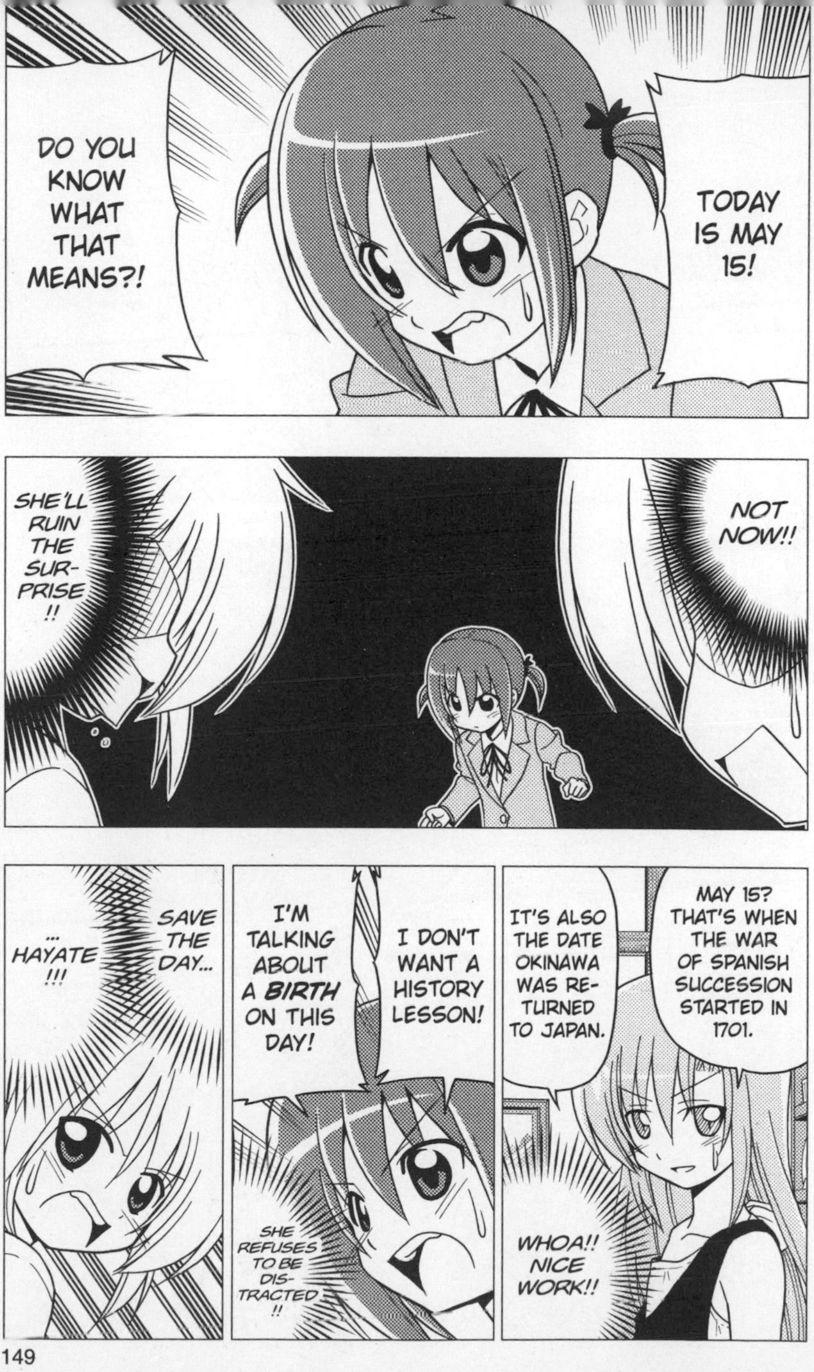

TODAY IS MAY 15!
DO YOU KNOW WHAT THAT MEANS?!
NOT NOW!!
SHE'LL RUIN THE SURPRISE!!
MAY 15? THAT'S WHEN THE WAR OF SPANISH SUCCESSION STARTED IN 1701.
IT'S ALSO THE DATE OKINAWA WAS RETURNED TO JAPAN.
WHOA!! NICE WORK!!
I DON'T WANT A HISTORY LESSON!
I'M TALKING ABOUT A *BIRTH* ON THIS DAY!
SHE REFUSES TO BE DISTRACTED!!
SAVE THE DAY...
...HAYATE!!!

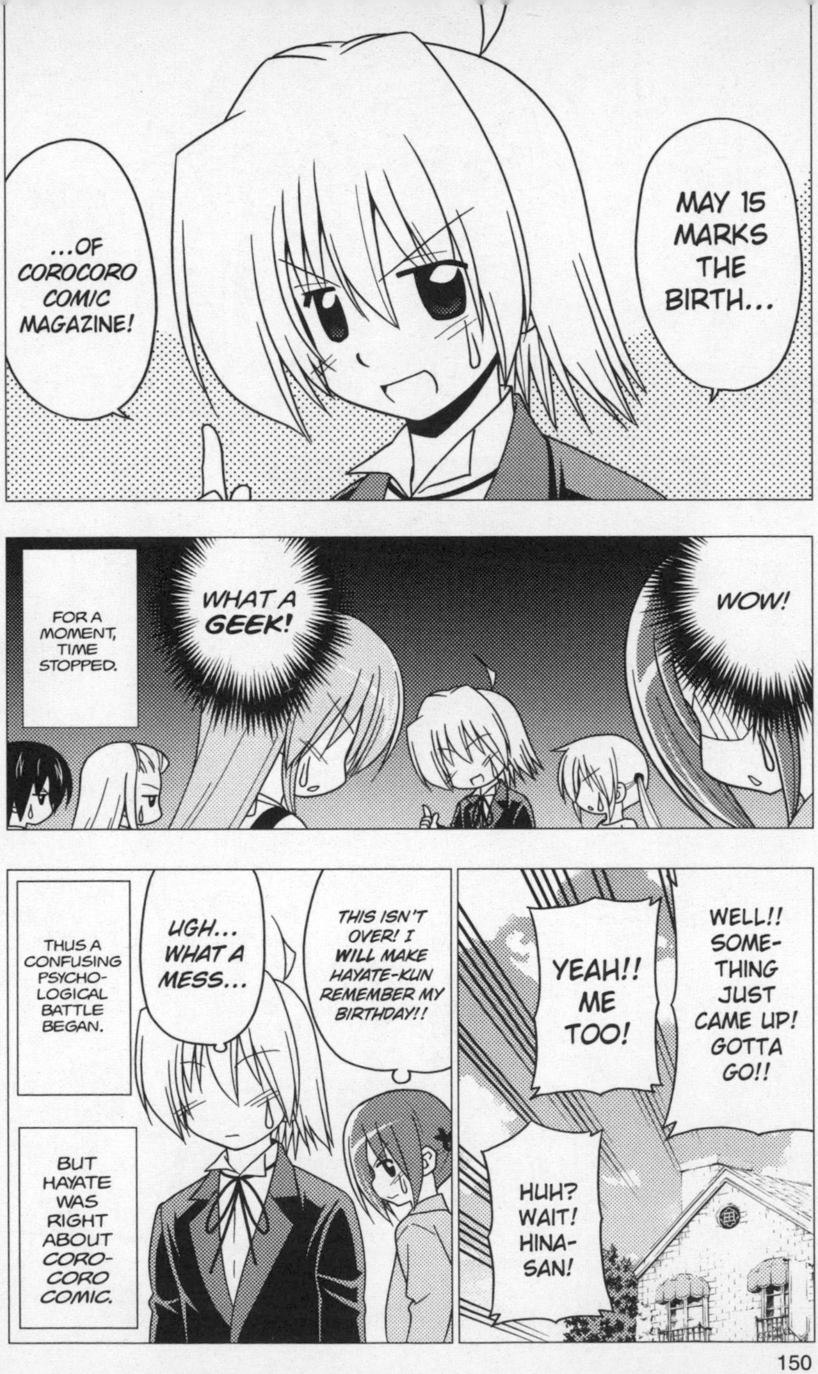
MAY 15 MARKS THE BIRTH...
...OF COROCORO COMIC MAGAZINE!
WOW!
WHAT A GEEK!
FOR A MOMENT, TIME STOPPED.
WELL!! SOMETHING JUST CAME UP! GOTTA GO!!
YEAH!! ME TOO!
HUH? WAIT! HINA-SAN!
THIS ISN'T OVER! I WILL MAKE HAYATE-KUN REMEMBER MY BIRTHDAY!!
UGH... WHAT A MESS...
THUS A CONFUSING PSYCHOLOGICAL BATTLE BEGAN.
BUT HAYATE WAS RIGHT ABOUT COROCORO COMIC.

Episode 10:
"Happy Birthday to Me!"

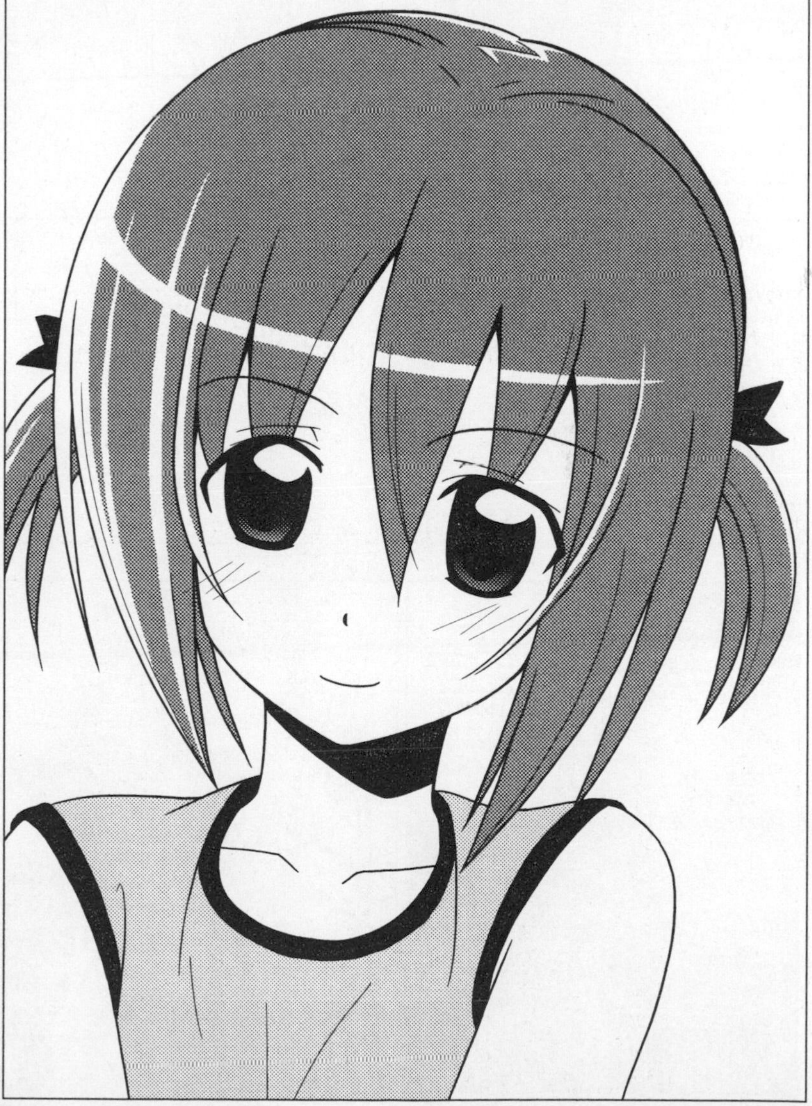

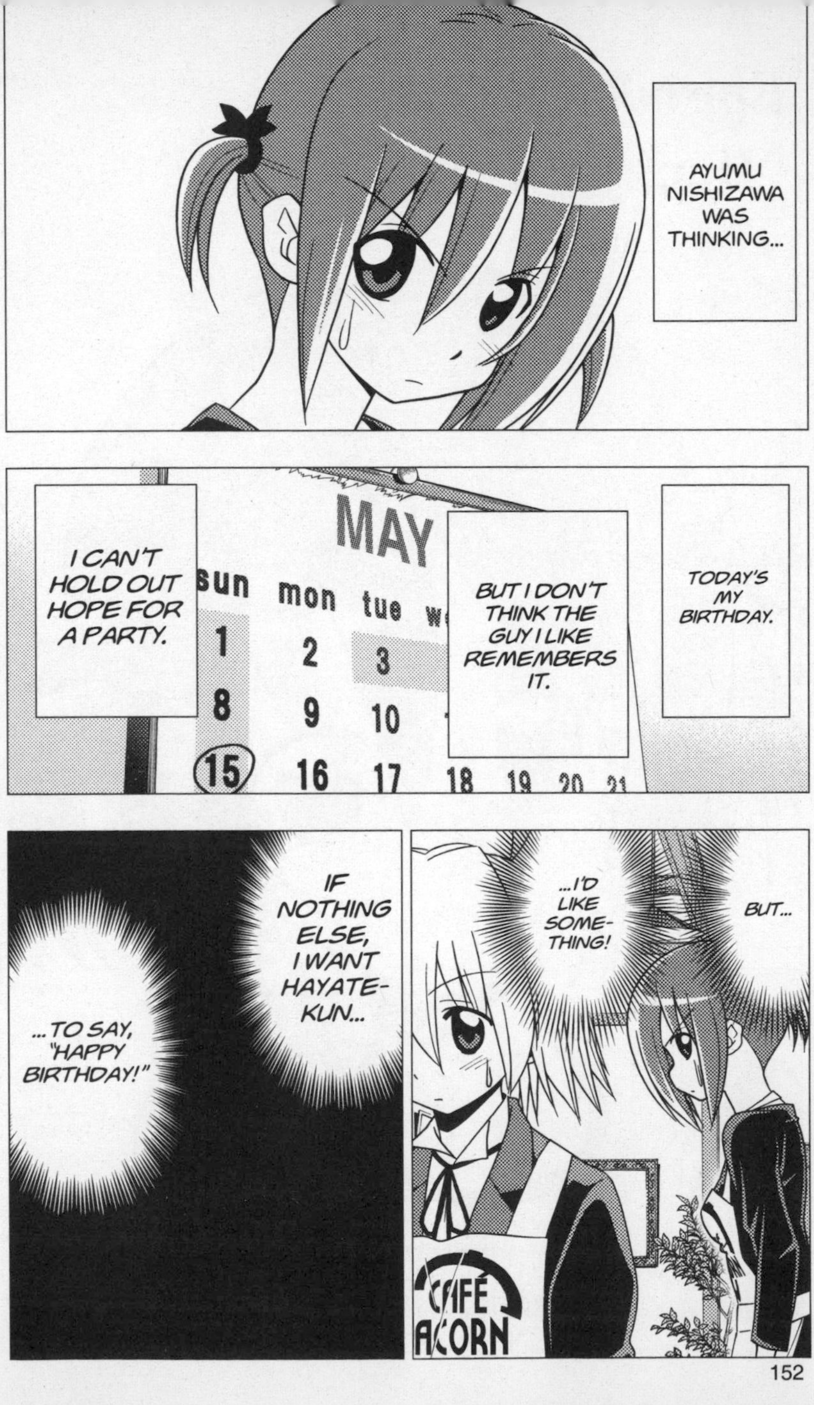
AYUMU NISHIZAWA WAS THINKING...
TODAY'S MY BIRTHDAY.
BUT I DON'T THINK THE GUY I LIKE REMEMBERS IT.
MAY
I CAN'T HOLD OUT HOPE FOR A PARTY.
BUT...
...I'D LIKE SOME-THING!
CAFÉ ACORN
IF NOTHING ELSE, I WANT HAYATE-KUN...
...TO SAY, "HAPPY BIRTHDAY!"

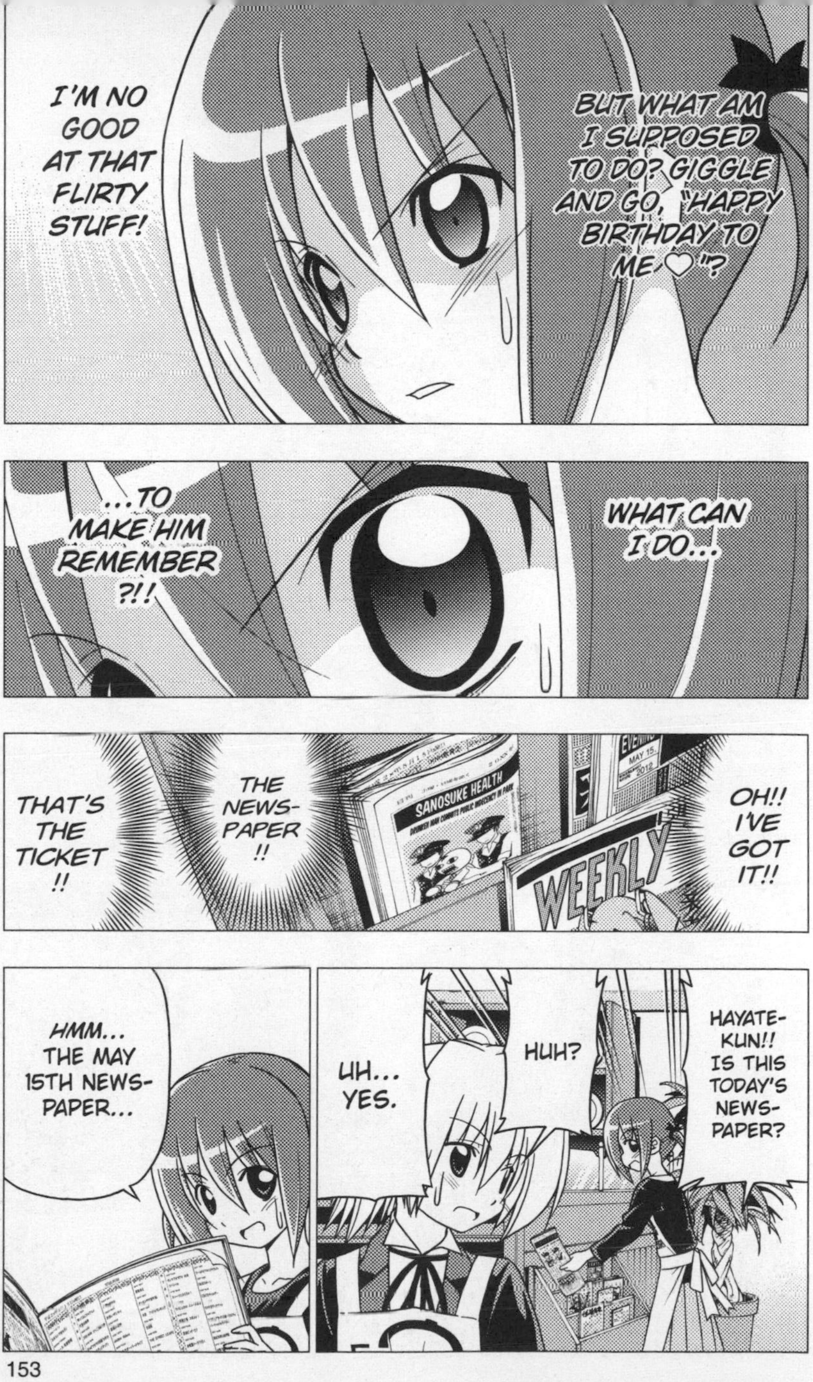
BUT WHAT AM I SUPPOSED TO DO? GIGGLE AND GO, "HAPPY BIRTHDAY TO ME ♡"?
I'M NO GOOD AT THAT FLIRTY STUFF!
WHAT CAN I DO...
...TO MAKE HIM REMEMBER?!!
OH!! I'VE GOT IT!!
MAY 15. 2012
SANOSUKE HEALTH
WEEKLY
THE NEWSPAPER!!
THAT'S THE TICKET!!
HAYATE-KUN!! IS THIS TODAY'S NEWSPAPER?
HUH?
UH... YES.
HMM... THE MAY 15TH NEWSPAPER...

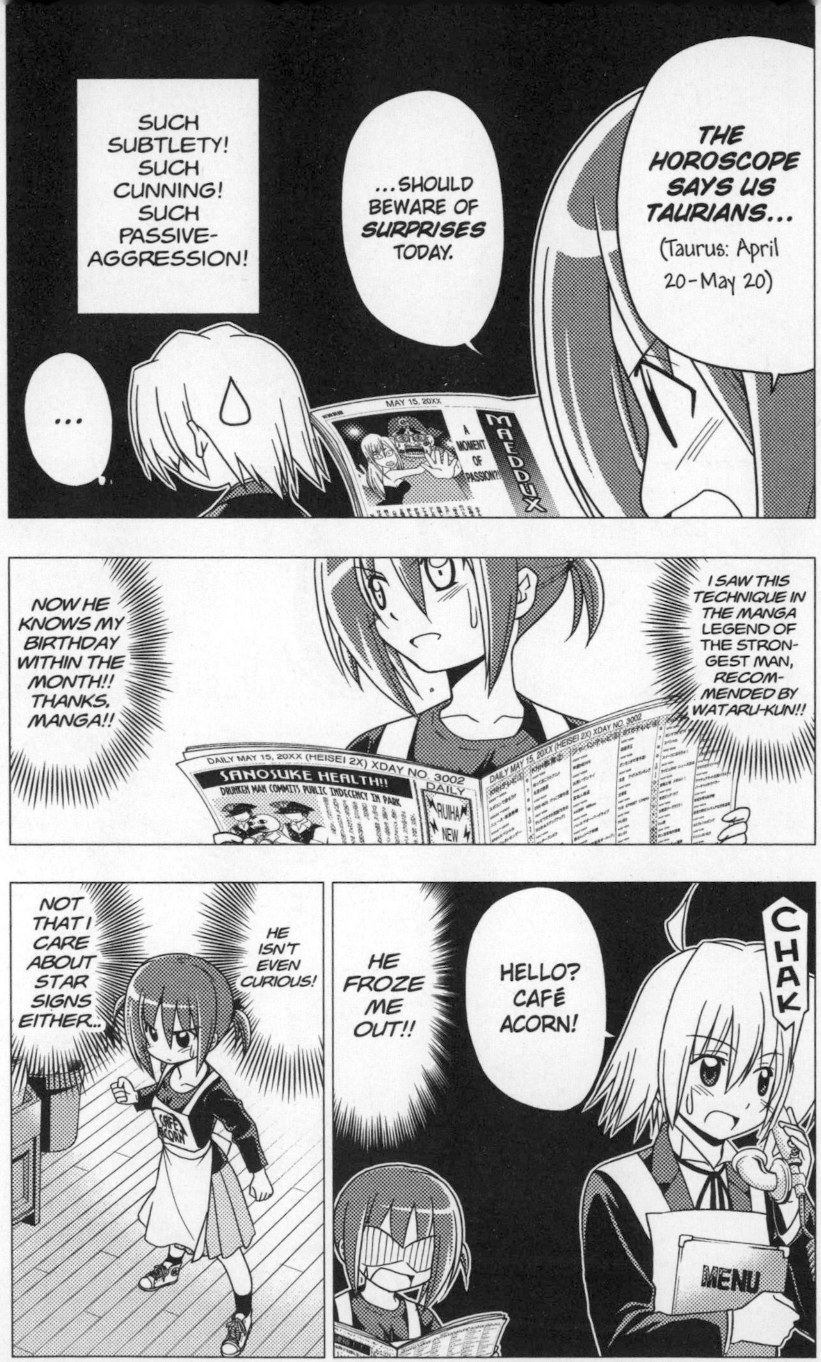
THE HOROSCOPE SAYS US TAURIANS...
(Taurus: April 20-May 20)
...SHOULD BEWARE OF SURPRISES TODAY.
SUCH SUBTLETY! SUCH CUNNING! SUCH PASSIVE-AGGRESSION!
...
MAY 15, 20XX
MAEDDUX
A MOMENT OF PASSION!!
I SAW THIS TECHNIQUE IN THE MANGA LEGEND OF THE STRONGEST MAN, RECOMMENDED BY WATARU-KUN!!
NOW HE KNOWS MY BIRTHDAY WITHIN THE MONTH!! THANKS, MANGA!!
DAILY MAY 15, 20XX (HEISEI 2X) XDAY NO. 3002
SANOSUKE HEALTH!!
DRUNKEN MAN COMMITS PUBLIC INDECENCY IN PARK
DAILY
RUIHA NEW
CHAK
HELLO? CAFÉ ACORN!
HE FROZE ME OUT!!
MENU
HE ISN'T EVEN CURIOUS!
NOT THAT I CARE ABOUT STAR SIGNS EITHER...
CAFE ACORN

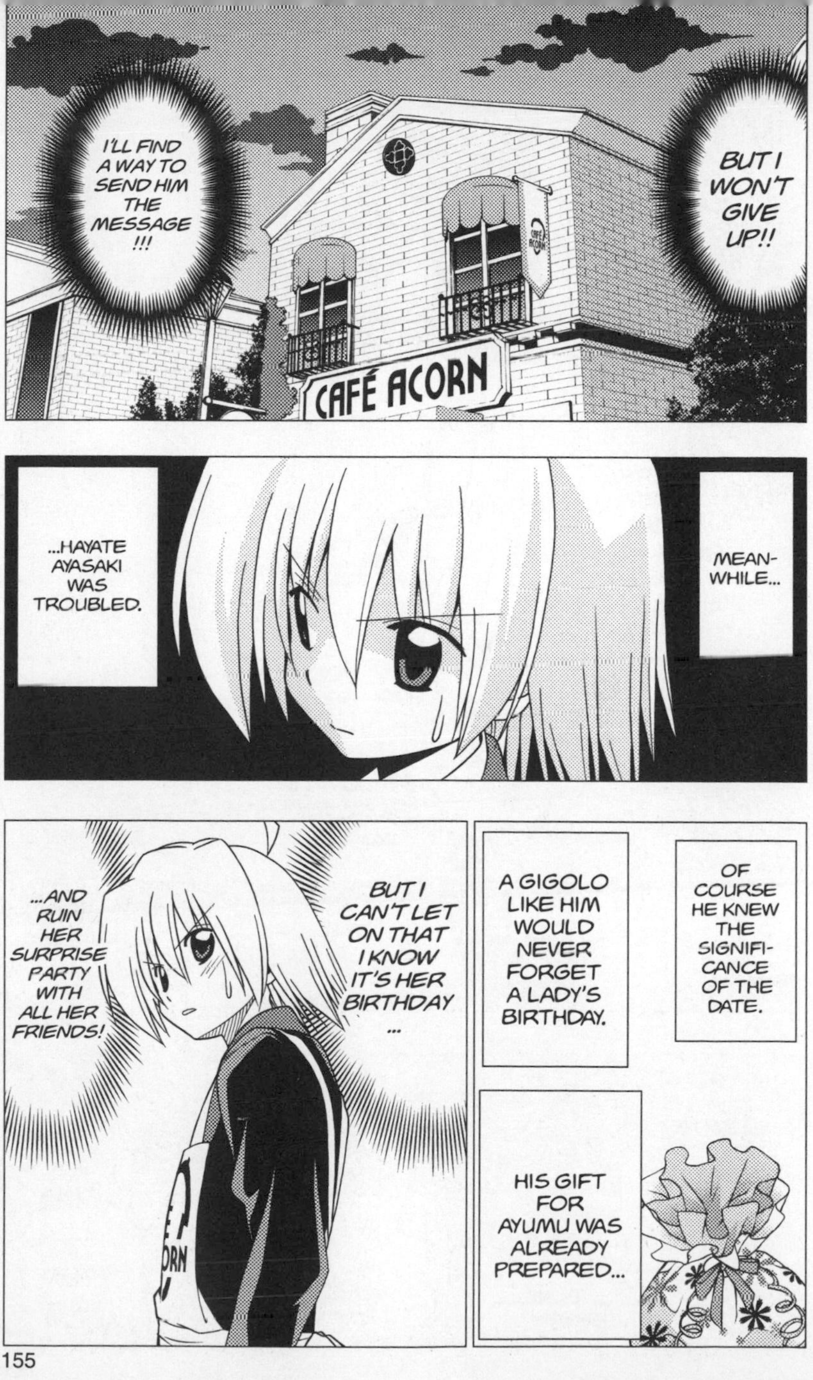
BUT I WON'T GIVE UP!!
I'LL FIND A WAY TO SEND HIM THE MESSAGE!!!
CAFÉ ACORN
MEAN-WHILE...
...HAYATE AYASAKI WAS TROUBLED.
OF COURSE HE KNEW THE SIGNIFI-CANCE OF THE DATE.
A GIGOLO LIKE HIM WOULD NEVER FORGET A LADY'S BIRTHDAY.
HIS GIFT FOR AYUMU WAS ALREADY PREPARED...
BUT I CAN'T LET ON THAT I KNOW IT'S HER BIRTHDAY...
...AND RUIN HER SURPRISE PARTY WITH ALL HER FRIENDS!

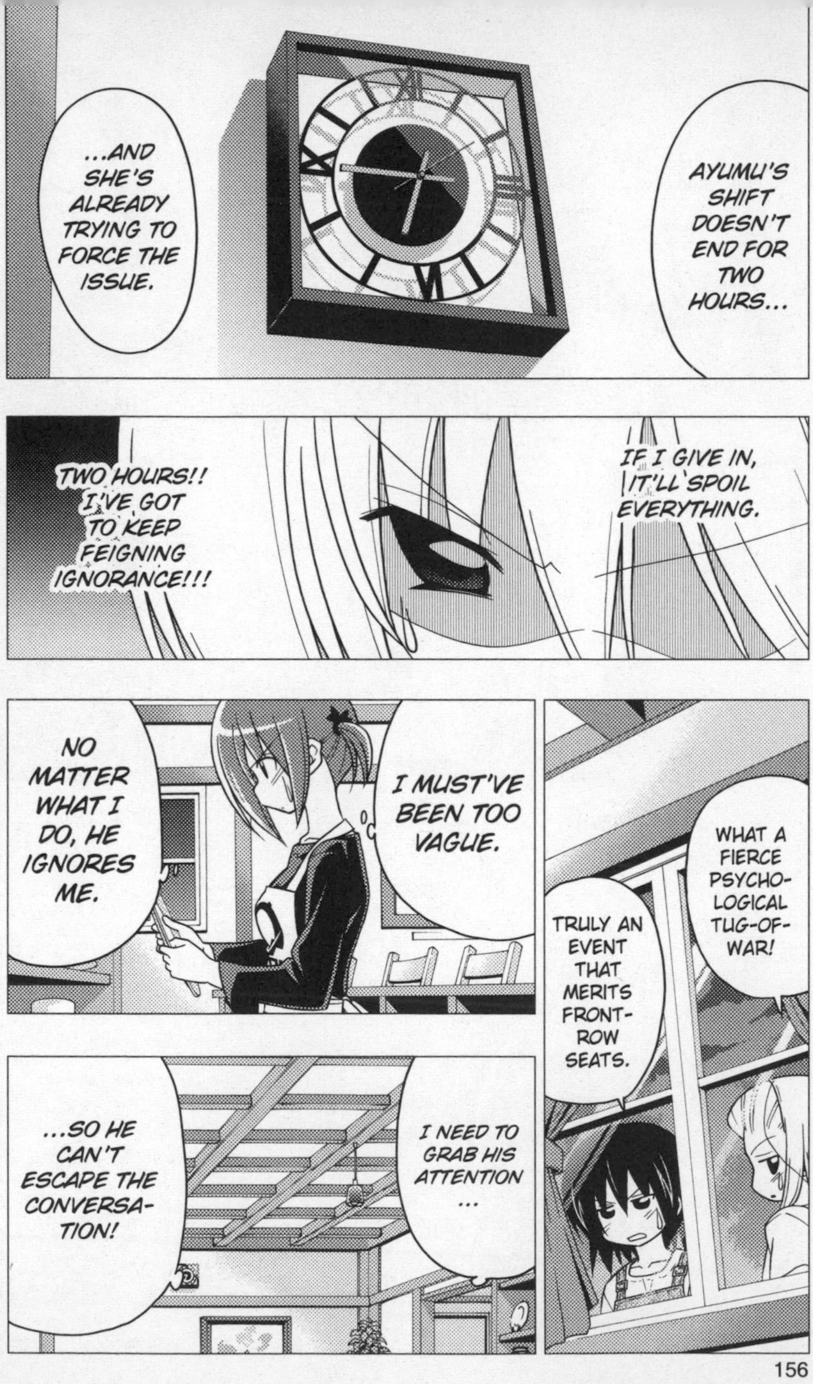
AYUMU'S SHIFT DOESN'T END FOR TWO HOURS...
...AND SHE'S ALREADY TRYING TO FORCE THE ISSUE.
IF I GIVE IN, IT'LL SPOIL EVERYTHING.
TWO HOURS!! I'VE GOT TO KEEP FEIGNING IGNORANCE!!!
WHAT A FIERCE PSYCHOLOGICAL TUG-OF-WAR!
TRULY AN EVENT THAT MERITS FRONT-ROW SEATS.
I MUST'VE BEEN TOO VAGUE.
NO MATTER WHAT I DO, HE IGNORES ME.
I NEED TO GRAB HIS ATTENTION...
...SO HE CAN'T ESCAPE THE CONVERSATION!

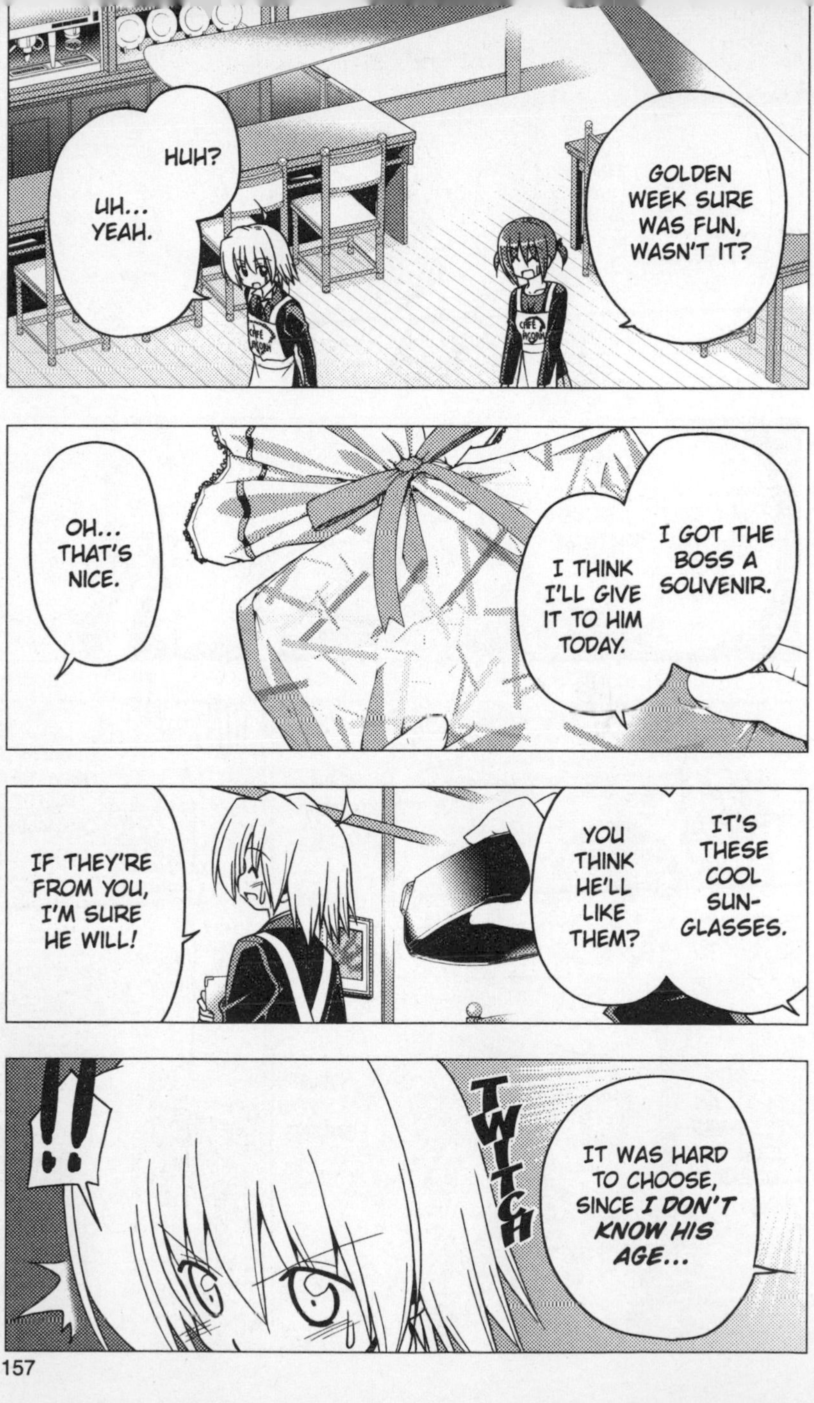
GOLDEN WEEK SURE WAS FUN, WASN'T IT?
HUH?
UH... YEAH.
I GOT THE BOSS A SOUVENIR.
I THINK I'LL GIVE IT TO HIM TODAY.
OH... THAT'S NICE.
IT'S THESE COOL SUN-GLASSES.
YOU THINK HE'LL LIKE THEM?
IF THEY'RE FROM YOU, I'M SURE HE WILL!
IT WAS HARD TO CHOOSE, SINCE *I DON'T KNOW HIS AGE...*
TWITCH
!!

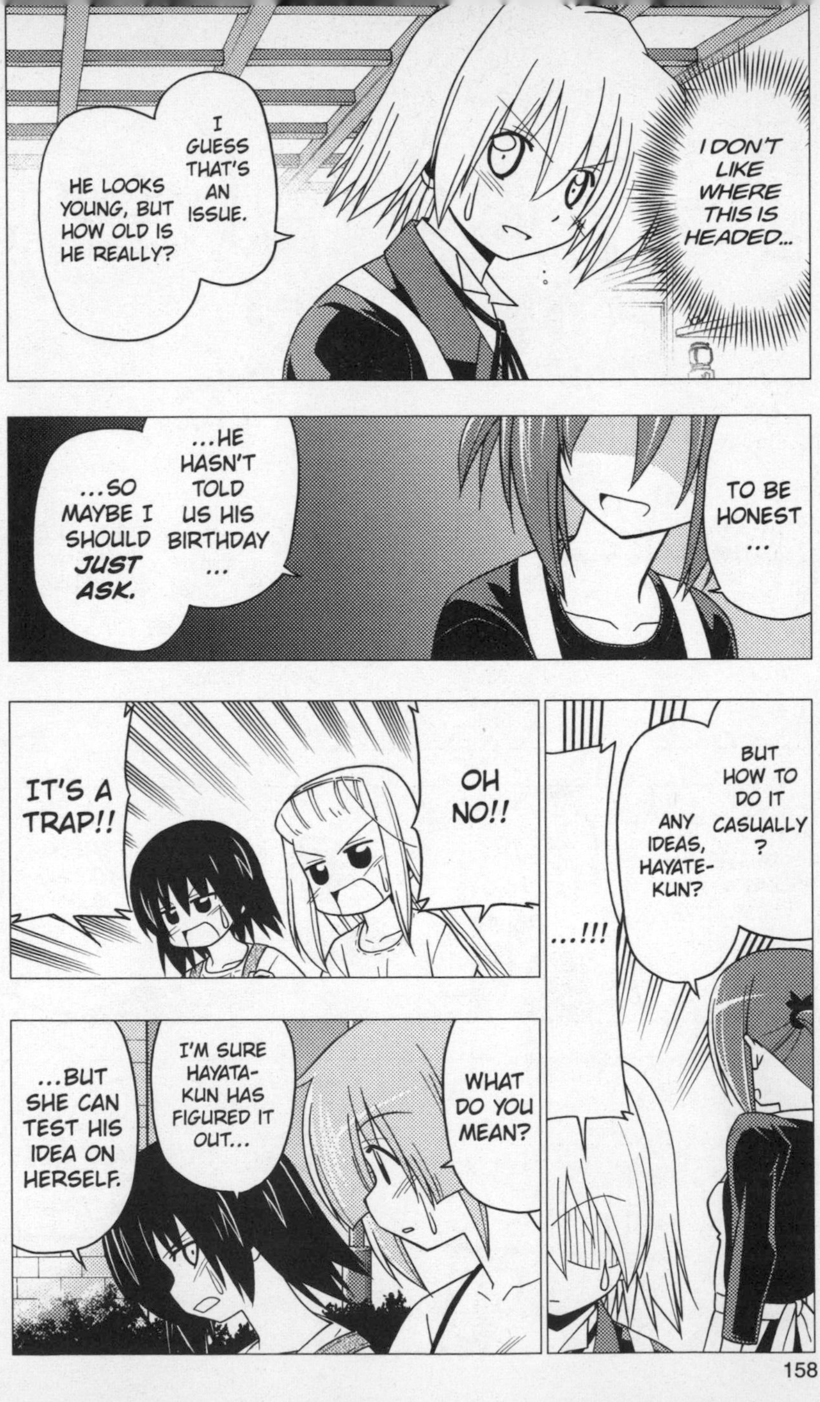
I DON'T LIKE WHERE THIS IS HEADED...
I GUESS THAT'S AN ISSUE.
HE LOOKS YOUNG, BUT HOW OLD IS HE REALLY?
TO BE HONEST...
...HE HASN'T TOLD US HIS BIRTHDAY...
...SO MAYBE I SHOULD JUST ASK.
BUT HOW TO DO IT CASUALLY?
ANY IDEAS, HAYATE-KUN?
...!!!
OH NO!!
IT'S A TRAP!!
WHAT DO YOU MEAN?
I'M SURE HAYATA-KUN HAS FIGURED IT OUT...
...BUT SHE CAN TEST HIS IDEA ON HERSELF.

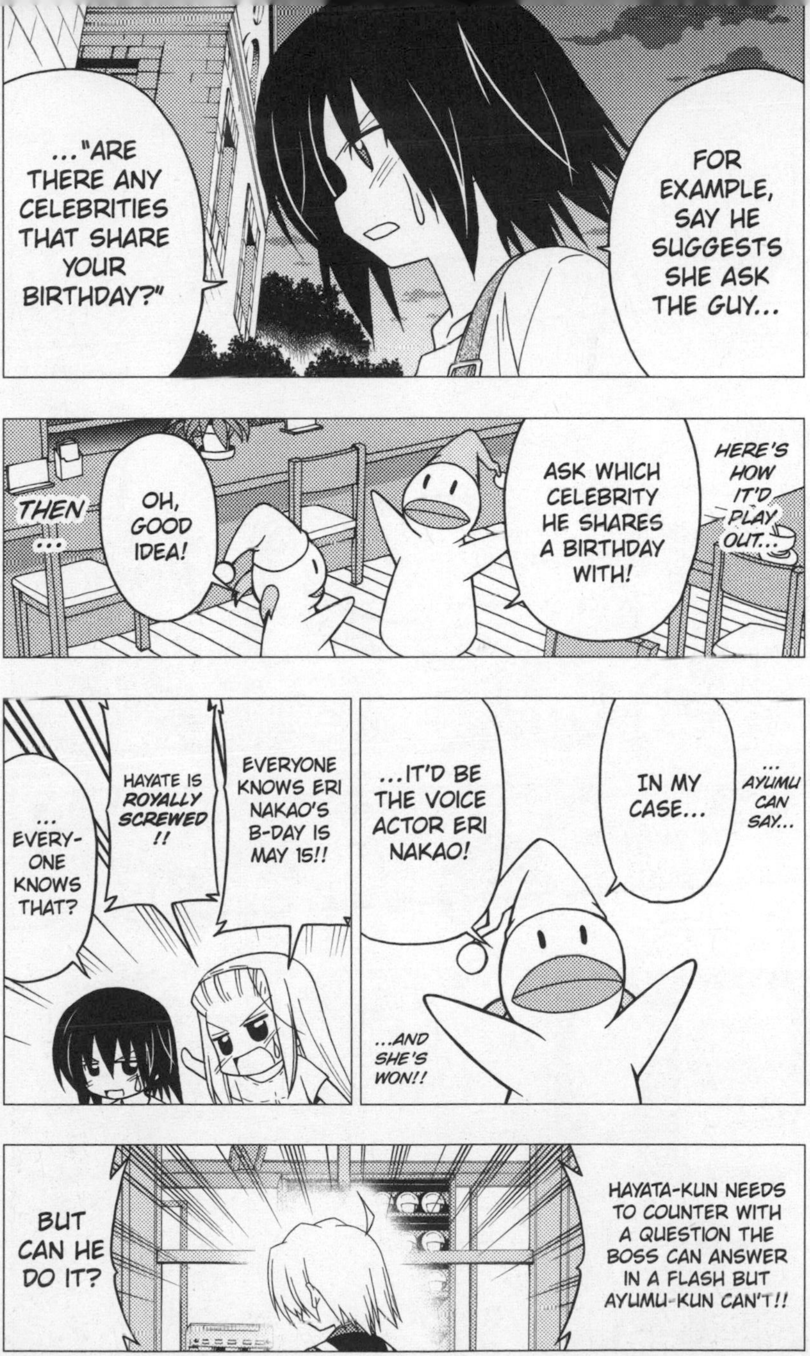
FOR EXAMPLE, SAY HE SUGGESTS SHE ASK THE GUY...
..."ARE THERE ANY CELEBRITIES THAT SHARE YOUR BIRTHDAY?"
HERE'S HOW IT'D PLAY OUT...
ASK WHICH CELEBRITY HE SHARES A BIRTHDAY WITH!
OH, GOOD IDEA!
THEN...
...AYUMU CAN SAY...
IN MY CASE...
...IT'D BE THE VOICE ACTOR ERI NAKAO!
...AND SHE'S WON!!
EVERYONE KNOWS ERI NAKAO'S B-DAY IS MAY 15!!
HAYATE IS ROYALLY SCREWED!!
...EVERY-ONE KNOWS THAT?
HAYATA-KUN NEEDS TO COUNTER WITH A QUESTION THE BOSS CAN ANSWER IN A FLASH BUT AYUMU-KUN CAN'T!!
BUT CAN HE DO IT?

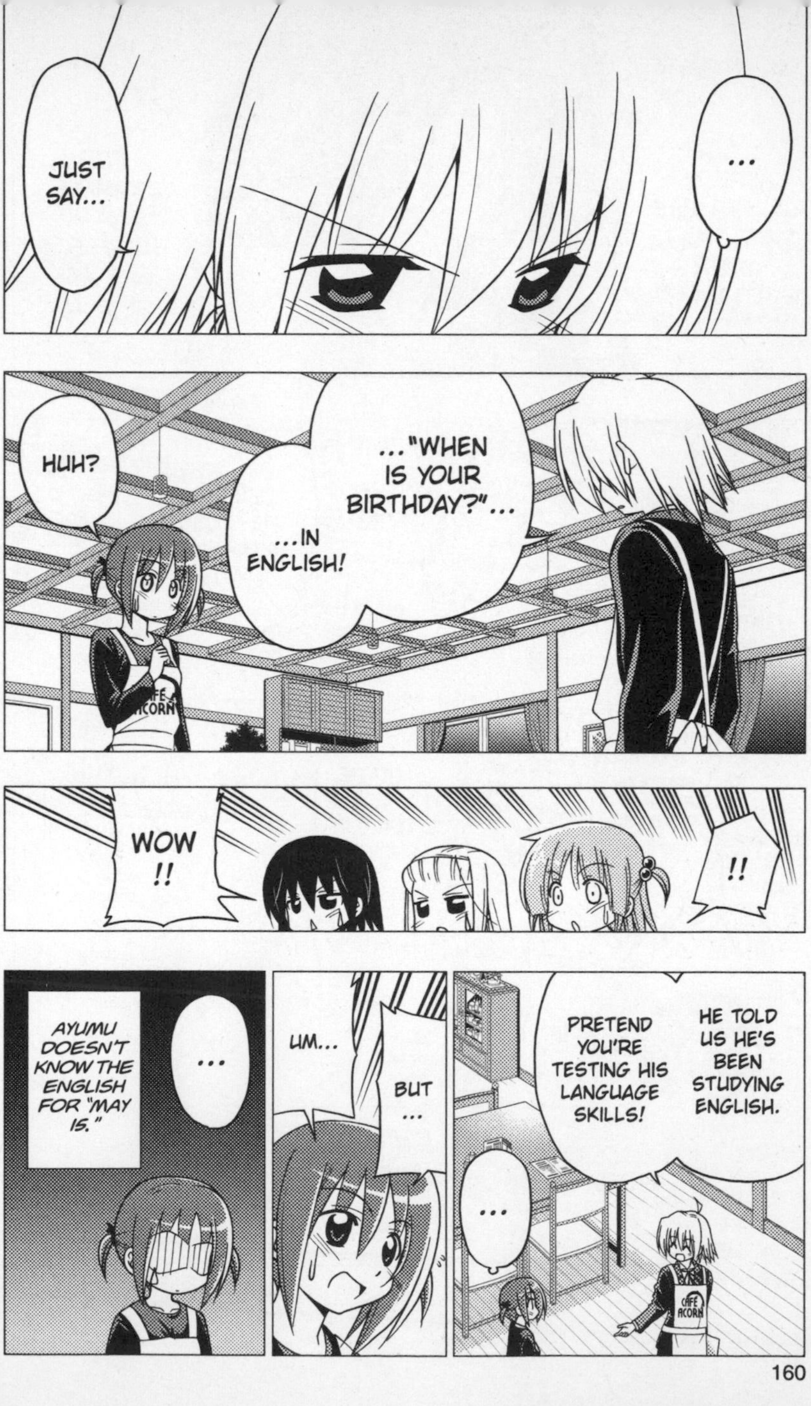
...
JUST SAY...
..."WHEN IS YOUR BIRTHDAY?"...
...IN ENGLISH!
HUH?
!!
WOW !!
HE TOLD US HE'S BEEN STUDYING ENGLISH.
PRETEND YOU'RE TESTING HIS LANGUAGE SKILLS!
...
UM...
BUT ...
...
AYUMU DOESN'T KNOW THE ENGLISH FOR "MAY IS."

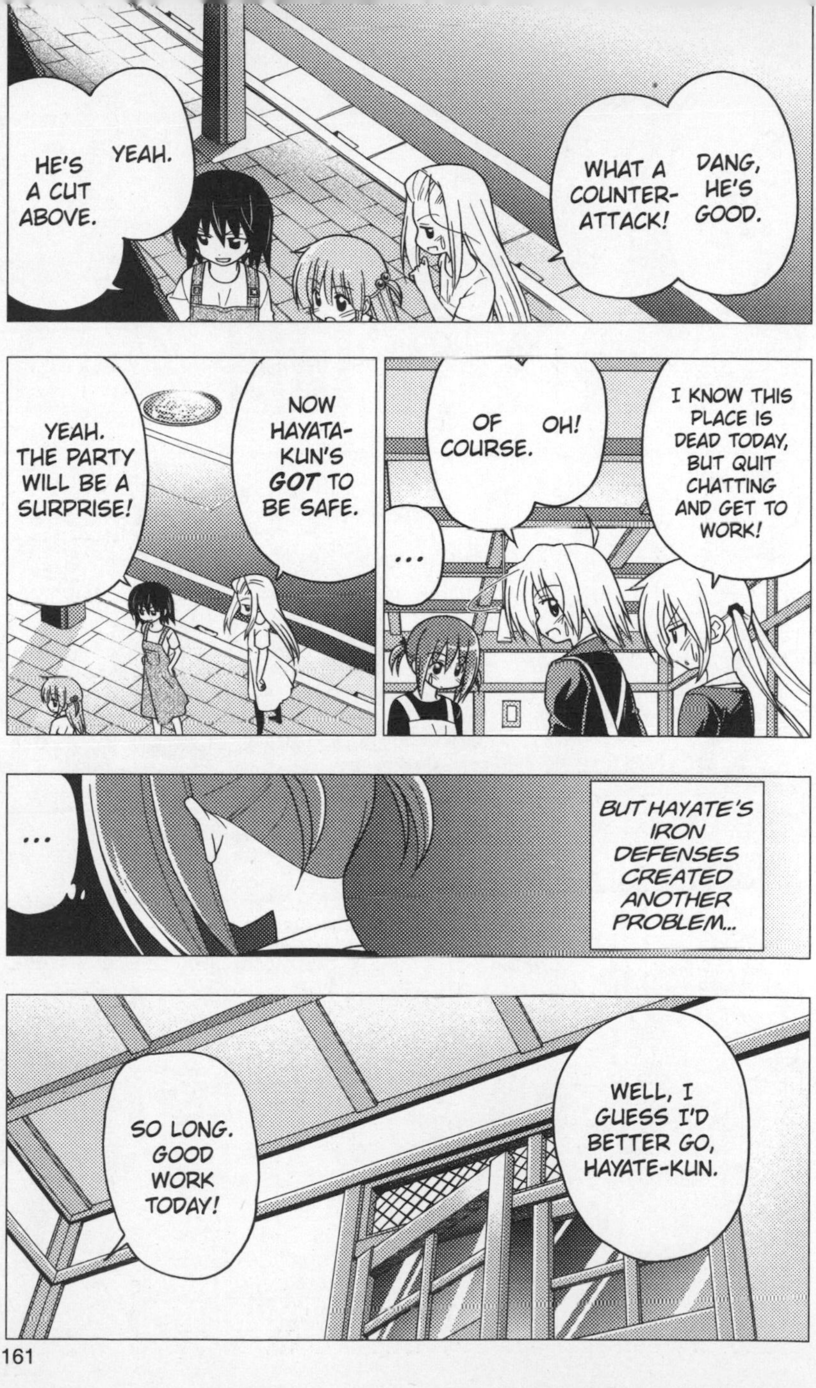
DANG, HE'S GOOD.
WHAT A COUNTER-ATTACK!
YEAH.
HE'S A CUT ABOVE.
I KNOW THIS PLACE IS DEAD TODAY, BUT QUIT CHATTING AND GET TO WORK!
OH!
OF COURSE.
...
NOW HAYATA-KUN'S *GOT* TO BE SAFE.
YEAH. THE PARTY WILL BE A SURPRISE!
BUT HAYATE'S IRON DEFENSES CREATED ANOTHER PROBLEM...
...
WELL, I GUESS I'D BETTER GO, HAYATE-KUN.
SO LONG. GOOD WORK TODAY!

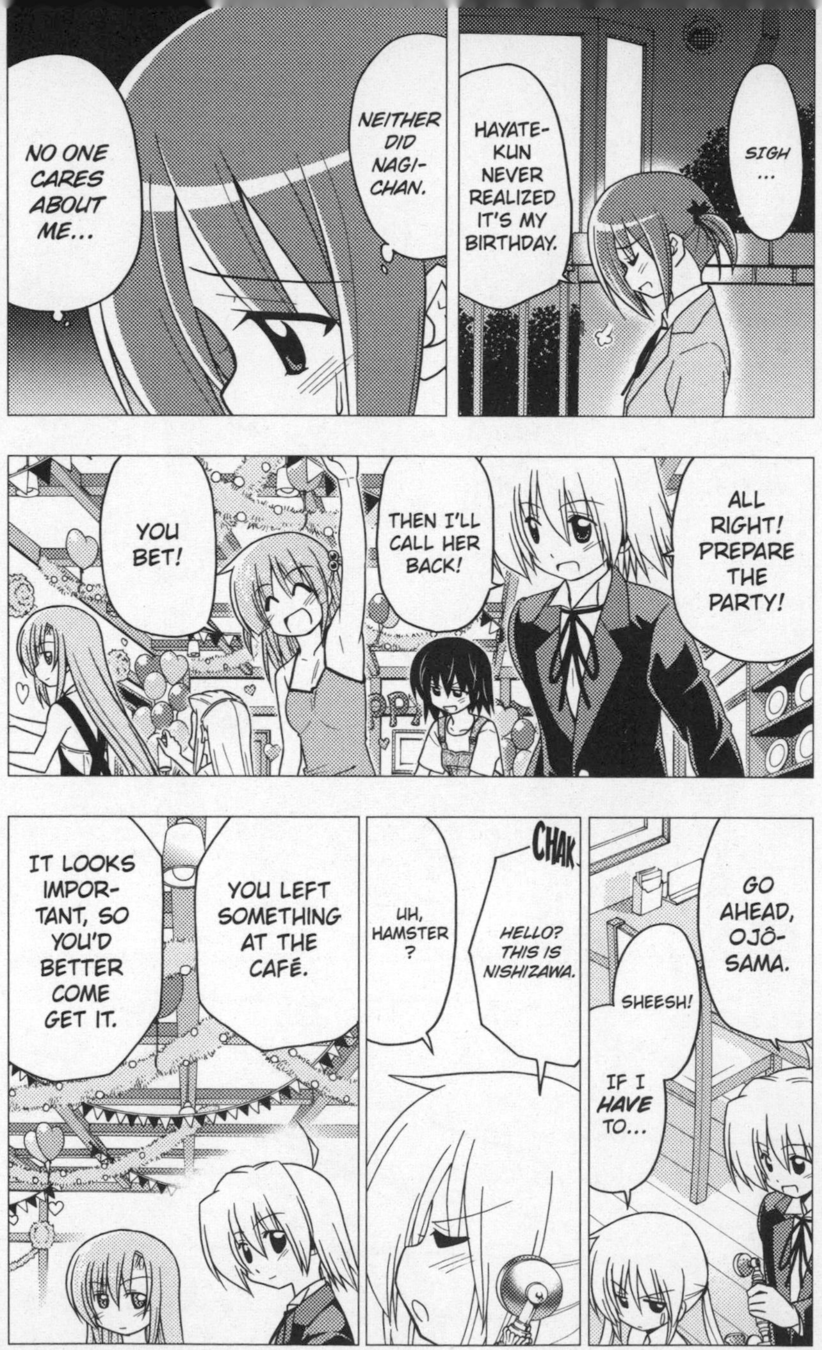
SIGH...
HAYATE-KUN NEVER REALIZED IT'S MY BIRTHDAY.
NEITHER DID NAGI-CHAN.
NO ONE CARES ABOUT ME...
ALL RIGHT! PREPARE THE PARTY!
THEN I'LL CALL HER BACK!
YOU BET!
GO AHEAD, OJÔ-SAMA.
SHEESH!
IF I *HAVE* TO...
CHAK
HELLO? THIS IS NISHIZAWA.
UH, HAMSTER?
YOU LEFT SOMETHING AT THE CAFÉ.
IT LOOKS IMPOR-TANT, SO YOU'D BETTER COME GET IT.

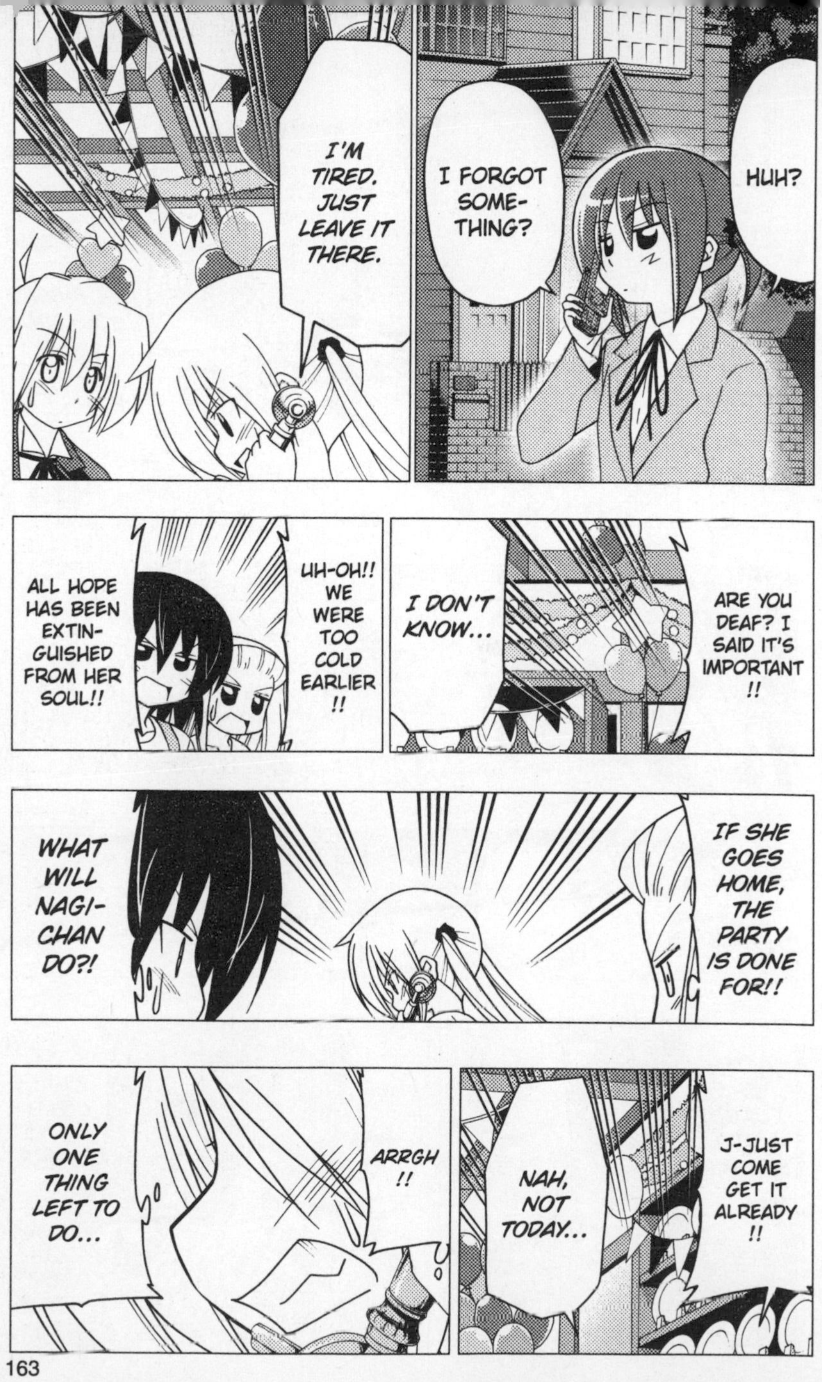
HUH?
I FORGOT SOME-THING?
I'M TIRED. JUST LEAVE IT THERE.
ARE YOU DEAF? I SAID IT'S IMPORTANT!!
I DON'T KNOW...
UH-OH!! WE WERE TOO COLD EARLIER!!
ALL HOPE HAS BEEN EXTIN-GUISHED FROM HER SOUL!!
IF SHE GOES HOME, THE PARTY IS DONE FOR!!
WHAT WILL NAGI-CHAN DO?!
J-JUST COME GET IT ALREADY!!
NAH, NOT TODAY...
ARRGH!!
ONLY ONE THING LEFT TO DO...

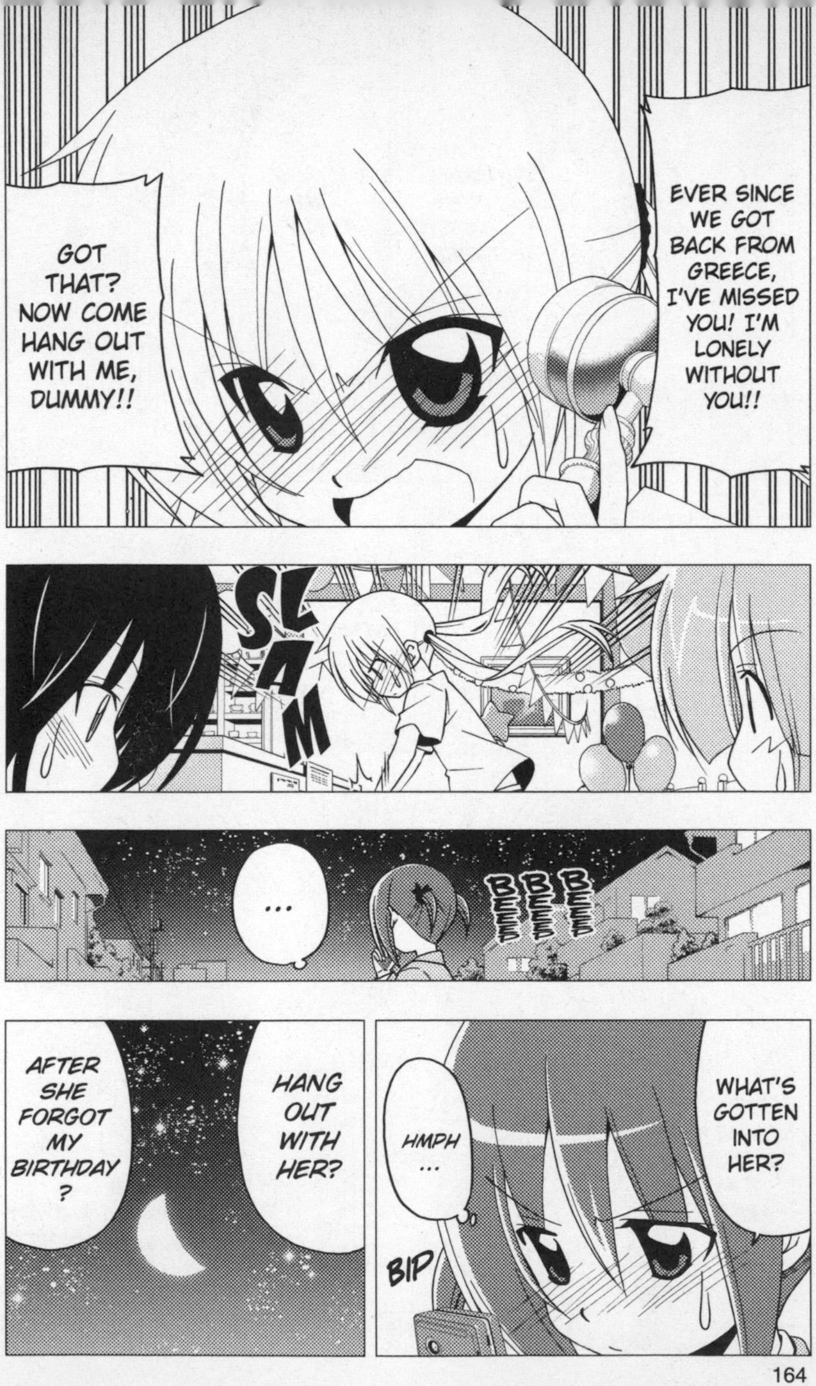
EVER SINCE WE GOT BACK FROM GREECE, I'VE MISSED YOU! I'M LONELY WITHOUT YOU!!
GOT THAT? NOW COME HANG OUT WITH ME, DUMMY!!
SLAM
BEEP
BEEP
BEEP
...
WHAT'S GOTTEN INTO HER?
HMPH ...
BIP
HANG OUT WITH HER?
AFTER SHE FORGOT MY BIRTHDAY ?

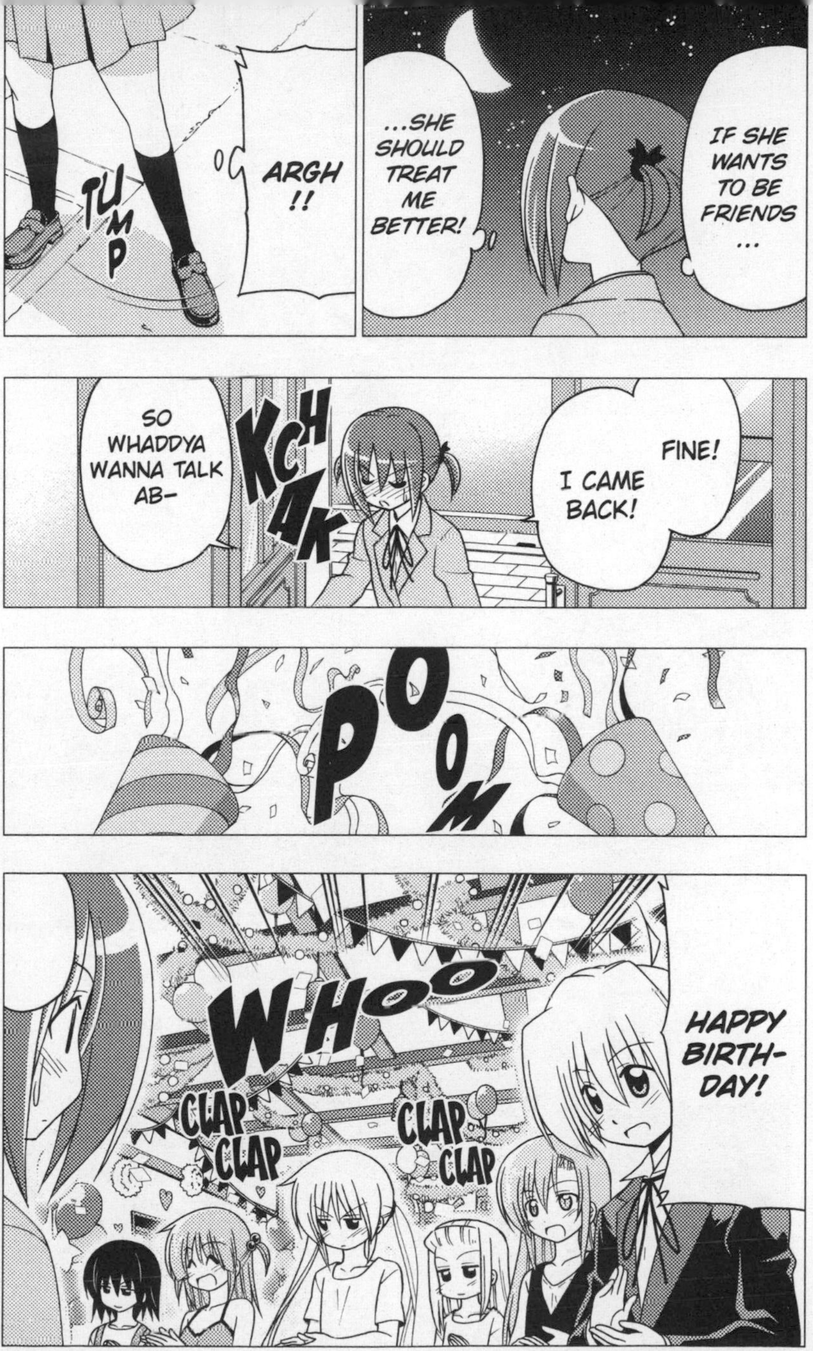
IF SHE WANTS TO BE FRIENDS ...
...SHE SHOULD TREAT ME BETTER!
ARGH !!
TUMP
FINE! I CAME BACK!
KCHAK
SO WHADDYA WANNA TALK AB-
POOM
HAPPY BIRTHDAY!
WHOOO
CLAP CLAP
CLAP CLAP

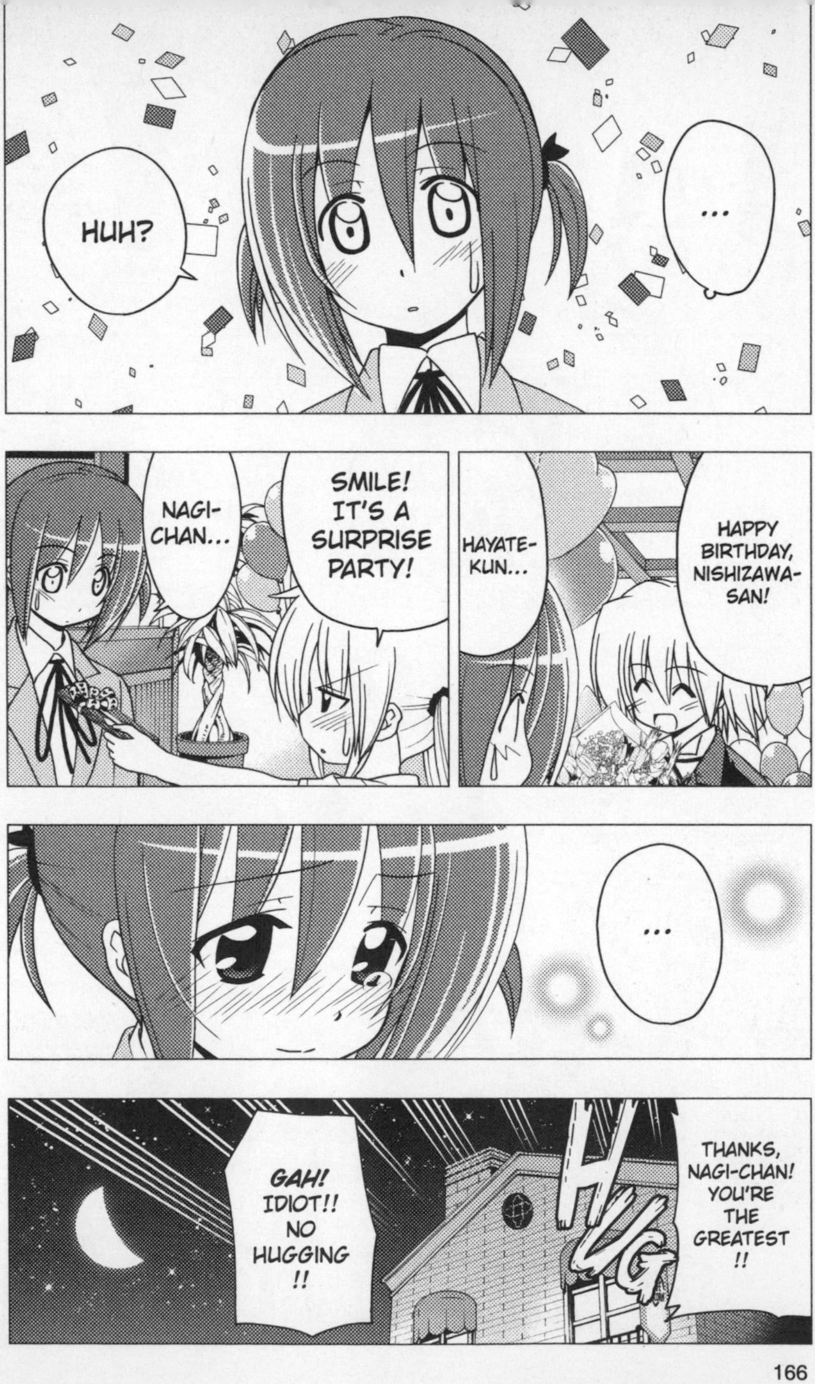
...
HUH?
HAPPY BIRTHDAY, NISHIZAWA-SAN!
HAYATE-KUN...
SMILE! IT'S A SURPRISE PARTY!
NAGI-CHAN...
...
THANKS, NAGI-CHAN! YOU'RE THE GREATEST!!
HUG
GAH! IDIOT!! NO HUGGING!!

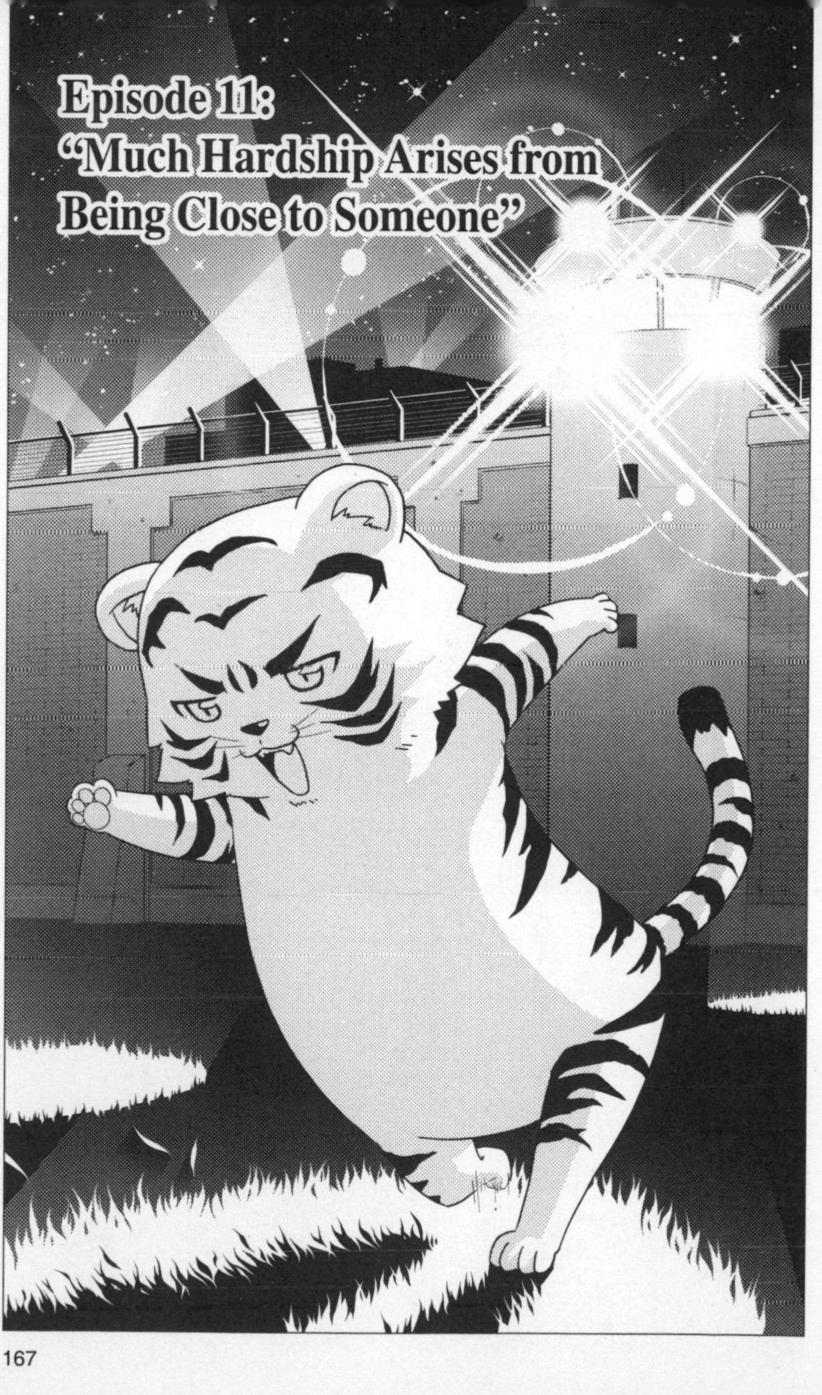
Episode 11:
"Much Hardship Arises from Being Close to Someone"

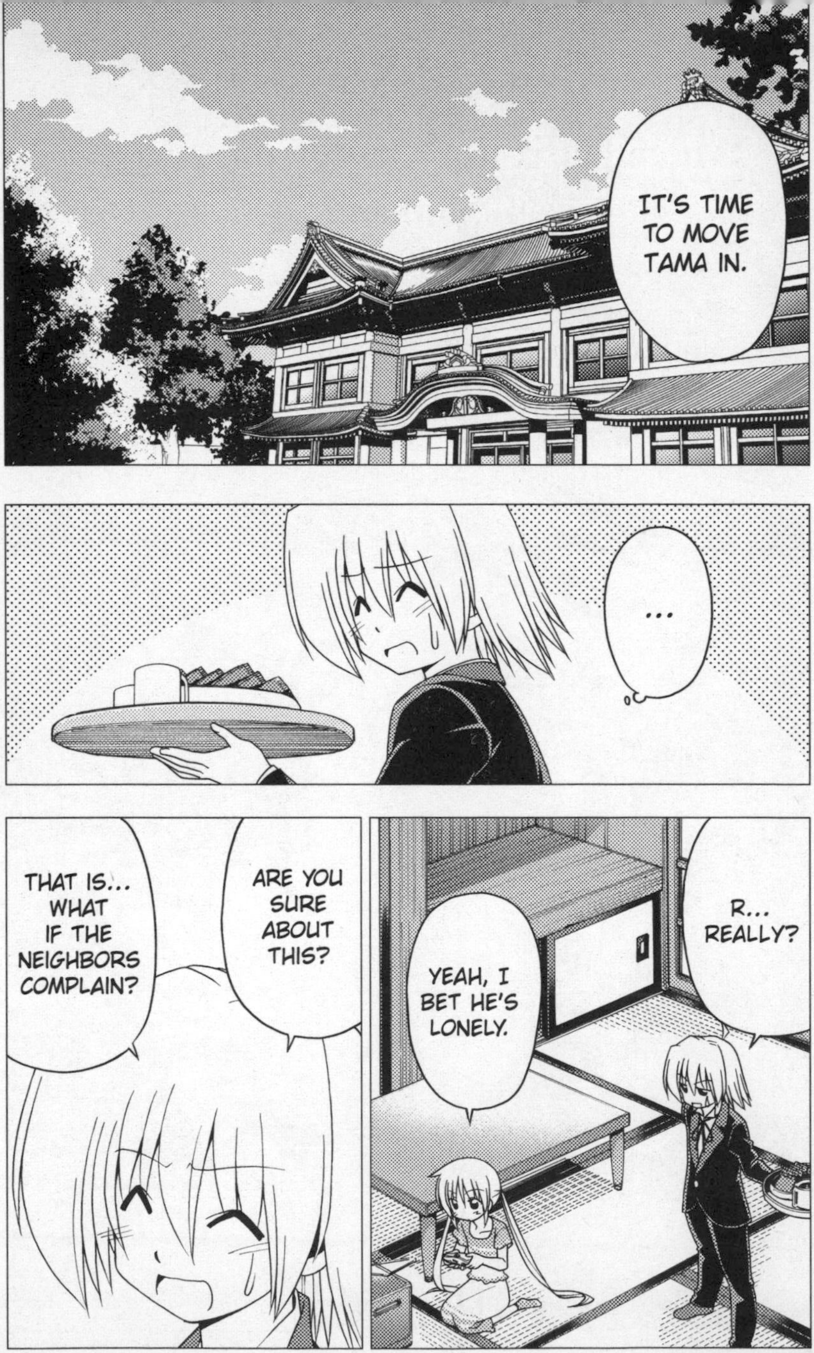
IT'S TIME TO MOVE TAMA IN.
...
R... REALLY?
YEAH, I BET HE'S LONELY.
ARE YOU SURE ABOUT THIS?
THAT IS... WHAT IF THE NEIGHBORS COMPLAIN?

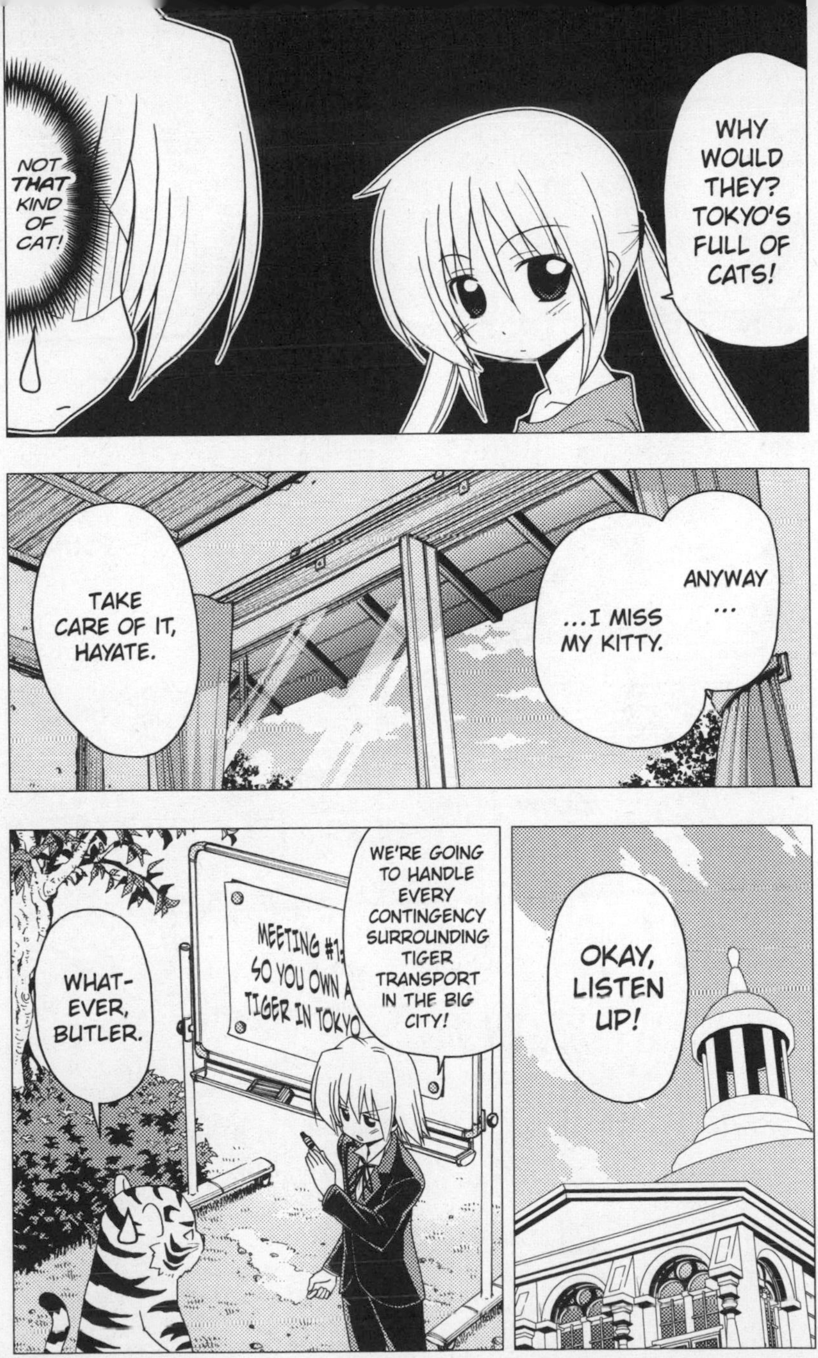
WHY WOULD THEY? TOKYO'S FULL OF CATS!
NOT THAT KIND OF CAT!
ANYWAY ...
...I MISS MY KITTY.
TAKE CARE OF IT, HAYATE.
OKAY, LISTEN UP!
WE'RE GOING TO HANDLE EVERY CONTINGENCY SURROUNDING TIGER TRANSPORT IN THE BIG CITY!
MEETING #1
SO YOU OWN
TIGER IN TOKYO
WHAT-EVER, BUTLER.

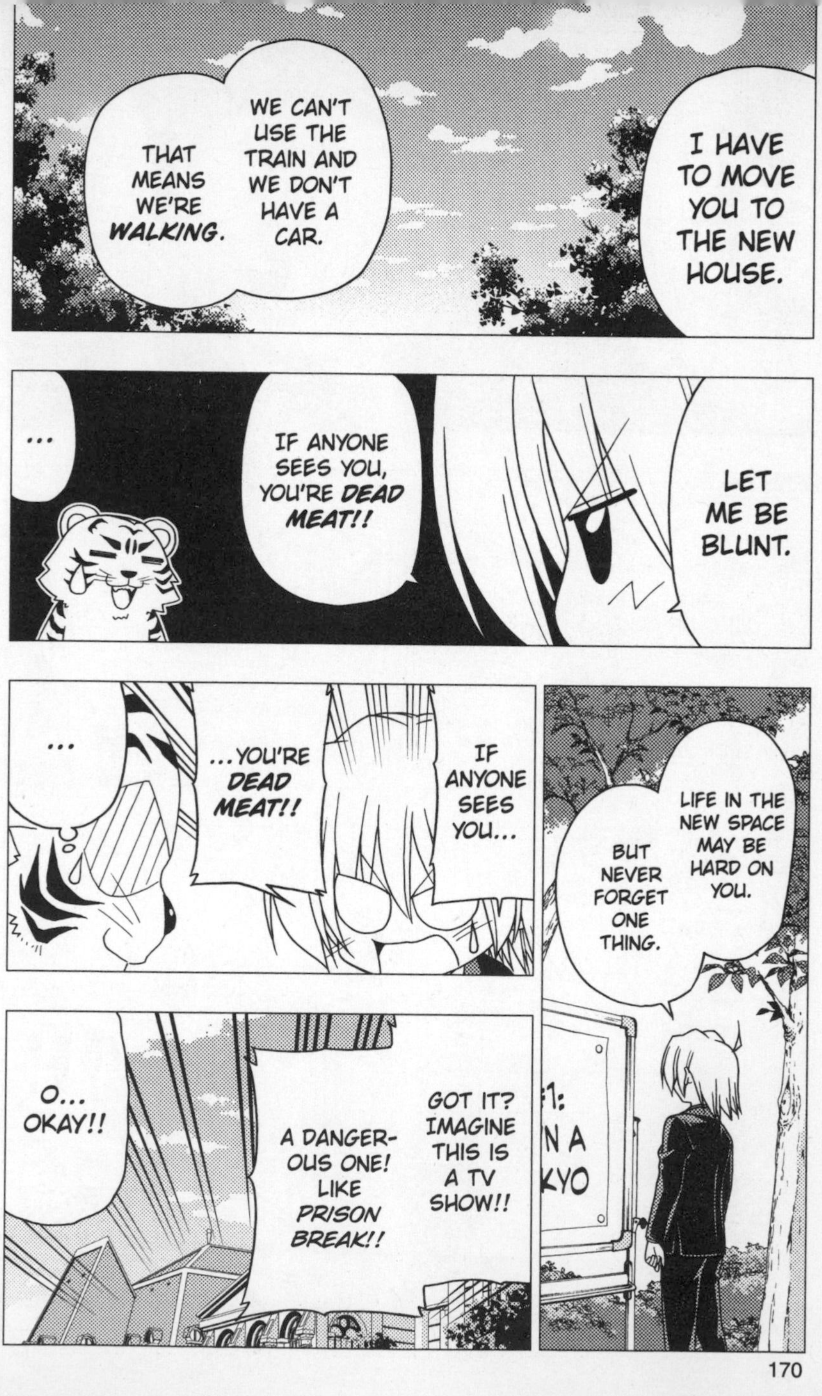

I HAVE TO MOVE YOU TO THE NEW HOUSE.
WE CAN'T USE THE TRAIN AND WE DON'T HAVE A CAR.
THAT MEANS WE'RE *WALKING*.
LET ME BE BLUNT.
IF ANYONE SEES YOU, YOU'RE *DEAD MEAT!!*
...
LIFE IN THE NEW SPACE MAY BE HARD ON YOU.
BUT NEVER FORGET ONE THING.
IF ANYONE SEES YOU...
...YOU'RE *DEAD MEAT!!*
...
GOT IT? IMAGINE THIS IS A TV SHOW!!
A DANGER-OUS ONE! LIKE *PRISON BREAK!!*
O... OKAY!!

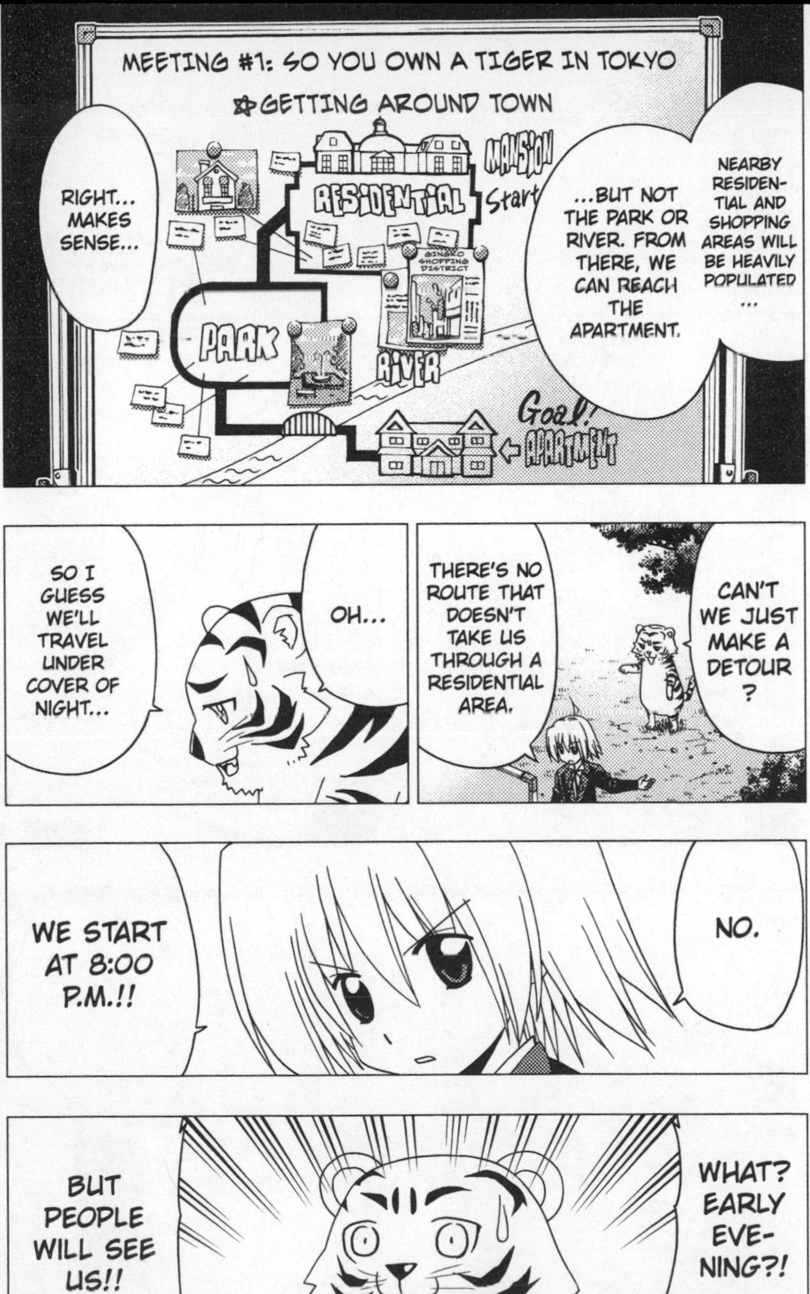
MEETING #1: SO YOU OWN A TIGER IN TOKYO
✲GETTING AROUND TOWN
MANSION
Start
RESIDENTIAL
GINGKO SHOPPING DISTRICT
PARK
RIVER
Goal!
APARTMENT
NEARBY RESIDENTIAL AND SHOPPING AREAS WILL BE HEAVILY POPULATED...
...BUT NOT THE PARK OR RIVER. FROM THERE, WE CAN REACH THE APARTMENT.
RIGHT... MAKES SENSE...
CAN'T WE JUST MAKE A DETOUR?
THERE'S NO ROUTE THAT DOESN'T TAKE US THROUGH A RESIDENTIAL AREA.
OH...
SO I GUESS WE'LL TRAVEL UNDER COVER OF NIGHT...
NO.
WE START AT 8:00 P.M.!!
WHAT? EARLY EVENING?!
BUT PEOPLE WILL SEE US!!

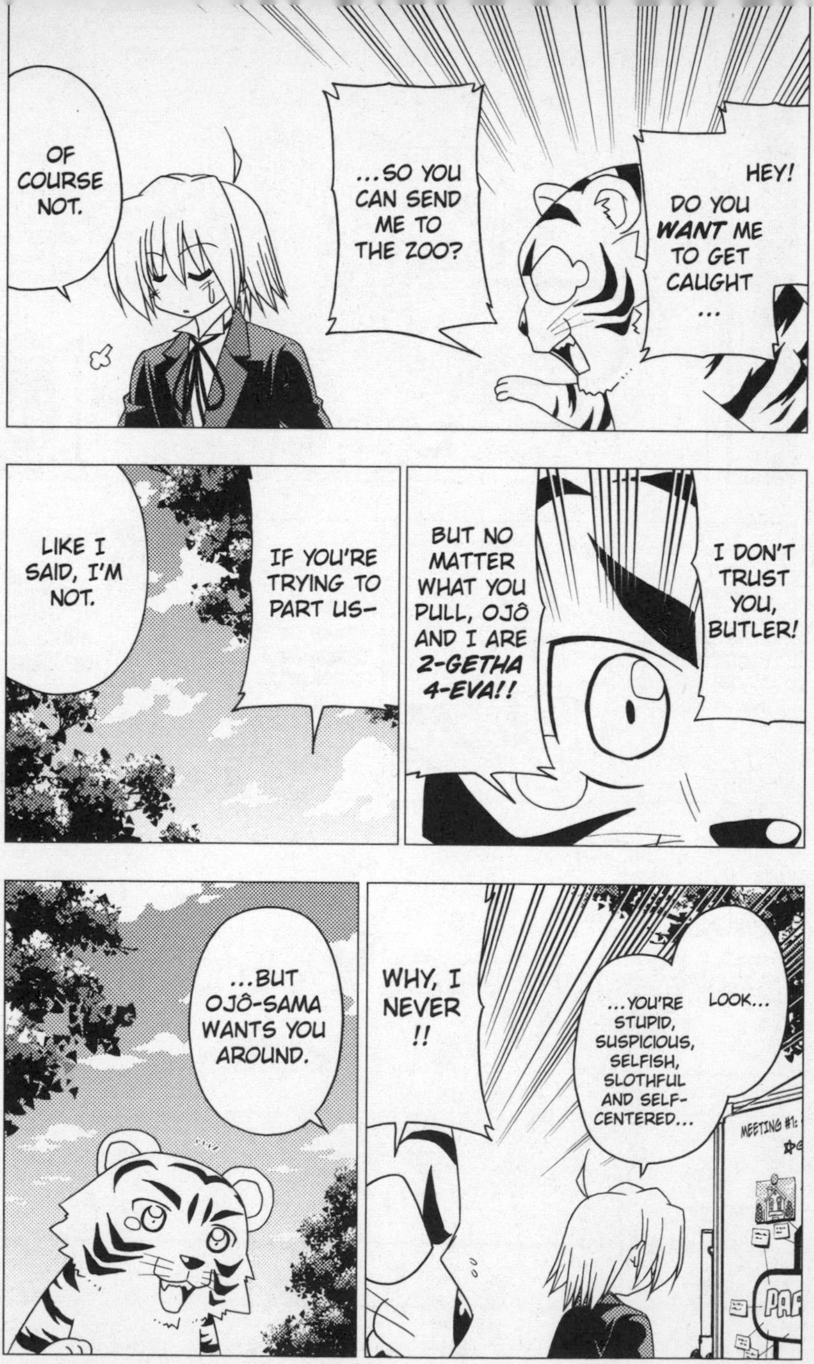
HEY! DO YOU WANT ME TO GET CAUGHT...
...SO YOU CAN SEND ME TO THE ZOO?
OF COURSE NOT.
I DON'T TRUST YOU, BUTLER!
BUT NO MATTER WHAT YOU PULL, OJÔ AND I ARE 2-GETHA 4-EVA!!
IF YOU'RE TRYING TO PART US—
LIKE I SAID, I'M NOT.
LOOK...
...YOU'RE STUPID, SUSPICIOUS, SELFISH, SLOTHFUL AND SELF-CENTERED...
MEETING #1:
WHY, I NEVER!!
...BUT OJÔ-SAMA WANTS YOU AROUND.

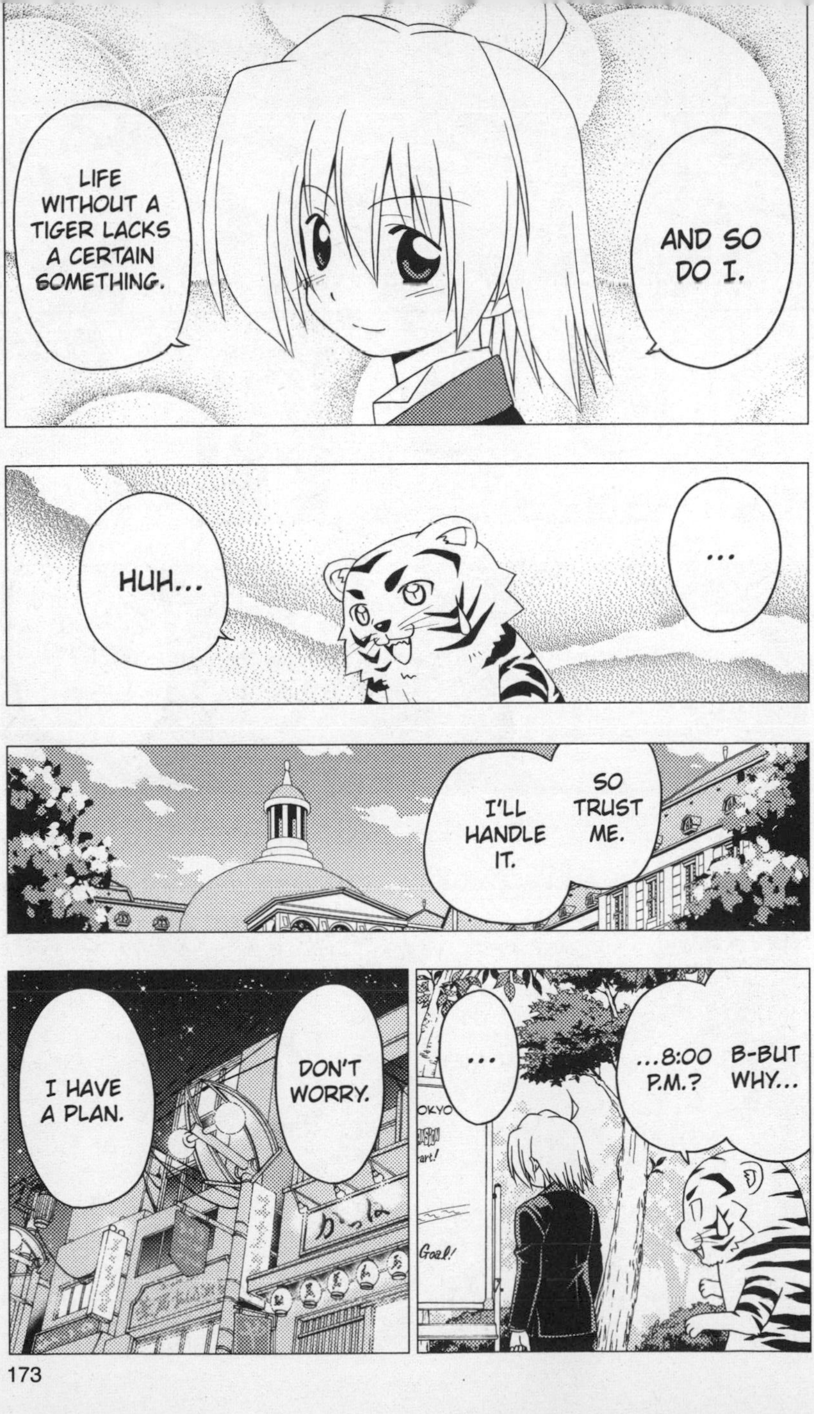
AND SO DO I.
LIFE WITHOUT A TIGER LACKS A CERTAIN SOMETHING.
...
HUH...
SO TRUST ME.
I'LL HANDLE IT.
B-BUT WHY...
...8:00 P.M.?
...
Goal!
DON'T WORRY.
I HAVE A PLAN.

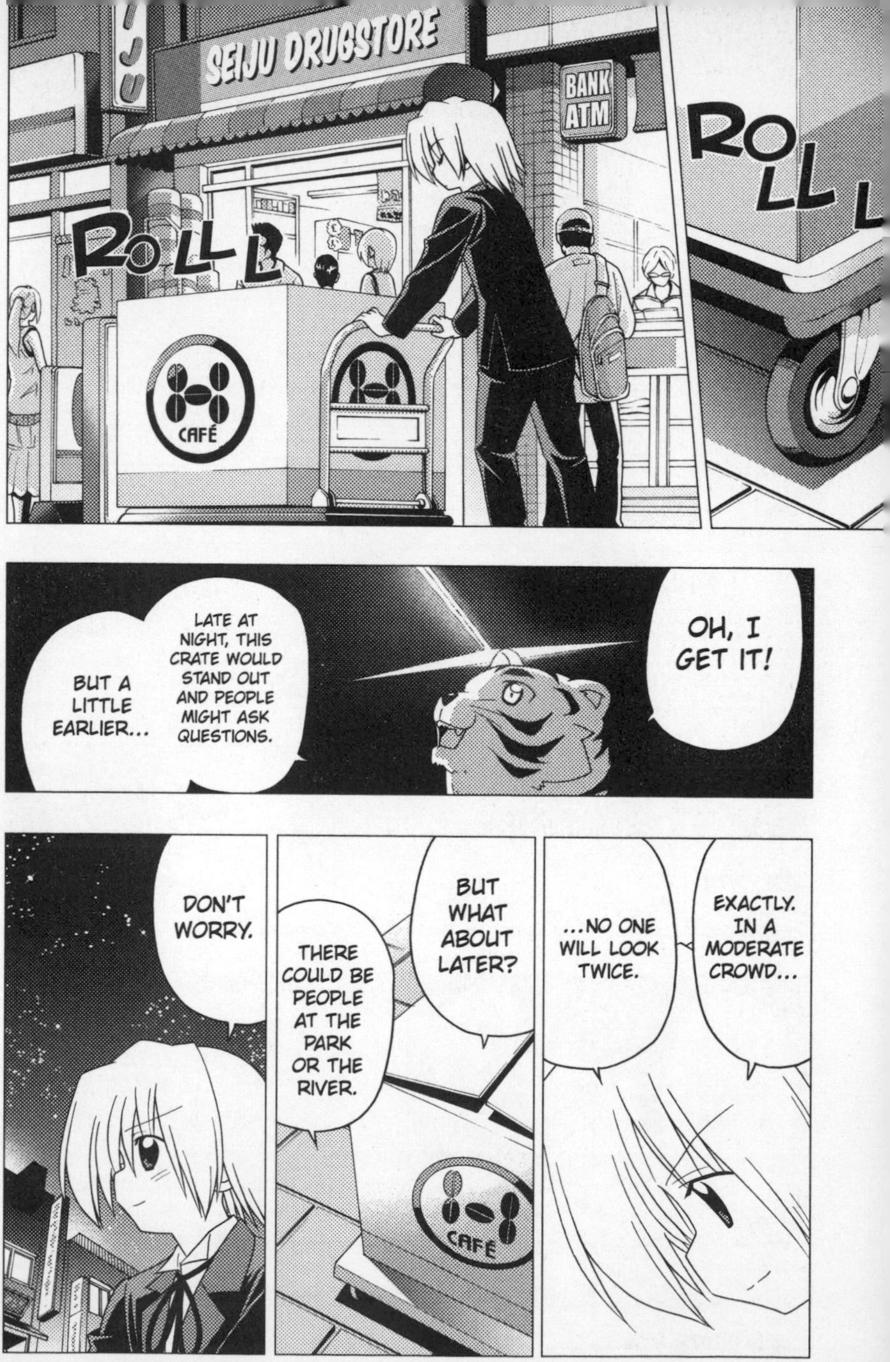
ROLLL
SEIJU DRUGSTORE
BANK ATM
ROLLL
CAFÉ
OH, I GET IT!
LATE AT NIGHT, THIS CRATE WOULD STAND OUT AND PEOPLE MIGHT ASK QUESTIONS.
BUT A LITTLE EARLIER...
EXACTLY. IN A MODERATE CROWD...
...NO ONE WILL LOOK TWICE.
BUT WHAT ABOUT LATER?
THERE COULD BE PEOPLE AT THE PARK OR THE RIVER.
CAFÉ
DON'T WORRY.

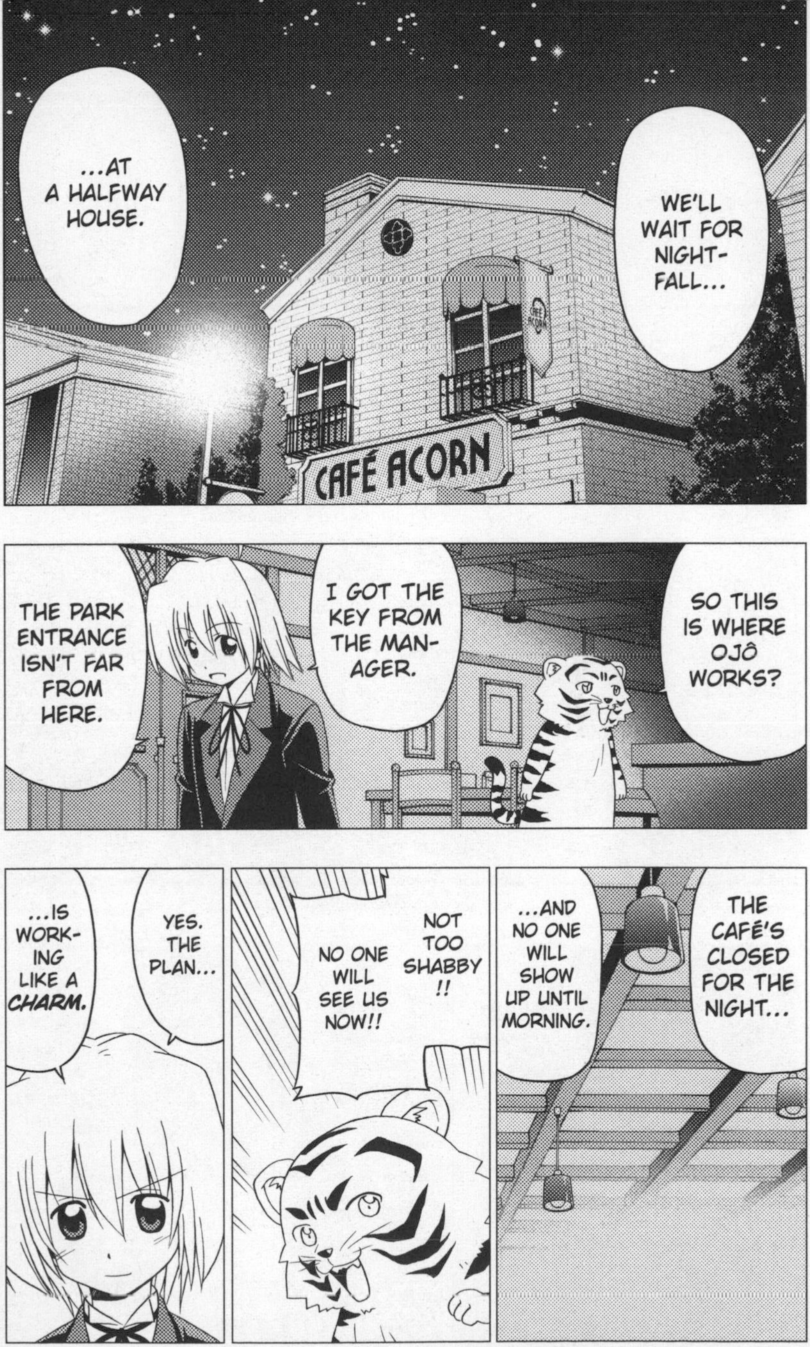
WE'LL WAIT FOR NIGHT-FALL...
...AT A HALFWAY HOUSE.
CAFÉ ACORN
SO THIS IS WHERE OJÔ WORKS?
I GOT THE KEY FROM THE MAN-AGER.
THE PARK ENTRANCE ISN'T FAR FROM HERE.
THE CAFÉ'S CLOSED FOR THE NIGHT...
...AND NO ONE WILL SHOW UP UNTIL MORNING.
NOT TOO SHABBY!!
NO ONE WILL SEE US NOW!!
YES. THE PLAN...
...IS WORKING LIKE A ***CHARM***.

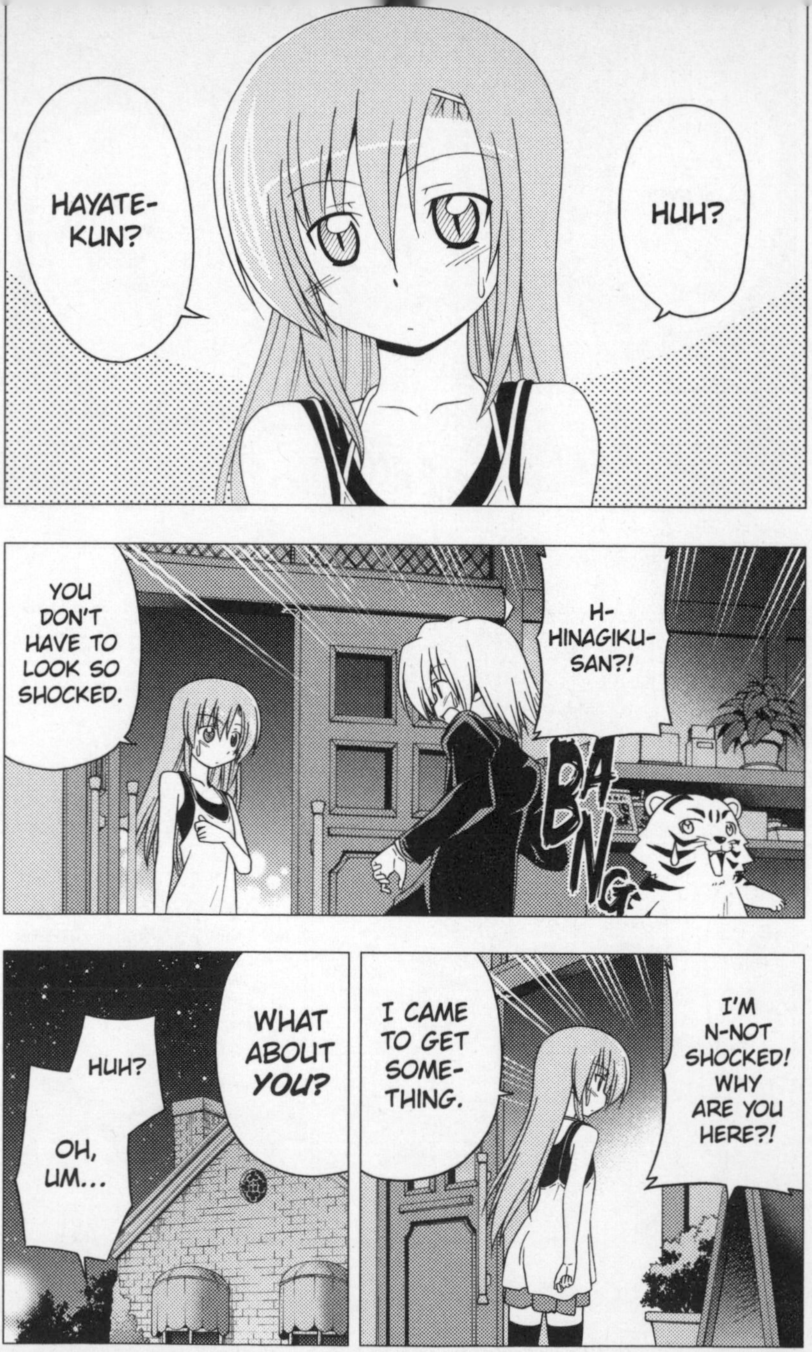
HUH?
HAYATE-KUN?
H-HINAGIKU-SAN?!
BANG
YOU DON'T HAVE TO LOOK SO SHOCKED.
I'M N-NOT SHOCKED! WHY ARE YOU HERE?!
I CAME TO GET SOMETHING.
WHAT ABOUT *YOU*?
HUH?
OH, UM...

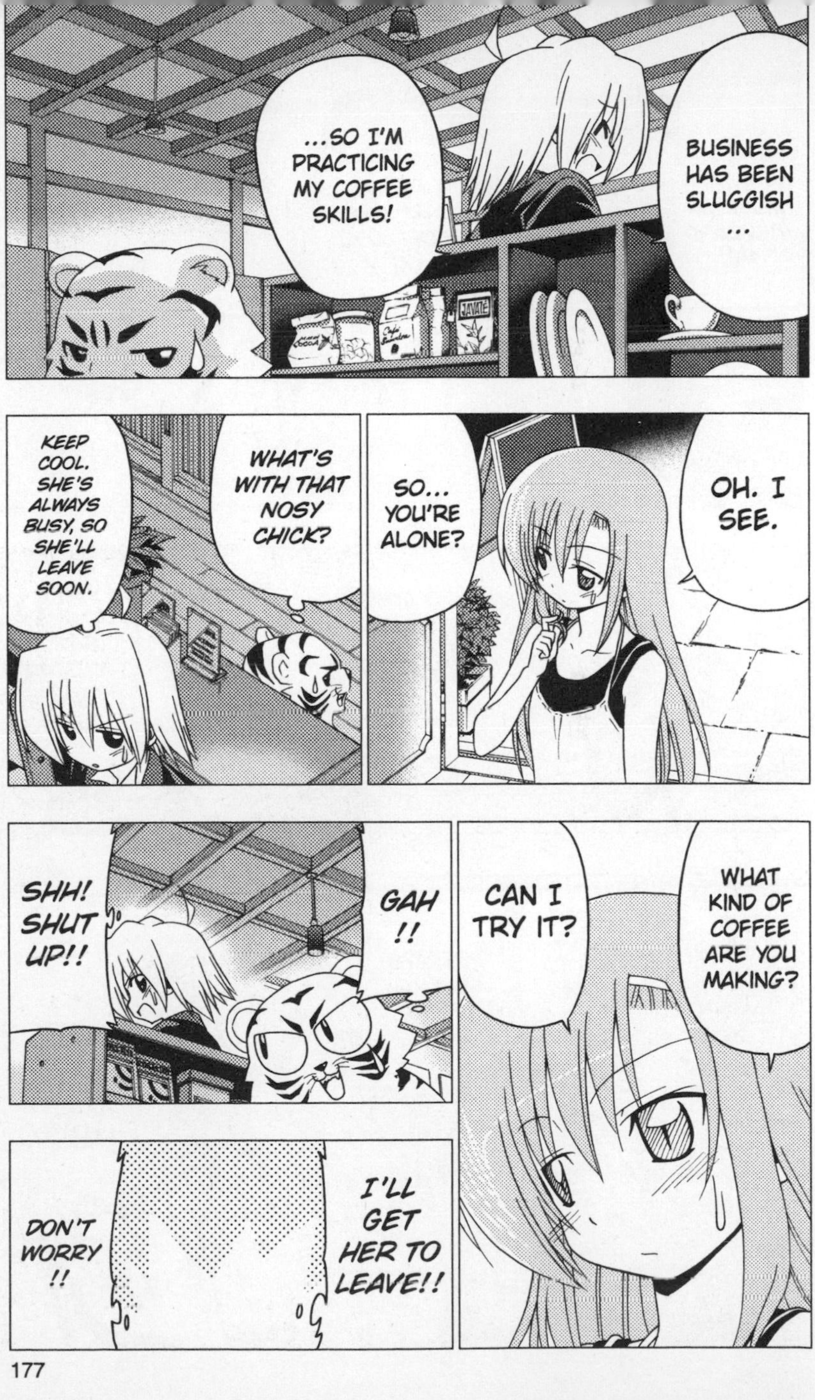
BUSINESS HAS BEEN SLUGGISH ...
...SO I'M PRACTICING MY COFFEE SKILLS!
JAVATE
OH. I SEE.
SO... YOU'RE ALONE?
WHAT'S WITH THAT NOSY CHICK?
KEEP COOL. SHE'S ALWAYS BUSY, SO SHE'LL LEAVE SOON.
WHAT KIND OF COFFEE ARE YOU MAKING?
CAN I TRY IT?
GAH !!
SHH! SHUT UP!!
I'LL GET HER TO LEAVE!!
DON'T WORRY !!

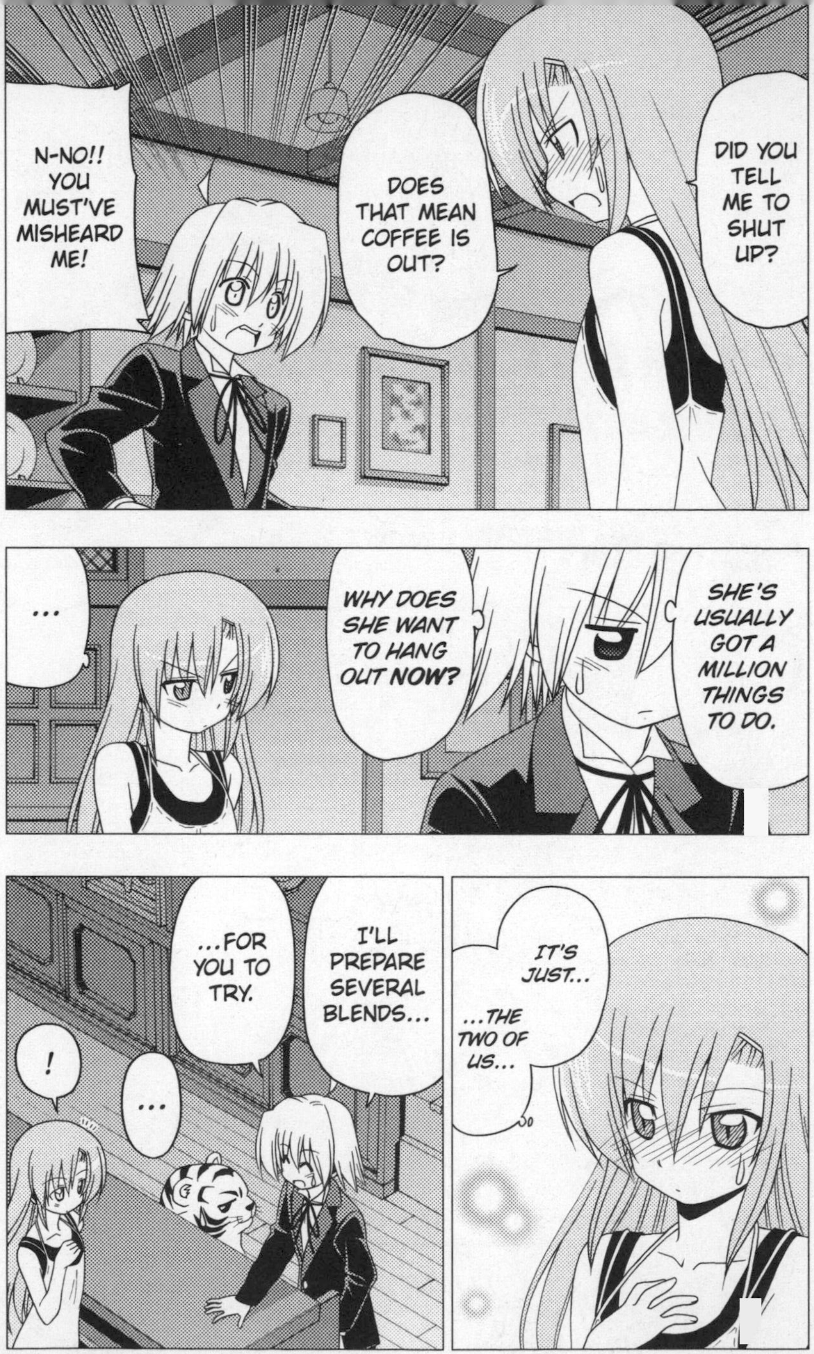
DID YOU TELL ME TO SHUT UP?
DOES THAT MEAN COFFEE IS OUT?
N-NO!! YOU MUST'VE MISHEARD ME!
SHE'S USUALLY GOT A MILLION THINGS TO DO.
WHY DOES SHE WANT TO HANG OUT NOW?
...
IT'S JUST...
...THE TWO OF US...
I'LL PREPARE SEVERAL BLENDS...
...FOR YOU TO TRY.
...
!

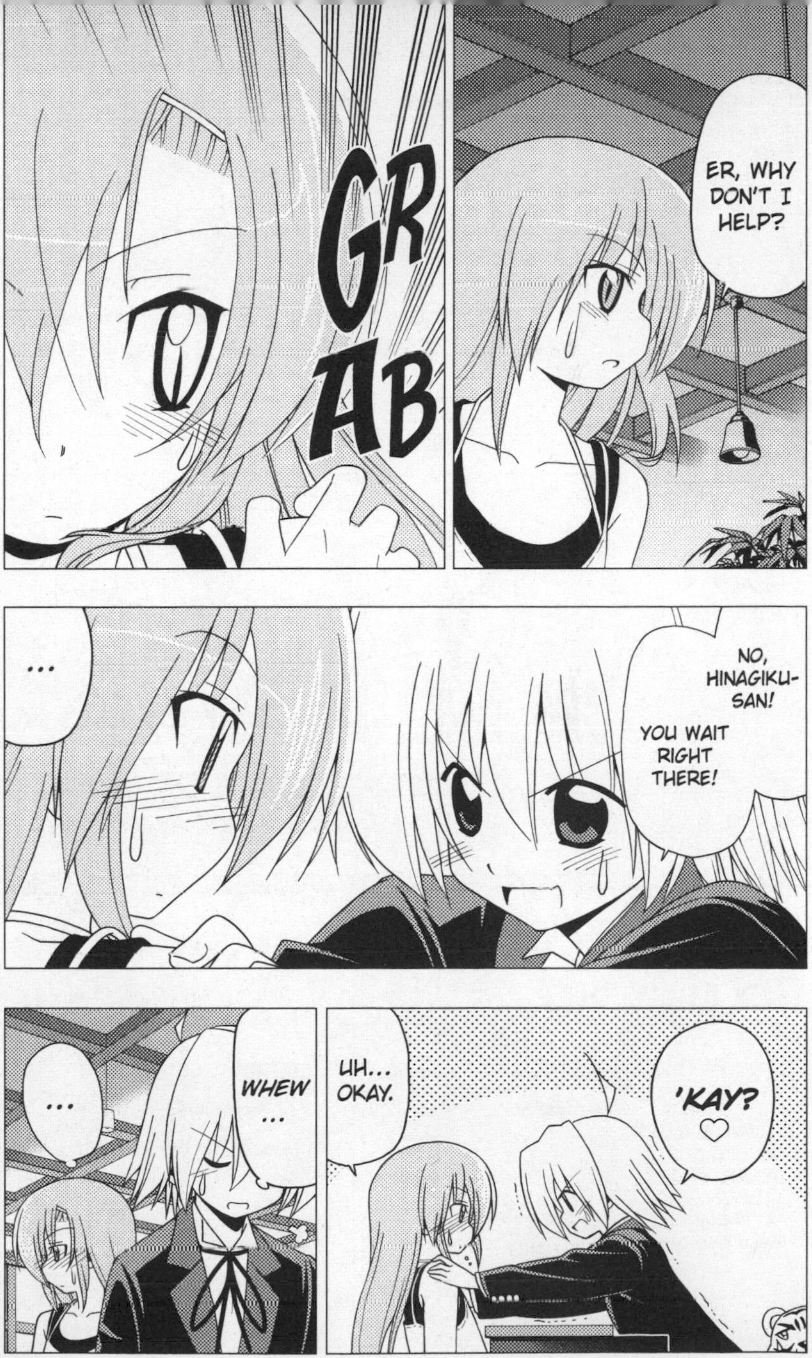
ER, WHY DON'T I HELP?
GRAB
NO, HINAGIKU-SAN!
YOU WAIT RIGHT THERE!
...
'KAY? ♡
UH... OKAY.
WHEW ...
...

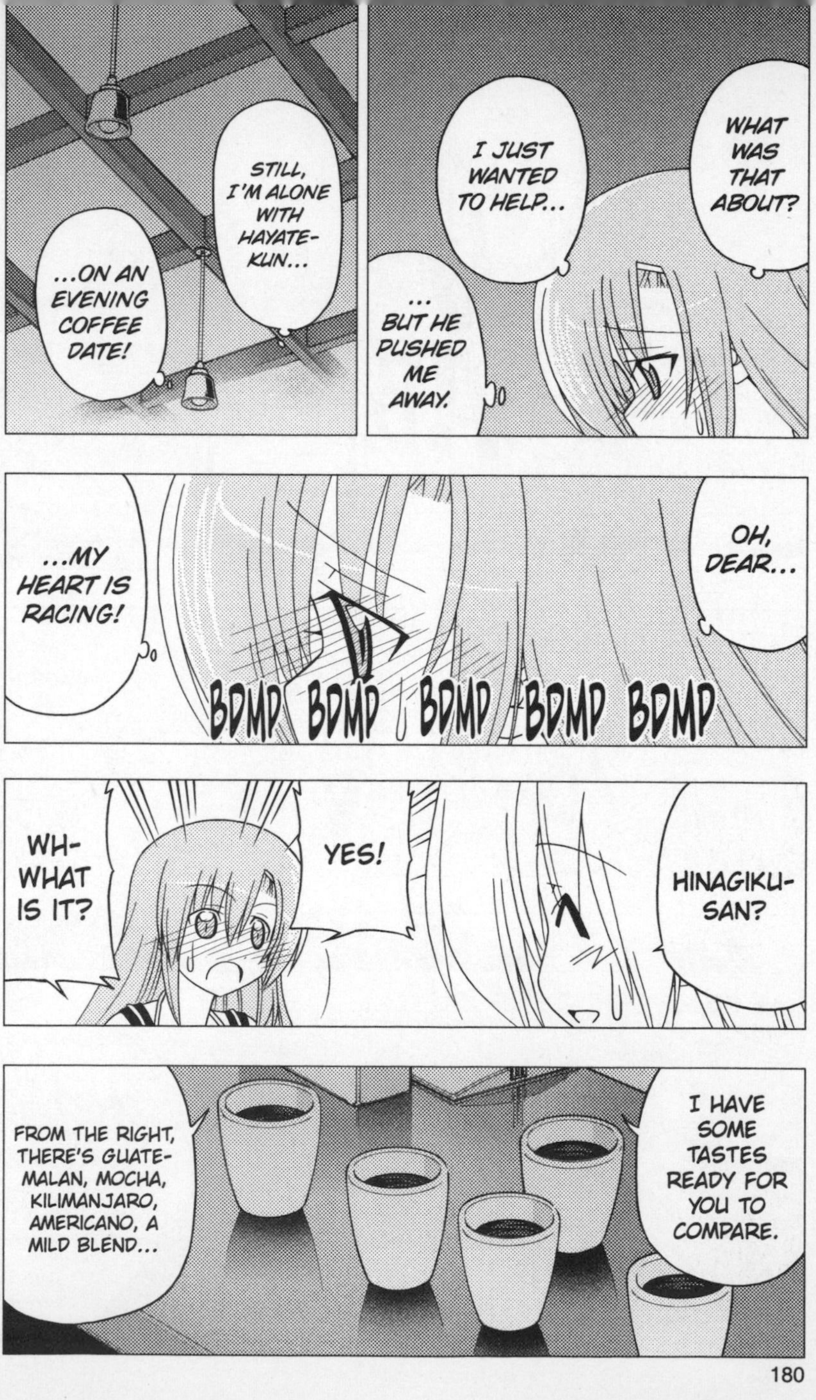
WHAT WAS THAT ABOUT?
I JUST WANTED TO HELP...
...BUT HE PUSHED ME AWAY.
STILL, I'M ALONE WITH HAYATE-KUN...
...ON AN EVENING COFFEE DATE!
OH, DEAR...
BDMP BDMP BDMP BDMP BDMP
...MY HEART IS RACING!
HINAGIKU-SAN?
YES!
WH-WHAT IS IT?
I HAVE SOME TASTES READY FOR YOU TO COMPARE.
FROM THE RIGHT, THERE'S GUATE-MALAN, MOCHA, KILIMANJARO, AMERICANO, A MILD BLEND...

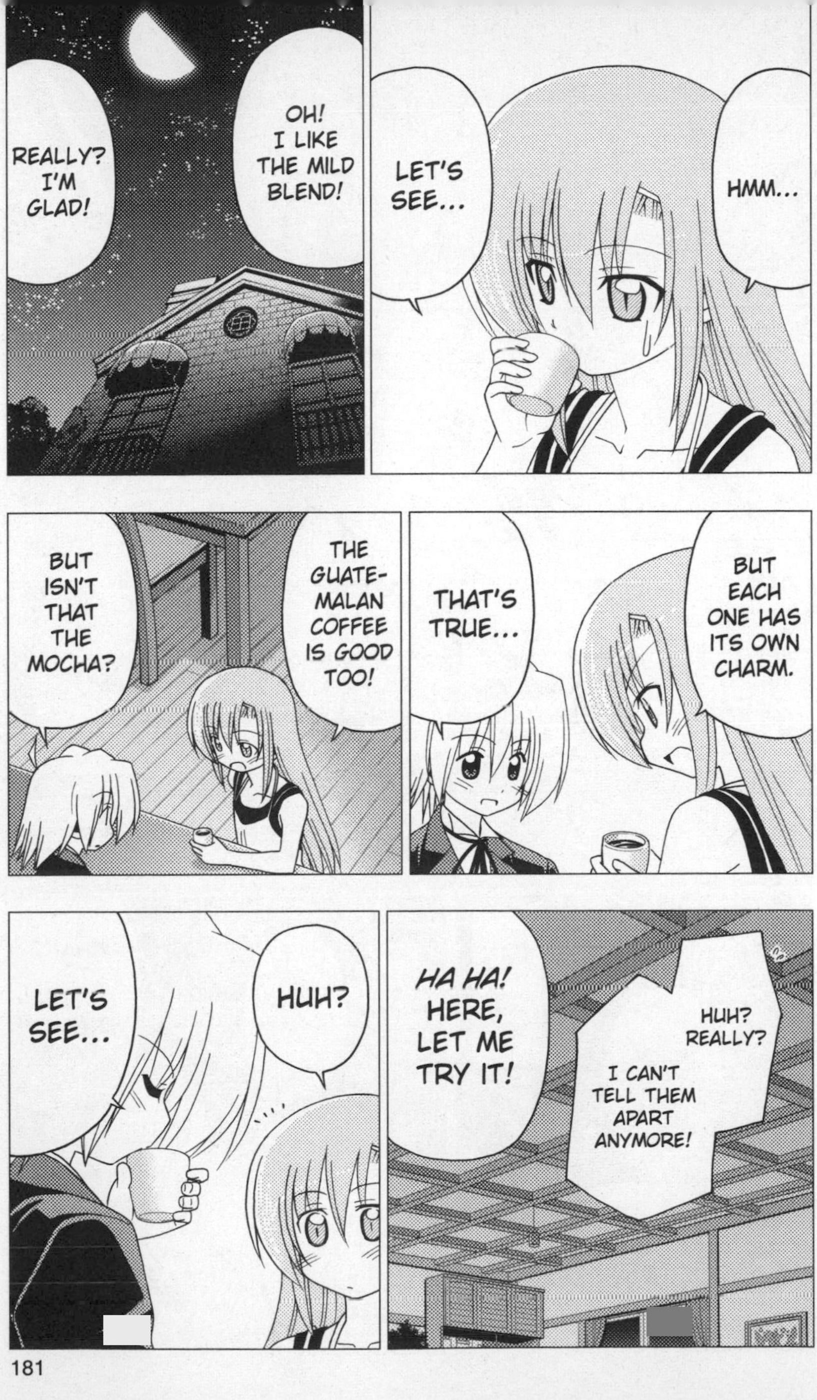
HMM...
LET'S SEE...
OH! I LIKE THE MILD BLEND!
REALLY? I'M GLAD!
BUT EACH ONE HAS ITS OWN CHARM.
THAT'S TRUE...
THE GUATE-MALAN COFFEE IS GOOD TOO!
BUT ISN'T THAT THE MOCHA?
HUH? REALLY?
I CAN'T TELL THEM APART ANYMORE!
HA HA! HERE, LET ME TRY IT!
HUH?
LET'S SEE...

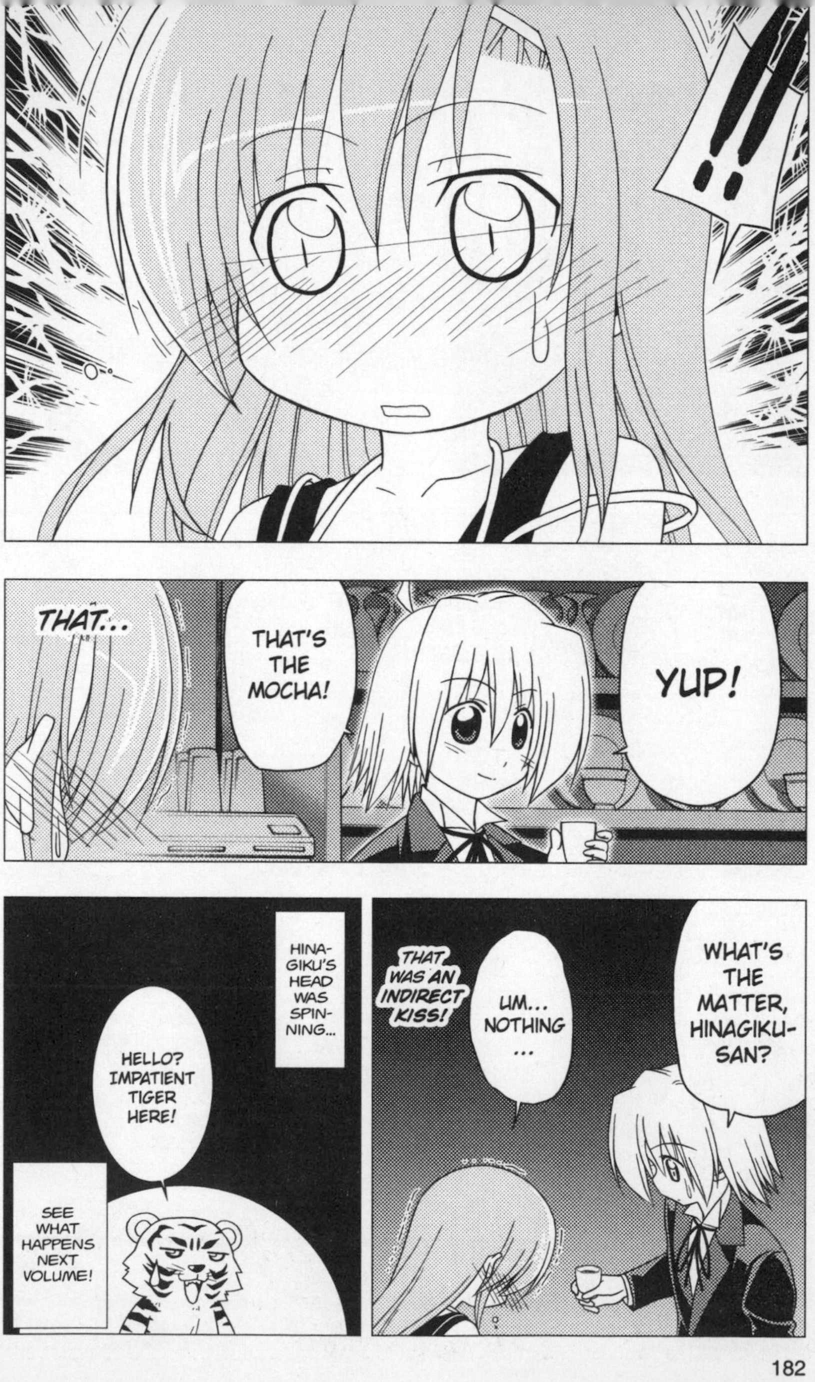
!!
YUP!
THAT'S THE MOCHA!
THAT...
WHAT'S THE MATTER, HINAGIKU-SAN?
UM... NOTHING ...
THAT WAS AN INDIRECT KISS!
HINA-GIKU'S HEAD WAS SPIN-NING...
HELLO? IMPATIENT TIGER HERE!
SEE WHAT HAPPENS NEXT VOLUME!

HAYATE THE COMBAT BUTLER!

TITLE CALLIGRAPHY BY RITSUKO HATA
(HER GLASSES COST 90,000 YEN)

BONUS PAGES

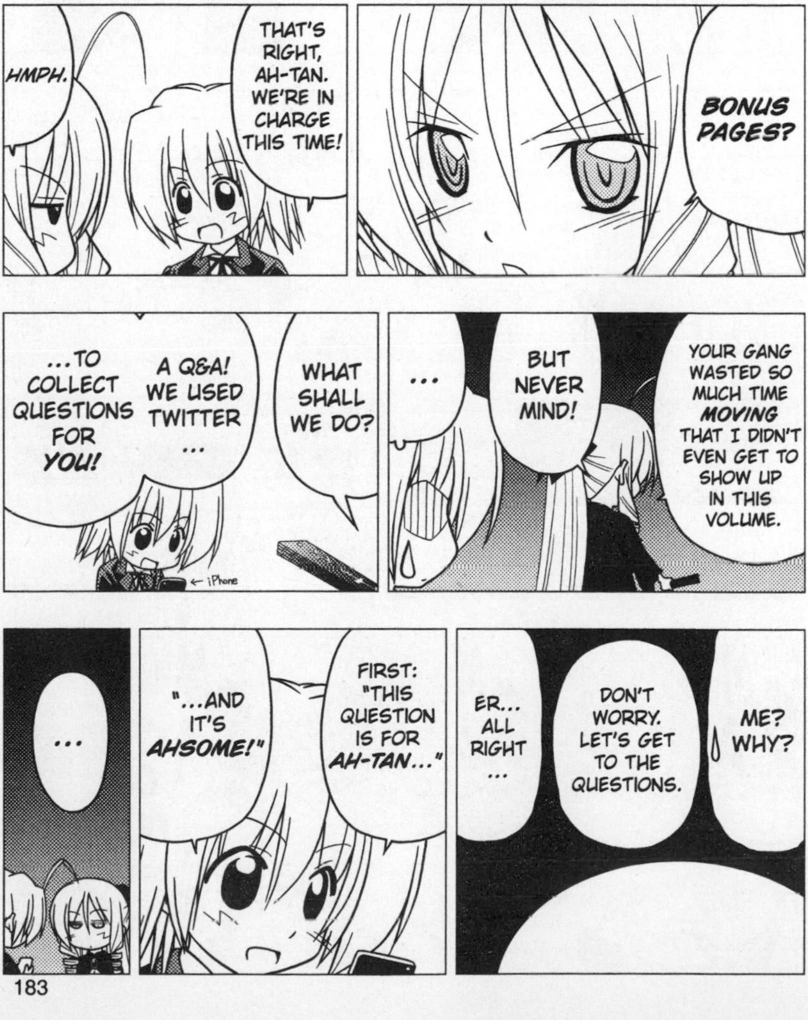
BONUS PAGES?
THAT'S RIGHT, AH-TAN. WE'RE IN CHARGE THIS TIME!
HMPH.
YOUR GANG WASTED SO MUCH TIME MOVING THAT I DIDN'T EVEN GET TO SHOW UP IN THIS VOLUME.
BUT NEVER MIND!
...
WHAT SHALL WE DO?
A Q&A! WE USED TWITTER ...
...TO COLLECT QUESTIONS FOR YOU!
← iPhone
ME? WHY?
DON'T WORRY. LET'S GET TO THE QUESTIONS.
ER... ALL RIGHT ...
FIRST: "THIS QUESTION IS FOR AH-TAN..."
"...AND IT'S AHSOME!"
...

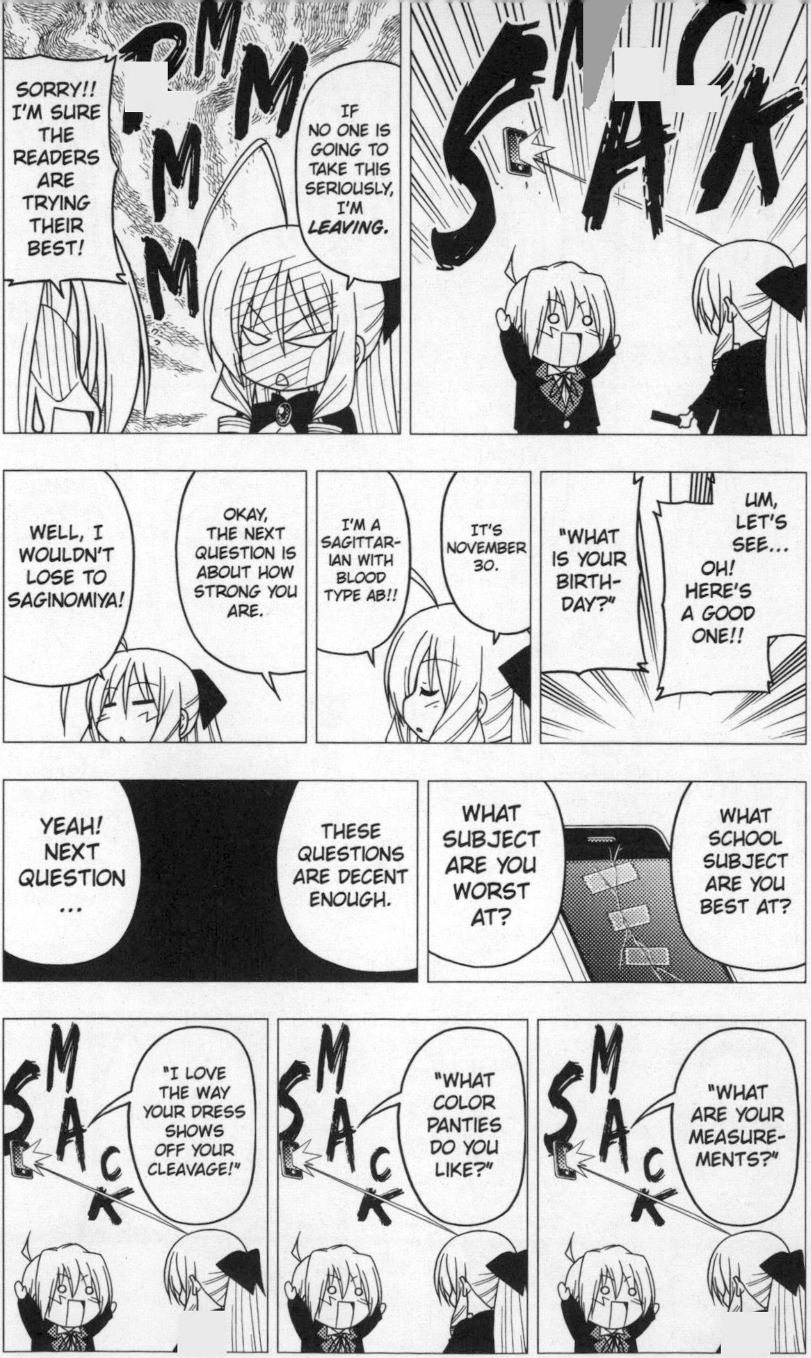
SMACK
IF NO ONE IS GOING TO TAKE THIS SERIOUSLY, I'M *LEAVING*.
SORRY!! I'M SURE THE READERS ARE TRYING THEIR BEST!
UM, LET'S SEE... OH! HERE'S A GOOD ONE!!
"WHAT IS YOUR BIRTHDAY?"
IT'S NOVEMBER 30.
I'M A SAGITTARIAN WITH BLOOD TYPE AB!!
OKAY, THE NEXT QUESTION IS ABOUT HOW STRONG YOU ARE.
WELL, I WOULDN'T LOSE TO SAGINOMIYA!
WHAT SCHOOL SUBJECT ARE YOU BEST AT?
WHAT SUBJECT ARE YOU WORST AT?
THESE QUESTIONS ARE DECENT ENOUGH.
YEAH! NEXT QUESTION ...
"WHAT ARE YOUR MEASUREMENTS?"
SMACK
"WHAT COLOR PANTIES DO YOU LIKE?"
SMACK
"I LOVE THE WAY YOUR DRESS SHOWS OFF YOUR CLEAVAGE!"
SMACK

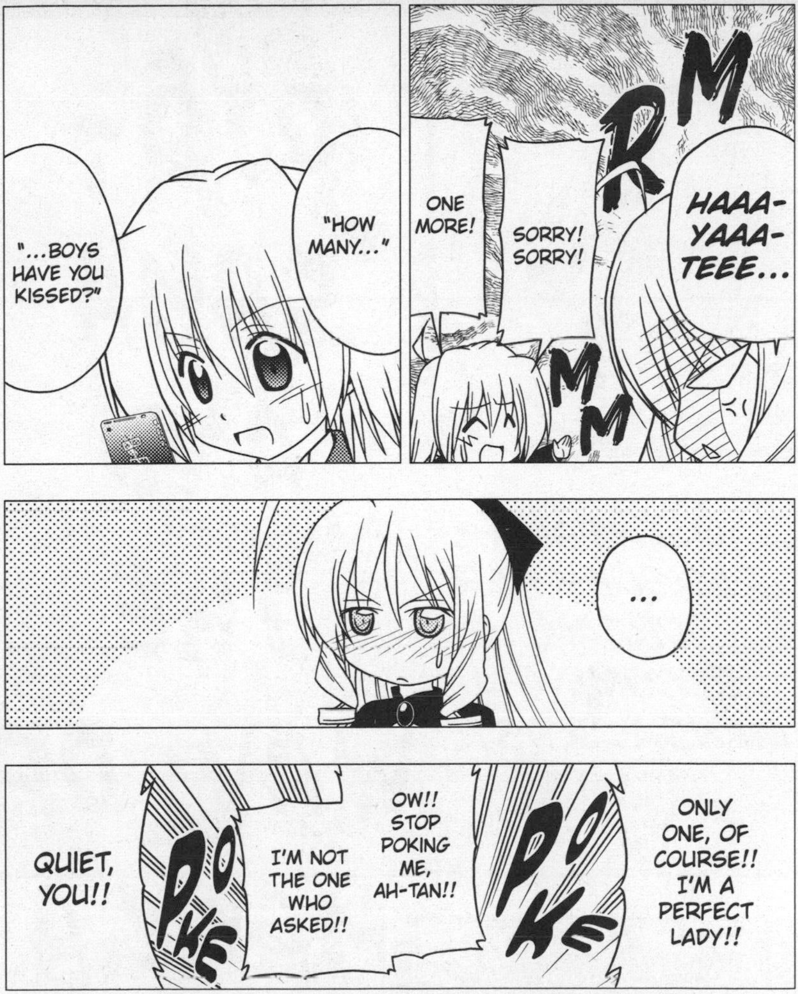
HAAAA-YAAA-TEEE...
RMM
SORRY! SORRY!
ONE MORE!
"HOW MANY..."
"...BOYS HAVE YOU KISSED?"
...
ONLY ONE, OF COURSE!! I'M A PERFECT LADY!!
POKE
OW!! STOP POKING ME, AH-TAN!!
I'M NOT THE ONE WHO ASKED!!
POKE
QUIET, YOU!!

SO HOW DID YOU LIKE VOLUME 26? THE JAPANESE VERSION CAME IN A LIMITED EDITION WITH A BONUS ILLUSTRATION OF MARIA. I WORKED HARD ON IT, SO I HOPE THOSE OF YOU WHO BOUGHT THE SPECIAL EDITION LIKED IT!

NEXT YEAR THIS MANGA IS GOING TO BE ADAPTED INTO A LIVE-ACTION DRAMA IN TAIWAN. IT ISN'T SCHEDULED TO AIR IN JAPAN YET, BUT I HOPE EVERYONE IN TAIWAN LOVES IT! ★ AND...AND...I'LL HAVE ANOTHER BIG ANNOUNCEMENT IN THE NEAR FUTURE. BRACE YOURSELVES!

WE'RE ALMOST UP TO THE 300TH CHAPTER! I PLAN TO KEEP WORKING HARD ON HAYATE, SO PLEASE KEEP READING! ★ AND IF YOU WANT TO FOLLOW ME ON TWITTER, I'M @HATAKENJIRO.

SEE YOU IN VOLUME 27!

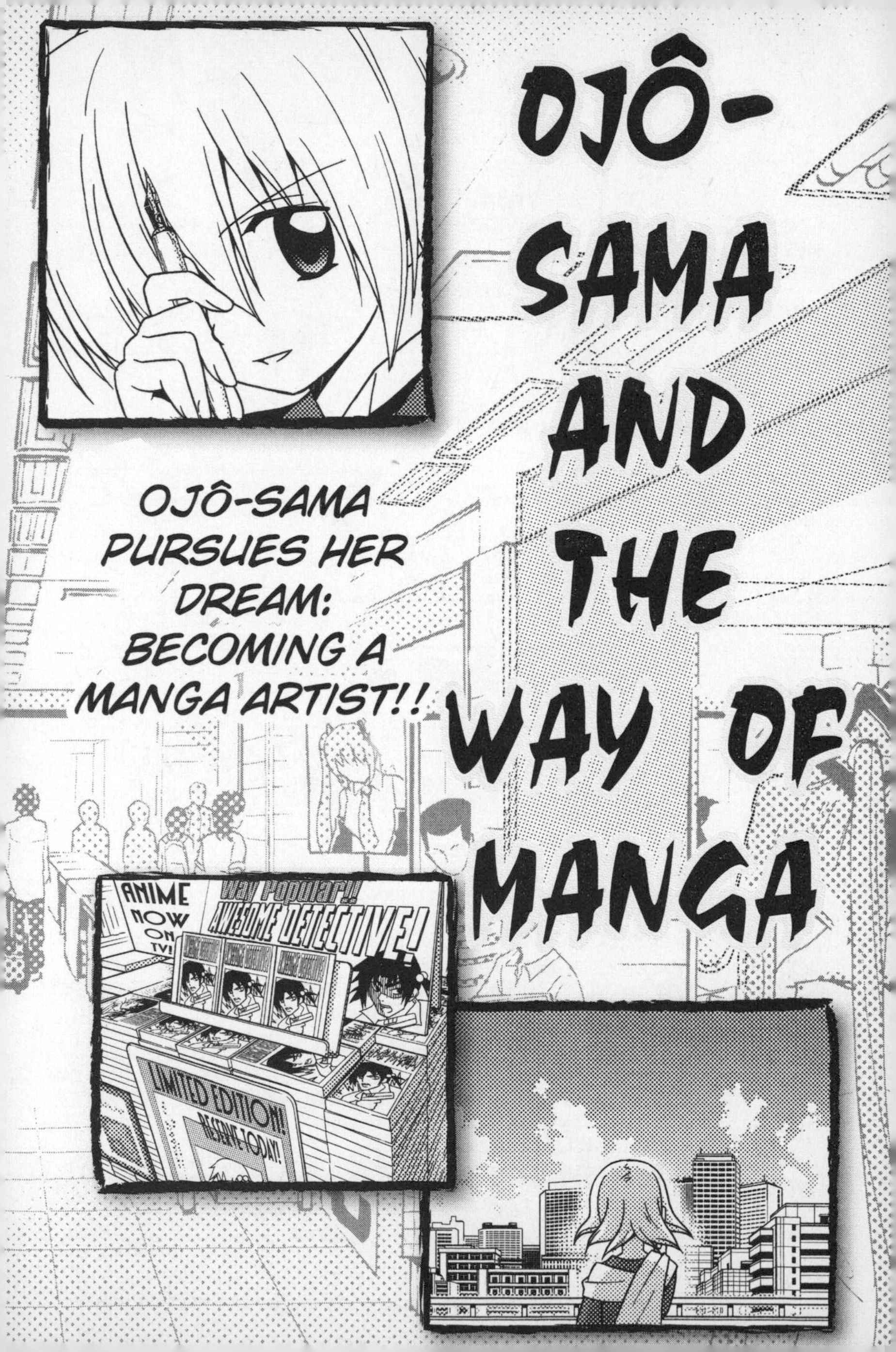
OJÔ-SAMA AND THE WAY OF MANGA
OJÔ-SAMA PURSUES HER DREAM: BECOMING A MANGA ARTIST!!
Way Popular!!
AWESOME DETECTIVE!
ANIME NOW ON TV!
LIMITED EDITION! RESERVE TODAY!

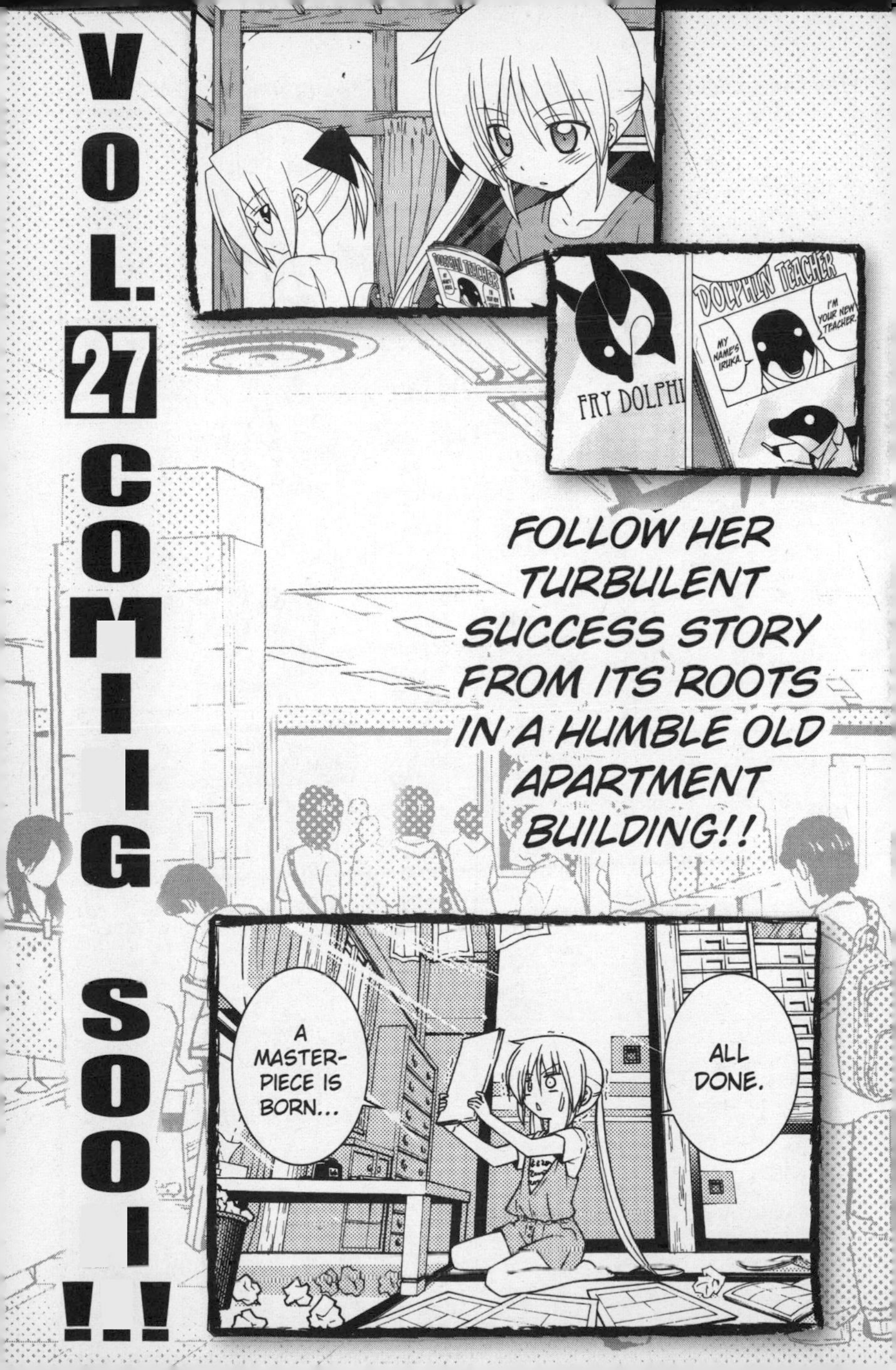
VOL. 27 COMING SOON!!
DOLPHIN TEACHER
I'M YOUR NEW TEACHER.
MY NAME'S IRUKA.
FRY DOLPHI
FOLLOW HER TURBULENT SUCCESS STORY FROM ITS ROOTS IN A HUMBLE OLD APARTMENT BUILDING!!
ALL DONE.
A MASTER-PIECE IS BORN...

The Sun Smiles All Year

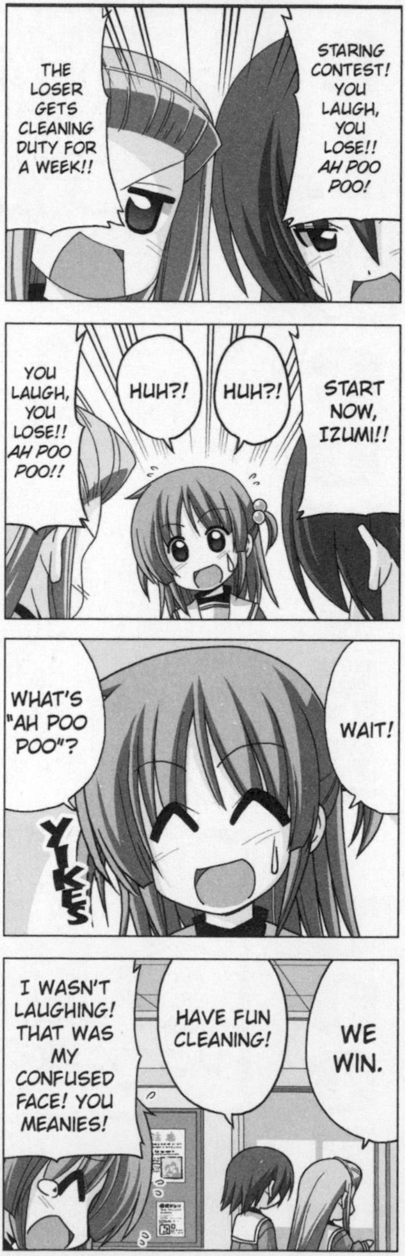
STARING CONTEST! YOU LAUGH, YOU LOSE!! *AH POO POO!*
THE LOSER GETS CLEANING DUTY FOR A WEEK!!
START NOW, IZUMI!!
HUH?!
HUH?!
YOU LAUGH, YOU LOSE!! *AH POO POO!!*
WAIT!
WHAT'S "AH POO POO"?
YIKES
WE WIN.
HAVE FUN CLEANING!
I WASN'T LAUGHING! THAT WAS MY CONFUSED FACE! YOU MEANIES!

The Sun Smiles All Year... A Sketch

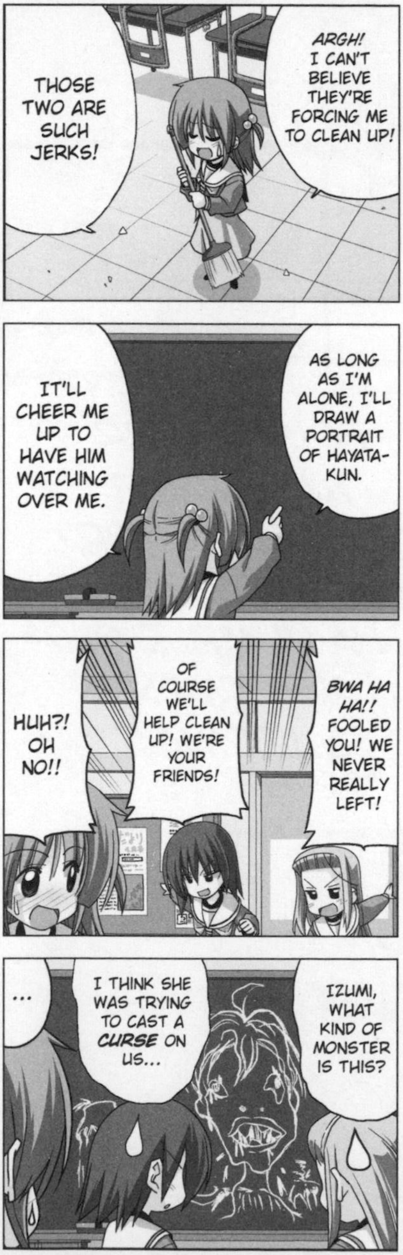
ARGH! I CAN'T BELIEVE THEY'RE FORCING ME TO CLEAN UP!
THOSE TWO ARE SUCH JERKS!
AS LONG AS I'M ALONE, I'LL DRAW A PORTRAIT OF HAYATA-KUN.
IT'LL CHEER ME UP TO HAVE HIM WATCHING OVER ME.
BWA HA HA!! FOOLED YOU! WE NEVER REALLY LEFT!
OF COURSE WE'LL HELP CLEAN UP! WE'RE YOUR FRIENDS!
HUH?! OH NO!!
IZUMI, WHAT KIND OF MONSTER IS THIS?
I THINK SHE WAS TRYING TO CAST A *CURSE* ON US...
...

HAYATE THE COMBAT BUTLER

—BAD END ⑪—

"What a cute kitty!"

"Shall we keep her?"

MEOW?

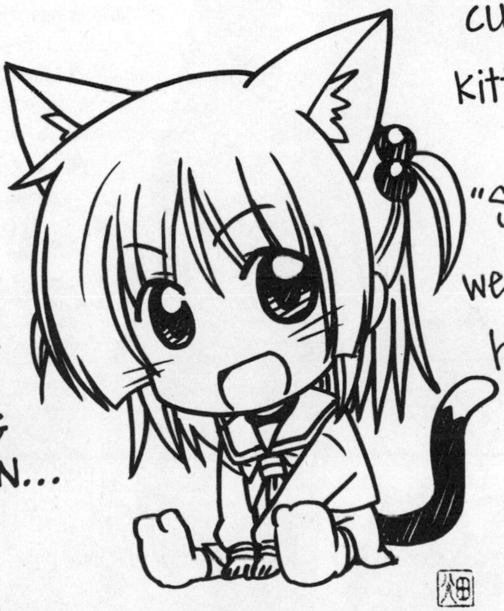

NOT THE MOST ROUSING CONCLUSION...

...BUT SHE'LL BE HAPPY, RIGHT?